the mozza cookbook

the Mozza cookbook

RECIPES FROM LOS ANGELES'S FAVORITE
ITALIAN RESTAURANT AND PIZZERIA

nancy silverton

with matt molina and
carolynn carreño

PHOTOGRAPHS BY SARA REMINGTON

ALFRED A. KNOPF · NEW YORK · 2011

This Is a Borzoi Book Published by Alfred A. Knopf

Copyright © 2011 by Nancy Silverton

Photographs copyright © 2011 by Sara Remington

All rights reserved. Published in the United States by Alfred A. Knopf, a division of Random House, Inc., New York, and in Canada by Random House of Canada Limited, Toronto.

www.aaknopf.com

Knopf, Borzoi Books, and the colophon are registered trademarks of Random House, Inc.

Library of Congress Cataloging-in-Publication Data
Silverton, Nancy.
The Mozza cookbook : recipes from Los Angeles's favorite Italian restaurant and pizzeria by Nancy Silverton, with Matt Molina and Carolynn Carreño; photographs by Sara Remington. —1st ed.
p. cm.

ISBN 978-0-307-27284-3
1. Cooking, Italian. 2. Cooking—California—Los Angeles. 3. Osteria Mozza. 4. Pizzeria Mozza. I. Molina, Matt. II. Carreño, Carolynn. III. Title.
TX723.S484 2011
641.5945—dc22   2011014599

Jacket photograph by Sara Remington

Jacket design by Abby Weintraub

Manufactured in China

First Edition

this book is dedicated to la famiglia mozza

contents

foreword

If you'd asked me ten years ago if I'd be part-owner of an Italian
restaurant in La La Land, I would have laughed in your face. If you'd
then asked me if I'd be part-owner of *three* Italian restaurants, well,
then I'd have said you were just wacky. And "wacky" is a good word to
describe what I thought of most Left Coasters up until about four years
ago. It's not that they're actually crazy, but let's face it—a good deal are
diet-crazed, low-carb-obsessed and think an 8:30 p.m. reservation is
for club kids and too late to dine. But the most important and perhaps
"real" reason I never went out West is that I've always been staunchly
opposed to opening any restaurant that's too far for me to get to on my
Vespa.

So what changed my cynical view of Angelenos and the way I like
to set up my business? Nancy Silverton and Matt Molina did.

We didn't always plan on working together to open Mozza but I've
always regarded Nancy's talent in the kitchen as nothing short of perfect. Her unique take on the dishes she has created over the years has
always been inspiring and just plain delicious. I have known this since
the eighties, but I initially got in touch with Nancy in 2005 to ask her
to join the nascent Del Posto in New York City in our pastry and bread
department. And that conversation was the beginning of our partnership in a restaurant and pizzeria in Los Angeles—Osteria Mozza
and Pizzeria Mozza. Despite all of my skepticism about anything
L.A.-related, the *only* way a West Coast project would work was if
Nancy was running the show. And even though I had never done any
business with her, I had an innate trust in her process.

That trust was not only about Nancy's ability to run a successful
business but also about the confluence of thought with the food and
menu. We share a similar philosophy when it comes to Italian food—
fresh, straightforward, seasonal—but more significantly, *simple*. And it's
my belief, and I know it is Nancy's, too, that if you share this core ide-
ology, the rest pretty much takes care of itself—provided you also have
a guy like Matt Molina in the kitchen.

I first met Matt when I did a dinner at the justly famous Campanile,
maybe fifteen years ago. He was clearly talented, but he also had a flair
for simplicity and the confidence a typical L.A. kitchen *cholo* often displayed. Later, we took a "tour de tortellini" in and around Bologna
with a few friends, and it was there that I really saw what sets him
apart. Immutable sense of perfect flavor and texture is something a
lot of people write about, but few possess. Matt has both, as well as a

pitch-perfect understanding of acid balance. What distinguishes the food at Osteria and Pizzeria Mozza from a lot of the food in the United States is the wine-friendly, slightly high acid tone in the finish of many of the dishes. The food that we serve at most of my restaurants on the East Coast has this in common as well. It usually happens in the last seconds as you finish a dish before serving it, and it makes a subtle but important difference. Watch and learn in this book.

And so it began . . . this partnership, which has only flourished over the years. Since the day it opened, Mozza has been a huge success. People flock to the restaurants for the food, of course, but also to see Nancy, an iconic figure in the L.A. food scene, doing the boogie-woogie at her Mozzarella Bar. Sitting at the Mozzarella Bar and watching the queen of the delicious do her thing with her unique style (big red hair, big jewelry, and bohemian dresses) is theater with benefits—the food.

At the Aspen Food and Wine Classic in 2009, Nancy and I did a demonstration of several recipes from Mozza. Nancy prepared a Burrata with Speck, Peas, and Mint, a variation of which you'll find in this book. That demo and our unrehearsed banter was the most fun I have had onstage and maybe ever legally in the United States. Nancy doesn't just ooze Italian with her words—her Italian pronunciation can be off a bit (she is from Los Angeles, after all)—but there's still something so visceral about listening to her talk and watching her cook and create with a definite sexy flair. It is always a joy to watch someone who is really good at something just go to work. Why else are spectator sports so popular? This cookbook takes the spectator sport out of cooking and puts you in the game. I am ecstatic that Nancy has now written a cookbook to share all of the dishes that make dining at Mozza better than a ride on Space Mountain. From antipasti to dessert, every recipe has a story, but more importantly, it is the sharing of the tricks, the lore, and the love of the raw ingredients from Nancy's point of view that make this book smart and yet easy to use.

And that's what I love about our Mozza group. The food here is not just about taste—it's got a history, a reason, and a thought process. And that alone exemplifies everything I love about Nancy, Matt, their collective cooking, and, of course, this cookbook. It embraces true Italian *cucina* while living in L.A. amidst the movie stars, the earthquakes, and the theme parks. And do not for a moment think I am not jealous of the spectacular farmers and purveyors, whose story may just be another book altogether.

mario batali october 2010

the mozza cookbook

introduction

If there's one thing I've learned in the last few years, it's that you just don't know where life is going to take you. If someone had asked me when I finished my last book if I would write another cookbook, I would have said, "No way!" Then again, if someone had told me that I would have two restaurants of the size and level of success that I have today, the side-by-side Pizzeria Mozza and Osteria Mozza in Los Angeles, I never would have believed that either.

I started brainstorming what became Mozza about three years before it opened, in 2004. I wasn't actively involved in any restaurant or business at the time, having recently sold my active partnership in Campanile. I wasn't looking for anything, but I just knew that I wasn't done with the food business—there was something else out there for me. I just didn't know what that something was. I would have to wait until the right idea brewed up inside me.

That summer I went to Italy, where I have a house on a country road about 100 yards outside the walls of a tiny medieval hill town called Panicale, in Umbria. While I was there I found out that Jeremiah Tower, the chef who is largely credited, along with Alice Waters, with inventing "California Cuisine," was living in a town nearby. Jeremiah wasn't a close friend—more of a business associate—but I'd always liked him, and when I learned that he was close by I thought it would be nice to have him over for lunch.

Earlier that week I had made a trip to one of my favorite local *caseificio,* or cheese makers, in the area in the nearby town of Todi. They now have a retail shop, but back then the cheese was sold right on the farm where the milk was produced and the cheese was made. They produce a variety of fresh cheeses, all from cow's milk, that I brought home with me, including ricotta, burrata, and mozzarella in various shapes and sizes. I decided to make these cheeses the star of the lunch I was serving for Jeremiah. I presented them on a big olivewood board along with a variety of *condimenti*—delicious savory complements—including pesto made with fresh basil from my little patio garden, olive oil pressed from the trees that grow on the hill above my house, a confit of garlic using the delicious sweet garlic that I buy at one of the two markets in town, roasted torpedo onions, oven-dried *pomodorini* (cherry tomatoes), marinated olives, toasted, salted almonds, sliced mortadella, prosciutto, and salami, and to sop up all the flavor, grilled bread.

It was a very simple lunch, but it was exactly the kind of meal that, from my experience, food-obsessed people want to eat: seasonal, light, tasty, and unpretentious. I know Jeremiah was pleased. He said he felt that I had truly captured the spirit of eating at someone's home in Italy on a hot summer afternoon. He had recently eaten at a place in Rome that had just opened, called Obika, a "mozzarella bar," which, he said, was like a sushi bar that served mozzarella instead of fish. Having eaten the lunch I'd served him, he told me I had to go see what they were doing. We weren't talking about what I should do next, or trying to come up with a new restaurant concept for me. He just saw the way I had prepared and served that lunch, built around those cheeses, and he thought I would appreciate what they were doing at Obika. As it would turn out, Obika would be the inspiration for Mozza.

On my way back to California from Italy, I always stop in Rome for a night or two to eat, and on that trip, I went to Obika. Until I found out otherwise, I assumed that it was a Japanese company, both because the name sounds Japanese to me and because it really did look exactly like a sushi bar with the long counters and the short window displays where you could see the product. What Jeremiah Tower had said when he explained the restaurant's concept to me was that they had a great idea, but that he thought I could take that idea to a different level. When I saw the way the restaurant worked, I understood exactly what he meant.

They served the cheeses with an accompaniment of your choice, so you could order mozzarella with, for example, shaved radicchio, arugula, *pomodorini,* or prosciutto. None of the accompaniments were cooked. The presentations were so simple and straightforward that it was almost like fast food. I loved it. I loved that it was such a focused concept, like a pizzeria or a hamburger joint. By the time I got back to Los Angeles, I knew I was going to open a mozzarella bar. It suited me perfectly. I've always liked working behind a counter, where I can interact with guests while I'm preparing food. I'm much more comfortable doing that than walking around a dining room greeting customers while they're in the middle of a meal. And I liked the concept of a mozzarella bar specifically because mozzarella's mild, milky flavor lends itself to so many combinations.

I didn't have a name for my restaurant yet, but I knew exactly what I wanted: just a little place—picture your neighborhood hole-in-the-wall sushi bar—with a ten-seat counter and two or three tables, if any, with me working behind the counter assembling room-temperature dishes. I might have one prep cook and a dishwasher, but I would make every dish and hand every customer his or her plates myself, just like a sushi chef. I hoped that my customers and I would have that same kind of interaction that you have with a sushi chef, only I would prefer my customers to send me red wine instead of beer. It would be a small, homespun, uncomplicated business. I thought I might have investors, but definitely no partners.

About a year before this, Mario Batali, whom I knew only from food industry events, had asked me if I was interested in running the baking program at his New York restaurant, Del Posto. I toyed with the idea. I lived in New York from 1985 to 1986 to work at a restaurant, now closed, called Maxwell's Plum and have always fantasized about moving back to New York or being bicoastal. But my youngest son, Oliver, was still living at home, so I couldn't just pick up and leave, and the idea of going back and forth was just not realistic. So I'd said to Mario, joking, "Why don't you move to L.A. and we can open a restaurant together?" I really was joking, but it wouldn't have mattered anyway because Mario was not about to open a restaurant in Los Angeles. He was under the impression, partially correct, that people in L.A. don't eat in restaurants as often as they do in New York, and that when they do eat out, they are finicky, fat-conscious, calorie-counting eaters who watch everything they eat and don't eat anything at all after nine o'clock. You probably don't need me to tell you that this mentality did not interest Mario. Then, shortly after I'd eaten at Obika, I ran into Mario at a food event and told him about my idea for a mozzarella bar. I remember very clearly that the next words out of his mouth were, "I'm *in*!" And Mario being Mario, that was the beginning of a very different mozzarella bar story.

I was already testing out the concept on Monday nights at my friend Suzanne Tracht's steakhouse, Jar. I developed a menu that included items I might put on a mozzarella-bar menu and served them from behind the bar on what we called Mozzarella Mondays. I wanted to see if people in Los Angeles would go for my idea, and I also wanted to practice what I was doing. People did like it and Mozzarella Mondays became such a success that customers would stand three-deep at the bar waiting for a seat.

The week after I mentioned the idea to Mario, his partner Joe Bastianich, whom I'd never even met, called and told me to start looking around for a space in L.A. With three people involved, obviously my little sushi-bar-size concept was not going to cut it. The mozzarella bar would have to be part of something larger, a real restaurant. In many ways, circumstances dictated the kind of restaurants we ended up opening. While we were looking at real estate, David Shaw, the late, wonderful writer and my friend, wrote a story for the *Los Angeles Times* titled "What's Next for Nancy Silverton?" After the story hit the stands, real estate agents and restaurateurs started calling with locations they wanted me to look at, one of which was an Italian restaurant with a pizzeria attached on what some called a "cursed corner" in the Hancock Park area of Los Angeles.

While I originally had no intention of opening a pizzeria, the idea of a pizzeria appealed to me. The experience of going to a pizzeria is a big part of my life in Italy. There is a pizzeria, called Il Pellicano, down the hill from Panicale, that we go to just about every night we're there. It looks like nothing and I drove by it for years until my friend Vinnie discovered it. The morning after he first ate there, we were sitting at Aldo's, the bar in the *piazza* where my friends and family and I all find each other every morning, and Vinnie told me, "You've gotta check this place out. All the locals are there. It's like a big party." I loved it. Not just the food but also the spirit and the energy of the place.

Also, learning to make pizza, I mean to really perfect the art of pizza, had been on my list of things I wanted to do before I die (more on this in the Pizza chapter, page 121). And I knew it was something I would never do unless I was somehow forced to. I had had a similar experience with La Brea Bakery. I'd known I wanted to learn to make bread someday, and when my dad found the building where La Brea Bakery is now located, it seemed like the perfect opportunity. When I saw the Hancock Park restaurant space with the pizzeria attached, I knew that this was my chance to make pizza. And once I saw the space, it was the only one I wanted.

The deal took a long time to close, but a year later, the space on the corner of Melrose and Highland, a fairly large restaurant and a pizzeria attached, was ours.

As I write this book—a compilation of sweet and savory recipes from both restaurants—the Pizzeria is more than four years old and the Osteria has been open for four years. In 2009, next door to the Osteria, we opened a take-out shop with a small retail storefront, Mozza2Go. In 2010, we opened outposts of Pizzeria Mozza and Osteria Mozza in Singapore, and we currently have a Pizzeria Mozza under construction in Orange County. In Los Angeles, we were busy on day one and we have only grown busier with time. We take reservations a month out and that's more or less how long it takes to get one. The seats at the bars in both restaurants—the Wine Bar and the Pizza Bar in the Pizzeria and the Mozzarella Bar and the Amaro Bar (named after the selec-

tion of *amari*, or bitters, that line its shelves) in the Osteria—are reserved for walk-in customers and usually fill up the minute we open.

We hadn't been open for three months when the first customers began asking me when I was going to write *The Mozza Cookbook*. I honestly thought that I would never do it. I had just finished writing *A Twist of the Wrist*, and I always say that writing a cookbook is like childbirth. But the real reason for my hesitancy was that I didn't know what I had to offer the home cook. There are so many Italian restaurant cookbooks on the shelves, I thought, the world doesn't need one more. But the thing that changed my mind was very simple: the food.

our food

The foods we serve and the styles of cooking at Pizzeria Mozza and Osteria Mozza are very different from each other. At the Osteria, the dishes are very involved. Nothing we do is fancy or ornate, but each dish involves several steps and often takes several days, a fair amount of prep, and a lot of attention to detail in terms of the way the dish is finished and presented. It's a more polished restaurant and the food reflects that. The Pizzeria, on the other hand, is very casual. The menu is built around the pizzas, with selections for *affettati*, or sliced meats; salads; and a large selection of antipasti. The feel of the Pizzeria is convivial and loud—customers who sit at the bar or the pizza counter often end up talking to the people sitting next to them—and the food reflects that. What binds the two restaurants, and thus the recipes in this book, is that it is all Italian cuisine. Not "Cal-Ital," or "Ital-inspired," which is how I would describe food I've cooked in the past. The food at Mozza, a term I will use to collectively describe both restaurants, is traditionally Italian, and that has everything to do with Mario and Joe.

While Italian food is without question my favorite cuisine and while Italy has had a tremendous effect on my style as a cook and a baker, I am not an expert on Italian cuisine, and I never envisioned myself opening a traditional Italian restaurant, or even felt I was qualified to do so. But Mario probably knows more about Italian food than any other person alive, or at least anyone I know. And Joe is *the* Italian wine authority in this country. So with them on board, we were already leaning in that direction.

I had already chosen Matt Molina, whom I had worked with for years previously, to be our executive chef. Before we opened, Matt spent six months in New York City working at Mario and Joe's Italian fine dining restaurant, Del Posto. He learned so much about traditional Italian food while he was there, and got so excited about what Mario and his team of cooks were doing, it was clear that Osteria Mozza was going to be a traditional Italian restaurant. With Mario and Joe on board and Matt in the kitchen, I knew I was in good hands, and that I could do this.

When I say that Mozza is a "traditional" Italian restaurant, I should add that I mean traditional as seen through the eyes of the restaurants' American owners and chefs. Italians, when it comes to all things food—what they eat, how they cook it, when they eat, and in what order—are traditional to the point of being almost superstitious. They do things the same way they've been doing them since the beginning of time, without asking why and without, it would seem, the temptation to change anything. What's more, the cuisine is extremely region-specific. In my town and throughout Umbria, there are about five specialty ingredients, including lentils from Castelluccio, which we serve at both restaurants; some of the best olive oil in Italy, which we use exclusively; local prosciutto; aged sheep's milk cheese; and a variety of things made with *cinghiale,* or wild boar, that is hunted in the hills around Panicale. And there are about five regional dishes, two of which are on the menu at the Osteria: Wild Boar Ragù (page 185) and what may be the official *secondo,* or main dish, of my town, roasted guinea hen served on a big piece of toasted bread and smothered with a rich, liver-enhanced gravy (see Guinea Hen *Crostone* with Liver and Pancetta Sauce, page 218). Not only are there very few dishes but also these dishes do not change. Ever.

I love these culinary traditions and idiosyncrasies in Italy, but cooking within these parameters would be extremely limiting; I could never cook this way. My favorite thing to do in the kitchen is to tinker. I hesitate to say that what we do at Mozza is improve upon traditional dishes, since I would like to be welcome in my town after this book is published, but if I had to define my style as a cook, I would say that I take traditional dishes and elements of those dishes and then tweak them. I make additions and adjustments that make them more exciting to *me.* Besides having cultural permission to deviate from convention, another advantage we have at Mozza is access to really good ingredients. Twenty years ago chefs and other food-obsessed Americans talked about how great the raw ingredients were in Italy, but today we have access to the same quality ingredients, sometimes even better.

The first time I rented a house in Italy, more than twenty years ago, we bought all of our produce from roadside stands, but I don't see many of those stands anymore. Now a big truck comes to town a couple of times a week, delivering produce that was grown who knows where to the two stores in town. One store sells only this produce, while the other sells a combination of what comes off those trucks and what the storeowners pull from their own garden. So in that regard, Italy seems to be transitioning in a direction we don't want to go. Meanwhile, in Southern California, we have long growing seasons and access to a wider variety of locally grown produce every year. Chris Feldmeier, the chef de cuisine in the Osteria, and Dahlia Narvaez, the pastry chef for both restaurants, go to the Santa Monica farmers' market every Wednesday morning.

Although we shop at farmers' markets, Mozza is not a market-driven restaurant in that we don't change our menus every day or every week depending on what we find at the market. The way we build our menus is something we adopted from Mario—and it's more of a European model. You can go to a restaurant in Rome that you visited twenty years ago and find the same dish that you remember them for, and, if everything goes your way, the dish will be just as you remembered it. Mario is obviously very creative and he loves when he comes up with something new to put on one of his menus, but he doesn't want to get rid of anything. He knows that a customer like me will go to Babbo just for the octopus, so he keeps it there, and when he comes up with something new, he just adds. We do the same thing. At the Pizzeria, our list of pizzas and antipasti has doubled since we opened, and we offer twice as many *primi* and *secondi* in the Osteria. Before we put an item on the menu, we work on it and work on it until we feel that we have taken that dish to the point where it is as delicious and as visually appealing as we believe it could possibly be, and I believe that consistency is one of the reasons for our success.

One of the marks of a great restaurant for me is that I wake up and think, "I *have* to have x dish from y restaurant." Whether it's the Meatballs *al Forno* (page 107), any of the pizzas, or the Butterscotch *Budino* with Caramel Sauce and Maldon Sea Salt (page 272) in the Pizzeria; or the Duck *al Mattone* with Pear *Mostarda* (page 223), Garganelli with Ragù Bolognese (page 189), or *Torta della Nonna* (page 276) in the Osteria, I like to believe that there are people who wake up and think, "I *have* to have that!"

Once I get excited about a subject—I mean really into the intricacies and subtleties of it—I want to spread the gospel. When I started writing this book, the Pizzeria had been open for two years and the Osteria was a year and a half old. I finally felt that what we were doing at both restaurants was special enough that it warranted sharing with the world. I also knew that the public really liked what we were doing, and by then I had been asked for the cookbook enough times that I was convinced that people wanted to cook our food at home. Now as I finish, I have no trepidation whatsoever about sharing our recipes in a cookbook. In fact, I can't wait for people to cook from this book and share our food with their family and friends.

our recipes

If you are one of those readers who flip through the pages of a cookbook to see how long a recipe is in order to gauge its difficulty, I hope that you won't be deterred by the length of some of the recipes in this book. While I was working on the book, I sat on a panel discussion in Los Angeles on how people cook today. One of the most interesting things that came out of this panel was a discussion of Julia Child's recipes. As anyone who has ever looked at her books knows, Julia Child's recipes are lengthy. I remember when my mom would cook from *Mastering the Art of French Cooking,* she would be so proud when she had successfully completed a dish. She would always say, "Look at what I had to do to get here." And then she would show my sister and me all of the pages in the book that constituted that one recipe. Julia was so passionate about her mission to introduce French food to her American readers that she wouldn't let you fail. Her recipe writing— and as a result, the length of her recipes—reflects that. Although I assume my readers have at least a basic understanding of Italian cuisine, I feel the same way. I don't want to let you fail.

When I decided to write this book, I wanted to be sure that it would not just be a memento, something for fans to buy and put on their coffee tables to remind themselves that they ate at Mozza. Of course, I'd like that, too. But if I was going to call this a *cookbook,* I wanted the recipes to include all the information the reader would need to successfully replicate our food at home. And I think that, with the assistance of Matt, Dahlia, my co-author, Carolynn Carreño, and a team of recipe testers, I've achieved that. So, yes, some of the recipes are long, but think of them as roadmaps of the Italian countryside—detailed, long, and sometimes winding—but they *will* get you where you want to go. And as you embark on the journey, remember that they have all been done before, and in the spirit of Julia Child, know that we are all in the kitchen with you, cheering you on.

In the restaurant business, you are only as good as the people you attract to work for you, and now more than at any other time in my career, I rely on those individuals to help me execute my creative visions. I could name a long list of people who help me do what I do. In fact, I could name every one of Mozza's nearly 300 employees, as well as people from Mario and Joe's camp who come in every few weeks, bringing their expertise to help us improve and grow. But my own little team, those who were on board with this project before I even knew what it was going to be, and without whom I can tell you without hesitation Mozza would not be the restaurant it is today, includes Matt Molina, Mozza's executive chef; Dahlia Narvaez, the pastry chef; and David Rosoff, whose title General Manager does not begin to describe the impact he has had at Mozza.

First, about Matt: When people ask me if I cook at my restaurants, I like to tell them that I assemble food. I work five nights a week behind the Mozzarella Bar, putting together dishes with fresh cheeses as the star. But when customers come up to me at the bar and say, "Our dinner was fantastic!" I grab Matt and tell them, "He's the chef." I never make any bones about the fact that I am not the chef at Mozza, because it's the truth. I understand food. I understand flavors. I know how I like food to taste and to look, but I don't always have the skills necessary to get there.

When my mozzarella-bar concept grew so much grander than I initially envisioned, it became evident that I would need a real live chef. Matt, whom I'd worked closely with in the past, was my number one choice. Not only is he young, energetic, and enthusiastic, but he has a special ability to taste food. My standard line about Matt is that he cooks like a woman. What I mean is that he resists the temptation to show off and instead understands the beauty of keeping things simple. We have very similar styles and visions, and the way we work together, as you will read in many of the headnotes to these recipes, is a true collaboration. Oftentimes, I will tell Matt about something I ate in a local restaurant or on a trip and he will try to re-create it based on my description. Or I might say, "I'd like to put rabbit on the menu and I would like it to have x, y, and z qualities." Matt will take it from there, and what he comes back with is sometimes like a miracle, in that I'm not sure exactly how he did it. Another quality that makes Matt the ideal collaborator for me is that he knows when something is not good. He is always open to my input, and he is never defensive about his cooking, which is rare for a chef. Nothing goes on the menus until it passes my approval.

I work a little differently with Dahlia than I do with Matt because I am a trained pastry chef—I have more skills and confidence in dessert making—so we often work out recipes together. I chose Dahlia, whom, like Matt, I had worked with for many years, because she is hardworking, she pays great attention to detail, and she loves what she does. Dahlia also has the same sensibility as I have, which means I can trust her completely to execute desserts the way I would want them. She is also such a perfectionist that she will do something over and over again, taking my input, until she gets it right. I wish Dahlia got more recognition for what she does at Mozza, but I also understand that this is the nature of the business. She will be rewarded one day, and she will deserve it.

Last but not least, David Rosoff. As the idea of Mozza grew, I also needed a front-of-house person: someone who knew service, knew how to put together a wine list, and most critically, knew numbers and how to manage a budget. I knew right away that David Rosoff was that person. I'd worked with David before and knew him to be one of a dying breed of individuals in this country who treat the service profession not only seriously but also with pleasure. He was the opening manager for the Pizzeria, hiring and putting systems in place. Once that restaurant was running smoothly, he did the same for the Osteria. The motto with which he directs his staff in both restaurants, which I believe he executes successfully, is: "Every customer is a VIP."

In addition to being a great manager, David is exceptionally knowledgeable when it comes to wine. He built the wine lists for both restaurants and, more important, he has a unique ability to talk about wine in such a way that even someone like myself with limited wine knowledge and vocabulary is able to understand. Continuing in his tradition of going above and beyond in the service of others, David has made wine-pairing suggestions throughout this book. So before you begin to cook from this book, pour yourself a glass of Prosecco and raise that glass to David.

the traditional italian meal

When I first started to travel in Italy, I always tried to follow the principles for eating a traditional Italian meal—starting with an antipasto; following it with a *primi,* or first course, which is pasta, risotto, gnoc-

chi, or soup; and finishing with a *secondi,* which is what we think of as a main course. I felt guilty anytime I didn't do the multicourse thing. I had read in guidebooks and I had heard seasoned travelers talk about how the waiter would look down on you if you ordered a *primi* as your main course or if you made a meal of only one course. I imagined myself being kicked out of the restaurant or humiliated if I didn't have the full meal.

Only recently did I learn that Italians don't even eat that way anymore. It is still the template of a proper meal, and it's how an Italian family would eat on special occasions or Sundays, but on a daily basis, they do not eat all three courses plus a dessert. So, although the Osteria menu was set up so that people can order an antipasto, a *primo,* and then a *secondo,* finished with something sweet—even the portion sizes are based on this—we don't expect our customers to necessarily have all three courses. When customers ask us how to order, we might explain the courses of a traditional Italian meal. But then we'll ask, "How hungry are you?" Or, "How many courses were you planning on having?" From there, we might suggest they share a selection of antipasti or a plate of *affettati misti*—sliced meats—followed by a *primi* and then a *secondo* to share. The Pizzeria is a completely different story. That menu is built on sharing. People share pizzas so they can try different toppings. The salads are mountainous and meant for more than one person. And to round out their meal, diners often get a selection from the antipasti portion of the menu.

In using this book, I hope you will have fun with the idea of the traditional Italian meal when it suits you, maybe take the time to make and serve handmade pasta or the long-cooked *Brasato* al Barolo with Polenta and Horseradish Gremolata (page 230) on a lazy Sunday afternoon. But I hope you will also be as creative with cooking from the book as our customers are in ordering from our menus. Following are some menu ideas that I would serve, and in some cases have served, at home. Some an Italian would approve of, like the *tavola fredda,* which means "cold table," and is the name for the tables of room-temperature antipasti displayed in many restaurants in Italy; and others, such as the Holiday Dinner, might leave them scratching their heads. In any case, enough talk. *A tavola!*

mozzarella bar

Selection of *latticini* (pages 58-61)
Basil Pesto (page 62)
Salsa Romesco (page 63)
Black Olive Tapenade (page 65)
Fett'Unta (page 65)
Olives *al Forno* (page 37)
Toasted Almonds with Sea Salt (page 38)
Affettati Misti (pages 92-93)
Prosciutto-wrapped Breadsticks (page 39)

sunday supper

Affettati Misti (pages 92-93)
Francobolli di Brasato al Pomodoro with Basil
and Ricotta Salata *al Forno* (page 177)
Veal Breast *Stracotto* (page 235)
Tricolore with Parmigiano-Reggiano
and Anchovy Dressing (page 98)
Torta della Nonna (page 276)

tray-passed cocktail party

Prosciutto-wrapped Breadsticks (page 39)
Pancetta-wrapped Figs with Aged *Balsamico*
Condimento (page 52)
Fried Squash Blossoms with Ricotta (page 40)
Selection of biscotti (pages 320-327)

holiday dinner

Olives *al Forno* (page 37)
Ribollita "Da Delfina" (page 115)
Grilled Quail Wrapped in Pancetta
with Sage and Honey (page 221)
Cauliflower *Gratinate* (page 258)
Brussels Sprouts with Sherry Vinaigrette
and Prosciutto Bread Crumbs (page 256)
Pumpkin and Date Tart with Bourbon Gelato (page 280)

We're fortunate in Los Angeles, and in this country, to have access to quality imported ingredients that weren't available to the home cook ten years ago. But I think the consumer is often confused by the huge variety offered at most stores. When I opened Mozza2Go, in addition to the take-out portion of the business, I wanted to have a tiny storefront whose walls were lined with products, and I wanted to limit those products to what we use every day at Mozza and that contribute to making the food at Mozza as good as it is. These are those products.

anchovies: I prefer salt-packed anchovies to those packed in oil, but of all the salt-packed anchovies, the most special are Alici di Menaica from Salerno. *Menaica* is the name of a type of net that has been used for fishing anchovies since ancient Roman times, which has small holes in it, so small bycatch can escape. Few fishermen use this method because it is slower than modern nets, but it is better for the preservation of anchovy populations. Also, Menaica anchovies are bled in a particular way that yields a sweeter, more flavorful product. Alici di Menaica are on the ARC list of products, which is a sort of endangered species list for foods, protected by the organization Slow Food. Whatever kind of anchovies you buy, salt-packed anchovies are sold whole, so you have to fillet them, discard the spines, and remember when using them in recipes that each anchovy is two anchovy fillets.

balsamic vinegar: Balsamic vinegar may be the most misunderstood condiment of our time. True balsamic is a thick, syrupy, reduced condiment that has been made in the Modena and Reggio Emilia regions of Italy since the Middle Ages. The names "Aceto Balsamico Tradizionale di Modena" and "Aceto Balsamico Tradizionale di Reggio Emilia" have DOP status (Denominazione di Origine Protetta), meaning that only those products made in the traditional way in one of these two regions can be called "traditional balsamic vinegar." This grade of balsamic, which is aged for a minimum of twelve years and as long as twenty-five years or more, is sold in small bulbous jars, nestled in individual boxes like bottles of perfume. *Balsamico condimento* has some of the same sweetness, viscosity, and much of the same complex flavor as *balsamico tradizionale* but at a considerably lower price; in some instances the only reason for the lower grade is that it is produced outside Modena and Reggio Emilia or without consortium approval. In Italy, both *tradizionale* and *condimento* are typically drizzled over Parmigiano-Reggiano and mortadella, grilled meat and fish, strawberries, and vanilla gelato. A third product, called "Aceto Balsamico di Modena," is produced in huge batches and is not the artisanal product that the *tradizionale* and *condimento* are. This is the stuff you find on supermarket shelves for as little as two dollars a bottle (*tradizionale* and *condimento* are often locked behind glass). We use this to cook with and to make marinades. The *balsamico* that we use for finishing dishes, and that we sell at Mozza2Go, is a *condimento*-grade product called Manicardi "Oro." It has that viscous quality, without being terribly expensive. If your budget allows, of course, the first choice would be the *tradizionale*. Although it is expensive, keep in mind that you will use it sparingly, in eye-dropper-like portions.

bench mate: To give our pastries the unique flavor of Italian pastries, I use Bench Mate, the brand name of an Italian leavening agent, in my *Pasta Frolla* (page 276), or pastry dough. You can find Bench Mate at many Italian specialty food stores or you can buy it from Mozza2Go. If you can't get it, use the recommended combination of leavening that I give in the recipes as a substitute. It won't be quite the same because Bench Mate contains vanillin, a synthetic flavoring that I excuse in the name of authenticity.

champagne vinegar: We use champagne vinegar exclusively wherever white wine vinegar might normally be used, such as in Lemon Vinaigrette (page 29), our basic salad dressing. It adds another dimension of flavor that you wouldn't get from white wine vinegar.

calabrian bomb: We import this spicy Calabrian condiment paste to enhance the garlic mayonnaise that we serve with Mussels *al Forno* (page 109), and to spread on grilled panini made with smoked scamorza cheese and Armandino's mole salami—a delicious salami made with the Mexican combination of chile and chocolate. The Calabrian Bomb is one of the rare artisanal products that is so special that we can justify using it rather than trying to make a version ourselves. If you can't find it, use a spicy red pepper paste in its place.

capers: I prefer salt-packed capers to those packed in vinegar, because they carry the distinct, slightly bitter taste of capers and not just the flavor of vinegar. Soak the salt-packed capers in water for at least 15 minutes before using them in recipes to remove the excess salt.

fennel pollen: I discovered fennel pollen fairly recently and just love it. I use fennel pollen when I want a concentrated slightly sweet fennel flavor. It's expensive, but like so many of these products, a little goes a long way. It's essential to our Fennel Sausage (page 137), and the Fennel Sausage, *Panna,* and Scallion pizza (page 144).

hazelnuts: We made a conscious decision not to name sources on our menus because that is not something restaurants in Italy do, but we made an exception in the case of the hazelnuts from Trufflebert

Farms in Eugene, Oregon. These hazelnuts have so much more flavor than other hazelnuts I've tasted that I felt I had to credit the grower. We blanch the hazelnuts, then toast them and toss them in hazelnut oil before using them in salads and other dishes where they are prominently featured. We use conventional hazelnuts in baked goods and other instances where they do not play as big a role.

mostarda: A traditional Northern Italian condiment made with fruit or sometimes onions, *mostarda,* also called *mostarda di frutta,* is traditionally served with *bollito misto,* a boiled meat dish, and has more recently been adopted as a condiment for cheese. The closest thing to *mostarda* would probably be chutney, but what makes *mostarda* unique, and what also gives it its name, is the presence of mustard seed oil, a very sharp, spicy oil that goes straight through your nose the way wasabi does. The essential oil is sold in pharmacies in Italy but it's illegal in the United States, so making a true *mostarda* here would be impossible, or at least illegal. The *mostarda* that we use—Mostarda Mantovana by Casa Forcello, from Mantova, in Lombardy—is one of the few products in the restaurant that we buy rather than make. It is artisanally produced and an example of a product we don't think we could improve upon by making ourselves. The variety we use most is pear *mostarda,* which we serve alongside Duck *al Mattone* (page 223). We also serve crab apple *mostarda* on our cheese plate, and plum *mostarda* with house-made *coppa,* or hard salami.

olive oil: There are so many delicious imported olive oils available now, and while that's a good thing for the consumer, it can also be confusing. In general, with olive oil, price can be a pretty good indicator of quality, meaning the more expensive the oil, the better it's likely to be. But that isn't always the case, and everyone's taste is different. People ask me all the time, "What kind of olive oil should I buy?" My standard response is that you should taste a bunch of them, and buy what tastes good to you. Maybe you like the spicy, throat-burning quality that Tuscan olive oil is known for, or the fruity flavor of Ligurian olive oil. Whatever you choose, you want to keep it out of the sunlight, and keep it for no more than a year. Unlike wine, olive oil does not age well. We use only three types of olive oil, and unless you are an olive oil fanatic, that's all you need as well.

We use a good quality extra-virgin olive oil, sold in 3-quart cans, for cooking and vinaigrettes. The brand we use is Spoleto, but any quality olive oil will do. We use what I refer to in these recipes as "finishing-quality olive oil" for drizzling over mozzarella-bar items, cooked meats such as Grilled Beef *Tagliata* (page 227), and Grilled Quail Wrapped in Pancetta (page 221), and to drizzle over pasta dishes to emulsify the sauce. The finishing oil we use is an Umbrian oil, Monini DOP. I have an olive grove on the hillside that stretches above my house in Italy, which my neighbor Franco manages for me. Every November after the harvest, he takes my olives to a co-op that presses them into olive oil, and both he and the co-op take a portion as payment. Monini buys from this co-op, so I like to think that some of the olives from my own trees were pressed into the oil I am drizzling behind the mozzarella bar.

The third type of olive oil that we use is *olio nuovo,* or new oil. The name refers to the fact that it is the oil pressed from newly harvested olives. In Italy during the olive harvest in November and December there are signs all over the countryside advertising the new oil. Italians get so excited about it—they talk about the nuances of the year's oil and how it differs from last year's oil—and so do I. You can recognize new oil by its bright green color and pronounced peppery flavor, both of which fade with time. What I want to make clear here is that new oil is special only when it's new. A couple of months after the oil is pressed, it's just olive oil. It may still be really good olive oil, but it's not new. The two brands of *olio nuovo* I like and that are available here are Pasolivo, from Paso Robles on the Central Coast of California (*Sideways* country), and Cappezana, from Tuscany.

oregano: Oregano is the one herb that we also use in its dry form, because the leaves are even more flavorful dried and that's the way oregano is used in Italy. It's important to note that not all dried oreganos are created equal; most dried oregano that you buy in supermarkets is old and no longer fragrant. When making something like Oregano Vinaigrette (page 97), we use dried oregano from Penzeys, a well-known source for quality herbs and spices. We use dried oregano, imported from Sicily, that comes still on the branch for finishing dishes, such as the pizza with Tomato, Sicilian Oregano, and Extra-virgin Olive Oil (page 133). To use the oregano, we brush the leaves from the branch so they fall onto whatever we are seasoning. It's kind of fun to do. I recommend you keep one of these branches on your kitchen counter for this cookbook and other uses.

pasta: At the Osteria, in addition to the many fresh pasta shapes that we make ourselves, we serve two brands of dried pasta—Rustichella d'Abruzzo and Setaro—for dishes such as Linguine with Clams (page 199) and Spaghetti *alla Gricia* (page 198), where we want the toothsomeness you can get only from dried pasta. Both of these producers make pasta in small batches and use bronze dies, which don't heat up and melt the pasta, to extrude the shapes. The resulting pastas have a slightly rough wonderful texture that I appreciate.

peppercorns: At Mozza we grind all of our pepper fresh. When the flavor of the pepper is central to the dish, such as in Bavette *Cacio e Pepe* (page 201), we use Tellicherry peppercorns, a particularly flavorful variety grown on the coast of India. In addition to having a pepper grinder, you might find it convenient to grind a handful of pepper in a spice grinder to keep in a small dish to use when you're cooking.

porcini: These mushroom delicacies when dried add a subtle, distinct flavor to dishes, such as our *Brasato* al Barolo with Polenta and Horse-radish Gremolata (page 230) and are the base of the seasoning we rub on our rib-eye steak (see Porcini-rubbed Rib-eye *Bistecca*, page 232).

saba: This condiment is made from Sardinian grape must that has been reduced to a syrup consistency. Traditionally, it is drizzled on desserts and grilled meats. If you can't find *saba*, substitute *vin cotto*, another sweet, syrupy condiment that means "cooked wine," or *balsamico condimento* where it is called for.

salt: Several years ago my dad, who is an avid woodworker, made me a beautiful saltbox with two compartments: one for Maldon sea salt and one for kosher salt. I use my saltbox daily at the Mozzarella Bar and take it with me anywhere I cook. I use Maldon sea salt for sprinkling on finished dishes and kosher salt for everything else. I prefer Maldon to any of the other sea salts available because I like the way the large flakes of salt sit on top of a finished dish. And in instances where I don't want the crunchy texture from the large flake, unlike rock salt, I can easily crush Maldon between my fingers.

tomato paste: We use tomato paste to add a touch of sweetness and a hint of tomato flavor to sauces that aren't otherwise tomato-based, such as ragù bolognese (see Garganelli wih Ragù Bolognese, page 189) and Lentils Castellucciano (page 264). We use double-concentrated tomato paste, which comes in a tube and has a richness that you don't get from domestic tomato paste. The brand we like, Mutti, is available at Italian import stores and specialty food stores such as Whole Foods. Occasionally I've seen triple-concentrated Mutti tomato paste instead of double-concentrated. If that's what you find, use it. More concentrated means more flavor.

truffle salt: This mixture of sea salt and shaved truffles has the flavor of truffles without the funky taste you get from truffle oil or the high price tag of whole truffles. The product we use, Casina Rossa, contains 5 percent truffles. We use it primarily to make truffle butter, which we use in Prosciutto-wrapped Breadsticks (page 39). Truffle salt is also delicious with eggs, but whatever you use it on, sprinkle it only on finished dishes, as the truffle flavor disappears when it is heated.

One of the reasons our food is so memorable is that each dish contains many layers of flavor, but that layering takes time. At the restaurant, we have a staff of chefs, prep cooks, and pastry cooks, who prepare the ingredients we need, which is how we are able to put together in minutes each of the dishes on our menu. Chris Feldmeier, chef de cuisine in the Osteria and the chef you're most likely to find standing behind the pasta station expediting orders at dinnertime, likes to say that what he and his line cooks do is heat up everything that the morning sous chef, Erik Black, and his guys made during the day.

Obviously, a staff of prep cooks is not a luxury the home cook has access to, but you can take advantage of some of the techniques we use to make executing the recipes in this book quicker and easier.

- Read the recipes through to see which components can be made in advance, and use those as a way to spread your cooking tasks out over a period of time.
- Trim and salt meats for braising and making ragùs a day in advance. Salting the meat enhances its flavor, and by doing this small step, when you cook the meat, it will already be unwrapped, trimmed, and seasoned, so you can get to work.
- Braise meats, such as for the lamb ragù (see Stinging Nettle Tagliatelle with Lamb Ragù, Taggiasche Olives, and Mint, page 192) and the *Brasato* al Barolo with Polenta and Horseradish Gremolata (page 230), two or three days ahead of time. They are better the day (or days) after they're made.
- Freeze ragùs so you can turn them into last-minute pasta dinners.
- Keep Basic Chicken Stock (page 27), *Passata di Pomodoro* (page 25), Basic Tomato Sauce (page 24), and Soffritto (page 28) in your refrigerator and/or freezer at all times.
- Prepare *gelati* and *sorbetti* bases as well as cookie dough up to three days in advance.
- Keep *Pasta Frolla* (page 276) in the freezer for last-minute desserts.

The recipes that follow are the "mother sauces" of our kitchen—the ingredients that, built upon one another, provide those layers of flavor I mentioned earlier.

- Basic Tomato Sauce
- *Passata di Pomodoro*
- Roasted Roma Tomatoes
- Basic Chicken Stock
- Soffritto
- Lemon Vinaigrette

basic tomato sauce

Like the name suggests, this is a basic tomato sauce that we use in a variety of dishes. You can keep it in the freezer for up to six months, so you may want to double the recipe and freeze the extra. The only "secret" to this sauce is that you start with good canned tomatoes. Our preference, hands down, is San Marzano, a variety of plum tomatoes from Campania praised for its tart flavor and bright red color.

MAKES ABOUT 2 QUARTS

Heat the olive oil in a medium saucepan over medium heat. Add the onion, sprinkle with the salt and the pepper, and cook the onion, stirring occasionally, until it is tender and translucent, about 10 minutes. Add the garlic and cook 1 to 2 minutes to soften , stirring constantly so it doesn't brown. Add the carrot and thyme leaves and cook, stirring occasionally, until the carrot is soft, 6 to 8 minutes. Add the tomatoes, including their juices; bring the liquid to a boil, reduce the heat, and simmer the sauce, stirring often, for about 30 minutes, until it has thickened slightly. (Be careful: the tomato sauce can burn easily if you don't stir it often enough or if you have the heat too high.) When the sauce is done, pass it through a food mill into a large bowl. Taste for seasoning and add more salt or pepper, if desired. Use the sauce or set it aside to cool to room temperature, then transfer it to an airtight container and refrigerate for up to several days or freeze for up to several months.

¼ cup extra-virgin olive oil

1 large Spanish onion, finely diced (about 2 cups)

1 tablespoon kosher salt, plus more to taste

½ teaspoon freshly ground black pepper, plus more to taste

4 garlic cloves, thinly sliced

Half of a medium carrot, peeled and shredded in a food processor or on a box grater

3 tablespoons fresh thyme leaves

2 28-ounce cans whole peeled plum tomatoes, including their juices (preferably San Marzano)

passata di pomodoro

*P*assata *comes from the word* passare, *which means "to pass" in Italian, and* passata di pomodoro, *often referred to as* passata, *is the name given to tomatoes that have been passed through a food mill, or through a gadget made especially for the task called a* passapomodoro, *or "tomato passer." Anyone who has ever successfully tried to grow tomatoes or who has ever visited a farmers' market in the late summer knows that when the time comes, you get all the tomatoes you could ever dream of—more than you could possibly eat or give away—and you get them all at once. During this time in the Italian countryside, they pass the tomatoes through the* passapomodoro, *which extracts the skin and seeds, and bottle the sauce that is extracted. A typical Italian larder might contain dozens of these bottles, which look like wine bottles and which allow cooks to use "fresh" tomato sauce year-round. Our* passata *is a little different from a traditional* passata *in that we cook it and season it to enhance the flavor, but it is still a very pure product.*

MAKES ABOUT 1 QUART

*P*ass the tomatoes, including their juices, through a food mill into a large bowl.

Heat the oil in a large sauté pan over medium-high heat until the oil is almost smoking and slides easily in the pan, 2 to 3 minutes. Add the tomato purée slowly as it will splatter when it hits the oil. Stir in the sugar, salt, and pepper, and cook until the sauce thickens slightly, about 30 minutes. Use the *passata* or set it aside to cool to room temperature, then transfer it to an airtight container and refrigerate for up to several days or freeze for up to several months.

2 28-ounce cans whole peeled plum tomatoes, including their juices (preferably San Marzano)

¼ cup extra-virgin olive oil

1 tablespoon sugar, plus more as desired

1 scant tablespoon kosher salt

1 heaping teaspoon freshly ground black pepper

roasted roma tomatoes

hese tomatoes are part of the arsenal of ingredients that we reach for to bring layers of flavor to other dishes. They add not just the flavor of tomatoes but also the slightly charred flavor that you get from cooking the tomatoes at very high heat. The tomatoes need to fit snugly on a baking sheet, which is why this recipe calls for you to roast four pounds of them. But you can always freeze them to use at a later date. I recommend you freeze them in batches of four halves, as we always call for them in multiples of four.

MAKES ABOUT 2 QUARTS

*P*reheat the oven to 450°F.
  Put the tomatoes, thyme, and garlic on a baking sheet. Drizzle with the olive oil, sprinkle with the salt and pepper, and toss the tomatoes to distribute the ingredients and coat them with the seasonings. Turn the tomatoes so they are cut side down and slip the garlic cloves under a few of them.

Place the baking sheet in the oven to roast the tomatoes until they are shrunken and dark brown in places, about 40 minutes. Remove the baking sheet from the oven and set aside. When the tomatoes are cool enough to touch, remove the skin from each tomato half and discard. Use the tomatoes or cool them to room temperature, transfer the contents of the baking sheet, including the garlic, thyme, and juices, into an airtight container or sealable plastic bags and refrigerate for up to several days or freeze for up to several months.

4 to 4 1/2 pounds fresh plum tomatoes, halved length-wise through the core, stem ends removed and discarded
1 bunch of fresh thyme (10 or 20 sprigs)
8 whole garlic cloves
1/2 cup extra-virgin olive oil
1 tablespoon kosher salt
1/2 teaspoon freshly ground black pepper

basic chicken stock

This is a neutral chicken stock that doesn't contain any seasonings other than peppercorns. We keep it simple because we use it in a variety of dishes, each of which will contain its own seasonings. We go through an astonishing amount of this stock and as you cook from this book, you will, too.

MAKES ABOUT 2 QUARTS

Put the chicken in a tall stockpot (10 quarts) and fill the stockpot with 10 cups water, or enough to cover the chicken liberally. Bring the water to a boil over high heat, skim off and discard the gray foam that rises to the top, and continue to boil until you have skimmed the foam two or three more times. Add the onion, carrot, celery, and peppercorns, reduce the heat, and simmer the stock for about 2 hours, until the water has reduced by half. Pour the stock through a fine-mesh strainer and discard the chicken and vegetables. Use the stock or set it aside to cool to room temperature. Transfer the stock to an airtight container, or several smaller containers, and refrigerate for up to several days or freeze for up to several months.

5 pounds chicken feet
and chicken wings

1 Spanish onion, quartered

1 large carrot, peeled
and cut into large pieces

1 celery rib, cut into
large pieces

1 tablespoon black
peppercorns

soffritto

offritto is a combination of sautéed onions, celery, and carrots, and it is the base of much Italian cooking. We start many of our dishes by sautéing these ingredients, and then we have this, a very dark soffritto, that we cook for four hours, after which the vegetables are transformed into a rich, thick paste. We make the soffritto in big batches and use it as a starting point for many of our ragùs, such as the duck ragù (see Gnocchi with Duck Ragù, page 187), the wild boar ragù (see Maltagliati *with Wild Boar Ragù, page 185), and the ragù bolognese (see Garganelli with Ragù Bolognese, page 189). We also use it to make a rich* contorni—*Yellow Wax Beans* Stracotto *in Soffritto with Salsa Verde (page 260)—that we serve in the Osteria. This soffritto might seem oily, but don't let that scare you as it's used to start dishes where olive oil would normally be used. At the restaurant, we chop the carrots and celery in a food processor, but we chop the onions by hand to avoid their becoming a watery purée.*

MAKES ABOUT 3 CUPS

*H*eat the olive oil in a large sauté pan over medium-high heat until the oil is almost smoking and slides easily in the pan, 2 to 3 minutes. Add the onions and cook for about 20 minutes, stirring frequently, until they are tender and translucent. Add the carrots and celery, reduce the heat to medium, and cook the vegetables, stirring often, for about 3 hours, until the soffritto is a deep brown caramel color and the vegetables are almost melted. If the vegetables start to sizzle and stick to the bottom of the pot, reduce the heat to low and continue cooking. Use the soffritto or let it cool to room temperature, then transfer it to an airtight container and refrigerate for up to a week or freeze for up to several months.

2 cups extra-virgin olive oil

2 pounds Spanish onions, finely chopped (about 7 cups)

1 pound carrots, peeled and finely chopped (about 3½ cups)

1 pound celery ribs, finely chopped (about 3¼ cups)

lemon vinaigrette

This is our most basic vinaigrette, used to dress many of our salads, and as a starting point to make other dressings, such as the mustard vinaigrette that is spooned over leeks in one of our most popular Mozzarella Bar items, Burrata with Leeks Vinaigrette and Mustard Bread Crumbs (page 72). Because it contains shallots, which can get a bit of an "off" flavor, you don't want to keep it for more than two or three days.

MAKES 1 CUP

Combine the shallots, lemon juice, vinegar, and salt in a small bowl. Set the bowl aside for 5 to 10 minutes to marinate the shallots. Add the olive oil in a slow, steady stream, whisking constantly to combine. Stir in the pepper. Taste for seasoning and add more salt or pepper, if desired. Use the vinaigrette or transfer it to an airtight container and refrigerate it for up to three days. Bring the vinaigrette to room temperature and whisk to recombine the ingredients before using.

¼ cup minced shallots
¼ cup fresh lemon juice
1 tablespoon champagne vinegar
1 teaspoon kosher salt, plus more to taste
½ cup extra-virgin olive oil
½ teaspoon freshly ground black pepper, plus more to taste

a note on presentation

I believe that we taste as much with our eyes as we do with our tongues, and for that reason, I think that the way food is presented is almost as important as the way it's prepared. I am very deliberate about the way I plate things, but this does not mean that the food is carefully placed. My standard line when I am training new people behind the bar is that I want the finished composition to look like it either fell from the sky or grew from the plate. I think food is pretty in its natural state, so I like it to look organic, not molded or manipulated. When I'm making Mozzarella Bar items, I like to treat each one individually. Each artichoke is a different size and shape, so I take that into consideration when I'm putting it on a *crostino*. It's as if I'm painting, and the *mise en place* in front of me—the cheeses and pestos, the leeks and roasted tomatoes, the breads and bread crumbs—are my paint. In this book, I tried to give you as detailed instructions for the presentations as for the preparations of these dishes. And I hoped to avoid the word *place*, which I never do, in favor of more accurate *nestle, drop, drape, drizzle, fold, lay, layer, build, rumple, scatter, sprinkle*, and *spoon*. You get the idea.

aperitivi and stuzzichini

*O*ne of the things I enjoy most about my time in Italy is the rituals that punctuate every day—a particular favorite being cocktail hour. In my town, in the summertime, every afternoon at around six o'clock, the entire population descends on the one bar in town, Bar del Gallo, which everyone refers to as Aldo's, after its owner, for an *aperitivo.* In the hour or two between a postlunch nap and dinner, we sit at the tables that spill out from the bar into the *piazza* and enjoy relaxed conversation at a slow pace that I rarely experience here.

The primary difference between Italian cocktail hour and American cocktail hour is that Italians don't eat. Italians might have seven salty peanuts at the bar, or they might indulge in a little cube of mortadella or mozzarella at a stand-up reception. The word for these little bites is *stuzzichini,* which comes from the word *stuzzicare,* meaning "to tease" or "to whet." The idea is to stimulate the appetite, not ruin it. But Italians would never, as we might, turn cocktail snacks into dinner.

All that said, when we host private parties in the Primo Ministro room, the private dining room in the Osteria, or in the Scuola di Pizza, the special-events room attached to Mozza2Go, our customers request to start with a cocktail hour that includes tray-passed *stuzzichini.*

But since Mozza is, as I've said, an Italian restaurant as seen through the eyes of American owners, the *stuzzichini* that we offer are a bit more substantial and flavorful than cubes of mortadella. We serve bite-size morsels that are easy to eat with a cocktail in one hand, such as crostini (pages 44–49) and Pancetta-wrapped Figs (page 52). You probably won't find anything so rich or filling at a cocktail hour in Italy, but we hope you enjoy these. And for you purists, forgive us the transgression, and enjoy your peanuts.

Italians are deeply habitual when it comes to what they eat and drink and in what order. They would never, for instance, have a glass of wine after they've had a *digestivo,* or after-dinner drink. During cocktail hour, there are only a few acceptable options, the most common of which is a glass of Prosecco, or Italian sparkling wine. At Mozza, we greet guests for private parties with a glass of Prosecco and one of our sommeliers carries a magnum of Flor Prosecco around the dining room, refilling glasses and greeting regular customers with complimentary glasses. For those who prefer a cocktail, we offer some, also included in this chapter, conceived in an Italian spirit and executed in an American one.

facing page: sculaccione cocktail

sugar plum

MAKES ENOUGH POMEGRANATE REDUCTION FOR 8 COCKTAILS

To make the pomegranate reduction, combine the pomegranate juice and sugar in a small saucepan and bring the mixture to a boil over high heat. Reduce the heat and simmer until the sugar dissolves and the juice thickens to the consistency of thin syrup. Turn off the heat and set aside to cool the syrup to room temperature before using. Store refrigerated in an airtight container for up to a week.

To make each cocktail, combine the vodka, grapefruit juice, and pomegranate reduction in a shaker filled with ice and shake vigorously. Strain the cocktail into a martini glass and serve.

for the pomegranate reduction
¼ cup pomegranate juice
¼ cup sugar

for each cocktail
2 ounces vodka (or gin)
1 ounce fresh grapefruit juice
1½ teaspoons pomegranate reduction

il postino

I don't rent out my house in Italy but I do let friends stay there. The "rent" that I charge is always the same: one book and one DVD. Our collection of both is pretty random, but thankfully someone at some time thought to bring the movie Il Postino, *one of my all-time favorites.*

MAKES ENOUGH HONEY SYRUP FOR 8 COCKTAILS

To make the honey syrup, combine the honey and water in a small saucepan and bring the mixture to a boil over high heat. Reduce the heat and simmer until the honey is the consistency of thin syrup. Turn off the heat and set aside to cool the syrup to room temperature before using. Store refrigerated in an airtight container for up to a week.

To make each cocktail, combine the rum, lime juice, and honey syrup in a shaker with ice and shake well. Add the Prosecco and shake again. Strain the cocktail into a champagne flute, adding more Prosecco, if necessary, to fill the glass. Garnish with a lime twist and serve.

for the honey syrup
3 ounces mild-flavored honey, such as clover or wildflower honey
2 tablespoons water

for each cocktail
1 ounce light rum
1 tablespoon fresh lime juice
1 tablespoon honey syrup
3 ounces Prosecco, plus more as needed
Lime twist, for garnish

sculaccione

MAKES ENOUGH SIMPLE SYRUP FOR 4 TO 6 COCKTAILS

To make the simple syrup, combine the sugar and water in a small saucepan and bring the mixture to a boil over high heat. Reduce the heat and simmer until the sugar is dissolved. Turn off the heat and set aside to cool the syrup to room temperature. Store refrigerated in an airtight container for up to a week.

To make each cocktail, combine the tequila, lime juice, grapefruit juice, Campari, bitters, and simple syrup in a shaker filled with ice and shake vigorously. Fill an old-fashioned glass with ice, strain the cocktail into the glass, and garnish with a lime wheel.

for the simple syrup
1/4 cup sugar
1/4 cup water

for each cocktail
2 ounces Blanco tequila
1 1/2 tablespoons fresh lime juice
1 tablespoon fresh grapefruit juice
1 tablespoon Campari
Dash of Angostura bitters
1 tablespoon simple syrup
Lime wheel, for garnish

meletti smash

This cocktail is named after the brand of amaro, or bitters, that we use to make it. You could use another bitters if you can't find Meletti.

MAKES ENOUGH SIMPLE SYRUP FOR 4 TO 6 COCKTAILS

To make the simple syrup, combine the sugar and water in a small saucepan and bring the mixture to a boil over high heat. Reduce the heat and simmer until the sugar is dissolved. Turn off the heat and set aside to cool the syrup to room temperature. Store refrigerated in an airtight container for up to a week.

To make each cocktail, use a wooden pestle or wooden spoon to muddle the mint leaves in an old-fashioned glass. Add the mint bitters and fill the glass with crushed ice. Combine the Amaro Meletti, rum, lime juice, and simple syrup in a shaker filled with ice and shake vigorously. Strain the cocktail into the glass with the mint leaves, garnish with a sprig of fresh mint, and serve.

for the simple syrup
1/4 cup sugar
1/4 cup water

for each cocktail
10 fresh mint leaves, plus 1 sprig for garnish
Dash of Fee Brothers mint bitters
1 ounce Amaro Meletti
1 ounce Black Seal rum
1 1/2 tablespoons fresh lime juice
1 tablespoon simple syrup

gordon's cup

This refreshing cocktail is a play on the traditional British cocktail, Pimm's Cup, made with gin instead of Pimm's.

MAKES ENOUGH SIMPLE SYRUP FOR 4 TO 6 COCKTAILS

To make the simple syrup, combine the sugar and water in a small saucepan and bring the mixture to a boil over high heat. Reduce the heat and simmer until the sugar is dissolved. Turn off the heat and set aside to cool the syrup to room temperature. Store refrigerated in an airtight container for up to a week.

To make each cocktail, use a wooden pestle or wooden spoon to muddle 6 of the cucumber slices in an old-fashioned glass and fill the glass with ice cubes. Combine the gin, lime juice, and simple syrup in a shaker filled with ice and shake vigorously. Strain the cocktail into the glass with the muddled cucumbers, garnish with the remaining cucumber slices, and serve.

for the simple syrup
1/4 cup sugar
1/4 cup water

for each cocktail
9 thin slices cucumber (preferably Japanese cucumber)
2 ounces Plymouth gin
1 ounce fresh lime juice
1 1/2 tablespoons simple syrup

olives al forno

In the Italian tradition of stuzzichini, *I don't like to put out so many appetizers that my guests will ruin their appetites, but two things that I must serve whenever I entertain are roasted olives and toasted almonds tossed with olive oil and sea salt. These olives, which are tossed with citrus zest and garlic confit, are as beautiful as they are delicious. If we get an unusual olive variety, we might throw that in, but normally the combination we use is Lucques, Castelvetrano, Taggiasche, and Picholine. You can use whatever combination of olives you want or have access to, as long as they're not the canned pitted things I grew up with. Also, keep in mind that it's ideal to have a variety of colors and sizes.*

You can prepare the olives up to a month in advance. Keep them in the refrigerator and roast them just before serving. If you are preparing them in advance, however, omit the garlic confit and garlic oil, as they will cause the olives to spoil more quickly. Prepare the olives with only the regular olive oil, and add the garlic and garlic oil up to several days before you are ready to roast them.

MAKES 1 QUART OF OLIVES

SUGGESTED WINE PAIRING: LAMBRUSCO *BIANCO* I.G.T. (EMILIA-ROMAGNA)

Combine the olives in a large bowl. Add the olive oil, orange rind, lemon rind, bay leaves, and rosemary. Add the Garlic Confit, including the chiles, and toss to combine.

Adjust the oven rack to the middle position and preheat the oven to 500°F.

Transfer the olives to a large shallow baking dish or several small shallow baking dishes. Place the baking dish on a baking sheet to catch any oil that bubbles over, and place the olives in the oven until the oil is sizzling and the olives are light golden brown on top, 8 to 10 minutes. Remove the olives from the oven and drizzle the balsamic vinegar over them while they're still hot. Serve warm.

4 cups mixed unpitted olives (such as 1 cup each Lucques, Castelvetrano, Taggiasche or Niçoise, and Picholine), drained
1 cup extra-virgin olive oil
Wide zest strips of 1 orange (peeled using a vegetable peeler)
Wide zest strips of 1 lemon (peeled using a vegetable peeler)
4 dried bay leaves
1/2 cup fresh rosemary needles
Garlic Confit (page 38)
1/4 cup balsamic vinegar

garlic confit

MAKES ³/₄ CUP

*C*ombine the garlic, chiles, and olive oil in a small saucepan. Add enough oil to come three-fourths of the way up the sides of the garlic.

Heat the oil over high heat until it just starts to bubble; you will start to hear the first sizzling noises and the first rapid bubble start to come up. Reduce the heat and simmer the garlic until it's deep golden brown, soft, buttery, and spreadable. Keep a careful eye on the garlic cloves and don't overcook them; they burn easily and will continue to brown as they cool. Set the garlic aside to cool to room temperature and use or transfer the contents of the saucepan to an airtight container and refrigerate for several days. To store the garlic for a longer period of time, add enough oil to completely cover the cloves and refrigerate them for up to several weeks.

1 cup garlic cloves
3 dried whole arbol chiles
¹/₂ cup extra-virgin olive oil, or more as needed

toasted almonds with sea salt

*T*his isn't really a recipe, just a method for toasting almonds, but I felt that it was important to talk about almonds since, as I've said, they are my favorite thing to set out before a meal, not to mention to snack on while setting up at work or at home. Toasting the almonds enhances their flavor, and then tossing them with olive oil and sea salt turns them into something really worth eating. We call for toasted almonds in various recipes, such as Burrata with Asparagus, Brown Butter, Guanciale, and Almonds (page 76). Anytime we ask for toasted almonds I suggest you make more than what the recipe calls for, as I know you'll want some to snack on.

*T*o toast almonds, adjust the oven rack to the middle position and preheat the oven to 325°F. Spread the almonds on a baking sheet and toast for 12 to 15 minutes, or until they are fragrant and golden brown. Remove the almonds from the oven, drizzle them with the olive oil, sprinkle with sea salt, and toss to coat the almonds with the seasonings. Transfer the almonds to a pretty bowl, and serve.

1 cup raw almonds
1 tablespoon olive oil
¹/₂ teaspoon Maldon sea salt

prosciutto-wrapped breadsticks

At the restaurant we call these Love Sticks, because everyone loves them so much. Before I tried them, I might have thought it was lily gilding to serve butter with prosciutto, even though ham and butter has always been one of my favorite sandwich combinations. And I never would have considered truffles and prosciutto together, because truffles are so pungent and are usually paired with mild flavors. In fact, the combination is so perfect that I'm sorry to have to admit that I did not invent it. These are something Matt brought home from Del Posto. They are also really fun to eat and make for the ideal handheld appetizer. If you have leftover truffle butter, wrap what you don't use tightly in plastic and refrigerate to make Love Sticks, spread it on a ham sandwich, or shave it over scrambled eggs. It will last for several days, after which the truffle flavor may begin to fade.

MAKES 48 STICKS

SUGGESTED WINE PAIRING: EXTRA-DRY PROSECCO (FRIULI)

Combine the butter and truffle salt in a small bowl and mix with a spoon to thoroughly combine.

Break each breadstick in half. Smear 2 teaspoons of the truffle butter on the last 3 to 4 inches of the broken end of each breadstick. Rip a slice of prosciutto in half and loosely drape it around the breadstick over the truffle butter. Repeat with the remaining breadsticks and prosciutto.

Lay the breadsticks down on a cutting board or a serving platter, crossing the undressed portion of the sticks in an x formation. Lay two more breadsticks in the same way on top of the first, creating a long line of crossed breadsticks, and serve.

½ cup (1 stick) unsalted butter, at room temperature
½ teaspoon truffle salt
24 long *grissini* (breadsticks)
24 thin slices of prosciutto (about 6 ounces)

fried squash blossoms with ricotta

I have never met anyone who doesn't like these squash blossoms. It would seem like it would be hard to go wrong, considering the combination of deep-fried batter and ricotta cheese, but I find that rarely do restaurants get the filling right. It took us a lot of tries to come up with ours, but luckily Matt and I both knew what we wanted and we both wanted the same thing, which was a light fluffy filling that also had a melting component, which is why we added mozzarella. We dip the blossoms in tempura batter because we like how light and crunchy tempura is. I try not to be brand-specific in my recipes, but in this case we recommend you use Mochiko rice flour, which you can find at conventional grocery stores, and which we think makes for the crispest finished product.

MAKES 40 SQUASH BLOSSOMS

SUGGESTED WINE PAIRING: PROSECCO DI VALDOBBIADENE (VENETO)

Combine the ricotta, mozzarella, Parmigiano-Reggiano, egg, salt, and nutmeg in a medium mixing bowl and stir to combine. Taste for seasoning and add more salt or nutmeg, if desired. Use the filling or transfer to an airtight container and place it in the refrigerator for up to three days.

Trim all but the last 1 inch of the squash blossom stems and discard. Use a small sharp knife to gently cut an incision the length of a blossom to open it. Gently open the flower to reveal the stamen and use the knife to cut it off and discard. Repeat with the remaining blossoms.

Working one at a time, lay a squash blossom on your work surface, open it up, and spoon about 1 tablespoon of the filling inside. Some blossoms may take more or less filling, depending on their size. You don't want to overstuff the blossoms; you want the filling to come up to just where the blossom starts to break off into multiple petals. Close the blossom and press it gently in the palm of your hand to squeeze the filling down toward the stem. With your other hand, grab the petals at the top and twist them slightly to close the blossoms and seal the cheese inside. Repeat with the remaining blossoms and filling.

Prepare a large bowl of ice water. Put the flour in a bowl smaller than that with the ice water. Add the sparkling water and whisk until smooth. It should be the consistency of thin pancake batter; add more water if it is too thick. Place the bowl with the batter in the ice bath to keep it cold.

1 cup fresh ricotta

1 cup small-cubed low-moisture mozzarella (about 5½ ounces)

½ cup freshly grated Parmigiano-Reggiano

1 extra-large egg, lightly beaten

1 teaspoon kosher salt, plus more to taste

½ teaspoon freshly grated nutmeg, plus more to taste

40 squash blossoms

2 cups rice flour (preferably Mochiko brand)

2 cups sparkling water

Grapeseed oil or another neutral-flavored oil, such as canola oil, for frying

1 lemon, halved, for squeezing over the blossoms

Maldon sea salt or another flaky sea salt, such as fleur de sel

Fasten a deep-fry thermometer to the side of a medium saucepan and fill the saucepan 3 to 4 inches deep with the oil. Heat the oil over medium-high heat until the thermometer registers 350°F. While the oil is heating, line a baking sheet with paper towels.

Working in batches of about six at a time, carefully drop the squash blossoms in the batter and gently turn to coat them all over. Pick one blossom out of the batter, give it a twist to close it again, and carefully drop it stem first into the oil. Repeat with the remaining blossoms that are in the batter and fry until they are golden brown, turning them so they brown evenly, 3 to 4 minutes. Use a slotted spoon to remove the blossoms from the oil and transfer them to the paper towels to drain. Squeeze a drop of lemon juice on each blossom, season with the sea salt, and serve immediately.

Use a slotted spoon to clean the cooked bits out of the oil. Add more oil to the pan if it has dropped below 3 inches and wait for the oil to heat to 350°F. Repeat, battering and frying the remaining blossoms in the same way, until you've fried all of the squash blossoms.

homemade ricotta

Ricotta means "recooked," and is so named because it is a by-product of making mozzarella. This version is only cooked once, so it really isn't ricotta at all. Still, the result is a creamy and delicious fresh cheese, which you can use in any recipes in this book that call for ricotta. (If you are making the Ricotta Ravioli, however, you need to strain the cheese for at least 24 hours.) I especially like the cheese still warm, fresh after it's made. The recipe can be doubled or quadrupled, depending on how much you need.

MAKES ABOUT 8 OUNCES

Without stirring, pour the milk, cream, lemon juice, and salt in a small heavy-bottomed stainless steel saucepan and bring to a boil. Turn off the heat and set the saucepan aside until the mixture cools slightly, 5 to 10 minutes. (You'll see the "ricotta" separating into curds.) Line a strainer or colander with cheesecloth and place it in the sink. Scoop the curds out of the saucepan (don't pour, as you don't want to break up the curds) and into the strainer to drain. You can use the ricotta while it's still warm, or tie the cheesecloth on to the handle of a long wooden spoon. Place the spoon over a bowl or saucepan so the bundle is hanging over the bowl, and place it in the refrigerator to drain until you are ready to use it, or for up to two days.

4 cups whole milk
1 cup heavy whipping cream
2 tablespoons fresh squeezed, strained lemon juice
1 1/2 teaspoons kosher salt

arancine alla bolognese

*U*p *until we opened Mozza I had eaten only meatless versions of* arancine. *Those I'd had were mostly in* cichetti, *the shoebox-size stand-up wine and* stuzzichini *bars in Venice, where cone-shaped versions are a staple, and in Sicily, where they're much larger and round, like a tangerine. Both were made of plain risotto with cheese in the middle. In Rome,* arancine *are often called "suppli al telefono," meaning telephone cords, because the ideal is that the cheese inside melts and stretches like an old-fashioned telephone cord. Matt and I worked hard to achieve that ideal and I think we did. I suggest you make these when you have leftover bolognese because, as good as they are, it would be a herculean effort to make bolognese for just the ½ cup you need to make these. Besides, that is what an Italian grandmother would do.*

MAKES ABOUT 4 DOZEN RICE BALLS

SUGGESTED WINE PAIRING: SANGIOVESE DI ROMAGNA (EMILIA-ROMAGNA)

*T*o make the risotto, bring the stock to a boil in a medium pot. Reduce the heat to low to barely keep the stock warm. Combine the onion, 2 tablespoons of the olive oil, and ½ teaspoon of the salt in a risotto pot or large saucepan over medium-high heat and sauté until the onion is tender and translucent, about 10 minutes. Add the water and continue to cook the onion, stirring frequently and taking care not to let it brown, until the water has evaporated and the onion looks oily again, about 3 minutes. Stir in the rice, drizzle with 2 tablespoons of the remaining olive oil, and toast the rice for 4 minutes, stirring frequently, until it starts to make a light crackling sound. Here is where the famous risotto process of stirring constantly begins.

Add the wine, reduce the heat to low, and simmer for 5 to 6 minutes, stirring frequently, until the pan is dry and the rice begins to stick to the pot; you will hear the rice faintly begin to crackle in the pan. Ladle in ½ cup of the stock, or enough to just cover the rice, and ½ teaspoon more of the salt. Cook the rice, stirring constantly and wiping down the sides of the pan with a spatula, until the pan is once again dry and the rice again begins to stick to it, about 3 minutes. Add ¼ cup more stock and cook the rice for 5 minutes, adding ¼ cup more stock whenever the liquid gets below the level of the rice. Stir in the bolognese and cook the rice with the bolognese for 8 to 10 minutes, stirring

for the risotto

4 cups Basic Chicken Stock (page 27) or water

½ large yellow Spanish onion, finely chopped (about 1 cup)

¼ cup plus 2 tablespoons (6 tablespoons) extra-virgin olive oil

1 teaspoon kosher salt

2 tablespoons water

1 cup carnaroli or arborio rice

1 cup dry white wine

½ cup ragù bolognese (see Garganelli with Ragù Bolognese, page 189)

1 tablespoon unsalted butter

½ cup freshly grated Parmigiano-Reggiano

½ cup small-diced fontina (about 3 ounces)

½ cup small-diced low-moisture mozzarella (about 3 ounces)

constantly and adding ½ cup more stock when the pan is dry, until the rice is al dente.

Turn off the heat, add the butter and the remaining 2 tablespoons of olive oil, and stir vigorously with a risotto spoon or a wooden spoon for about 2 minutes to emulsify the risotto. (This is probably the most important detail of all the details to making risotto. Here the rice is releasing its starches, leaving it suspended in its rich and creamy liquid.) Stir in the Parmigiano-Reggiano and set the risotto aside to cool to room temperature. When the risotto is cool, gently fold in the fontina and mozzarella. Transfer the risotto to a tightly covered container and place it in the refrigerator to chill for at least 1 hour and up to overnight.

Using a spoon, scoop up ¾ ounce (about 1 tablespoon) of the risotto, and gently compress it by cupping it tightly in your fingers, then roll it into a ball. Fry the *arancine* immediately or cover in plastic and refrigerate until you are ready to fry them or for up to one day.

To fry and serve the *arancine,* heat the *passata* in a medium saucepan over low heat, stirring occasionally to keep it from sticking to the pan while you fry the *arancine.*

Pour the flour into a medium bowl or pie pan. Whisk the eggs into a separate medium bowl and pour the bread crumbs into a third medium bowl or another pie pan. Dredge a rice ball into the flour, making sure to coat it all over. Shake off the excess flour and place the ball into the egg mixture, making sure it is completely covered in egg. Lastly, put the ball in the bread crumbs to coat evenly. Place the prepared *arancine* on a baking sheet and repeat with the remaining balls.

Fasten a deep-fry thermometer to the side of a medium saucepan and fill the saucepan 3 to 4 inches deep with the oil. Heat the oil over medium-high heat until the thermometer registers 350°F. While the oil is heating, line a baking sheet with paper towels.

Working in batches and taking care not to crowd the pan, carefully drop the *arancine* into the oil in a single layer and fry until they are golden brown, turning them so they brown evenly, 3 to 4 minutes. Use a slotted spoon or tongs to remove the balls from the oil and transfer them to the paper towels to drain. Season them with salt immediately.

Add more oil to the pan if it has dropped below 3 inches deep and wait for the oil to heat to 350°F before frying the remaining batches of *arancine* in the same way.

Spoon the *passata* in a thin layer on individual dishes or on a large serving dish. Place the *arancine* on top of the *passata,* use a microplane or another fine grater to grate Parmigiano-Reggiano over the top, and serve.

for frying and serving

1 cup *Passata di Pomodoro* (page 25) or tomato sauce

1 cup unbleached all-purpose flour

4 extra-large eggs

2 cups finely ground unseasoned bread crumbs (from about 10 ounces of crustless bread)

Grapeseed oil or another neutral-flavored oil, such as canola oil, for frying

Kosher salt

Wedge of Parmigiano-Reggiano, for grating

In Tuscany and Umbria a plate of crostini *misti* or bruschette *misti* is the standard snack to enjoy before a meal, but I have never quite figured out the difference between the two. The common American conception is that crostini are made on slices of bread that are smaller and thinner than those used to make bruschette, and bruschette are so closely identified with the chopped tomatoes that often top them that in some supermarkets, chopped tomato with garlic and basil is sold as "bruschetta." When I taught a class with Mario at *Food & Wine* magazine's annual event in Aspen, Mario told the students that the difference between crostini and bruschette is that crostini tend to be smaller and can be cold, and bruschette are larger and hot. "You can, however, have a hot *crostino*. But you will never have a cold *bruschetta*." At the restaurant, we serve these crostini in groups of three and those in the Mozzarella Bar in pairs. These recipes have much larger yields, which makes them convenient for a party. If you serve crostini for a party, I think it's nice to offer a selection.

white beans alla toscana with extra-virgin olive oil and saba

The crostini selection served at just about every restaurant near my house in Italy includes toppings of chicken livers, chopped tomatoes, and white bean purée, such as this one. We simmer the beans with tons of garlic and olive oil, and drizzle the crostini with saba, Sardinian grape must. If you can't find saba, substitute vin cotto, a sweet, syrupy condiment that means "cooked wine," or aged balsamico condimento. It is a nice option for vegetarians. We grill the radicchio for these crostini but gave instructions for cooking it on the stovetop because it would be unrealistic to light the grill just to cook a few leaves of the radicchio. That said, if you happen to have the grill on . . .

MAKES 24 CROSTINI

 WINE PAIRING SUGGESTION: VERNACCIA DI SAN GIMIGNANO (TUSCANY)

o make the white bean purée, drain the soaked beans and put them in a large saucepan with enough water to cover by 1½ inches. (Cooking them in just enough water yields richer, creamier beans than if you were to boil them in tons of water.) Wrap the carrots, celery, garlic cloves, onion, and chiles in a doubled piece of cheesecloth and tie it into a closed bundle with kitchen twine. Add the bundle to the pot with the beans, stir in the olive oil and salt, and bring the water to a boil over high heat. Reduce the heat and simmer the beans until they are very tender and creamy, adding more water to the pot as needed, but never covering them by more than an inch to an inch and a half. (The time will vary depending on how long you soaked the beans, from 1 hour to as long as 4.) Turn off the heat and set the beans aside to cool slightly in their liquid. Remove and discard the cheesecloth bundle and drain the beans, reserving the cooking liquid.

Transfer the beans to the bowl of a food processor fitted with a metal blade or the jar of a blender and purée, adding some of the reserved liquid if necessary, to form a spoonable paste that is smooth with some texture. (Alternatively, you can mash the beans using a mortar and pestle or using a wire whisk as you would a potato masher to smash the beans.) Taste for seasoning and add more salt, if desired. Use the beans or transfer to an airtight container and refrigerate for up to three days. Bring the beans to room temperature before serving.

To prepare the radicchio, combine the vinegar, oil, salt, and pepper in a large bowl. Add the radicchio leaves and massage the marinade into the leaves. Set aside to marinate the leaves for at least 15 minutes and up to several hours.

Preheat a cast-iron pan or a grill pan over high heat. Place the radicchio leaves in the pan and cook for 1½ to 2 minutes, turning occasionally, until they are deep brown and caramelized in places but not crisp.

To assemble, lay the Garlic Crostini oiled side up on a work surface. Rip each radicchio leaf in half and drape the half on each *crostino,* leaving the edges of the bread visible. Spoon 1 heaping tablespoon of the white bean purée on top of the radicchio on each *crostino,* leaving the radicchio visible around the edges. Create a small crater in each serving of white beans, drizzle the finishing-quality olive oil in the craters and about ½ teaspoon of the *saba* in and around each crater. Sprinkle the thyme and grind the pepper over the crostini, and serve.

for the white bean purée

1 cup dried white beans, soaked 1 to 4 hours
2 large carrots, peeled and halved
2 celery ribs, halved
16 garlic cloves
½ yellow Spanish onion, halved
2 dried whole arbol chiles
½ cup extra-virgin olive oil
2 tablespoons kosher salt, plus more to taste

for the radicchio

2 tablespoons balsamic vinegar
2 tablespoons extra-virgin olive oil
½ teaspoon kosher salt
½ teaspoon freshly ground black pepper
12 radicchio leaves

for assembling the crostini

24 Garlic Crostini (page 46)
Finishing-quality extra-virgin olive oil
Saba, for drizzling (see headnote)
Fresh thyme leaves
Fresh coarsely ground black pepper

garlic crostini

These crispy toasts are a staple of our kitchen. If you have a sandwich press, you can use it instead of the oven to toast the bread slices.

MAKES 8 CROSTINI

Adjust the oven rack to the middle position and preheat the oven to 350°F, or preheat a sandwich press.

Place the bread slices on a baking sheet, brush the tops with olive oil, and bake for 15 to 20 minutes, until they're golden brown and crisp. Alternatively, brush both sides of the bread slices with olive oil and toast them in a sandwich press. Remove the crostini from the oven and rub the oiled sides of the crostini lightly with the garlic.

8 ½-inch-thick slices from a *bâtard,* or fat baguette, or 4 slices from a large round of rustic white loaf, halved
Extra-virgin olive oil, for brushing the bread
1 garlic clove

chicken livers, capers, parsley, and guanciale

Just when I think we have perfected a dish, I come across a version that someone has done better, and that's what happened here. I always thought we did a great job with the chicken liver pâté we served at the Pizzeria, and it is one of the most raved-about items we serve. The combination of pancetta, lemon, and capers is delicious, and we hand-chop it, which gives it great texture, so I was totally happy with these crostini until I went to the Spotted Pig in New York City and had theirs. April Bloomfield, the chef, served her chicken livers on bread that was doused with—not drizzled and not brushed, but drowned *in—olive oil, which made the chicken liver taste that much better. When I came back from that trip, we started doing the same thing, drowning the toast for our chicken liver pâté in the best finishing-quality olive oil we have. After I copied April's bread, I think our version of chicken liver crostini went back to number one—or at least we're tied for first place.*

MAKES 2 CUPS PÂTÉ, OR ENOUGH FOR 24 CROSTINI

WINE PAIRING SUGGESTION: CERASUOLO ROSATO (ABRUZZI)

Use a small knife to remove the connective veins from the chicken livers, discard the veins, and place the chicken livers on a plate lined with paper towels. Pat them with paper towels to get out the excess moisture, and discard the towels. Season the livers very generously with salt and pepper and toss to coat them all over with the seasoning.

Heat ¼ cup of the olive oil in a large sauté pan over medium-high heat until the oil is almost smoking and slides easily in the pan, 2 to 3 minutes. One by one, carefully add the chicken livers to the pan. (By adding them one at a time the pan doesn't cool down too much, and it also ensures you will have room for all of the livers, as they shrink immediately when they hit the pan. You should be able to fit them all in the pan at the same time.) Cook the livers for about 3 minutes per side, until they're deep brown. Add the pancetta, reduce the heat to low, and cook for 1 to 2 minutes, until the fat is rendered from the pancetta. Add the garlic and cook for about 1 minute, stirring constantly to prevent it from browning. Add the brandy, shake the pan or stir the livers to deglaze the pan, and cook for about 30 seconds to burn off the alcohol. Turn off the heat and turn the contents of the pan out onto a large cutting board, making sure to get all the bits out of the bottom of the pan.

Pile the parsley, shallots, capers, and lemon zest on top of the mound of chicken livers and pancetta and drizzle with the lemon juice and ¼ cup of the olive oil. Run a large knife through the mound five or ten times to roughly chop the livers and all the other ingredients. Drizzle another ¼ cup of olive oil over the mound and continue to chop, gathering the ingredients into a mound from time to time. Add the remaining ¼ cup of olive oil and chop until the livers are the consistency of a coarse paste, almost puréed. Serve the chicken liver spread or transfer to an airtight container and refrigerate for up to three days; bring to room temperature before assembling the crostini.

When you are ready to serve the crostini, adjust the oven rack to the middle position and preheat the oven to 350°F.

Place the *guanciale* slices on a baking sheet and put in the oven until they are cooked through but not crisp, 3 to 5 minutes. Remove the *guanciale* from the oven and transfer to paper towels to drain.

To assemble, lay the crostini oiled side up on a work surface and spoon a heaping tablespoon of the chicken liver spread in an uneven layer on the toast, leaving the edges exposed. Tear 1 piece of *guanciale* in half and lay both halves at an angle on top of the chicken liver, slightly overlapping in a natural-looking way. Repeat with the remaining crostini, chicken liver, and *guanciale,* and serve.

1 pound chicken livers
Kosher salt and freshly ground
    black pepper
1 cup extra-virgin olive oil
2 ounces pancetta, chopped
2 garlic cloves, finely chopped
2 tablespoons brandy or
    Cognac
2 tablespoons finely chopped
    fresh Italian parsley leaves
2 tablespoons finely chopped
    shallots
2 tablespoons capers
    (preferably salt-packed),
    soaked for 15 minutes if
    salt-packed, rinsed, and
    drained
Grated zest of 1 lemon, plus
    1 tablespoon fresh lemon
    juice
12 thin slices *guanciale* or
    pancetta (about 6 to
    8 ounces)
24 Crostini *Bagnati* (page 48)

crostoni and crostini bagnati

The difference between crostoni *and* crostini *is that* crostoni *are big and* crostini *are small. Here, both are bathed in olive oil. We use them when we want the bread to be part of the flavor of the dish, not just a vehicle for other flavors. If you have a sandwich press, you can use it to toast these instead of toasting them in the oven.*

MAKES 4 LONG *CROSTONI* OR 8 SMALLER *CROSTINI*

Adjust the oven rack to the middle position and preheat the oven to 350°F or preheat a sandwich press.

Place the bread slices on a baking sheet, brush the tops with olive oil, and bake them for 15 to 20 minutes, until they're golden brown and crisp. Alternatively, brush both sides of the bread slices with olive oil and toast them in a sandwich press. Remove the *crostoni* from the oven and rub the oiled sides of the *crostoni* with the garlic. Drizzle 1 tablespoon of the finishing-quality olive oil over each *crostono* or ½ tablespoon on each crostini, and sprinkle liberally with the sea salt.

4 ½-inch-thick slices from a loaf of *pane rustica* or another large, flat loaf of rustic white bread, such as ciabatta; or 8 slices from a *bâtard,* or fat baguette, cut on an extreme bias to yield very long slices

Extra-virgin olive oil, for brushing the bread

1 garlic clove

4 tablespoons finishing-quality extra-virgin olive oil

Maldon sea salt or another flaky sea salt, such as fleur de sel

bacalà mantecato

*M*antecato *means "churned," and* bacalà mantecato, *essentially an Italian version of French brandade, is salt cod potato purée. We started making these crostini to use the salt cod we had left from the* Bacalà al Forno *(page 215) at the Pizzeria. It's so popular that we now make extra salt cod for this dish.*

MAKES 24 CROSTINI

SUGGESTED WINE PAIRING: SOAVE CLASSICO (VENETO)

*T*o prepare, place the *bacalà* in a large bowl. Fill the bowl with water and soak the *bacalà* for 1 hour, changing the water two or three times during that period. Remove the *bacalà* from the water and cut it into three segments.

Heat the olive oil and garlic in a medium saucepan over medium heat, season with salt, and cook, stirring constantly, to flavor the oil with the garlic and sweat the garlic without browning it, about 2 minutes. Add the potatoes and cook for 1 minute to coat them with seasonings. Add the milk, increase the heat to high, and cook until the milk begins to bubble. Reduce the heat and simmer the potatoes in the milk until they're tender, about 20 minutes. Add the *bacalà* and simmer until the fish is cooked through and the potatoes have begun to break down, thickening the milk to a saucelike consistency, about 6 minutes. Pass the contents of the saucepan through a food mill into a mixing bowl and stir to combine the ingredients. Transfer half of the purée to the bowl of a food processor fitted with a metal blade or the jar of a blender and purée until smooth. Return the puréed *bacalà* to the bowl with the unpuréed cod and stir to combine. Add more milk if necessary to obtain a spoonable consistency. Taste for seasoning and add more salt, if desired. Serve the *mantecato* or transfer it to an airtight container and refrigerate for up to three days. Before serving, warm the *mantecato* in a small saucepan over low heat, adding enough milk to obtain the desired consistency.

To assemble, lay the crostini oiled side up on a work surface and spoon a heaping tablespoon of the *bacalà mantecato* into an uneven layer onto each *crostino,* leaving the edges of the bread visible. Create a small crater in the center of each mound of *bacalà* and spoon ¼ teaspoon of the tapenade into each crater. (If you are using olives instead of tapenade, nestle one olive in each crater and drizzle with ⅛ teaspoon of the finishing-quality olive oil.) Sprinkle with the parsley and serve.

for the *bacalà mantecato*

6 ounces salted *bacalà* (salt cod; see *Bacalà al Forno,* page 215, or use store-bought)

¼ cup extra-virgin olive oil

12 large garlic cloves, minced

Kosher salt

6 ounces russet potatoes, peeled and cut into 1-inch dice

1½ cups whole milk, plus more as needed

for assembling the crostini

24 Garlic Crostini (page 46)

2 tablespoons Black Olive Tapenade (page 65); or 24 whole Moroccan oil-cured black olives, pitted and chopped, plus finishing-quality extra-virgin olive oil

¼ cup thinly sliced fresh Italian parsley leaves

roasted baby peppers stuffed with tuna

When the Pizzeria first opened we hosted a book signing for Lidia Bastianich's book Lidia's Italy, *and we served Lidia's peppers as an antipasto. I found myself nibbling on them all evening. Shortly after, I spotted tiny, bright-colored peppers in a grocery store. They were so pretty, with red, yellow, and orange colors mixed in one bag. Motivated by those peppers, I decided to put a version of Lidia's peppers on the Pizzeria menu. For the stuffing, we start by poaching tuna in olive oil, but you could use quality olive oil–packed tuna. If you don't want to make 48 peppers, save the excess tuna stuffing and serve it on a salad of arugula dressed with lemon vinaigrette.*

MAKES 48 PEPPERS

SUGGESTED WINE PAIRING: VITOVSKA (CARSO, FRIULI)

To prepare the peppers, adjust the oven racks so one is in the middle position and preheat the oven to 350°F.

Place the peppers on a baking sheet, rub them all over with the olive oil, sprinkle with salt, and spread them out in a single layer. Roast the peppers for about 30 minutes, turning them occasionally, until their skins are wrinkled and slightly charred in places. Remove the peppers from the oven, leaving the oven on at the same temperature, and set aside to cool to room temperature.

To prepare the stuffing, cut the tuna into 1-inch-thick slices, season with the salt and pepper, and place the slices in a small saucepan. Arrange the lemon slices and rosemary around the tuna and pour in enough olive oil to cover. Place the saucepan in the oven to cook the tuna for about 10 minutes, until medium-rare. (To test, split one of the slices with a fork to see the center.) Remove the tuna from the oven and let it cool to room temperature in the oil.

Combine the Garlic Mayonnaise, parsley, capers, mustard, anchovies, vinegar, and lemon juice in a large bowl. Remove the tuna from the oil and break it into the bowl with the mixture. Use a wire whisk as you would a potato masher to break up any large chunks but you do want the tuna to have texture. Fold the tuna and other ingredients until they are thoroughly combined.

for the peppers

48 baby peppers (preferably assorted colors), stems attached

3 tablespoons extra-virgin olive oil

Kosher salt

for the tuna stuffing

1 pound albacore tuna

½ teaspoon kosher salt

¼ teaspoon freshly ground black pepper

1 lemon, sliced into ¼-inch rounds

1 long sprig of rosemary, broken into a few pieces

6 cups extra-virgin olive oil, or enough to cover the tuna

¾ cup Garlic Mayonnaise (recipe follows)

2 heaping tablespoons finely chopped fresh Italian parsley leaves

2 heaping tablespoons capers (preferably salt-packed), soaked for 15 minutes if salt-packed, rinsed, drained, and finely chopped

1½ tablespoons Dijon mustard

3 anchovy fillets (preferably salt-packed), rinsed, backbones removed if salt-packed, and finely chopped

2½ teaspoons apple cider vinegar

2 teaspoons fresh lemon juice

To assemble, slice each pepper almost in half lengthwise, leaving them attached on one side. Carefully scrape out and discard the seeds, and spoon a scant tablespoon of stuffing into each pepper. Arrange the peppers on a platter. Scatter the arugula over them, drizzle with the finishing-quality olive oil and the juice of the lemon, sprinkle with sea salt, and serve.

for assembling the peppers
2 cups loosely packed arugula
(preferably wild)
Finishing-quality extra-virgin
olive oil
1 lemon, halved
Maldon sea salt or another
flaky sea salt, such as
fleur de sel

garlic mayonnaise

*W*e serve this mayonnaise alongside many dishes, including the Bacalà al Forno *(page 215) and, mixed with spicy red chile paste,* Mussels al Forno *(page 109). The goal in making it is to form an emulsion, and there is only one way to do this: by whisking vigorously as you add the oil as slowly as humanly possible. When it looks like you have successfully formed an emulsion, you can begin to add the oil a bit more rapidly, but not quickly, by any means. If you get impatient, just remember: it's easier to go slow than it is to fix a broken emulsion.*

MAKES ABOUT 1 CUP

*C*ombine the egg yolk, vinegar, lemon juice, garlic, and salt in a medium bowl and whisk to combine. To keep the bowl steady as you whisk, wet a kitchen towel, squeeze out the excess water, and roll it up on the diagonal. Lay the rolled towel in a ring on your work surface and set the bowl in the center of the ring. Combine the grapeseed oil and olive oil and add the oils a few drops at a time, whisking constantly to form an emulsion. When you've added about half of the oil, begin to drizzle the oil in a slow steady stream, continuing to whisk constantly, until all of the oil has been added. Taste for seasoning and add more salt, if desired. The garlic mayonnaise can be made up to three days in advance; transfer it to an airtight container and refrigerate until you are ready to use it.

1 extra-large egg yolk
2 teaspoons champagne
vinegar
2 teaspoons fresh lemon juice
1 large garlic clove, grated
or minced
1 teaspoon kosher salt,
plus more as needed
¾ cup grapeseed oil or
another neutral-flavored oil,
such as canola oil
¼ cup extra-virgin olive oil

pancetta-wrapped figs with aged balsamico condimento

Bacon-wrapped dates—a more elegant version of rumaki, the 1950s appetizer of chicken liver wrapped in bacon with a water chestnut in the middle—have taken Los Angeles by storm ever since Suzanne Goin started serving them at her restaurant, AOC. I didn't want to copy hers, but I like them so much that I wanted to make a version for Mozza using figs, which are so abundant in my town in Italy that you almost forget they are a delicacy. Although I've never been served anything like these in Italy, I certainly didn't invent the idea of contrasting the sweetness of figs with something piggy and salty: figs and prosciutto is a classic. At the Osteria, we serve these as an antipasto on a tangle of wilted dandelion greens, but they also make a great bite-size snack for cocktail hour, which is how we have presented them here.

MAKES 12 FIG HALVES

SUGGESTED WINE PAIRING: NERO D'AVOLA (SICILY)

Use a microplane or another fine grater to cut 12 very thin slices from the wedge of Parmigiano-Reggiano.

Prepare a hot fire in a gas or charcoal grill or preheat a grill pan or heavy-bottomed skillet over high heat.

Wrap a strip of pancetta tightly around each fig half. Place the fig halves flat side down on the grill for 2 to 3 minutes per side, until the pancetta is golden brown and crispy.

Place the figs on a platter and drizzle with the *balsamico*. Place one slice of Parmigiano-Reggiano on top of each fig half, grind a few turns of fresh black pepper over each, and serve.

Wedge of Parmigiano-Reggiano, for slicing
12 thin slices pancetta (6 to 8 ounces)
6 ripe figs, halved lengthwise
Aged *balsamico condimento,* for drizzling
Freshly ground black pepper

mozzarella

facing page: (clockwise from top right) smoked mozzarella, mozzarella *di bufala*, imported burrata, domestic burrata, buricotta, cow's milk ricotta, sheep's milk ricotta, fior di latte, ovalini, bocconcini, ciliegini, nodini

*A*nyone who knows Italian culinary culture and who is paying close attention knows that what I call a "mozzarella bar" is really a *latticini* bar. *Latticini* refers to the family of fresh-milk products that includes mozzarella, burrata, and ricotta cheeses—the stars of the dishes in this chapter. In the countryside, a traditional old-fashioned *latteria* is built on the Italian dairy farm where the cows are milked, and the cheese is made in a little factory right behind the shop. For many months before we opened, Mario and Joe and I thought the name of our restaurant was going to be Latte, after the word *latteria*. We finally gave that up because nobody we told about it could get past the idea of the coffee drink. In the end we decided on Mozza, which, in case it's not obvious, is short for *mozzarella.*

As I've said, a big inspiration for me in opening the Mozzarella Bar was the restaurant Obika that I visited in Rome. At Obika, they feature mozzarella from various producers in the region. Here in Los Angeles, we are lucky that we have a few local cheese makers, and, then, of course, I import some cheeses. Still, I knew that a restaurant featuring only mozzarella would not be enough; I would have to expand the definition somehow, which is how I decided to include the entire *latticini* family. In the end, I'm much happier this way, showcasing all of these varieties, as it gives me more opportunities to be creative and it allows customers to be introduced to cheeses they might not know.

In creating each dish on the Mozzarella Bar menu, I chose ways of dressing them that highlight the flavor and texture of the featured cheese. With the really special cheeses, such as the imported mozzarella *di bufala,* I tried to keep the condiments simple so you can really taste the complex flavors of the cheese. I complemented milder flavored cheeses, such as cow's milk ricotta, with bolder condiments like those featured in the Buricotta with Braised Artichokes, Pine Nuts, Currants, and Mint Pesto (page 69).

If you've ever seen me work behind the Mozzarella Bar, you may have noticed that what I'm doing is not cooking but assembling various components—bacon, prosciutto, and other sliced meats; vegetable preparations such as braised artichokes or grilled escarole; toasted nuts or bread crumbs; and sauces, including pestos and vinaigrettes—into *latticini*-based creations. The entire palette of ingredients that I have in front of me has been prepared by a team in the kitchen earlier that day or that week. What this means for you, the home cook, is that each dish requires some preparation. The good news is that the vast majority of items can be prepared in advance, and throughout these recipes I've told you which items those are and how far in advance you can prepare them. So if, like me, you plan ahead, when your guests arrive or dinner is served, all you'll have to do is put the components together. It'll look like there was nothing to it.

latticini: an introduction to the family of italian fresh cheese

The following cheeses are the members of our *latticini* family. I hope they inspire you as they did me. Choosing quality cheese is important. In each recipe in this chapter I call for a specific type of cheese, but I also recognize that you might not have access to each one. As a rule, it's better to use a good-quality cheese than an inferior version of the specific cheese that I call for. For instance, if you have access to really fresh, supple, artisanally produced cow's milk mozzarella, but only inferior, mass-produced versions of mozzarella *di bufala,* use the cow's milk cheese. The best way to find out what cheeses are good is to taste them. Make it a research project. Grill up some *Fett'Unta* (page 65). Buy a bottle of good olive oil. And open a bottle of good wine. It's a research project that you should enjoy.

mozzarella *di bufala*

Fresh mozzarella cheese made with the milk of the water buffalo is the original fresh mozzarella. It comes from Naples, also home to Neapolitan pizza, which is traditionally topped with this cheese. In 1993, Mozzarella di Bufala di Campagna was granted Denominazione di Origine Controllata (DOC), which means that those cheeses marked with this status are produced according to specific guidelines and are the highest quality you can buy. The *bufala* produced and sold in Italy is made with unpasteurized milk, it is never refrigerated, and it is usually eaten within two or three days, whereas the *bufala* that they make in Italy to export to the United States must be pasteurized and, of course, is refrigerated. So even with imported Italian *bufala,* you don't get quite the same tangy flavor and creamy texture as you would in Italy. But just think of it as an excuse to go to Italy. There are some domestic producers of mozzarella *di bufala,* but I prefer the imported varieties. Mozzarella made from buffalo milk has a distinct, tangy flavor, so I use it in ways that allow the flavor of the cheese to dominate. If you can't find it, you can substitute good-quality cow's milk mozzarella (fior di latte).

fior di latte

The cow's milk equivalent of mozzarella *di bufala,* which is much easier to find here, is known in Italy not as mozzarella but as fior di latte, or "flower of milk." There are several good domestic producers of cow's milk mozzarella. When buying fior di latte, you want to make sure it's packed in water. (Low-moisture mozzarella, which is wrapped in plastic, is not a good substitute, though we do use it when we want a stringy melting cheese, such as on our pizzas.) Those varieties of mozzarella that are sold behind a deli counter rather than packaged in a deli case tend to be the fresher, artisanally produced options.

Fresh mozzarella can come in many shapes. Mimmo Bruno, one of our burrata makers, says that the different sizes are meant to be paired with corresponding-sized tomatoes. In addition to the most common 8-ounce ball, simply referred to as fior di latte, the following are some other sizes you can expect to find:

- Ovolini are named for their egg-like shape, literally meaning "little eggs" (4-ounce balls).
- Bocconcini means "little bites" and is named for its one-bite size (1- to 2-ounce balls).
- Ciliegini means "little cherries," and these are the smallest offered; they should be the size of a Sweet 100 tomato (⅓-ounce balls).
- Nodini, "little knots," are a tradition of Puglia and one of many novelty shapes you'll find in Italy.

smoked mozzarella

Also called mozzarella *affumicato,* this is fresh mozzarella that has been smoked. We use smoked mozzarella *di bufala,* imported from Italy, but you will more likely find smoked cow's milk mozzarella. Good smoked mozzarella gets its flavor from burning wood, as opposed to lesser varieties flavored with liquid smoke. Ours has visible grid marks on each ball of cheese from where it sat on a rack while being smoked. I serve the grid side facing up because I like the way the marks look and what they signify. We also serve smoked scamorza, which is low-moisture, aged mozzarella that becomes even firmer after it is smoked.

burrata

Of all the cheeses I feature at the Mozzarella Bar, burrata, which is a cream-filled mozzarella sack, is by far the biggest seller. People's eyes just light up when they read "burrata" on the menu. Burrata was invented a relatively short time ago, not more than forty years, in Puglia, Italy's boot heel, as a way to use the scraps of curds left over after twisting balls of mozzarella. The scraps are pulled into shreds and then mixed with *panna,* or cream, and a thin skin of mozzarella is stretched around it. When you cut into a ball of good burrata, the insides slowly spill out—it's a creamy, decadent experience. The story of burrata in this country is remarkable in that ten years ago hardly anyone had ever heard of it, and today it's a household name. Los

Angeles is an especially burrata-obsessed town, and my two favorite domestic producers, DiStefano and Gioia, are located here. (Both are available at specialty food stores nationwide.) We also use a third variety of burrata, one imported from the source, Puglia. This one is made in the traditional shape, which is like a beggar's purse of mozzarella, that holds the cheese. Traditionally the "purse" was tied with a thin strand of leek, so you could judge the cheese's freshness; when the leek was brown, the cheese was bad. Today, that leek has been replaced by a green string, but I still think it looks very pretty.

stracciatella

There are three culinary types of stracciatella, meaning "shreds," that I know of, this one being the shredded mozzarella and cream mixture that makes up the inside portion of burrata. Stracciatella is also the name given to gelato with chocolate shreds in it, and to an Italian version of egg-drop soup. Here in Los Angeles, you'll find stracciatella at cheese stores because it's sold by the same producers who make burrata. Outside Los Angeles, you may not find it, but you can substitute regular burrata.

ricotta

Meaning "recooked" in Italian, ricotta is so named because it is made by recooking the whey, or milky liquid, that is left from making mozzarella. The whey is cooked with an acidic substance, such as citric acid or vinegar, causing it to curdle into ricotta cheese. In Italy, ricotta is often eaten the same day it is made. It's sold in little baskets that are set inside a plastic container, so the whey that continues to ooze from the cheese is constantly draining out and the cheese stays fresh and firm. Here, when people think of ricotta, they think of the flavorless stuff that we smear in between layers of lasagne. And Italians don't even use ricotta in their lasagne! But good ricotta is so delicious and has a light, delicate texture—all of which is lost in the grocery-store stuff.

Try to get your ricotta from a cheese shop or specialty food shop if possible, and look for one made by a cheese maker as opposed to a factory. If all you can get is grocery-store ricotta, I have another suggestion, but I want to make sure you are sitting down before I tell you: cottage cheese. I know it might sound weird, since we're used to seeing cottage cheese with canned pineapple on top, but it's not as big a stretch as you might imagine. Just as ricotta is made from the whey left over from making mozzarella, cottage cheese is made from the by-products of making butter. It was so named because it was usually made in small cottages. When I taste-tested ricotta to recommend for this book, I found that more than any of the inferior grocery-store varieties, cottage cheese has the milky richness of good ricotta, as well as big, loose curds, which I like. Naturally I urge you to buy the best you can find, such as those made by a few cottage-industry cottage cheese producers here, such as Cowgirl Creamery in Northern California.

sheep's milk ricotta

Sheep's milk ricotta has a much more complex flavor than cow's milk ricotta. In this country, you will find mostly cow's milk ricotta, but in Italy, sheep's milk ricotta is at least as common and, in some places such as Sicily and Sardinia, more common. There are a few domestic cheese makers, such as Bellweather Farms, that make sheep's milk ricotta. While it is good, we use sheep's milk ricotta from Rome in instances when you can really notice the flavor of the cheese. We use cow's milk ricotta, which we get from a local fresh cheese producer in Los Angeles, Gioia, when the cheese is accompanied by other bold flavors. If you can find sheep's milk ricotta, I think it's safe to say that anything that tastes good with ricotta would be even better with sheep's milk ricotta. Regardless of what kind you buy, the first thing I recommend you do before you use the ricotta is to taste it. If the texture is too dry, stir in heavy whipping cream to loosen it up a bit.

buricotta

Ricotta-stuffed mozzarella sacks, buricotta is like burrata, with ricotta in place of the stracciatella. It was invented in Los Angeles by cheese makers from Puglia while they waited for the permits they needed to make burrata. I like the inventiveness behind it. When they finally were able to make burrata, they kept buricotta on the market. I like to use buricotta because I can cut clean, pretty slices to lay on crostini. Outside of Los Angeles you may not be able to find this cheese, so use ricotta instead. The resulting dish may not be quite as elegant, but as long as you use quality ricotta it will be as delicious.

stracchino

I fell in love with stracchino, a rich, rindless creamy cheese (also called crescenza) from Lombardy when I had it in a sandwich at Aldo's, the bar in my Italian hometown. The sandwich was made on *torta al testo*, the bread of the region, with nothing but arugula and this cheese, which has a mild flavor and texture similar to Brie. It was so delicious and yet very simple—just the kind of combination that I get excited about. I asked Mimmo if he could make it for me, and he did. You can buy it, sold by the commercial cheese maker Belgioioso, at most grocery stores. Now I am able to offer the same sandwich at Mozza2Go. I add sliced red onion to the sandwich in honor of the delicious red torpedo onions that are in season in the summer when I am in Italy.

bufala mozzarella with basil pesto, salsa romesco, and black olive tapenade

At the Mozzarella Bar, we offer a plate that consists of fresh mozzarella di bufala *accompanied by three condiments, Basil Pesto, Salsa Romesco, Black Olive Tapenade, and caperberry relish and served with Fett'Unta—grilled bread drowned in olive oil—on the side. Here I give you recipes for all but the relish, which I included in* A Twist of the Wrist. *So if you want to serve it, you'll have to buy the book! I love the flexibility of giving our customers this pure ball of very special* bufala *and letting them do whatever they want with it. With these condiments, you can create your own mozzarella bar for a party at home, which I often do when I entertain. I love the idea of personalizing your own food, the way everyone has his or her own way of dressing a hamburger. I think people enjoy eating this way, and it loosens them up and makes for a livelier party.*

SUGGESTED WINE PAIRING: RAVELLO BIANCO COSTA D'AMALFI (CAMPANIA)

basil pesto

When we started working on this book, I had a battle with Matt and Carolynn about whether to ask for the various pestos that we use to be made using a mortar and pestle or in a food processor. I always make pesto using a mortar and pestle, and I feel strongly that pesto tastes better this way. That said, as Matt was so kind to remind me, when I make pesto, it's usually because I'm in Italy in the summer, where it gets light at five, dark at ten, and I have all the time in the world. At the restaurant we make pesto in such volume that we have to do it by machine; it would not be practical for us to make it by hand. "This is a restaurant cookbook," Matt said, "and how we do it at the restaurant is in a food processor." I'm sorry to say that Carolynn took Matt's side. "Save that for the Lazy Days in Panicale *cookbook," she said. Although here they gave you instructions for how to make it in a blender, I'm hoping you'll prove me right by taking the extra time and using elbow grease to make yours with a mortar and pestle from time to time.*

MAKES ABOUT 1 1/2 CUPS

Combine the pine nuts, garlic, salt, and half of the olive oil in the bowl of a food processor fitted with a metal blade or the jar of a blender. Add half of the basil and pulse until it is finely chopped. Turn off the machine and scrape down the sides of the bowl

2 tablespoons toasted pine nuts (recipe follows)

2 garlic cloves, minced or grated if you are making the pesto using a mortar and pestle

1 teaspoon kosher salt, plus more to taste

1 cup extra-virgin olive oil, plus more as needed

4 packed cups whole fresh basil leaves

1/4 cup freshly grated Parmigiano-Reggiano

1 teaspoon fresh lemon juice, plus more to taste

with a rubber spatula. Add the remaining basil, the Parmigiano-Reggiano, and the remaining olive oil and purée, stopping as soon as the ingredients form a homogenous paste, and adding more olive oil if necessary to obtain a loose, spoonable pesto. (You want to stop the machine as soon as you achieve the desired consistency, as the blade will heat the garlic and give it a bitter flavor. Also, overprocessing the pesto will incorporate too much air, making the pesto fluffy and too smooth. I like to see some flecks of herbs in my pesto.) Turn the pesto out into a bowl and stir in the lemon juice. Taste for seasoning and add more salt or lemon juice if desired. Use the pesto or transfer it to an airtight container and refrigerate for up to two days—any longer and it will lose its pretty green color and vibrant flavor. Bring the pesto to room temperature, stir to recombine the ingredients, and taste again for seasoning before serving.

toasted pine nuts

*T*oasting pine nuts brings out their subtle, nutty flavor. Because they are so small and oily, they go from toasted to burnt in no time, so keep a close eye on them. Pine nuts turn rancid very quickly so try to buy them from a source with high turnover and store them in the refrigerator.

*T*o toast pine nuts, adjust the oven rack to the middle position and preheat the oven to 325°F.
Scatter the amount of pine nuts that you need for your recipe on a baking sheet and place it in the oven to toast the pine nuts, shaking the pan occasionally, for 8 to 10 minutes, or until they are fragrant and golden brown. Remove the pine nuts from the oven and set them aside to cool to room temperature.

salsa romesco

*R*omesco is a Catalan condiment traditionally made of fried bread and dried peppers, and served with seafood. We make our Romesco using roasted red peppers because we love their charred, sweet flavor. We serve it with mozzarella because we love the way it contrasts with the mild flavor of the cheese—and because we are a mozzarella restaurant! If you happen to have Garlic Confit, use it in this recipe; but if not, your Romesco will still be delicious without it.

*P*repare a hot fire in a gas or charcoal grill or preheat a grill pan or heavy-bottomed skillet over high heat.

Place the peppers on the grill and cook them, turning occasionally, until they are blackened on all sides and the flesh is tender, 8 to 10 minutes. (Alternatively, you can cook the peppers over the direct flame of a gas stove.) Place the peppers in a plastic bag or a large bowl. Close the bag or seal the bowl tightly with plastic wrap and set the peppers aside to steam until they are cool enough to handle. Using a clean kitchen towel, remove the charred skin from the peppers and discard. Remove and discard the cores and seeds. (The peppers can be prepared to this point up to three days in advance. Refrigerate the peppers in an airtight container and drain the liquid released from the peppers before using them.)

Adjust the oven rack to the middle position and preheat the oven to 325°F.

Spread the hazelnuts and almonds on a baking sheet in two separate piles and place them in the oven to toast until golden brown and fragrant, 12 to 15 minutes, shaking the pan occasionally so the nuts brown evenly. Remove the nuts from the oven and set them aside until they are cool enough to touch. Gather the hazelnuts into a clean dishtowel and rub them together to remove the skins.

Warm 3 tablespoons of the oil in a small skillet over medium heat. Add the bread slices and fry them until they are lightly browned on both sides, about 2 minutes per side. Remove the bread to a paper towel to drain.

Combine the hazelnuts and almonds in the bowl of a food processor or the jar of a blender and pulse until the nuts are finely ground and start to coat the sides of the bowl, but not so long that they turn into a paste. Add the fried bread and pulse until it is finely ground. Add the peppers and purée to form a smooth paste, scraping down the sides of the bowl with a spatula occasionally. With the machine running, add the vinegar, salt, Garlic Confit if you are using it, fresh garlic, and cayenne and continue to purée until the sauce is very smooth. With the food processor still running, add the remaining 3 tablespoons olive oil in a steady stream to emulsify the Romesco. Add more olive oil if necessary to form the consistency of a thick, almost spoonable sauce. Turn the Romesco into a bowl, taste for seasoning, and add more salt, if desired. Serve, or transfer the Romesco into an airtight container and refrigerate for up to three days. Bring the Romesco to room temperature and taste again for seasoning before serving.

5 red bell peppers

¾ ounce hazelnuts (about 22 nuts)

¾ ounce almonds (about 18 nuts)

6 tablespoons extra-virgin olive oil, plus more as needed

½ ounce bread (about 3 thin slices from a baguette)

2½ tablespoons red wine vinegar

1 teaspoon kosher salt, plus more to taste

3 cloves of Garlic Confit (page 38; optional)

2 small garlic cloves or 1 large clove, minced or grated (about 1½ teaspoons)

½ teaspoon cayenne

black olive tapenade

*T*his is a classic olive tapenade spruced up with the zest of oranges and lemons, and I have to say that it's the best version I've ever had. Note when buying olive purée to look for a product that has just olives or olives and olive oil, such as the olive pâté made by Rustichella d'Abruzzo.

MAKES ABOUT 1 CUP

*C*ombine the olive purée, olives, anchovies, orange zest, lemon zest, lemon juice, and capers in a medium bowl and stir to thoroughly combine. Stir in the olive oil, adding more if necessary to obtain a loose, spreadable consistency. Use the tapenade or transfer it to an airtight container and refrigerate for up to several weeks. Stir in the parsley just before serving.

1 cup olive purée

¼ cup sliced, pitted Ligurian olives or another black olive, such as Taggiasche or Niçoise

2 anchovy fillets (preferably salt-packed), rinsed, backbones removed if salt-packed, finely chopped, and smashed with the flat side of a knife

Grated zest of 1 large orange

Grated zest and fresh juice of 1 lemon

1 tablespoon capers (preferably salt-packed), soaked for 15 minutes if salt-packed, rinsed, drained, and chopped

2 tablespoons extra-virgin olive oil, plus more as needed

¼ cup thinly sliced fresh Italian parsley leaves

fett'unta

*W*hen we first opened the Pizzeria, we made a choice not to offer bread, but we often had customers who requested it. We served breadsticks, but we didn't want to get involved with bread service. We asked Mario for his advice about people wanting bread, and he said, "They want bread, give them bread. But make it into something and charge them." And then he told us about fett'unta, *sliced bread that is grilled and then drowned in olive oil. The word comes from* fetta, *or "slice," and* 'unta, *which means "oily." Matt made some in the pizza oven, we both loved it, and we added it to the menu immediately. Today, we offer* fett'unta *at both restaurants. At the Pizzeria, we suggest people order it when they want items that have sauce to sop up, such as the Eggplant Caponata (page 104), Mozza Caprese (page 66), or to accompany a plate of prosciutto. At the Osteria we serve it with a sampler of mozzarella. We serve this bread year-round, but my favorite time for it is late fall and early winter, just after the olive harvest in Italy, when* olio nuovo—*green, peppery "new olive oil"—is released. If you happen to have a charcoal grill lit, that is my first choice for making this, but you can also make it in a grill pan or sandwich press—but be prepared for a bit of smoke. At home it's always part of my Umbrian* tavola.

SERVES 4

SUGGESTED WINE PAIRING: CHIANTI COLLI SENESI (TUSCANY)

fett'unta *(continued)*

*P*repare a hot fire in a gas or charcoal grill or preheat a grill pan or heavy-bottomed skillet over high heat or a sandwich press.

Brush the bread slices liberally on both sides with olive oil. Place the bread on the grill and cook it until crisp and golden brown, about 2 minutes per side. Remove the bread from the heat and rub the garlic clove over one side of each piece. Pour 3 tablespoons of finishing-quality olive oil over the same side of each toast and season the oiled sides generously with the sea salt. Cut the bread on an angle into halves or thirds and serve.

4 1½-inch-thick slices from a large loaf of crusty white bread (we use white table bread from La Brea Bakery)

Extra-virgin olive oil, for brushing the bread

1 garlic clove

¾ cup (12 tablespoons) finishing-quality extra-virgin olive oil

Maldon sea salt or another flaky sea salt, such as fleur de sel

mozza caprese

*F*or me, a "tell" for a restaurant I probably don't want to eat in is seeing a Caprese salad on the menu when tomatoes are out of season. I knew I wanted to serve a Caprese at the Pizzeria, both because everyone loves it and because it is an icon of a casual, inexpensive Italian restaurant. Since we opened in November, when tomatoes were no longer in season, I took it as a challenge to figure out how to present these flavors in a way that was every bit as good as a Caprese made with sweet, vine-ripened summer tomatoes, even when such tomatoes were nowhere to be found. This adaptation, which I first named Winter Caprese, consists of fresh burrata cheese, basil pesto, and cherry tomatoes on the vine that have been slow-roasted to concentrate their sweetness and flavor. I changed its name to Mozza Caprese when winter ended, tomatoes came into season, and it had become so popular that I could not take it off the menu. I suggest you serve it with Fett'Unta (page 65) to sop up the wonderful, juicy flavors left on your plate. The recipe for slow-roasted tomatoes makes enough for six or more of these salads, and the pesto recipe will give you more than enough pesto for that many. So, to expand the number of servings you make, just increase the amount of burrata you buy.

SERVES 6

SUGGESTED WINE PAIRING: ERBALUCE DI CALUSO (PIEDMONT)

Cut the burrata into six equal-size segments and lay each segment, cut side up, on a salad plate. Season the burrata with sea salt and spoon 1 teaspoon of pesto over each portion of cheese. Use scissors to cut the tomatoes into clusters of one, two, or three tomatoes. Carefully lift the tomatoes by the stems and gently rest one cluster atop each serving of cheese, choosing the largest clusters. Stack another cluster on top of the first, with the stem at an opposing angle, and then stack the remaining clusters on top of the first, creating a small pile of tomatoes two to three stacks high, with about five to seven tomatoes per serving. (The idea is for the tomatoes to look pretty and like they are comfortably nestled into the burrata.) Drizzle about ½ teaspoon of the finishing-quality olive oil over each salad, scatter the micro or miniature basil leaves or use scissors to snip one large basil leaf over each salad, and serve with the *Fett'Unta* on the side, if desired.

1 ½ pounds fresh burrata

Maldon sea salt or another flaky sea salt, such as fleur de sel

¼ cup plus 2 tablespoons Basil Pesto (page 62)

30 to 40 Slow-roasted Cherry Tomatoes (recipe follows)

Finishing-quality extra-virgin olive oil

30 to 40 fresh micro or miniature basil leaves or 6 large fresh basil leaves, for garnish

Fett'Unta (optional; page 65)

slow-roasted cherry tomatoes

For these beautiful, sweet tomatoes on the vine, we start with Sunsweet tomatoes, which you can find sold in plastic boxes in grocery stores. I love the delicate, organic look of the small tomatoes dangling from the long stems. This recipe makes more than you will need for four servings of the Mozza Caprese. We did this to tailor the recipe to the size of the boxes the tomatoes are sold in and because you are sure to lose some tomatoes to anyone who walks by after they are out of the oven. If you can find tomatoes on the vine at your local famers' market, even better.

MAKES ABOUT 1 POUND, OR ABOUT 36 TOMATOES

Adjust the oven rack to the middle position and preheat the oven to 300°F.

Place a wire rack on top of a baking sheet. Gently lift the tomatoes out of the boxes, taking care to keep the tomatoes attached to the stems as much as possible. Brush the tomatoes with the olive oil and season with the salt and pepper. Place the tomatoes in the oven to roast until their skins are shriveled but the tomatoes are still plump, about 1½ hours. Remove the tomatoes from the oven and allow them to cool to room temperature. Use the tomatoes, or cover with plastic wrap and store at room temperature for up to one day or refrigerate for up to three days. Bring the tomatoes to room temperature before serving.

2 9-ounce packages Sunsweet tomatoes on stems, or 1 pound sweet small tomatoes

1 tablespoon extra-virgin olive oil

1 teaspoon kosher salt

½ teaspoon freshly ground black pepper

buricotta with braised artichokes, pine nuts, currants, and mint pesto

I love the way the funky flavor of artichokes complements the mild flavor of buricotta cheese in these crostini. The currant and pine nut relish on top of the buricotta adds a touch of sweetness and acidity, and a little mint pesto livens up the whole story. The result: one of the most popular offerings at the Mozzarella Bar, and one I always recommend to vegetarians.

MAKES 12 CROSTINI

 SUGGESTED WINE PAIRING: MALVASIA DI CAGLIARI SECCO (SARDINIA)

Combine the pine nuts, garlic, salt, and half of the olive oil in the bowl of a food processor fitted with a metal blade or the jar of a blender. Add the parsley and pulse until it is finely chopped. Turn off the machine and scrape down the sides of the bowl with a rubber spatula. Add the mint, Parmigiano-Reggiano, and the remaining olive oil and purée, stopping as soon as the ingredients form a homogenous paste, and adding more olive oil if necessary to obtain a loose, spoonable pesto. (You want to stop the machine as soon as you achieve the desired consistency, as the blade will heat the garlic and give it a bitter flavor. Also, overprocessing the pesto will incorporate too much air, making the pesto fluffy and too smooth.) Turn the pesto out into a bowl and stir in the lemon juice. Taste for seasoning and add more salt or lemon juice if desired. Use the pesto or transfer it to an airtight container and refrigerate for up to two days—any longer and it will lose its pretty green color and vibrant flavor. Bring the pesto to room temperature, stir to recombine the ingredients, and taste again for seasoning before serving.

To assemble, lay the crostini oiled side up on your work surface. If you are using ricotta, place it in a medium bowl and stir vigorously with a spoon to fluff it up. Lay 1 slice of buricotta, or spread 2 tablespoons of ricotta in an uneven layer on each *crostino*, leaving the edges of the bread visible. Season the buricotta or ricotta with salt and spoon 1 teaspoon of pesto on top. Cut off the long stems from the braised artichokes, leaving ½ inch of stem on each and reserving the stems to snack on. Open up the artichokes like a flower, and set 1 artichoke on top of each *crostino*, sticking the stems into the buricotta like stakes to secure them. Season the artichokes with salt and spoon 1 teaspoon of relish over each artichoke. Sprinkle each *crostino* with ½ teaspoon of the bread crumbs if you are using them, and serve.

for the mint pesto

1 tablespoon toasted pine nuts (page 63)

1 garlic clove, grated or minced if you are making the pesto using a mortar and pestle

½ teaspoon kosher salt, plus more to taste

½ cup extra-virgin olive oil, plus more as needed

½ cup whole fresh Italian parsley leaves

1½ cups whole fresh mint leaves

1 tablespoon freshly grated Parmigiano-Reggiano

¾ teaspoon fresh lemon juice, plus more to taste

for assembling the crostini

12 Garlic Crostini (page 46)

1 pound buricotta, sliced into ¾-inch disks, or 1½ cups fresh ricotta

Kosher salt

12 Braised Artichokes (page 70)

¼ cup Currant and Pine Nut Relish (page 71)

6 teaspoons Toasted Bread Crumbs (optional; page 74)

braised artichokes

It takes a lot of olive oil to make these artichokes, but that's what gives them their buttery texture and delicious flavor. The good news is that you can use the oil a second time for the same purpose. For this recipe you want to use baby artichokes. If you use the bigger artichokes that are commonly found in grocery stores, you'll have to remove the choke before braising the artichokes and the final result won't be quite as pretty. If you like sweetbreads, make a double batch and use half for the Veal Sweetbreads Piccata with Artichokes (page 239), one of the stars on our secondo *menu.*

MAKES 12 ARTICHOKE HEARTS

Fill a large bowl with water. Cut 2 of the lemons in half, squeeze the lemon into the water, and drop the lemon halves into the water.

Remove the outer leaves from the artichokes until you are left with only the light green centers. Cut off and discard the tough stem ends of the artichokes, leaving as much as 1 or 2 inches of stem attached. Using a vegetable peeler or a small sharp knife, shave the artichoke stems, revealing the light green inner stems. Cut ½ inch to ¾ inch off the tip ends of the artichoke leaves so they have flat tops and discard all of the trimmed leaves and bits. Place the trimmed artichokes in the lemon water as you finish them. (You can prepare the artichokes to this point up to a day in advance. Leave them in the lemon-water until you're ready to braise them.)

Pour ¼ cup of the olive oil into a large sauté pan; add the onion and garlic, season with salt, and cook over high heat for about 2 minutes, until the onion just begins to soften. Add the artichokes and season with salt. Turn off the heat. Pour in enough olive oil to cover the artichokes; the amount will vary depending on the size of the pan you're cooking them in. Squeeze the remaining lemon into the pan with the artichokes and drop the squeezed halves into the olive oil. Add the rosemary sprigs. Place a large paper coffee filter or a piece of cheesecloth on top of the artichokes and pat it down to saturate the paper or cloth with the oil so that it rests directly on the surface of the oil to help keep the artichokes submerged. Turn the heat on high to heat the oil until it begins to boil just around the edges of the pot; you don't want the oil at a rolling boil. Reduce the heat to low and cook the artichokes without tending them for 25 to 35 minutes, until they are just

3 lemons
12 baby artichokes
¼ cup extra-virgin olive oil, plus more as needed (2 or more cups)
1 large Spanish yellow onion, sliced
12 large garlic cloves, sliced
Kosher salt
2 fresh rosemary sprigs

barely tender when pierced with a small, sharp knife; they will continue gently cooking as they sit in the oil, making them very tender and buttery. Remove the pot from the heat, remove and discard the coffee filter or cheesecloth, and let the artichokes cool in the oil to room temperature. Drain the artichokes in a colander, reserving the oil. Remove and discard the onion, garlic, and lemon. Store the artichokes in the oil and transfer them to an airtight container and refrigerate for up to one week. Bring the artichokes to room temperature and drain before using them.

currant and pine nut relish

I've been making a version of this condiment for as long as I can remember. Currants and pine nuts are a traditional Sicilian combination, so anytime I use this I feel like I am making a Sicilian dish.

MAKES ABOUT 1 CUP RELISH

Warm the olive oil in a small sauté pan over medium-high heat, add the onion, chile, and rosemary, and season with the salt. Sauté, stirring often to prevent the onion from browning, for about 5 minutes, until the onion is tender and translucent. Add the garlic and cook for 1 minute, stirring constantly to prevent it browning.

Meanwhile, place the currants in a small saucepan. Add the vinegar, making sure there is enough to cover. Bring the vinegar to a simmer over high heat, reduce the heat, and simmer for about 5 minutes, until they are soft and plump. Add the currants and vinegar to the sauté pan with the onion. If there is so much vinegar that the relish is runny, bring the vinegar to a boil over medium-high heat and boil it until there is just enough liquid to bind the currants. Turn off the heat and allow the currants to cool to room temperature. Remove and discard the chile and rosemary and stir in the pine nuts just before serving. Note: In order to ensure that they keep their crunchy texture, you want to add pine nuts only to the amount of relish you will be using at the time. Transfer the remaining relish to an airtight container and refrigerate for up to one week.

2 tablespoons extra-virgin olive oil
1 cup medium-diced red onion (about 1 small onion)
1 dried arbol chile
1 small fresh rosemary sprig
1/2 teaspoon kosher salt, plus more to taste
2 large garlic cloves, grated or minced
1/3 cup dried currants
1/4 cup balsamic vinegar, plus more as needed
1/3 cup Toasted Pine Nuts (page 63)

burrata with leeks vinaigrette and mustard bread crumbs

I love leeks, and I especially love the traditional French preparation of leeks vinaigrette—boiled or steamed leeks served cold and dressed with a sharp vinaigrette. This is my Mozzarella Bar take on that classic. All of the Mozzarella Bar dishes have some kind of crunchy bread as a contrast to the soft cheese. Some are served on crostini, but those that aren't are topped with some kind of crouton or, in this case, bread crumbs, which really finish this dish.

SERVES 6

 SUGGESTED WINE PAIRING: RIBOLLA GIALLA (FRIULI)

To prepare the bread crumbs, adjust the oven rack to the middle position and preheat the oven to 275°F.

Put the mustard seeds in a small skillet and toast them over high heat, shaking the pan and taking care not to let them smoke or burn, until they begin to smell fragrant and toasty like popcorn and brown slightly, about 2 minutes. Set the mustard seeds aside to cool slightly.

Stir the mustard seeds, mustard, wine, salt, and pepper together in a medium bowl. Drizzle in the oil, whisking constantly. Add the bread and use your hands to massage the marinade into the bread so that all the marinade is absorbed. Scatter the bread on a baking sheet and toast it in the oven for about 1½ hours, until the croutons are crunchy and toasted all the way through, but not browned. Remove the baking sheet from the oven and set aside to cool the croutons to room temperature. Transfer the croutons to a food processor and grind them until they are the consistency of coarse crumbs; you want them to have some texture, not to be powder.

To make the mustard vinaigrette, spoon the mustard into a medium bowl and slowly pour in the Lemon Vinaigrette, whisking to keep it emulsified. The mustard should be spoonable, but not as thick as mayonnaise. If it is too thick, add more vinaigrette. Use the vinaigrette or transfer it to an airtight container and refrigerate it for up to three days. Bring the vinaigrette to room temperature and whisk to recombine the ingredients before using.

To serve, lay two leek halves side by side, root sides together, on each of six salad plates or in pairs on one long serving platter and

for the mustard bread crumbs

- 1 tablespoon yellow mustard seeds
- 2 tablespoons whole-grain Dijon mustard
- 2 tablespoons white wine
- ½ teaspoon kosher salt
- ½ teaspoon freshly ground black pepper
- 2 tablespoons grapeseed oil or another neutral-flavored oil, such as canola oil
- 1 pound rustic bread, crust removed and torn into 1-inch chunks (about 8 loosely packed cups)

for the mustard vinaigrette

- ¼ cup whole-grain Dijon mustard
- ½ cup Lemon Vinaigrette (page 29), plus more as needed

to finish and serve the dish

- 6 Braised Leeks (12 halves; recipe follows)
- Maldon sea salt or another flaky sea salt, such as fleur de sel
- 12 ounces burrata
- 1 tablespoon thinly sliced fresh Italian parsley leaves

sprinkle them with the sea salt. Spoon 1½ tablespoons of the mustard vinaigrette on the leeks close to the root ends and, using the back of the spoon, smear the vinaigrette over the length of the leeks. Cut the burrata into six equal-size segments and lay one segment of burrata on each serving of leeks, closer to one end or the other rather than in the center. Pile 2 tablespoons of the bread crumbs on each serving of burrata, and sprinkle with the parsley.

braised leeks

We should call these "Lyn's Leeks" because Lyn, who tested many of the recipes in this book, had to make them several times before getting the recipe right. In each instance the leeks she made were delicious, but she pushed on until she achieved the caramel color and glazed look of those we serve in the restaurant.

SERVES 6

Adjust the oven rack to the middle position and preheat the oven to 350°F.

Peel away and discard the outer layer of each leek and trim and discard the hairy roots, leaving the very ends of the roots attached. One at a time, place the leeks on the cutting board and, with the white end pointing away from you, remove the dark green part of the leek, cutting it at an angle and rolling the leek a quarter-turn to repeat the same cut. Continue rolling and cutting in this manner until the tapered pale green ends resemble a sharpened pencil. Discard the dark green trimmings. Cut the leeks in half lengthwise, rinse to remove the fine grit, and pat dry.

Place the leeks in a shallow baking dish just large enough to hold them in a single layer, such as a 9 by 13-inch Pyrex dish. Drizzle the leeks with ¼ cup of the olive oil, sprinkle them with the salt and several turns of pepper, and toss to coat the leeks with the seasonings. Arrange the leeks cut side up in a single layer in the baking dish and pour in the stock, adding more if necessary for it to come three-fourths of the way up the sides of the leeks. Drizzle the remaining ½ cup of olive oil over the leeks, and lay the lemon slices and scatter the thyme sprigs over them. If you have industrial-strength plastic wrap, which does not melt in the oven, cover the pan tightly with the plastic. In any

6 large leeks (about 1 pound), rinsed thoroughly
¾ cup extra-virgin olive oil
1 teaspoon kosher salt
Freshly ground black pepper
1½ cups Basic Chicken Stock (page 27), plus more as needed
½ lemon, thinly sliced
About 20 fresh thyme sprigs

case, cover the pan tightly with foil and place the leeks in the oven for 45 minutes. Remove the leeks from the oven and increase the temperature to 400°F. Remove and discard the foil, and plastic if you used it; remove and discard the lemon slices and thyme sprigs, and return the leeks to the oven until they are glazed and golden brown and the liquid has evaporated, about 1 hour 15 minutes. Cool to room temperature and serve, or wrap them in a single layer with plastic wrap, and refrigerate them for up to two days. Bring the leeks to room temperature before serving them.

toasted bread crumbs

*P*ain de mie *is a French-style bread shaped like a traditional, square-edged slicing loaf similar to a Pullman loaf.* Mie *means "crumb" and is a breadbaker's term that refers to the inside of bread—that which isn't the crust. This bread is so named because, baked in a loaf pan, it doesn't have a crust.* Pain de mie *contains a touch of sugar and butter so it makes for the most flavorful bread crumbs. If you can't get* pain de mie, *substitute brioche, which is even more buttery.*

MAKES ¹⁄₂ CUP CRUMBS

*A*djust the oven rack to the middle position and preheat the oven to 350°F.
Spread the bread crumbs in a single layer on a baking sheet and bake until they're golden brown and crunchy, 10 to 12 minutes, shaking the pan occasionally for even cooking. Remove the baking sheet from the oven and cool the crumbs to room temperature. Gradually drizzle half of the olive oil over the bread crumbs and add the salt. Stir to combine and add more olive oil as needed so the bread crumbs are moist but are not so wet that they clump together.

Use, or transfer the bread crumbs to an airtight container and store at room temperature for up to three days.

¹⁄₂ cup finely ground fresh bread crumbs, preferably from *pain de mie*, brioche (crust removed), or another white bread that has a touch of butter in it

1 tablespoon finishing-quality extra-virgin olive oil, plus more as needed

¹⁄₂ teaspoon kosher salt, plus more to taste

stracciatella with celery and herb salad and celery-leaf pesto

One of the principles of Italian cooking—and maybe this is true of all of European kitchens—is not to be wasteful. Italian cooks find a use for every edible component of each animal or vegetable they cook. In the Italian spirit, I use all parts of the celery in this dish. I slice the celery ribs for the salad, and I use the leaves, so often discarded, both in a salad the cheese is served on and to make a celery-leaf pesto that gets spooned onto the cheese. The result is a bright, flavorful, and textural salad that is equally pretty and unexpected. We peel celery using a vegetable peeler anytime we are serving it raw; it takes only a few seconds and the celery is so much more tender with the fibrous strings removed. The pesto recipe makes ¾ cup, which is more than you will need for this recipe, but it's difficult to make pesto in a smaller quantity. Spoon the leftovers over grilled chicken, fish, or vegetables; use in place of basil pesto to make a tomato and mozzarella salad; or simply double the salad and the stracciatella in this recipe to make eight salads. Since stracciatella is hard to find, feel free to substitute burrata in this dish.

I normally like to use only the pale green leaves from the celery hearts, but since this dish requires so many celery leaves, I call for you to use the darker green leaves for the pesto, reserving the light green leaves for the salad. If you were inclined to buy even more *celery, then use the light green leaves for both parts of this recipe—and use the excess celery ribs as inspiration to make Basic Chicken Stock (page 27), Soffritto (page 28), Lentils Castellucciano (page 264), or any of our other recipes that begin with sautéed diced celery.*

SERVES 4

SUGGESTED WINE PAIRING: SAUVIGNON (FRIULI)

Combine the pine nuts, garlic, salt, and half of the olive oil in the bowl of a food processor fitted with a metal blade or the jar of a blender. Add the parsley and pulse until it is finely chopped. Turn off the machine and scrape down the sides of the bowl with a rubber spatula. Add the celery leaves, the Parmigiano-Reggiano, and the remaining olive oil and purée, stopping as soon as the ingredients form a homogenous paste, and adding more olive oil if necessary to obtain a loose, spoonable pesto. (You want to stop the machine as soon as you achieve the desired consistency, as the blade will heat the garlic and give it a bitter flavor. Also, overprocessing the pesto will incorporate too much air, making the pesto fluffy and too smooth. I like to see some flecks of herbs in my pesto.) Turn the pesto out into a

for the celery-leaf pesto

1 tablespoon toasted pine nuts (page 63)

1 garlic clove, grated or minced if you're making the pesto in a mortar

¼ teaspoon kosher salt, plus more to taste

½ cup extra-virgin olive oil, plus more as needed

¼ cup packed fresh Italian parsley leaves

1¾ cups whole fresh celery leaves (preferably light green)

2 tablespoons freshly grated Parmigiano-Reggiano

¾ teaspoon fresh lemon juice, plus more to taste

for the salad

3 celery ribs, peeled and thinly sliced on an extreme bias

2 scallions, thinly sliced on an extreme bias starting at the green ends and moving toward the root ends (white and green parts)

¼ cup whole fresh pale green celery leaves from the hearts

½ cup fresh chervil leaves

½ cup fresh tarragon leaves

¼ cup fresh Italian parsley leaves

½ cup fresh micro or miniature basil leaves (or the smallest conventional basil leaves but do not tear or cut the leaves)

¼ cup 2-inch-long pieces fresh chives (about 10 chives)

Kosher salt

(continued)

bowl and stir in the lemon juice. Taste for seasoning and add more salt or lemon juice if desired. Use the pesto or transfer it to an airtight container and refrigerate for up to two days—any longer and it will lose its pretty green color and vibrant flavor. Bring the pesto to room temperature, stir to recombine the ingredients, and taste again for seasoning before serving.

To prepare the salad, combine the celery, scallions, celery leaves, chervil, tarragon, parsley, basil, and chives in a large bowl. Season with salt and toss to combine. Drizzle the salad with the vinaigrette and toss gently to coat it with the dressing. Taste for seasoning and add more vinaigrette or salt, if desired.

Pile the salad in the center of four salad plates or four large soup plates, dividing it evenly. Drizzle about 1 teaspoon of vinaigrette around each salad. If you are using burrata, cut it into four equal segments. Nestle one segment of burrata or pile the stracciatella, dividing it evenly, in the center of each salad. Use the back of a spoon to create a shallow crater in the center of each serving of burrata or stracciatella, spoon 1 tablespoon of the pesto into each crater, and serve.

2 tablespoons Lemon Vinaigrette (page 29), plus about 4 teaspoons for drizzling and more to taste

8 ounces stracciatella or burrata

burrata with asparagus, brown butter, guanciale, and almonds

From my vantage point behind the Mozzarella Bar I can see people's faces when they're eating, and their expressions when they bite into this dish are that they're wowed. I like brown butter with asparagus, and I like asparagus with almonds, but putting brown butter with burrata—that was a really indulgent decision and a combination I'm not even sure how I had the courage to put together. We use Sicilian almonds, which have a strong almond flavor and also a slight bitterness. If you can find them, use them.

When making brown butter, the trick is to brown it enough to get the delicious, nutty flavor that you want without letting it burn. It's best to do this in a stainless steel pan as opposed to a black-bottomed pan, so you can see the butter browning as it cooks.

SERVES 4

SUGGESTED WINE PAIRING: PETITE ARVINE (VALLE D'AOSTA)

Adjust the oven rack to the middle position and preheat the oven to 325°F.

Spread the almonds on a baking sheet and place them in the oven to toast for 12 to 15 minutes, until they are golden brown and fragrant, shaking the pan occasionally so the nuts brown evenly. Remove the almonds from the oven and set them aside to cool to room temperature. Drizzle the almonds with 1 tablespoon of the olive oil, sprinkle them with sea salt, and toss to coat them with the seasonings. Slice the almonds in half lengthwise.

After you put the almonds in the oven, lay the *guanciale* slices on a baking sheet and put it in the oven with the almonds until the *guanciale* is cooked through but not crisp, about 5 minutes. Remove the *guanciale* from the oven, transfer it to paper towels to drain, and cut each piece of *guanciale* in half on the diagonal.

Increase the oven temperature to 450°F.

Snap off the asparagus stems at the natural break and discard the stems. Put the asparagus spears on a baking sheet. Drizzle them with the remaining olive oil and sprinkle them with the kosher salt. Spread the asparagus out in a single layer and roast them in the oven until they start to brown but are still al dente, about 10 minutes. Remove the asparagus from the oven and set aside to cool to room temperature.

Place the butter in a medium saucepan (preferably stainless steel). Cook the butter over medium-high heat without stirring, but swirling the pan occasionally to brown the butter evenly, for 3 to 5 minutes, until the bubbles subside and the butter is dark brown with a nutty, toasty smell. (As you cook it, the butter will foam up and begin to brown, then the milk solids will drop to the bottom and the foam will subside. At this point the butter is done. Turn off the heat immediately, as the line between brown butter and burnt butter is a fine one.)

To serve, lay five to seven asparagus spears side by side on each of four plates (preferably oval or rectangular), pulling the tips of some of the spears so they aren't lined up evenly. Spoon 1 tablespoon of the brown butter along the length of each serving of asparagus spears to coat them with the butter. Cut the burrata into four equal segments and lay one segment on top of each serving of asparagus. Use the back of the tablespoon to create a small crater in each segment of burrata and spoon 1 tablespoon of the brown butter into each crater. Drop 1 tablespoon of bread crumbs in clumps, avoiding the butter (clumping them keeps them from getting soggy), over each serving of burrata and asparagus. Sprinkle the almonds over and around the asparagus and burrata, and lay two pieces of *guanciale* overlapping each other on top of each serving.

20 whole almonds (preferably Sicilian)

3 tablespoons extra-virgin olive oil

Maldon sea salt or another flaky sea salt, such as fleur de sel

2 ounces thinly sliced *guanciale* or pancetta

20 to 28 pencil-thin asparagus spears (depending on thinness)

Kosher salt

1 cup (2 sticks) unsalted butter

8 ounces burrata

¼ cup (4 tablespoons) Toasted Bread Crumbs (optional; page 74)

burrata with bacon, marinated escarole, and caramelized shallots

*I*f subtlety is your thing, this Mozzarella Bar creation is not for you. Each crostino *is composed of a really strong vinegar presence from the escarole, which is marinated before being grilled and again after; a strong flavor of smoke from the bacon; and sweetness from caramelized shallots. The role that the cheese plays is to tame those aggressive flavors but the result is by no means bland. The recipe for the shallots makes more than you will need for this recipe, but they are essentially pickled, so they will keep for several weeks in the refrigerator. You can use the leftovers on sandwiches or spooned over grilled beef, chicken, or pork.*

MAKES 12 CROSTINI

SUGGESTED WINE PAIRING: SANTA MADDALENA (ALTO ADIGE)

*T*o prepare the escarole for grilling, cut the heads in half through the core. Put the escarole in a large bowl. Combine the oil, garlic, and shallot in the jar of a blender and purée. Pour the marinade over the escarole, sprinkle with the salt, and toss to coat with the seasonings, massaging the marinade into the leaves to make sure the marinade gets in between the layers of the escarole. (You can prepare the escarole to this point up to several hours in advance. Refrigerate in an airtight container until you are ready to grill it.)

Prepare a hot fire in a gas or charcoal grill or preheat a heavy-bottomed skillet over high heat.

Place the escarole halves on the grill and grill until it is deep brown and charred in places, 8 to 10 minutes, turning it several times during the cooking time so the escarole cooks evenly. (If you are cooking the escarole on a grill, note that there is so much oil and water in the escarole that it will flare up, so use the perimeters of the grill to keep the flare-ups to a minimum.) Remove the escarole from the grill and put it in a large bowl. Cover the dish tightly with plastic wrap and set it aside for about 10 minutes to wilt the escarole.

To dress the escarole, cut off and discard the cores. Cut the leaves across the heads into 1½-inch pieces, and put the pieces in a large mixing bowl. Add the shallots, vinegar, garlic, and salt and toss to distribute the seasonings. Add the oil and toss the escarole again. Taste for seasoning and add more vinegar, oil, or salt, if desired.

To prepare the shallots, heat the oil in a large sauté pan over medium-high heat until it is almost smoking and slides easily in the

for preparing the escarole to grill

2 medium heads escarole (about 1¼ pounds), rinsed and dried well

¾ cup extra-virgin olive oil

6 garlic cloves, chopped

1 shallot, chopped

3 tablespoons kosher salt

for dressing the escarole

1 cup minced shallots

¼ cup champagne vinegar, plus more as needed

1 large garlic clove, minced or grated

1½ teaspoons kosher salt, plus more to taste

¼ cup extra-virgin olive oil, plus more as needed

(continued)

pan, 2 to 3 minutes. Add the shallots and sauté, stirring only as much as necessary to prevent them from burning, for about 5 minutes, until they're brown around the edges and soft. Add the balsamic vinegar, reduce the heat, and simmer the shallots, stirring frequently, until the bottom of the pan is dry, 6 minutes. Use the shallots or transfer them to an airtight container and refrigerate for up to several days. Bring the shallots to room temperature before serving. (This makes about ⅔ cup of shallots, which is more than you will need for this recipe. Serve the rest with grilled meat, fish, or pork.)

To assemble the crostini, adjust the oven rack to the middle position and preheat the oven to 350°F. Lay the bacon on a baking sheet and bake until it is cooked all the way through but not crisp, 15 to 17 minutes. Remove the bacon from the oven and transfer it to paper towels to drain.

Place the crostini oiled side up on your work surface. Mound ½ cup of the marinated escarole on top of each *crostino,* leaving the edges of the bread visible. Cut each slice of bacon in half on the diagonal and lay both halves side by side on each *crostino.* Cut the burrata into 12 equal segments and nestle one segment on top of each *crostino.* Drizzle each segment of burrata with the finishing-quality olive oil and spoon 1 teaspoon of the caramelized shallots on top of each serving of burrata. Coarsely grind black pepper over each *crostino,* and serve.

for the shallots

¼ cup extra-virgin olive oil

2 cups sliced shallots, thinly sliced lengthwise

½ cup balsamic vinegar

for assembling the crostini

12 thick slices (about 12 ounces) applewood-smoked bacon

12 Garlic Crostini (page 46)

1½ pounds burrata

Finishing-quality extra-virgin olive oil

Fresh coarsely ground black pepper

sheep's milk ricotta with hazelnut aillade, lemon, and roasted garlic vinaigrette

*W*hen the media review the Mozzarella Bar, they almost always mention having eaten this dish. It is composed of two special ingredients—large hazelnuts that we get from Trufflebert Farms in Eugene, Oregon, and sheep's milk ricotta imported from Italy—paired in an unusual way. Aillade is a French condiment of garlic pounded with some type of nuts, usually served as a condiment for duck or other meats. We make ours with hazelnuts; it's one of the few condiments that we make at the restaurant using a mortar and pestle because otherwise it comes out too smooth, like peanut butter.

SERVES 8

SUGGESTED WINE PAIRING: OFFIDA PECORINO (THE MARCHES)

To make the *aillade,* adjust the oven rack to the middle position and preheat the oven to 325°F.

Spread the hazelnuts for both the *aillade* and for serving the dish on a baking sheet and place them in the oven to toast until they're golden brown and fragrant, 12 to 15 minutes, shaking the pan occasionally so the nuts brown evenly. Remove the nuts from the oven and set them aside until they are cool enough to touch. Gather the hazelnuts into a clean dishtowel and rub them together inside the towel to remove the skins. Set them aside to cool to room temperature.

Put the 1 cup of hazelnuts for the *aillade* in a large mortar. Sprinkle the nuts with ¼ teaspoon salt and work the nuts with the pestle, scraping down the sides of the mortar with a rubber spatula, until they become the consistency of wet sand and you see the oil from the nuts leaching out. Add the lemon zest and garlic and work them in with the pestle. Add the hazelnut oil in a slow, steady stream, stirring with the pestle as you add it to keep it emulsified. Taste for seasoning and add more salt, if desired. (Use or transfer the *aillade* into an airtight container and refrigerate for up to several days. Bring it to room temperature before serving.)

Transfer the hazelnuts for serving to a bowl, drizzle them with the 2 tablespoons hazelnut oil, sprinkle with salt to taste, and toss to coat the nuts with the seasonings.

To make the vinaigrette, combine ¼ cup of Garlic Confit cloves (about 15 cloves), the lemon juice, and salt in the bowl of a food processor fitted with a metal blade or the jar of a blender and purée until smooth. With the motor running, drizzle the olive oil that the garlic was cooked in into the food processor, adding enough until you have the consistency of a loose paste. Transfer the vinaigrette to a bowl, taste for seasoning, and add more salt or lemon juice, if desired. Use the vinaigrette or transfer it to an airtight container and refrigerate for up to three days.

To serve, spoon 1 tablespoon of the vinaigrette in the center of each of eight salad plates or large soup plates. Put the ricotta in a medium bowl and stir it vigorously with a spoon to fluff it up. Spoon a rounded ⅓ cup of ricotta in an uneven pile on top of each serving of vinaigrette. Use a microplane or fine grater to zest a few gratings of lemon peel over each serving of cheese. Cut the larger Garlic Confit cloves in half lengthwise and scatter the garlic and hazelnuts around the ricotta, dividing them evenly. Smear 1 heaping tablespoon of *aillade* on each *crostino,* leaving the edges of the toast visible, and sprinkle the *aillade* with sea salt. Cut each slice of toast in half on an extreme bias, place two halves on the side of each plate, and serve.

for the *aillade*

1 cup hazelnuts
½ teaspoon kosher salt, plus more to taste
1 teaspoon finely grated lemon zest
½ teaspoon grated or minced garlic
¼ cup hazelnut oil

for the vinaigrette and for serving

1½ cups hazelnuts
2 tablespoons hazelnut oil
¼ teaspoon kosher salt, plus more to taste
Garlic Confit (page 38)
3 tablespoons fresh lemon juice, plus more to taste (juiced lemon reserved for grating the rind)
3 cups fresh sheep's milk or cow's milk ricotta
8 Garlic Crostini (page 46), brushed with oil left over from making the Garlic Confit
Maldon sea salt or another flaky sea salt, such as fleur de sel

burrata with speck, english peas, and parmigiano-reggiano

*P*eas, Parmigiano, and prosciutto are a combination that you see often in Italy, and one that, to me, says spring. The way we plate this dish it looks like a bird's nest, with half of a ball of burrata nestled into folds of speck, topped with a pile of peas, and then covered with a light dusting of Parmigiano that looks like fresh fallen snow. Although I prefer the smoky flavor of the speck, prosciutto is a fine substitute.

SERVES 4

SUGGESTED WINE PAIRING: PINOT BIANCO (ALTO ADIGE)

*F*ill a large saucepan with water, salt the water to taste like the ocean, adding approximately 1 tablespoon of salt to each quart of water, and bring it to a boil over high heat. Fill a bowl with ice water and line a plate or small bowl with paper towels. Place a wire strainer in the sink. Add the Engllish peas to the boiling water and cook them for about 1½ minutes, until they turn bright green but are still crunchy. Quickly drain the peas in the wire strainer and plunge them, still in the strainer, in the ice water to cool completely, about 1 minute. Transfer them to the paper towels to drain.

Pull the strings off the sugar snap peas, discard, and slice the sugar snap peas ⅛ inch thin on such an extreme bias that you are almost slicing them lengthwise. Put the peas, sugar snap peas, and mint in a medium bowl. Sprinkle with the grated Parmigiano-Reggiano, season with salt and pepper, drizzle with the olive oil, and toss to combine the ingredients and coat the vegetables with the seasonings.

Drape four slices of speck in a rosette-like pattern on each of four salad plates, dropping the slices onto the plate so they stand up slightly rather than placing the slices flat against the plate. Cut the burrata into four equal segments and nestle one segment in the center of each "rosette." Pile the dressed peas on top of the burrata, allowing a bit to fall onto the speck below, and use a microplane or another fine grater to grate a light layer of Parmigiano-Reggiano over each plate, and serve.

Kosher salt and freshly ground black pepper

⅓ cup shelled fresh English peas (about 20 pods, or 2½ pounds unshelled peas)

20 sugar snap peas

20 medium mint leaves, stacked and very thinly sliced lengthwise

3 tablespoons freshly grated Parmigiano-Reggiano, plus a wedge for grating an additional ¼ cup

2 tablespoons finishing-quality extra-virgin olive oil

16 thin slices of speck (about 2 ounces) or prosciutto (about 4 ounces)

8 ounces burrata

pane pomodoro with burrata, speck, pickled shallots, and tomato vinaigrette

*P*an con tomate *is a Catalan creation of grilled bread rubbed with garlic and raw tomato pulp, doused with olive oil, and sprinkled with coarse salt—and one of my favorite things to order at a tapas bar. So how do you serve your favorite Spanish snack at an Italian mozzarella bar? Add mozzarella, of course, or in this case, burrata, and give it an Italian name. We offer this dish only during tomato season. If the tomatoes have no flavor, the tomato bread will also have no flavor. And despite all the other delicious components, which include speck, pickled shallots, and tomato vinaigrette, the bread is, without question, the star. The recipe for the shallots makes more than you will need for this recipe, but they will keep for several weeks. Use the leftovers to make this recipe another time, or on sandwiches or grilled meat.*

MAKES 6 LONG CROSTONI

SUGGESTED WINE PAIRING: "TOCAI PLUS" (BASTIANICH WINERY, FRIULI)

*T*o prepare the shallots, trim the roots but leave enough of the root end intact to hold the layers of the shallots together. Starting at the root end, cut the shallots in half lengthwise. Peel the shallots and discard the peel and trimmed bits. Cut each shallot in half lengthwise again.

Combine the vinegar, sugar, fennel seeds, peppercorns, coriander seeds, bay leaf, chile, and 1 cup of water in a small saucepan and bring it to a boil over high heat. Have a slotted spoon or small strainer handy for lifting the shallots out of the water and a plate or baking sheet that will fit into your freezer. Add the shallots and return the liquid to a boil. Turn off the heat and lift the shallots out of the water and onto the plate or baking sheet. Place the shallots in the freezer for 15 to 20 minutes, until they cool to body temperature. Bring the liquid back to a boil and repeat, returning the shallots to the liquid, bringing the liquid to a boil again, straining and freezing the shallots again until they come to body temperature. Repeat, blanching and straining the shallots a third time and setting the liquid aside to cool to room temperature. When the shallots have cooled to room temperature for the third time, remove them from the freezer and return them to the liquid. Use the shallots or transfer them, along with the blanching liquid, to an airtight container and refrigerate them for up to several weeks. Bring the shallots to room temperature before serving.

for the shallots
½ pound shallots
1 cup champagne vinegar
1 cup sugar
1 teaspoon fennel seeds
1 teaspoon pink peppercorns
1 teaspoon coriander seeds
1 dried bay leaf
1 dried arbol chile

for the tomato vinaigrette
½ cup chopped good quality, ripe tomatoes (about 3 ounces)
3 large basil leaves, torn by hand
1 teaspoon red wine vinegar
½ teaspoon kosher salt, plus more to taste
½ teaspoon sugar, plus more to taste
1 tablespoon extra-virgin olive oil, plus more as needed
1 teaspoon thinly sliced Italian parsley

To make the vinaigrette, put the tomatoes, basil, vinegar, salt, and sugar in the bowl of a miniature food processor fitted with a metal blade or the jar of a blender and purée until it is fairly smooth with some texture. With the motor running, drizzle the olive oil through the feed tube, adding more oil if necessary to obtain the consistency of creamy vinaigrette. Turn off the machine, taste the vinaigrette for seasoning, and add more salt or sugar, if desired. Use the vinaigrette or transfer it to an airtight container and refrigerate it for up to three days. Bring the vinaigrette to room temperature and whisk to recombine the ingredients and taste for seasoning before using. Stir in the parsley just before serving.

To prepare the *pane pomodoro,* cut the tomatoes in half and smush the pulp of each tomato half on the same sides of the *crostono* you rubbed with garlic, using half of a tomato for each slice of toast, until you are left holding nothing but the tomato skin. Discard the skins. Drizzle 1 teaspoon of the finishing-quality olive oil over each *crostono* and sprinkle the *crostoni* liberally with the sea salt.

To assemble the *crostoni,* drape two slices of speck on each bread slice, leaving the bread peeking through each slice. Cut the burrata into 1-ounce segments and lay three segments on each *crostono,* spacing them evenly along the bread slice. Create a small crater in each portion of burrata and spoon a scant tablespoon of the vinaigrette into each. Fan one of the shallot quarters out on top of each segment of cheese. Coarsely grind black pepper over each *crostono,* place a parsley leaf, if using, on top of each segment of cheese, and serve.

for the *pane pomodoro*

3 large very flavorful, ripe tomatoes

6 *Crostoni Bagnati* (page 48)

6 teaspoons finishing-quality extra-virgin olive oil

Maldon sea salt or another flaky sea salt, such as fleur de sel

12 thin slices of speck or prosciutto (about 3 ounces)

1½ pounds burrata

Fresh coarsely ground black pepper

18 whole fresh Italian parsley leaves (optional)

mozzarella di bufala with bagna cauda, bottarga, and croutons

*W*hen I opened the Osteria, Joe Bastianich told me that one of his favorite combinations was fried mozzarella stuffed with anchovies—while I certainly trusted the guy and know he has great taste—let's just say that the combination sounded less than delicious to me. But since Joe said so, I tried it—and I loved it. What I didn't know is that bufala *and anchovies are actually a classic pairing. Here, the anchovies are in the* bagna cauda, *a delicious sauce from the Piedmont region and whose name translates "warm bath." In addition to anchovies, garlic, and olive oil, my version contains lemon and butter. Bottarga, a delicacy of Sicily and Sardinia, is cured pressed fish roe (usually from mullet or tuna) that has a pungent, fishy taste and is used sparingly, finely grated or very thinly sliced over dishes. You* *can purchase bottarga from specialty food stores and online food sources. This recipe for* bagna cauda *makes 1 cup—more than you will need. Spoon the leftovers over grilled fish or vegetables.*

SERVES 4

SUGGESTED WINE PAIRING: ROERO ARNEIS (PIEDMONT)

To make the croutons, heat the oil in a large sauté pan over medium-high heat until it is almost smoking and slides easily in the pan, 2 to 3 minutes. Line a plate with paper towels. Add the bread cubes to the oil and cook for 30 to 40 seconds, until they are golden brown. Use a slotted spoon to remove the croutons to the prepared plate and season them with salt. If the croutons appear greasy, transfer them to a clean paper towel to drain further.

To make the *bagna cauda,* heat the butter, olive oil, anchovies, and garlic in a large sauté pan over medium heat until the anchovies dissolve and the garlic is soft and fragrant, 5 to 6 minutes, stirring constantly so the garlic does not brown. Reduce the heat to low and cook the *bagna cauda* for another 2 minutes to meld the flavors. Proceed if you are going to use the *bagna cauda* right away. If you are preparing to use it later, set the *bagna cauda* aside to cool to room temperature, transfer it to an airtight container, and refrigerate for up to one week.

When you are ready to serve the *bagna cauda,* use a lemon zester to zest long strips from the lemon. Cut the two ends off the lemon and stand the zested lemon upright on a cutting board and use a serrated knife to cut away the peel, trying to maintain the integrity of the lemon shape while making sure that no pith remains. Cut the lemon into individual fillets, by cutting on either side of the membrane, removing and discarding the seeds as you go, and coarsely chop the fillets. Warm the *bagna cauda* over medium heat and stir in the lemon zest, chopped lemon fillets, and parsley.

To assemble the dish, place one ball or segment of mozzarella on each of four large salad plates or soup plates. Spoon 2 tablespoons of *bagna cauda* over each serving of mozzarella and sprinkle with the croutons, dividing them evenly and allowing them to fall over and around the mozzarella. Peel and discard the skin from the bottarga and use a microplane or another fine grater to grate a light layer of bottarga over each serving of mozzarella. Lay a parsley leaf on top of each serving of mozzarella, and serve.

for the croutons
¾ cup extra-virgin olive oil
¼ pound crustless sourdough bread, cut into ¼-inch cubes
Kosher salt

for the *bagna cauda*
¼ cup (½ stick) unsalted butter
¼ cup extra-virgin olive oil
10 anchovy fillets (preferably salt-packed), rinsed, backbones removed if salt-packed, and finely chopped
5 garlic cloves, minced
1 lemon
2 tablespoons thinly sliced fresh Italian parsley leaves

for serving
4 2- to 2½-ounce balls of mozzarella *di bufala* (or one 8- to 10-ounce ball, cut into 2- to 2½-ounce segments)
1 ounce red mullet bottarga
4 whole parsley leaves (optional)

peperonata with ricotta crostoni

*P*eperonata is a classic Italian *contorno, or side dish, of stewed sweet peppers. This version, which we serve with ricotta-topped crostini at the Osteria and to dress the Buricotta with Peperonata and Oregano (page 152) in the Pizzeria, is unusual and especially delicious because after the peppers are stewed, they are baked—an idea I got from Gino Angelini, a wonderful Italian chef in Los Angeles. Baking the peppers further caramelizes them, making them even richer and sweeter than you ever imagined a vegetable could be.*

MAKES 1 QUART

SUGGESTED WINE PAIRING: SALICE SALENTINO ROSATO (PUGLIA)

*A*djust the oven rack to the middle position and preheat the oven to 350ºF.

Heat the oil in a large sauté pan over medium-high heat until it is almost smoking and slides easily in the pan, 2 to 3 minutes. Add the onion and garlic, season with 1 teaspoon of the salt and several turns of pepper, and sauté, stirring occasionally to prevent the onion and garlic from browning, until the onion is tender and translucent, 5 to 7 minutes. Add the peppers, season with the remaining 1 teaspoon of salt, and sauté until they begin to soften, about 2 minutes. Add the vinegar, oregano, and sugar, and stir to combine the ingredients. Stir in the tomato sauce and cook for about 2 minutes to meld the flavors. Taste for seasoning and add more salt or pepper, if desired.

Transfer the peperonata to a large baking dish (at least 9 by 13 inches) or a large, ovenproof skillet and smooth the top with a wooden spoon or spatula to make it level. Place the peperonata in the oven to bake for 10 minutes. Remove the peperonata from the oven, stir in the olives, and return it to the oven for 30 to 35 minutes, until the top is charred, especially around the edges. Remove the peperonata from the oven and allow it to cool for at least 10 minutes before serving. Serve warm or at room temperature. If you are making the peperonata to serve later, set it aside to cool to room temperature, transfer to an airtight container, and refrigerate for up to two to three days. Bring the peperonata to room temperature and sprinkle the parsley over it before serving.

½ cup extra-virgin olive oil
1 large red onion, halved and sliced ¼ inch thick
¼ cup thinly sliced garlic cloves (about 10 large cloves)
2 teaspoons kosher salt, plus more to taste
Freshly ground black pepper
2 red bell peppers, cored, seeded, and sliced ¼ inch thick
2 yellow bell peppers, cored, seeded, and sliced ¼ inch thick
2 orange bell peppers, cored, seeded, and sliced ¼ inch thick
1 tablespoon Spanish sherry vinegar
1 tablespoon dried oregano
2 teaspoons sugar
1 cup Basic Tomato Sauce (page 24)
½ cup pitted Taggiasche, Umbrian, or Niçoise olives
2 tablespoons thinly sliced fresh Italian parsley leaves

ricotta crostoni

put this on the Mozzarella Bar menu following a visit to Chez Panisse Café, after which I became obsessed with ricotta toast. At the café, they served a garlic crostini with mounds of fresh, fluffy ricotta piled on top, and I just loved it at first sight. I was so excited about that toast that I had to find a way to work it into my repertoire at the Mozzarella Bar. I had been wanting to find a way to work peperonata—stewed peppers—onto the menu, since mozzarella and roasted peppers are a classic combination, but I just hadn't known how I wanted to serve it. The ricotta toast, or crostoni, *offered the perfect solution. While I drifted a bit from tradition, I feel I did that pairing justice. We serve the* crostoni *with the peperonata on the side, so guests can assemble the combination one bite at a time, with the toast in one hand and a forkful of peperonata in the other. I like being a two-fisted eater, and I just assume other people do too. Because the peperonata makes such a large amount, this is a great antipasto for a crowd. We gave you directions for serving this dish family style, but you could also spoon the peperonata onto individual serving dishes and give one to each guest.*

SERVES 12

Spoon the peperonata into a medium serving dish or individual serving dishes.

Put the ricotta in a medium bowl and stir vigorously with a spoon to fluff it up. Pile ¼ cup of ricotta in mounds on each *crostoni* and drizzle with finishing-quality olive oil. Sprinkle a teaspoon of parsley, a pinch of sea salt, and coarsely grind black pepper over each *crostono*. Arrange the *crostoni* on a serving platter or board, or rest one toast on the edge of each individual serving dish, and serve.

Peperonata (page 87)
3 cups fresh ricotta (preferably sheep's milk)
12 *Crostoni Bagnati* (page 48)
Finishing-quality extra-virgin olive oil
¼ cup thinly sliced fresh Italian parsley leaves
Maldon sea salt or another flaky sea salt, such as fleur de sel
Fresh coarsely ground black pepper

antipasti

clockwise from top left: mortadella, speck, molé salami,
genoa salami, *guiancale,* prosciutto-wrapped breadsticks,
lardo, hot sopressata, coppa

*P*asto" means "meal" in Italian, and antipasto is what comes before the meal—or what Americans think of as appetizers. Since Italians are practically obsessed with not spoiling their appetites, antipasti are usually very simple. A typical antipasto might be a plate of grilled or sautéed vegetables—things we might think of as side dishes. But the most popular antipasto in Umbria and Tuscany, where I spend my summers, is a plate of *affettati,* or sliced meats. Unlike Americans, Italians do not typically begin a meal with salad, much less make a meal of one, but I serve salads at both the Pizzeria and the Osteria (and thus have included them in this chapter) for one simple reason: I love them.

affettati misti:
an introduction to italian cured meats

Starting a meal with *affettati* is a tradition I have come to embrace when I dine and when I entertain, because it's so simple and delicious and it doesn't spoil my guests' appetites. Not long ago, the only cured meats you would find here were poor imitations of Italian varieties made by large American manufacturers. Today, cured meats are undergoing the same kind of revolution as artisan breads did twenty years ago. At Mozza, we currently have two pig-obsessed chefs, Erik Black, the sous chef in the Osteria, and Chad Colby, Chef de Cuisine at Mozza2Go, who always have several things hanging in the curing room located in the Scuola di Pizza. We import some of our meats from Italy; some we get from American artisan producers; and others we produce in-house. Mario's father, Armandino, is a pioneer of artisanal cured meats in America, and we get some of our meats from his Salumeria Artisan Cured Meats in Seattle. When I serve *affettati* at home, I serve them with *Fett'Unta* (page 65). While our selection changes depending on what Erik or Chad make or what we get in from Italy, below is a selection of what we may have at any time.

- *Mortadella,* identifiable by the white chunks of fat, and sometimes pistachios, that dot each slice, is a large sausage traditionally from Bologna, the original of which we call bologna.
- *Prosciutto* is Italian ham. Prosciutto *cotto,* or cooked ham, is similar to

the ham we would eat in a regular American sandwich. Prosciutto *crudo,* or "raw" ham, refers to ham that has been cured in salt and air-dried for at least fourteen months and as long as twenty-four— it's what you eat with melon.

- *Speck,* a tradition of the northern part of Italy near Austria, is essentially smoked prosciutto. I use speck whenever I want a touch of smoky flavor; you can substitute prosciutto wherever speck is called for.
- *Coppa,* also called capicola, is cured salami. The word *coppa* means "neck," and the meat is so named because it is made from the meat of the pig's neck.
- *Lardo* is cured fatback. When sea urchin are available, we often send special guests an olive oil–bathed *crostino* topped with sea urchin, a thin sheet of lardo, and Maldon sea salt—an idea I "borrowed" from a delicious version the chef Michael White serves at Marea in New York City.

nancy's chopped salad

was introduced to the concept of a chopped salad in the 1970s at La Scala Boutique, a casual offshoot, now closed, of the Beverly Hills institution La Scala. The salad, which they call the Jean Leon Chopped Salad (it's now available at the original La Scala restaurant), is made of iceberg lettuce, salami, and mozzarella, all so finely chopped that you almost don't have to chew it, then topped with ceci, or chickpeas, and a tangy red wine vinaigrette. I was totally addicted to that salad. I've been making chopped salads ever since, always with La Scala's version in mind, but the one we serve at the Pizzeria with aged provolone and Sweet 100 tomatoes is my best yet.

SERVES 4 AS A STARTER OR 2 AS A MAIN COURSE

 SUGGESTED WINE PAIRING: ORVIETO CLASSICO SUPERIORE (UMBRIA)

eparate the layers of the onion, stack two or three layers on top of one another, and slice them lengthwise $\frac{1}{16}$ inch thick. Repeat with the remaining onion layers. Place the onion slices in a small bowl of ice water and set them aside while you prepare the rest of the ingredients for the salad. Drain the onion and pat dry with paper towels before adding them to the salad.

Cut the iceberg in half through the core. Remove and discard the outer leaves from the head and remove and discard the core. Separate the lettuce leaves, stack two or three leaves on top of one another, and slice them lengthwise $\frac{1}{4}$ inch thick. Repeat with the remaining leaves and thinly slice the radicchio in the same way.

Cut the tomatoes in half, season them with salt, and toss gently to distribute the salt.

Combine the lettuce, radicchio, tomatoes, Ceci, provolone, salami, peperoncini, and onion slices in a large, wide bowl. Season with salt and toss to thoroughly combine the ingredients. Drizzle $\frac{1}{2}$ cup of the vinaigrette and squeeze the lemon juice over the salad, then toss gently to coat the salad with the dressing. Taste for seasoning and add more salt, lemon juice, or vinaigrette if desired. Pile the salad on a large platter or divide it among individual plates, piling it like a mountain. Sprinkle the dried oregano on top and serve.

Half of a small red onion
(halved through the core)
1 small head iceberg lettuce
1 medium head radicchio
1 pint small sweet cherry
tomatoes (such as Sun Golds
or Sweet 100s), halved
through the stem ends, or
cherry tomatoes, quartered
Kosher salt
1 $\frac{1}{2}$ cups cooked Ceci
(page 96)
4 ounces aged provolone,
sliced $\frac{1}{8}$ inch thick and cut
into $\frac{1}{4}$-inch-wide strips
4 ounces Genoa salami, sliced
$\frac{1}{8}$ inch thick and cut into
$\frac{1}{4}$-inch-wide strips
5 peperoncini, stems cut off
and discarded, thinly sliced
(about $\frac{1}{4}$ cup)
$\frac{1}{2}$ cup Oregano Vinaigrette
(page 97), plus more
to taste
Juice of $\frac{1}{2}$ lemon, plus
more to taste
Dried oregano, for sprinkling
(preferably Sicilian oregano
on the branch)

ceci

hese days it's almost old-fashioned to cook your own beans, even for restaurants. While canned are surprisingly good (I included many canned beans in recipes in my last book, A Twist of the Wrist*), homemade beans are so much better. The key to good dried beans is to cook them long enough so that they become creamy. Many restaurants undercook their beans, and frankly I would rather have canned beans than beans that are dry and chalky.*

MAKES 2 CUPS COOKED CECI

*rain the ceci and put them in a medium saucepan with enough water to cover them by 1½ inches, salt, and the olive oil. Place the carrot, celery, chile, garlic, and onion in a doubled piece of cheesecloth and tie it into a closed bundle with kitchen twine. Add the bundle to the pot with the ceci and bring the water to a boil over high heat. Reduce the heat and simmer the ceci until they are very tender and creamy, about 2 hours, adding more water to the pot as needed but never covering them by more than an inch to an inch and a half. (Cooking them in just enough water yields richer-tasting, creamier beans than if you were to just boil them in tons of water.) (Note: The time will vary greatly depending on how long you soaked the beans and how old the beans are; the time could be anywhere from 1 hour to as long as 4.) Turn off the heat and allow the ceci to cool in the cooking liquid. Remove and discard the cheesecloth bundle. The ceci can be prepared to this point up to a week in advance. If you are using the ceci now, drain them, reserving the cooking liquid to use as a hearty, ceci-flavored base for vegetable soup. To use later, transfer the ceci and the cooking liquid to an airtight container and refrigerate until you are ready to use. Bring the ceci to room temperature and drain them before using.

1 cup ceci (chickpeas),
   soaked overnight
2 tablespoons kosher salt
½ cup extra-virgin olive oil
1 large carrot, peeled
   and halved
1 celery rib, halved
1 dried arbol chile
16 garlic cloves
½ yellow Spanish onion,
   halved

oregano vinaigrette

*W*e put so much dried oregano in this vinaigrette that you might think it's a typo. It's not. Because the oregano is so prominent, look for sources such as Penzeys that specialize in dried herbs.

MAKES A LITTLE OVER 1 CUP

*C*ombine the vinegar, oregano, lemon juice, smashed garlic, grated garlic, salt, and pepper in a medium bowl and whisk to combine the ingredients. Set the vinaigrette aside to rest for 5 minutes to marinate the oregano. Add the olive oil in a slow, thin stream, whisking constantly to combine. Taste for seasoning and add more salt, pepper, or lemon juice, if desired. Use the vinaigrette or transfer it to an airtight container and refrigerate it for up to three days. Bring the vinaigrette to room temperature, whisk to recombine the ingredients, and taste again for seasoning before using.

2½ tablespoons red wine vinegar

2 tablespoons dried oregano

1 tablespoon fresh lemon juice, plus more to taste

2 garlic cloves, 1 smashed and 1 grated or minced

½ teaspoon kosher salt, plus more to taste

¼ teaspoon freshly ground black pepper, plus more to taste

1½ cups extra-virgin olive oil

tricolore with parmigiano-reggiano and anchovy dressing

he red, green, and white tricolore salad, traditionally composed of radicchio, frisée, and endive, is just one of the many ways that Italians celebrate their flag. I like tricolore salads, but this version, which is tossed in an anchovy-enhanced dressing with lots of grated Parmigiano-Reggiano, was my way of sneaking the flavors of a Caesar salad onto the Pizzeria menu without calling it a Caesar. In the rare instance that a Caesar salad is done well, it is one of my favorite salads, but Caesar salad is such a cliché on Italian-American menus—and it's not even Italian; it was invented in Tijuana—I could never have put it on my menu as such.

SERVES 4 AS A STARTER OR 2 AS A MAIN COURSE

To make the dressing, combine the anchovies, vinegar, lemon juice, garlic, salt, and pepper in the bowl of a food processor fitted with a metal blade or the jar of a blender and purée. With the motor running, add the olive oil in a steady stream through the feed tube to create an emulsion. Turn off the machine, taste for seasoning, and add more salt, pepper, or lemon juice, if desired. Use the dressing or transfer it to an airtight container and refrigerate for up to three days. Bring the dressing to room temperature, whisk to recombine the ingredients, and taste again for seasoning before using.

To prepare the salad, discard any brown or unappealing outer leaves from the endive and frisée. Pull the leaves away from the cores, putting them in a large, wide bowl, and discard the cores. Add the arugula, sprinkle with salt, and toss gently to combine the lettuces and distribute the salt evenly. Drizzle ½ cup of the dressing, sprinkle with ¼ cup of the Parmigiano-Reggiano, and toss gently to coat the lettuce leaves with the dressing. Taste for seasoning and add more salt or dressing, if desired.

Pile the salad on a large plate or divide it among four individual plates. Sprinkle with the remaining 3 tablespoons of the Parmigiano-Reggiano and serve.

for the dressing

5 anchovy fillets (preferably salt-packed), rinsed and backbones removed if salt-packed

1½ tablespoons red wine vinegar

1 tablespoon fresh lemon juice, plus more to taste

1 large garlic clove, finely chopped

½ teaspoon kosher salt, plus more to taste

¼ teaspoon freshly ground black pepper, plus more to taste

½ cup extra-virgin olive oil

for the salad

3 large heads red Belgian endive, or 1 large head radicchio leaves, leaves torn into large pieces

3 large heads frisée

6 cups loosely packed arugula (preferably wild arugula)

Kosher salt

¼ cup plus 3 tablespoons freshly grated Parmigiano-Reggiano

rucola, funghi, and piave cheese

This mountain of arugula is layered with thinly sliced mushrooms and long thin shards of Piave, a hard cheese similar to but sweeter than Parmigiano—and much less expensive. It's important to use fresh, firm mushrooms; look for those with closed caps and no blemishes. If you can't find Piave, Parmigiano is a fine substitute.

SERVES 4 AS A STARTER OR 2 AS A MAIN COURSE

SUGGESTED WINE PAIRING: BIANCO DI CUSTOZA SUPERIORE (VENETO)

Wipe the mushrooms clean, trim the tough ends of the stems, and slice the mushrooms paper-thin, preferably using a mandoline, keeping the shape of the mushrooms intact. Use a large knife or the mandoline to cut 5 ounces of the cheese into very thin slices.

Put the arugula in a large, wide bowl, sprinkle with salt, and toss gently to distribute the salt evenly. Whisk the vinaigrette to recombine the ingredients, drizzle ½ cup over the arugula, and toss gently to coat the leaves with the vinaigrette. Taste for seasoning and add more salt or vinaigrette, if desired.

Building the salad in three layers, first arrange a layer of the mushroom slices in the center of a serving platter or on individual salad plates. Scatter a layer of the cheese slices on top of the mushrooms and pile ⅓ of the arugula on top of the cheese. Repeat, building two more layers just like the first and ending with a layer of the cheese. Drizzle a generous tablespoon of vinaigrette over the cheese and around the salad (for individual salads, drizzle 1 teaspoon per salad), coarsely grind black pepper over the salad(s), and serve.

5 ounces white button or cremini mushrooms

Wedge of Piave cheese or Parmigiano-Reggiano, for slicing (about 5 ounces)

8 cups loosely packed arugula (preferably wild arugula; about ½ pound)

Kosher salt and fresh coarsely ground black pepper

½ cup Lemon Vinaigrette (page 29), plus more to taste and for drizzling

little gem lettuce with summer squash, walnuts, and pecorino

ittle Gem lettuce, a smaller, sweeter, very crunchy variety of romaine, appeared recently in Los Angeles the way burrata did: one day nobody had heard of it and now it's everywhere. Also like burrata, I love it so much that I have found multiple uses for it in my restaurants. The first time I saw Little Gem lettuce was at the Atelier of Joël Robuchon in Paris seven or eight years ago, when I took my daughter Vanessa there for her birthday. A large percentage of Robuchon's perfectly simple, perfectly executed dishes came with a dressed quarter of this tiny oblong-shaped lettuce with a beautiful, pale green color; I fell in love with Little Gem at first bite.

SERVES 4 TO 6

SUGGESTED WINE PAIRING: FRIULANO (FRIULI)

*P*lace the onion slices in a small bowl of ice water and set them aside while you prepare the rest of the ingredients for the salad.

Adjust the oven rack to the middle position and preheat the oven to 325°F.

Scatter the walnut halves on a baking sheet and toast them for 10 to 12 minutes, shaking the pan occasionally for even toasting, until they're lightly browned and fragrant. Remove the walnuts from the oven and set them aside to cool to room temperature. Transfer the walnuts to a small bowl, drizzle with the walnut oil, sprinkle with salt, and toss to coat the nuts with the seasonings.

Drain the onion, pat dry with paper towels, and place it in a medium bowl. Add the squash, drizzle with 1 tablespoon of the vinaigrette, season with salt, and toss to coat the vegetables with the seasonings. Add the grated pecorino romano and toss gently to distribute the cheese. Taste for seasoning and add more vinaigrette or salt, if desired.

Discard any brown or unappealing outer leaves from the lettuce heads. Pull the leaves away from the cores, putting them in a large, wide bowl, and discard the cores. Season the lettuce with salt and toss gently to distribute the salt evenly. Drizzle the remaining ¼ cup of vinaigrette over the lettuce and toss, gently massaging the vinaigrette into the leaves. Taste for seasoning and add more vinaigrette or salt, if desired.

12 to 18 ⅛-inch-thin round slices of red onion

1 cup walnut halves

1 tablespoon walnut oil or extra-virgin olive oil

Kosher salt and fresh coarsely ground black pepper

¼ pound summer squash, thinly sliced on a mandoline (about 1 heaping cup)

¼ cup plus 1 tablespoon Lemon Vinaigrette (page 29), plus more to taste and for drizzling

¼ cup freshly grated pecorino romano, plus a wedge of pecorino romano for grating

4 heads Little Gem lettuce or 4 small hearts of romaine

Building the salads in three layers, place three of the largest lettuce leaves in the center of each of four plates like a triangle. Scatter one-third of the squash and onions on the leaves, dividing them evenly. Lay two onion rings and scatter several walnut halves on each salad. Build two more layers the same as the first, using the medium leaves for the second layers and reserving the smallest leaves for the top layers. Grate fresh pecorino romano and coarsely grind black pepper over each salad. Scatter the remaining walnuts around the salads, dividing them evenly, drizzle about a teaspoon of vinaigrette around each salad, and serve.

little gem lettuce with dates, red onion, and gorgonzola dolce

My two favorite salads in the world are a properly prepared Caesar salad and an iceberg wedge with blue cheese dressing, neither of which have any place in an Italian restaurant. Just as I sneaked the Caesar salad in under the guise of a tricolore (see page 98), here I disguised the iceberg wedge sufficiently so that my customers don't realize that I'm serving a wedge salad, an American classic, in a Pizzeria. I don't know where I got the idea to throw the dates on the salad, but the contrast of their sweetness with the pungent Gorgonzola really makes this.

SERVES 4 TO 6

 SUGGESTED WINE PAIRING: OLTREPO PAVESE PINOT NERO SPUMANTE (LOMBARDY)

To make the dressing, combine 6 ounces of the Gorgonzola and the vinegar in a medium bowl and mash them together with a whisk until the cheese is smooth. Add the yogurt, buttermilk, lemon juice, thyme, garlic, salt, and pepper, and use the whisk to stir to combine. Taste for seasoning and add more lemon juice, salt, or pepper, if desired. Break the remaining gorgonzola into

for the dressing

10 ounces Gorgonzola *dolce*

2 tablespoons plus 1 teaspoon Spanish sherry vinegar

2 cups strained whole-milk Greek yogurt

1/4 cup buttermilk

small pieces into the bowl and stir gently with a rubber spatula to incorporate the chunks into the dressing but not so much that they become smooth.

To prepare the salad, place the onion slices in a small bowl of ice water and set them aside while you prepare the rest of the ingredients.

Remove the rough outer leaves from the lettuce and cut off and discard the rough caps at the bottom of the cores, leaving the heads intact. Starting at the core, cut each head of lettuce in half lengthwise. If you are making four individual salads, spoon ¼ cup of the dressing on each of four plates; otherwise, spoon 1 cup of the dressing in the center of a long platter and use the back of a spoon to spread the dressing along the length of the platter. One by one, spoon 2 tablespoons of the dressing over each half head, using the back of the spoon to spread it along the cut sides of the lettuce halves, leaving the edges of the heads visible. As you dress the halves, place them face up on the dressed plates, as the dressing on the plates will help keep the lettuce in place. For individual salads, place one lettuce head half, cut side up, on each plate. To build the salad on a platter, place the lettuce head halves along the length of the platter backgammon style, with one facing one direction and the one next to it facing the other direction. Tear the dates into thin strips and scatter the strips over the salad(s). Drain the onion slices, pat them dry with paper towels, and scatter over the salad(s). Sprinkle the thyme and coarsely grind pepper over the salad(s), and serve.

2 teaspoons fresh lemon juice, plus more to taste

2 teaspoons chopped fresh thyme leaves

4 large garlic cloves, grated

1 tablespoon kosher salt, plus more to taste

½ teaspoon fresh coarsely ground black pepper, plus more to taste

for the salad

12 to18 ⅛-inch-thin slices of red onion

3 heads Little Gem lettuce or 1 head iceberg lettuce, quartered, or 3 small hearts of romaine

3 Medjool dates, pits removed

1 teaspoon fresh thyme leaves

Fresh coarsely ground black pepper

eggplant caponata

Caponata, a traditional Sicilian eggplant preparation, is the perfect example of agrodolce, *the Italian word for combining sweet and sour flavors in savory dishes. When people order this antipasto at the Pizzeria, we suggest they also get an order of* Fett'Unta *(page 65) to absorb the delicious flavors of the caponata. Caponata is an ideal dish to serve at a party, because you can prepare it in advance and serve it at room temperature.*

SERVES 4

 SUGGESTED WINE PAIRING: MARSALA SUPERIORE SECCO (SICILY)

Place the eggplant cubes in a bowl, sprinkle with the salt and pepper, and toss to coat the eggplant with the seasonings.

Heat ¼ cup of the olive oil in a large sauté pan over medium-high heat until it is almost smoking and slides easily in the pan, 2 to 3 minutes. Add the eggplant cubes. (Don't worry if the pan is crowded, as the eggplant will cook down quickly.) Cook the eggplant undisturbed for 2 minutes until it begins to brown. You want the eggplant to get a deep brown color, so really try to resist the temptation to stir it while it cooks. Drizzle ¼ cup of the remaining olive oil over the eggplant and cook for another 6 to 7 minutes, until the eggplant is brown all over, shaking the pan and turning the eggplant to brown the pieces evenly, and adding the last ¼ cup of olive oil midway through that time.

Use a slotted spatula to remove the eggplant to a plate and reduce the heat to medium. Add the onion to the pan and cook, stirring constantly so the water released from the onion deglazes the pan you cooked the eggplant in, until the onion is translucent, about 3 minutes. Add the garlic, currants, and red pepper flakes and cook for 1 to 2 minutes, until the garlic is fragrant, stirring constantly so it doesn't brown. Add the *passata*, balsamic vinegar, thyme, and sugar, and stir to combine. Return the eggplant to the pan and add 2 tablespoons of the pine nuts. Stir gently to combine the ingredients, cover, and cook for 5 minutes. Remove the lid and cook for another 5 minutes, or until almost all of the liquid is evaporated. Taste for seasoning and add more salt or sugar, if desired. Serve or set the caponata aside to cool to room temperature, transfer it to an airtight container, and refrigerate for up to three days. Bring the caponata to room temperature and sprinkle the remaining tablespoon of pine nuts over the top just before serving.

1½ pounds eggplant, cut into
1-inch cubes (about 8 cups)

2 teaspoons kosher salt,
plus more to taste

¼ teaspoon freshly ground
black pepper

¾ cup extra-virgin olive oil

½ large yellow Spanish onion,
cut into 1-inch dice (about
1 cup)

2 garlic cloves, thinly sliced

2 tablespoons dried currants

½ teaspoon red pepper flakes

½ cup *Passata di Pomodoro*
(page 25) or tomato sauce

¼ cup balsamic vinegar

1 teaspoon fresh thyme leaves

½ teaspoon sugar, plus
more to taste

3 tablespoons Toasted Pine
Nuts (page 63)

fave or asparagus al forno with speck and parmigiano-reggiano

The first place I was served fava bean pods, as opposed to shelled beans, was at Zuni Café in San Francisco. When they came to the table, I thought it was such an interesting idea, and when I tasted them I found them delicious. When you serve them this way, you want to use only tender, young, small pods, as larger pods will be tough and fibrous. If you can't get young fave, *use jumbo asparagus instead. In either case, this is a spring dish.*

SERVES 4

 SUGGESTED WINE PAIRING: KERNER (ALTO ADIGE)

Place a baking sheet under the broiler and preheat the broiler at its hottest setting.

If you are preparing asparagus, snap off the stems at the natural break and discard the stems. Place the *fave* or asparagus in a large bowl, drizzle with the olive oil, sprinkle with the salt, and coarsely grind the pepper over them. Toss to coat the vegetables with the seasonings. Open the broiler and spread the vegetables in a single layer on the baking sheet, taking care as it will be very hot. (We are trying to imitate the effect of a pizza oven.) Roast the vegetables for 12 to 15 minutes, until they are browned but still al dente, turning them occasionally so they brown evenly.

To serve, drape one slice of speck in a semicircle on each of four plates and lay one fava pod or asparagus spear on each slice of speck. Drape another slice of speck on the fava or asparagus and lay another fava pod or asparagus spear on the speck at a 45-degree angle to the first. Repeat, draping a slice of speck and laying the third fava pod or asparagus spear at a different angle than the others to create an irregular stack. Drizzle 1 tablespoon of finishing-quality olive oil, coarsely grind black pepper, and use a microplane or another fine grater to grate a light layer of Parmigiano-Reggiano over each serving.

24 small fava bean pods or 12 jumbo asparagus spears
¼ cup extra-virgin olive oil
1 tablespoon kosher salt
Fresh coarsely ground black pepper
12 thin slices of speck (about 3 ounces)
¼ cup finishing-quality extra-virgin olive oil
Wedge of Parmigiano-Reggiano, for grating

meatballs al forno

*W*hen I was building the Pizzeria menu, I wanted it to be a true Italian pizzeria experience with a nod to the Italian-American pizzerias that I grew up eating in. With those American pizzerias in mind, I felt that we had to offer meatballs. What I really wanted to serve was a meatball sandwich, but as strongly as I argued for it, Matt argued against it. He softened over time and finally, two years after the Pizzeria opened, I got my meatballs—not as a sandwich, but as an antipasto: a bowl of meatballs served with buttered semolina toast on the side. Today they are the most popular antipasto in the restaurant.

MAKES 24 MEATBALLS OR 8 SERVINGS

SUGGESTED WINE PAIRING: CESANESE DEL PIGLIO (LAZIO)

*P*ut the day-old bread in a small bowl, pour in the milk, and set aside to soak the bread for about 5 minutes.

Combine the 1½ cups Parmigiano-Reggiano, onion, parsley, eggs, garlic, ground red pepper flakes, salt, and pepper in a large bowl and stir to thoroughly combine. Add the pork, veal, and pancetta. Squeeze the bread in your fist to press out the milk, discarding the excess milk. Add the bread to the bowl with the other ingredients and use the tips of your fingers as if you were playing the piano to combine the ingredients without overworking them, which makes for heavy meatballs. Divide the meat into 2-ounce portions and roll each portion into a ball.

Pour the flour into a large bowl or another dish convenient for dredging. Dredge the meatballs in the flour, shake off any excess, and place them on a baking sheet. Cover the pan with plastic wrap and refrigerate the meatballs for at least an hour or overnight. (Refrigerating allows the fat in the meats to solidify so the meatballs maintain their shape when cooked.)

Adjust the oven rack to the middle position and preheat the oven to 350°F.

Pour the olive oil into a large Dutch oven or ovenproof skillet and add more if needed to cover the bottom of the pan to ¼ inch deep. Heat the oil over medium-high heat until it is almost smoking and slides easily in the pan, 2 to 3 minutes. Working in two batches, place the meatballs in a single layer in the pan and sear them until they are lightly browned all over, being gentle when turning them so they don't fall apart, about 6 minutes. Remove the meatballs to a plate. Add more

¾ cup diced day-old, crustless bread

¼ cup whole milk

1½ cups freshly grated Parmigiano-Reggiano (about 6 ounces), plus a wedge of Parmigiano-Reggiano for grating

½ large yellow Spanish onion, minced (about 1 cup)

⅔ cup finely chopped fresh Italian parsley leaves

2 extra-large eggs

4 large garlic cloves, minced

2 to 3 teaspoons pure ground red pepper flakes, plus more to taste

2 teaspoons kosher salt

1 teaspoon freshly ground black pepper

1 pound ground pork (preferably pork butt)

1 pound ground veal

6½ ounces pancetta, finely chopped or minced in a miniature food processor

All-purpose flour, for dredging (about 2 cups)

(continued)

oil to the pan and heat it until it's almost smoking before cooking the second batch in the same way. Turn off the heat and wipe the oil and browned bits from the pan. Return the meatballs to the pan. Combine the *passata* and chicken stock and pour the liquid over the meatballs. The amount of sauce you need will vary depending on the size of the vessel you are pouring it into, so add more or less as needed; you want them to be submerged but not drowning in the liquid. Add the bay leaves and chile pods and place the meatballs in the oven to braise for 1 hour. Remove the meatballs from the oven and allow them to rest in the sauce for at least 10 minutes. The meatballs can be prepared to this point up to two days in advance. Set them aside to cool to room temperature, then transfer the meatballs and the sauce to an airtight container, or several containers, and refrigerate until you're ready to serve them. Warm the meatballs and the sauce together in a saucepan over medium heat before proceeding with the recipe.

To serve, remove the meatballs to a plate and skim off and discard the fat from the sauce. Spoon a thin layer of sauce on a serving platter or individual plates, lay the meatballs on top of the sauce, serving 3 meatballs if you are using individual plates. Use a microplane or another fine grater to grate a thin dusting of Parmigiano-Reggiano over the meatballs. Serve with the semolina toast on the side, if desired.

¼ cup extra-virgin olive oil, plus more as needed
1 quart *Passata di Pomodoro* (page 25) or tomato sauce
1 quart Basic Chicken Stock (page 27)
3 dried bay leaves
3 dried arbol chiles
Buttered semolina toast (optional)

mussels al forno with salsa calabrese

After we signed our lease, Mario took a critical look at the Pizzeria, and the first thing he said was "There's no kitchen!" For a second I panicked, until he added, "It's perfect! Everything you make in the Pizzeria should come out of the pizza oven." With few exceptions, we have stayed true to that rule. We are always looking for creative, unexpected ways to use the oven, and these mussels, served with Salsa Calabrese, a red pepper–spiked mayonnaise, is a perfect example. The salsa recipe makes more than you will need for the mussels. Serve the rest on the side, and use what you have left on a sandwich or as a condiment for grilled fish, chicken, or meat.

SERVES 4

 SUGGESTED WINE PAIRING: CIRO BIANCO (CALABRIA)

To make the Salsa Calabrese, stir the mayonnaise and Calabrian Bomb together in a small bowl. Use the salsa or transfer it to an airtight container and refrigerate for up to three days.

To prepare the mussels, adjust the oven rack to the middle position and preheat the oven to 400°F.

Scrub the mussels to clean them thoroughly and pull off and discard the beards if they are still attached.

Combine the mussels, olive oil, wine, garlic, red pepper flakes, and ¼ cup of the parsley in a bowl and toss to combine. Reserving the marinade left in the bowl, arrange the mussels in a baking dish, an ovenproof sauté pan (such as a cast-iron skillet), or four individual baking dishes, with the pointed ends up. You want to use a dish or pan that holds the mussels snugly in a single layer. Pour the remaining marinade over the mussels and bake them for 10 to 15 minutes, until all, or all but a very few, of the mussels have opened. Remove the mussels from the oven and discard any that haven't opened. Drizzle ¼ cup of the salsa over the mussels, sprinkle with the remaining parsley, and serve in the dish you baked them in, with the crostini and the remaining salsa on the side.

for the salsa calabrese
Garlic Mayonnaise (page 51)
¼ cup Calabrian Bomb or another red chile paste or harissa

for the mussels
48 Prince Edward Island mussels or other fresh mussels
¼ cup extra-virgin olive oil
¼ cup dry white wine
4 large garlic cloves, minced (1 heaping tablespoon)
½ teaspoon red pepper flakes
¼ cup plus 1 heaping tablespoon finely chopped fresh Italian parsley leaves
8 Garlic Crostini (page 46)

grilled octopus with potatoes, celery, and lemon

I order octopus every time I go to Babbo and have done so since long before I partnered with Mario and Joe, so when Mozza came about I knew I wanted to include an octopus dish on the Osteria menu. Most people's experience of octopus is eating it raw at sushi bars, and we all know how chewy it can be, but, like Mario's version at Babbo that I love so much, ours is tender and not at all rubbery. That tenderness doesn't come without considerable effort, but as much effort as it is, the finished dish is certainly worth it. It's our most popular non-mozzarella antipasto.

In Italy people do all kinds of things to tenderize fresh octopus. They pound it with a meat pounder, they hit it with hammers, they throw it against rocks. Matt's solution is to start with frozen octopus; freezing helps break down the octopus's flesh the same way that pounding it does. He then sears the octopus, poaches it in olive oil, marinates it, and, lastly, chars it in a wood-fired grill. The wine cork in the recipe is something we do on Mario's orders. He claims that in Italy they say the wine cork tenderizes the octopus. I think it must be an old wives' tale, but it doesn't hurt to throw it in there, so we do. Note: This recipe requires a huge sacrifice of oil. You can keep the oil and reuse it once to make the octopus again within a week.

SERVES 4

SUGGESTED WINE PAIRING: VERDICCHIO DEI CASTELLI DI JESI
(THE MARCHES)

To poach the octopus, adjust the oven rack to the middle position and preheat the oven to 300°F.

In a braising pot just big enough to hold the octopus, heat 2 tablespoons of the olive oil over medium-high heat until it is almost smoking and slides easily in the pan, 2 to 3 minutes. Add the octopus and sear it for 8 to 10 minutes, turning to cook all sides evenly, until the octopus is burgundy all over and browned in places. Remove the octopus to a plate and wipe out the pot. In the pot you seared the octopus in, heat the garlic cloves with 2 tablespoons of the remaining olive oil and sauté the garlic over medium-high heat, stirring often, until it is golden brown, 2 to 3 minutes. Turn off the heat. Remove and discard the garlic cloves and return the octopus to the pot. Add the red pepper flakes, wine cork, and enough olive oil to cover the octopus. Put the lid on the pot and place it in the oven for 1½ to 2 hours, until

for poaching the octopus
8 cups plus ¼ cup extra-virgin olive oil, plus more as needed
1 2-pound frozen octopus, thawed and rinsed
10 garlic cloves, crushed
1 tablespoon red pepper flakes
1 wine cork

(continued)

the octopus is very tender; it will puncture and tear easily with a fork. Remove the pot from the oven, and set it aside to allow the octopus to cool to room temperature in the oil. Remove the octopus from the oil, reserving the oil to poach another octopus within a week, and place the octopus on a baking sheet. (If you are going to reuse the oil, strain it and refrigerate it until you are ready to use it.) Cover the baking sheet with plastic wrap and refrigerate the octopus overnight or for at least several hours.

Lay the octopus on a cutting board and spread out the tentacles like the petals of a flower. Use a large knife to cut the octopus in half through the body, keeping the tentacles intact. Working from the body outward as if you were cutting off the petals of the flower, cut each tentacle to remove it from the head. Turn the head inside out, scrape out and discard any guck left inside the head, and cut the head into quarters. Cut the body into 2-inch segments, leaving the ends of each tentacle long for their dramatic effect on the plate, and place all of the octopus pieces in a medium bowl or a large, nonreactive baking dish.

To make the marinade, combine the parsley, olive oil, garlic, and red pepper flakes in the bowl of a miniature food processor fitted with a metal blade or the jar of a blender and purée. Drizzle the marinade over the octopus and toss to coat it with the marinade. Cover the bowl or dish tightly with plastic wrap and refrigerate the octopus until you are ready to grill it or for up to three days.

To make the salad, steam the potatoes until they are tender when pierced with a small sharp knife, about 20 minutes. Remove the potatoes to a plate until they are cool enough to touch. Use a small, sharp knife to remove the peel from the potatoes and discard the peels. Slice the potatoes into ½-inch-thick rounds, place them in a small bowl, and set aside.

While the potatoes are cooking, fill a large saucepan with water, bring the water to a boil over high heat, and salt it to taste like the ocean, adding approximately 1 tablespoon of salt to each quart of water. Fill a bowl with ice water. Place the leek in a fine-mesh strainer and plunge into the boiling water to blanch it for 1 minute. Lift the strainer out of the water and immediately plunge the strainer into the ice water for about 1 minute to cool the leek. Remove the strainer from the water and turn the leek out onto paper towels to drain.

Prepare a hot fire in a gas or charcoal grill or preheat a grill pan.

Season the potatoes with the 1 teaspoon of kosher salt and toss to distribute the salt evenly over the potato slices. Add the leek, scallions,

for the marinade

1 cup whole Italian parsley leaves
½ cup extra-virgin olive oil
¼ cup garlic cloves
1 heaping teaspoon red pepper flakes

for the salad

¼ pound fingerling potatoes or other small potatoes
1 teaspoon kosher salt, plus more for the blanching water and to taste
1 medium leek, washed and sliced into ¼-inch rounds (white and light green parts only)
2 scallions, thinly sliced on an extreme bias starting at the green ends and moving toward the root ends
3 celery ribs, peeled and thinly sliced on an extreme bias
¼ cup whole fresh pale green celery leaves (from the hearts)
Freshly ground black pepper
¾ cup plus 2 tablespoons Lemon Vinaigrette (page 29), plus more to taste
1 lemon, halved
½ cup 3-inch-long chive batonettes (about 20)

sliced celery, and celery leaves to the bowl with the potatoes. Season the salad with salt and pepper, drizzle with ¼ cup plus 2 tablespoons of the vinaigrette, and toss to coat with the seasonings. Taste for seasoning and add more vinaigrette, salt, and pepper, if desired. Pile the salad in the center of four plates, dividing it equally and reserving any vinaigrette left in the bottom of the bowl.

Have the bowl with the reserved vinaigrette nearby and grill the octopus pieces until they are charred on all sides, about 3 minutes total. Remove the octopus pieces from the grill as they are done and place them in the bowl with the vinaigrette you tossed the salad with. Drizzle with another ¼ cup of the vinaigrette and toss to coat the octopus with the vinaigrette. Taste for seasoning and add more salt, if desired.

Stack the octopus pieces on top of the salads, dividing them evenly and reserving the long dramatic tentacles for the tops of the salads. Squeeze a few drops of lemon over each serving of octopus. Drizzle 1 tablespoon of the vinaigrette over and around each salad. Scatter a few chive batonettes over the top of each plate, and serve.

ribollita "da delfina"

*R*ibollita is a classic Tuscan soup traditionally made with leftover minestrone thickened with chunks of stale bread. This version is something quite different, and it's based entirely on the one they serve at Ristorante Da Delfina, a wonderful ristorante in a tiny village nestled in the hills just outside Florence. It was described to me as a fried soup, so the first time I ate it, I didn't know what to expect. I was pleasantly surprised to discover that they'd turned the soup into something wholly unsouplike that I could eat with a knife and fork. The way we make it, after cooking off the liquid, we thicken the soup with bread, we chill it, and then shape it into patties that we pan-fry in olive oil. We serve it as an antipasto but it could be a side dish or, served with a green salad, a light meal. I often recommend it to vegetarians, and to make it vegan, just omit the Parmigiano rind. One of our inveterate recipe testers, Tracey Harada, tested this recipe about eight times to get the flavors perfect. Cavolo nero, a variety of kale, is one of the defining ingredients of any ribollita. You can find it at specialty food stores and health-food stores, but if you can't find it, use another variety of kale.

SERVES 8

SUGGESTED WINE PAIRING: BARCO REALE DI CARMIGNANO (TUSCANY)

*C*ombine ½ cup of the olive oil, the onion, rutabaga, carrot, squash, and fennel in a large sauté pan over medium-low heat. Season with 2 teaspoons of the salt, and cook to sweat the vegetables for about 10 to 15 minutes, stirring occasionally to prevent them from browning, until they are tender. Reduce the heat to medium low and let the vegetables sweat in their own juices another 8 to 10 minutes, until they're very soft. Add the cabbage and *cavolo nero*, season with another 2 teaspoons of the salt, and cook to wilt the cabbages slightly, about 2 minutes. Reduce the heat to low, add ½ cup of the remaining olive oil, and cook without stirring until the juices released from the vegetables have boiled down and the pan is almost dry, about 15 minutes. Break the tomatoes up into the pan. Add the Parmigiano-Reggiano rind(s), and 1 cup of water, and cook the soup at a low simmer for 2½ to 3 hours, adding another cup of water from time to time so the vegetables are always barely covered with water, until the root vegetables are very tender but not disintegrated. When the vegetables are done, continue to cook until there is no water left in the pan and the soup is stiff enough that you can stand a wooden spoon straight up in it.

1 cup plus 2 tablespoons extra-virgin olive oil, plus more as needed

2 cups large-diced yellow Spanish onion (about 1 large onion)

1 cup large-diced peeled rutabaga (about 5 ounces)

1 cup large-diced peeled carrot (about 1 large carrot)

1 cup large-diced peeled butternut squash (about 6 ounces)

1 cup large-diced fennel (about ½ large bulb)

4 teaspoons kosher salt

3 packed cups coarsely chopped savoy cabbage (about ¼ medium head) or napa cabbage

(continued)

Transfer the soup to a large mixing bowl and remove and discard the Parmigiano-Reggiano rind(s). Add the bread and beat it vigorously into the soup with a wooden spoon so it breaks up and is suspended in the soup. If you have large chunks of bread in the soup, it will cause the patties to fall apart when you fry them. Set the soup aside to cool to room temperature, then cover the bowl tightly with plastic wrap or transfer the soup to an airtight container and refrigerate it overnight or for at least 1 hour. The soup can be made to this point up to five days in advance.

Adjust the oven rack to the middle position and preheat the oven to 400°F.

Scoop out 1 cup of soup and mold the soup between your palms as you would a hamburger patty, forming a square patty about 1 inch thick, and place it on a baking sheet. Repeat, forming the remaining soup patties in the same way. Cover the baking sheet tightly with plastic wrap and place it in the refrigerator to chill the patties for at least 30 minutes before frying them. The patties can be formed up to one day in advance.

Heat the remaining 2 tablespoons olive oil in a large nonstick skillet over medium-high heat until the oil is almost smoking and slides easily in the pan, 2 to 3 minutes. Add two or three of the soup patties, making sure to leave enough room so you can slide a spatula under and flip the patties. Fry the patties on the first side until they're crisp and almost black in places, 5 to 6 minutes. Carefully turn the patties and cook them on the second side for 2 minutes. Transfer the patties without turning them (the crisp side will be facing up) to a baking sheet and place them in the oven while you fry the remaining patties in the same way, adding more olive oil to the pan as needed, and adding the fried patties to the baking sheet in the oven as they're done. After the last patties have been fried, leave them all in the oven for 5 minutes to make sure the last batch is warmed through.

Remove the patties from the oven and place each one on a plate with the crisp side facing up. Drizzle each serving with 1 tablespoon of the finishing-quality olive oil. Use a microplane or another fine grater to grate a generous layer of Parmigiano-Reggiano over each patty, and serve.

3 packed cups *cavolo nero*, stems cut off and discarded, leaves coarsely chopped (about 1 bunch)

3 cups canned whole peeled tomatoes (preferably San Marzano)

1 or 2 rinds Parmigiano-Reggiano

1/2 pound stale, crustless bread, broken up into small chunks

Finishing-quality extra-virgin olive oil

Wedge of Parmigiano-Reggiano, for grating

steamed mussels with passata di pomodoro, chiles, and herbs

What I like most about this mussels preparation is that they are not simply steamed in white wine, like the vast majority of mussels you see in restaurants. We cook them with a light tomato sauce—and, yes, also white wine—and toss in piles of herbs after the mussels are cooked, so the herbs wilt only slightly. The finished dish manages to be original and familiar at the same time. It also couldn't be easier to make.

SERVES 4

 SUGGESTED WINE PAIRING: BIANCO D'ALCAMO (SICILY)

Combine the olive oil, garlic, scallions, and salt in a large sauté pan over medium-high heat, and sauté until the garlic starts to brown slightly, 2 to 3 minutes. Add the red pepper flakes, mussels, white wine, and *passata* and bring to a boil. Reduce the heat to medium, cover the pan, and steam the mussels for 3 minutes. Uncover the pan to check for doneness; if all but a few mussels have opened, discard those that did not open. If many mussels remain unopened, steam them another minute. Turn off the heat, add the basil, chives, and oregano, and stir to combine.

Spoon the mussels into four large bowls or soup plates, dividing them evenly, and ladle the broth over and around the mussels. Cut each *crostono* in half diagonally, place the two halves on the side of each plate or bowl, and serve.

½ cup extra-virgin olive oil

16 large garlic cloves, thinly sliced (about ½ cup)

4 scallions, thinly sliced on an extreme bias starting at the green ends and moving toward the root ends (white and green parts)

2 teaspoons kosher salt

2 teaspoons red pepper flakes

2 pounds Prince Edward Island mussels or other fresh mussels, scrubbed and beards removed

1 cup dry white wine

2 cups *Passata di Pomodoro* (page 25) or tomato sauce

1 cup fresh basil leaves, thinly sliced

40 chive spears, cut into 2-inch-long batonettes

½ cup fresh oregano leaves

4 *Crostoni Bagnati* (page 48)

red wine–braised squid
with garlic mayonnaise

For this dish, we braise squid in red wine and orange rind. The rind gives the sauce a slight bitterness that can seem overwhelming until you eat it on crostini with a dab of mayonnaise, and then it all comes together. We serve it as a condiment for pasta in the Osteria, which would be a perfect use for leftovers because when dressing pasta, a little goes a long way. We use calamarata, a short ring-shaped pasta that mimics the shape of squid rings, or paccheri, a long, tubular pasta that flattens when it cooks.

SERVES 4

 SUGGESTED WINE PAIRING: PIGATO RIVIERA LIGURE DI PONENTE (LIGURIA)

Rinse the squid thoroughly and remove and discard the cartilage and the beaks if they're still attached. Cut the squid into 2-inch pieces and place it in the refrigerator.

Combine the olive oil, onion, carrot, celery, and garlic in a large sauté pan over medium heat, season with the red pepper flakes, pepper, and 1 teaspoon of the salt, and sauté until the vegetables are soft, about 10 minutes, stirring often to prevent the vegetables from browning. Increase the heat to high, add the squid, season with the remaining teaspoon of salt, and stir to combine. Sauté the squid with the vegetables until the squid has released enough liquid to cover itself in the pan, about 5 minutes. Add the wine, *passata,* chopped orange, orange juice, and brandy, and stir to combine. Bring the liquid to a boil, reduce the heat, and simmer the squid for 1 hour, or until it is tender and the sauce has thickened to the consistency of thin gravy. Turn off the heat, drizzle in the finishing-quality olive oil, and stir vigorously to emulsify the sauce. Stir in the parsley.

Divide the squid and sauce evenly among four soup plates or large bowls. Place 2 crostini on the side of each plate or bowl and serve with a ramekin of mayonnaise on the side of each.

2½ pounds squid

½ cup extra-virgin olive oil

Half of a Spanish onion, cut into small dice (about 1 cup)

Half of a large carrot, peeled and cut into small dice (about ½ cup)

1½ celery ribs, cut into small dice (about ½ cup)

1 tablespoon chopped garlic (about 3 large cloves)

¼ teaspoon red pepper flakes

¼ teaspoon freshly ground black pepper

2 teaspoons kosher salt

2 cups dry red wine

¼ cup plus 2 tablespoons *Passata di Pomodoro* (page 25) or tomato sauce

Half of an orange, seeds removed and finely chopped, including rinds (about ½ cup)

1 tablespoon orange juice

1 tablespoon brandy

½ cup finishing-quality extra-virgin olive oil

½ cup thinly sliced fresh Italian parsley leaves

8 Garlic Crostini (page 46)

Garlic Mayonnaise (page 51)

OSTERIA

MOZZA

6602 Melrose Avenue, Los Angeles 90038
323.297.0100 · www.mozza-la.com

pizza

clockwise from top left: buricotta with peperonata and oregano; *funghi misti*; gorgonzola *dolce*, fingerling potatoes, radicchio, and rosemary; *bianca* with fontina, mozzarella, sottocenere *al tartufo,* and sage; pizza alla benno

*W*e welcome our customers' feedback through comment cards delivered with the check at both restaurants, and of all the comments we get from either restaurant, the overwhelming majority have to do with our pizza. Some love it and can't thank us enough for giving the gift of Pizzeria Mozza to Los Angeles. "When I die, I want to be buried with this pizza!" Others think that what we are serving isn't pizza at all and that it's their job to educate us—or me—as to what "real" pizza is.

I never quite know what to say when customers, colleagues, or journalists ask me—and they ask often—whether or not I serve "real pizza." Or when they ask me what style of pizza we make at Pizzeria Mozza. Is it New York pizza? Chicago style? Neapolitan? By "real," I assume that people are referring to pizza from its source, Naples. Pizza Napoletana follows a specific set of guidelines set forth by the Associazione Verace Pizza Napoletana. The pizza dough must be made with a specific type of flour, formed by hand, and not exceed a specific diameter and thickness. And the pizza topping must be made using specific types of tomatoes and cheese, and it must be baked in a wood-fired oven at 900°F for precisely 60 to 90 seconds.

I was often asked the same thing about bread when I first opened La Brea Bakery. My answer then was that the style was my own. I didn't set out to replicate French or Italian or German breads. I did study those, and I took in that information and created breads that satisfied me—my aesthetic and my palate, my perfect versions of whatever bread I was creating. The same is true for pizza. When I started developing the pizzas for Pizzeria Mozza, my goal was not to replicate the quintessential pizza Napoletana, or Chicago's deep-dish pizza, or traditional New York–style pizza. I simply set out to create pizzas that satisfied my taste and desires.

If there was any pizza that I did aspire to, it was a pie made by Chris Bianco, whose Pizzeria Bianco in Phoenix, Arizona, is a mecca for the pizza obsessed. The first time I ate Chris's pizza was several years before Pizzeria Mozza was conceived, when Suzanne Goin, the chef and owner of Lucques and AOC restaurants in Los Angeles, and David Lentz, chef and owner of the Hungry Cat restaurants, were married there. When I took a bite of Chris's pizza, I was speechless. So many of us at the wedding were cooks with high standards when it comes to food, and we all just walked around at the reception saying, "This. Pizza. Is. S O. *DELICIOUS*!" The crust had all the nuances of a perfectly crafted loaf of bread: it was crispy, chewy, airy, and flavorful. I was enamored of it. And eating it turned out to be a life-altering experience. My immediate response after savoring that first bite was "Someday I'm going to figure out how to do this." When we found the space we're currently in and there was a pizzeria attached, I knew that this was my chance to fulfill that dream.

As I embarked on the journey to create my perfect pizza, the first challenge I took on was the crust. Having eaten Chris Bianco's epic pizza and subsequently having fallen in love with the pizza crust at Roscioli Antico Forno, a bakery in Rome, I had begun to look at pizza differently. Where once I had thought that the crust was just a vehicle for the toppings, and that the toppings offered the chef the opportunity to shine, I now understood that a truly great pizza was one with a great crust and great toppings.

From a breadbaker's perspective, there were things I knew that I wanted in the pizza crust for Mozza. I wanted the crust to have an open hole structure, meaning that when the dough is baked there are irregular holes in it as you would see if you tore open a loaf of good, hearth-baked country white bread. I wanted the crust to be crisp but also chewy. And I wanted it to have flavor. Developing my first breads for La Brea Bakery took me quite a long time and quite a bit of practice, but with pizza, once I had the revelation that I was essentially working with bread dough, I was able to get what I wanted fairly quickly.

Before they bite into it, newcomers to Pizzeria Mozza often mistakenly think that the crust is thick because they're focused on the large rim, which in Italian is called a *cornice*, or "frame." Our *cornice* looks big, but that isn't the result of the dough's being thick. In fact, the dough is stretched very thin, but because it is a very active dough, without any toppings on it, the rim puffs up. Once they bite or tear into the *cornice*, people see that, rather than being doughy and solid, it is light, airy, and chewy with a thin, crisp exterior. Exactly what I wanted.

Once I developed the pizza crust that I wanted, it was time to think about toppings. Before we opened, Matt and I decided we wanted to open with ten different pizzas. We knew we would include a Margherita (page 133) because it's the classic. I wanted a clam pizza (see Littleneck Clams, Garlic, Oregano, Parmigiano-Reggiano, and Pecorino Romano, page 143) like the New Haven classic. And I knew I would create one with fennel sausage (see Fennel Sausage, Panna, and Scallions, page 144) modeled after one that they make at Pellicano, the pizzeria in Umbria that inspired Pizzeria Mozza. For the majority of the remaining pizzas I did what I like to do most—I got to work playing with different combinations of ingredients that I thought might make for a delicious and visually appealing, Italian-*ish* pizza.

Although the ingredients we include on our pizzas may not be traditional Italian pizza toppings, they are all Italian. You won't see barbecue chicken or Peking duck on these pies. There is also nothing that falls under the category of "create your own pizza." The combinations we offer are all the result of much deliberation and experimentation. We were very conscientious about picking ingredients that really work together and then, as we baked one pizza after another, changing an ingredient here or there, we scrutinized each one. Does it need anything else? Does it have too many toppings? Too many different flavors? We didn't stop until we felt we had created something that was absolutely great.

We do allow substitutions or for people to add or take away ingredients, but this isn't something I favor. It bothers me less when people take things away from a pizza because the look and flavor profile of the pizza remain more or less intact. But sometimes the pizzas people create look so unappetizing and crowded—my biggest pet peeve being adding tomato sauce to the mushroom pizza—I'll glance over and think, "What's *that*!?" At that point I just have to look away.

We use low-moisture mozzarella—mozzarella that has had the water pressed out of it—on all of our pizzas that contain cheese. The cheese, which is the supermarket variety that many of us are familiar with from our childhoods, is firmer than fresh mozzarella, and it is nice and gooey when it melts. Traditional Napoletana-style pizza uses fresh *bufala* mozzarella, but that pizza takes only 90 seconds to bake, at most, while our pizzas take as long as 12 minutes in the oven—by which time fresh mozzarella disappears and leaves a pool of water in its place. We cut the mozzarella into chunks and scatter them on the pizza, which looks really pretty when it melts. Using shredded cheese results in a pizza that looks like something you pulled from the freezer.

I know that seeing radicchio and a baked runny egg, or potato and Gorgonzola cheese, on pizza drives the purists just as crazy as my big, chewy *cornice* does. "Go back to Italy!" some of the comment cards read. And I think, "Gladly!" But that won't change how I make my pizza, or at least it won't make my pizza any more so-called authentic. The pizza we make at Mozza is exactly the pizza that I wanted to create. Some people love it, some people don't. Who knew it would generate such controversy?

nancy's pizza dough

The first thing I need to tell you about this pizza dough recipe is that it is not an exact replica of the pizza dough we use at Pizzeria Mozza. What I can promise you, however, is that when you make this dough at home, your pizza will be just as delicious as the one we serve. Dough reacts differently in different ovens, and when our restaurant dough is baked in a home oven the result is a thick and doughy crust—not at all like those that come out of our extremely hot wood-fired ovens. My challenge for this book was to come up with a recipe for a pizza dough that, when baked in a home oven, resulted in a crust that was as close to what we get out of our pizza ovens as possible. And with the invaluable help and relentless persistence of Jon Davis, a breadbaker whom I've worked with since I hired him at La Brea Bakery more than twenty years ago, we came up with this recipe.

The dough is made with a sponge, which means that half of the flour is fermented, or aged, for a period of time—in this case, for an hour and a half—before being mixed with the remaining ingredients. This is a breadbakers' trick to coax the subtle flavor characteristics from the flour in a relatively short period of time. I have also made this dough without the sponge, adding all of the flour and water at once and saving that hour and a half of fermenting time. If you are pressed for time, you can do this, and though you might lose a bit of flavor, it will still be better than most pizzas I've been served in the States. You will need a scale to make this recipe. Bread making, or in this case pizza dough making, is so specific, there is no way around it. When making the dough, it's important to time it so that it's ready when you want to make your pizzas.

MAKES ENOUGH DOUGH FOR 6 PIZZAS; EACH PIZZA SERVES ONE

*T*o make the sponge, put 15 ounces of the water and the yeast in the bowl of a standing mixer and let it sit for a few minutes to dissolve the yeast. Add 13 ounces of the bread flour, the rye flour, and the wheat germ. Stir with a wooden spoon to combine the ingredients. Wrap the bowl tightly in plastic wrap and tightly wrap the perimeter of the bowl with kitchen twine or another piece of plastic wrap to further seal the bowl. Set the dough aside at room temperature (ideally 68 to 70 degrees) for 1½ hours.

Uncover the bowl and add the remaining 7 ounces of water, the remaining 13 ounces of bread flour, and the barley malt. Fit the mixer with a dough hook, place the bowl on the mixer stand, and mix the dough on low speed for 2 minutes. Add the salt and mix on medium speed for 6 to 8 minutes, until the dough starts to pull away from the

22 ounces warm tap water
  (2 cups, 6 ounces)
½ ounce (1 tablespoon)
  compressed yeast or
  1 teaspoon active dry yeast
26 ounces unbleached bread
  flour, plus more as needed
½ ounce (1 tablespoon) dark
  rye flour or medium rye
  flour
1½ teaspoons wheat germ
1½ teaspoons barley malt or
  mild-flavored honey, such
  as clover or wildflower
½ ounce (1 tablespoon) kosher
  salt
Olive oil, grapeseed oil, or
  another neutral flavored oil,
  such as canola oil, for
  greasing the bowl

sides of the bowl. Note that the dough will not pull so much that it completely cleans the bowl, but if the dough is too sticky and is not pulling away from the sides at all, throw a small handful of flour into the bowl to make it less sticky. While the dough is mixing, lightly grease with olive oil a bowl large enough to hold the dough when it doubles in size. Turn the dough out of the mixer into the oiled bowl. Wrap the bowl as before. Set the dough aside at room temperature for 45 minutes. Dust your work surface lightly with flour and turn the dough out onto the floured surface. Acting as if the round has four sides, fold the edges of the dough toward the center. Turn the dough over and return it, folded side down, to the bowl. Cover the bowl again with plastic wrap and set it aside for 45 minutes.

Dust your work surface again lightly with flour and turn the dough out onto the floured surface. Divide the dough into six equal segments, each weighing approximately 7 ounces. Gently tuck the edges of each round of dough under itself. Cover the dough rounds with a clean dishtowel and let them rest for 5 minutes.

Lightly flour your hands and use both hands to gather each round of dough into a taut ball. Dust a baking sheet generously with flour and place the dough rounds on the baking sheet. Cover the baking sheet with the dishtowel and set them again at room temperature for 1 hour to proof the dough. (Or leave the dough on the counter to proof instead.) Follow "Nancy's Scuola di Pizza" instructions that follow to stretch the dough and bake the pizzas.

- Choose which pizza(s) you want to make and prepare all of the necessary ingredients.
- Remove the oven racks from the oven and place a pizza stone on the floor of the oven. A pizza stone absorbs and distributes heat evenly, which helps you achieve a crisp crust. Buy a quality stone that will not crack from extreme heat. In a pinch, use the underside of a thick baking sheet.
- Preheat the oven and the stone to 500°F, or as hot as your oven will go, for at least 1 hour.
- Create a pizza station that includes bowls full of olive oil, kosher salt, and the ingredients necessary to make the pizzas you have chosen.
- Have a bowl of flour ready for dusting your countertop.
- Have a bowl of semolina ready for dusting your pizza peel, a tool with a long handle and a large, flat metal or wood surface for sliding pizzas in and out of the oven.
- When your dough is ready, generously flour your work surface and place one round of dough in the center of the floured surface. Dust the dough lightly with flour. (If you haven't already, right about now you will want to pour yourself a glass of wine.)
- Using your fingertips as if you were tapping on piano keys, gently tap on the center of the dough to flatten it slightly, leaving a 1-inch rim untouched.
- Pick up the dough, ball both of your fists, and with your fists facing your body, place the top edge of the dough on your fists so the round stretches downward against the backs of your hands, away from them.
- Move the circle of dough around your fists like the hands of a clock so the dough continues to stretch downward into a circle.
- When the dough has stretched to about 10 inches diameter, lay it down on the flour-dusted surface.
- As instructed in the individual recipes, brush the rim of the dough with olive oil and sprinkle kosher salt over the surface of the dough.
- Dress the pizza according to the recipe you have chosen, making sure to leave a 1-inch rim with no sauce or topping around the edge.
- Dust a pizza peel with semolina and slide the pizza peel under the pizza with one decisive push. You are less likely to tear or misshape

the dough with one good push of the peel than several tentative pushes. Reshape the pizza on the peel if it has lost its shape. Shake the peel gently to determine whether the dough will release easily in the oven. If it is sticking to the peel, carefully lift one side of the dough and throw some more semolina under it. Do this from a few different angles until there is semolina under the entire crust.

- Open the oven door and slide the dough onto the preheated pizza stone. Again moving decisively, pull the peel toward you to leave the pizza on the stone.
- Bake the pizza until it is golden brown and the *cornice,* or rim, is crisp and blistered, 8 to 12 minutes. Cooking times vary depending on the power of your oven.
- While the pizza is in the oven, clear a space on a clean, dry cutting board or place an aluminum pizza round on the counter to put the baked pizza on.
- When the pizza is done, slide the peel under the crust, remove it from the oven, and place it on the cutting board or round.
- Use a rolling pizza cutter to cut the pizza. We cut ours into four wedges at the Pizzeria, but for parties we often cut them into six or eight wedges so that guests each get a slice of pizza while it is hot.
- Make another pizza.

margherita: mozzarella, tomato, and basil

Just as you would order a baguette to judge a bakery, Margherita is the pizza to order to judge a pizzeria. Not only is Pizza Margherita the original pizza Napoletana but it has all the elements you want to look at: the sauce, the cheese, and of course, the crust. It's our biggest seller.

MAKES 1 PIZZA (SERVES 1)

SUGGESTED WINE PAIRING: ISCHIA ROSSO (CAMPANIA)

Prepare and stretch the dough and preheat the oven according to the instructions given in "Nancy's Scuola di Pizza" (page 128). Brush the rim of the dough with olive oil and season the entire surface with salt. Ladle or spoon the sauce onto the center of the dough and use the back of the ladle or spoon in a circular motion to spread the sauce out over the surface of the dough, leaving a 1-inch rim without any sauce. Scatter the pieces of cheese over the pizza, slide it into the oven, and bake until the cheese is melted and the crust is golden brown and crispy, 8 to 12 minutes. Remove the pizza from the oven and cut it into quarters. Drizzle the pizza with the finishing-quality olive oil, scatter the tiny basil leaves or snip the large leaves over the top, and serve.

1 round of Nancy's Pizza Dough (page 126)

1 tablespoon extra-virgin olive oil

Kosher salt

¼ cup *Passata di Pomodoro* (page 25) or tomato sauce

3 ounces low-moisture mozzarella, cut into 6 cubes or clumps

Finishing-quality extra-virgin olive oil, about 1 tablespoon

Fresh micro or miniature basil leaves or 3 fresh large basil leaves

marinara: tomato, sicilian oregano, and extra-virgin olive oil

Marinara—pizza with tomato sauce and oregano and without cheese—is one of the two kinds of pizzas approved by the Associazione Verace Pizza Napoletana. At the tiny bakery in Panicale, they always have a sheet pan of tomato pizza and one of zucchini pizza on display, both sold at room temperature. It's so simple, but made with good sauce and fragrant oregano, it's delicious.

MAKES 1 PIZZA (SERVES 1)

SUGGESTED WINE PAIRING: FRAPPATO (SICILY)

repare the dough and preheat the oven according to "Nancy's Scuola di Pizza" (page 128).

Brush the rim of the dough with olive oil and season the entire surface with salt. Ladle or spoon the sauce onto the center of the dough and use the back of the ladle or spoon in a circular motion to spread the sauce over the surface of the dough, leaving a 1-inch rim without any sauce. Slide the pizza into the oven and bake until the crust is golden brown and crispy, 8 to 12 minutes. Remove the pizza from the oven and cut it into quarters. Drizzle the pizza with the finishing-quality olive oil, sprinkle it with the oregano, and serve.

1 round of Nancy's Pizza Dough (page 126)
1 tablespoon extra-virgin olive oil
Kosher salt
¼ cup plus 2 tablespoons *Passata di Pomodoro* (page 25) or tomato sauce
Finishing-quality extra-virgin olive oil, about 1 tablespoon
1 tablespoon dried oregano (preferably Sicilian, sold on the branch)

squash blossoms, tomato, and burrata

ur prettiest pizza, this is the one that customers are most likely to point to when they see it being carried through the dining room. The squash blossoms are laid out over the surface so they bake into the crust, and the pizza ends up looking like a painting. We put the burrata on after it comes out of the oven, and I love the cool creamy cheese on the hot, crispy pizza.

MAKES 1 PIZZA (SERVES 1)

SUGGESTED WINE PAIRING: BIFERNO ROSSO (MOLISE)

rim and discard the stems from the squash blossoms. Cut a slit down the side of the blossoms, open them up with your fingers, and cut out and discard the stamens.

Prepare and stretch the dough and preheat the oven according to the instructions given in "Nancy's Scuola di Pizza" (page 128).

Brush the rim of the dough with olive oil and season the entire surface with salt. Ladle or spoon the sauce onto the center of the dough and use the back of the ladle or spoon in a circular motion to spread the sauce over the surface of the dough, leaving a 1-inch rim without any sauce. Working from the outside of the pizza toward the center, and still leaving the rim clean, lay the squash blossoms in two concentric circles, plus 2 blossoms in the very center, with the outside of the blossoms facing up, covering the pizza in a single layer. Slide the pizza into the oven and bake until the crust is golden brown and crispy, 8 to 12 minutes. Remove the pizza from the oven and cut it into quarters. Cut the burrata into four equal segments, place one segment onto each quadrant of the pizza, drizzle the finishing-quality olive oil, grind the black pepper over the burrata, and serve.

10 to 12 fresh squash blossoms, or as needed
1 round of Nancy's Pizza Dough (page 126)
1 tablespoon extra-virgin olive oil
Kosher salt
¼ cup *Passata di Pomodoro* (page 25) or tomato sauce
4 ounces burrata
Finishing-quality extra-virgin olive oil, about 1 tablespoon
Freshly gound black pepper

prosciutto di parma, rucola, tomato, and mozzarella

This classic pizza is a Margherita with prosciutto draped on the pizza after it comes out of the oven. I added arugula because I love the combination of arugula and prosciutto.

MAKES 1 PIZZA (SERVES 1)

SUGGESTED WINE PAIRING: SANGIOVESE DI ROMAGNA (EMILIA-ROMAGNA)

Prepare and stretch the dough and preheat the oven according to the instructions given in "Nancy's Scuola di Pizza" (page 128).

Brush the rim of the dough with olive oil and season the entire surface with salt. Ladle or spoon the sauce onto the center of the dough and use the back of the ladle or spoon in a circular motion to spread the sauce over the surface of the dough, leaving a 1-inch rim without any sauce. Scatter the pieces of cheese over the pizza, slide it into the oven, and bake until the cheese is melted and the crust is golden brown and crispy, 8 to 12 minutes. Remove the pizza from the oven and cut it into quarters. Drape one slice of prosciutto onto each quadrant and pile the arugula in the center of the pizza. Drizzle the pizza with the finishing-quality olive oil, and serve.

1 round of Nancy's Pizza Dough (page 126)
1 tablespoon extra-virgin olive oil
Kosher salt
¼ cup *Passata di Pomodoro* (page 25) or tomato sauce
3 ounces low-moisture mozzarella, cut into 6 cubes or chunks
4 thin slices prosciutto (about 2 ounces)
1 cup loosely packed arugula (preferably wild arugula)
Finishing-quality extra-virgin olive oil, about 1 tablespoon

meat lover's: bacon, salami, fennel sausage, guanciale, tomato, and mozzarella

Pellicano offers a meat lover's pizza, so I felt I had to offer one, too. Our version should be called a "pork lover's pizza" because all four of the meats we put on it—fennel sausage, salami, guanciale, and bacon—are pork.

MAKES 1 PIZZA (SERVES 1)

SUGGESTED WINE PAIRING: LAMBRUSCO REGGIANO SECCO (EMILIA-ROMAGNA)

Prepare and stretch the dough and preheat the oven according to the instructions given in "Nancy's Scuola di Pizza" (page 128).

Brush the rim of the dough with olive oil and season the entire sur-

1 round of Nancy's Pizza Dough (page 126)
1 tablespoon extra-virgin olive oil

face with salt. Ladle or spoon the sauce onto the center of the dough and use the back of the ladle or spoon in a circular motion to spread the sauce over the surface of the dough, leaving a 1-inch rim without any sauce. Scatter the cheese on the pizza. Break the sausage into ½-inch pieces and scatter them over the pizza. Cut the bacon slices in half crosswise and rumple one half onto each quadrant of the pizza and scatter the salami slices and *guanciale* slices over the pizza. Slide the pizza into the oven and bake until the cheese is melted and the crust is golden brown and crispy, 8 to 12 minutes. Remove the pizza from the oven, cut it into quarters, making sure that each slice of pizza gets a piece of bacon, and serve.

Kosher salt

¼ cup *Passata di Pomodoro* (page 25) or tomato sauce

2 ounces low-moisture mozzarella, cut into ½-inch cubes

2 ounces Fennel Sausage (recipe follows)

2 thick slices applewood-smoked bacon

5 thin slices salami

¼ ounce thinly sliced *guanciale* or pancetta

fennel sausage

*W*e use this sausage on our Fennel Sausage, Panna, *and Scallions* pizza (page 144), Meat Lover's pizza (page 136), and to make our most popular pasta, Orecchiette with Fennel Sausage and Swiss Chard (page 180). It's easy to make and keeps well in the freezer. As our longtime sous chef Erik Black used to say, "Making sausage is like making chicken stock. It takes the same amount of time to make a big batch, so why wouldn't you? You know you'll end up using it."

MAKES 5 POUNDS

*T*oast the fennel seeds in a small skillet over high heat, shaking the skillet to keep the seeds from burning, until they are fragrant, about 1 minute. Pour the seeds onto a plate and set aside to cool to room temperature.

Cut the pork shoulder and fatback into 1-inch cubes and put the cubes in a large bowl. In a small bowl, combine the garlic, salt, sugar, pepper, paprika, fennel pollen, and toasted fennel seeds. Stir the seasonings together and sprinkle them over the pork and fatback. Toss to coat the meat with the seasonings, cover the bowl tightly with plastic wrap, and refrigerate for at least 24 hours and up to two days. (If you are in a hurry, you can put the meat in the freezer until it is ice cold, but not frozen.)

Fit a meat grinder with the largest die and have the bowl of a standing mixer handy. Remove the meat from the refrigerator (or freezer) and pass it through the grinder, catching the gound meat into the mixer bowl.

Fit the standing mixer with the paddle attachment. Combine the

3 tablespoons fennel seeds

4 pounds boneless pork shoulder

1 pound pork fatback

3 tablespoons finely chopped garlic (about 10 large cloves)

2 tablespoons kosher salt

2 tablespoons sugar

2 tablespoons freshly ground black pepper

2 tablespoons hot paprika

1 tablespoon fennel pollen (see page 19)

¼ cup red wine vinegar

¾ cup ice water

vinegar and ice water. Put the bowl with the ground meat in it on the standing mixer and mix them on low speed, gradually adding the vinegar and water until the meat is slightly sticky; you may not use all of the liquid. Use the sausage according to your recipe, or transfer it to an airtight container or several containers. Refrigerate the sausage for up to five days or in the freezer for up to three months.

pizza alla benno: speck, pineapple, jalapeños, mozzarella, and tomato

I created this pizza, an upgraded take on "Hawaiian pizza," typically made with Canadian bacon and canned pineapple, for my son, Ben. When he was growing up, that's the pizza he always ordered and I cringed at the combination every time. When I opened up my own pizzeria, I wanted to come up with a pizza using the same or similar ingredients that would please both Ben and me. We start with fresh pineapple and slice it paper-thin so it caramelizes in the oven, and we use speck in place of Canadian bacon. But what I think really makes this pizza is the addition of jalapeño peppers. Their heat cuts through the sweetness of the pineapple.

MAKES 1 PIZZA (SERVES 1)

SUGGESTED WINE PAIRING: GEWÜRZTRAMINER (ALTO ADIGE)

*P*repare and stretch the dough and preheat the oven according to the instructions given in "Nancy's Scuola di Pizza" (page 128).

Brush the rim of the dough with olive oil and season the entire surface with salt. Ladle or spoon the sauce onto the center of the dough and use the back of the ladle or spoon in a circular motion to spread the sauce over the surface of the dough, leaving a 1-inch rim without any sauce. Scatter the cheese and then the jalapeño slices over the pizza, lay 2 pineapple slices in each quadrant of the pizza, putting the halves together to look like a whole round, and lay the final slice in the center of the pizza. Slide the pizza into the oven and bake until the cheese is melted and the crust is golden brown and crispy, 8 to 12 minutes. Remove the pizza from the oven and cut it into quarters, making sure that each quadrant contains a whole slice of pineapple. Drape one slice of speck onto each quadrant, finely snip the chive over the pizza, and serve.

1 round of Nancy's Pizza Dough (page 126)

1 tablespoon extra-virgin olive oil

Kosher salt

¼ cup *Passata di Pomodoro* (page 25) or tomato sauce

2 ounces low-moisture mozzarella, cut into 1-inch cubes

8 very thin round slices jalapeño pepper

10 paper-thin pineapple slices (cut the skin off the pineapple, cut the pineapple in half lengthwise, and slice the pineapple on a mandoline, including core; about 2 ounces)

4 thin slices speck or prosciutto (about ½ ounce)

1 fresh chive

white anchovy, tomato, and spicy fresno chiles

*T**his is my answer to that controversial phenomenon of the main-stream pizza world—anchovy pizza. I use marinated white anchovies, which you can get at specialty stores both in the deli and in the fish departments. They are silvery and slightly plump, like sardines—very different from salt-packed anchovies or those sold in cans and jars. I love their flavor and vinegary quality.*

MAKES 1 PIZZA (SERVES 1)

 SUGGESTED WINE PAIRING: GRILLO (SICILY)

*T*o prepare the anchovies, lift them out of the brine they are packed in, discard the brine, and put them in a small bowl. Add the olive oil, lemon zest, parsley, and red pepper flakes, and gently toss to combine the ingredients, taking care not to tear the anchovies. Use the anchovies on the pizza or line them in a single row in an airtight container, drizzle with the seasonings, and refrigerate until you are ready to use them or for up to three days.

To make the pizza, prepare and stretch the dough and preheat the oven according to the instructions given in "Nancy's Scuola di Pizza" (page 128).

Brush the rim of the dough with olive oil and season the entire surface with salt. Ladle or spoon the sauce onto the center of the dough and use the back of the ladle or spoon in a circular motion to spread the sauce over the surface of the dough, leaving a 1-inch rim without any sauce. Scatter the chiles over the pizza, slide the pizza into the oven, and bake until the crust is golden brown and crispy, 8 to 12 minutes. Remove the pizza from the oven, cut it into quarters, and drape two anchovies on each quadrant, coiling one anchovy around the other. Sprinkle the parsley over the anchovies, drizzle the finishing-quality olive oil over the entire pizza, and serve.

for the anchovies
8 marinated white anchovies

2 tablespoons extra-virgin olive oil

Zested strips of 1/2 lemon (about 1 tablespoon)

1 teaspoon finely chopped fresh Italian parsley leaves

1/4 teaspoon red pepper flakes

for the pizza
1 round of Nancy's Pizza Dough (page 126)

1 tablespoon extra-virgin olive oil

Kosher salt

1/4 cup plus 2 tablespoons *Passata di Pomodoro* (page 25) or tomato sauce

1 heaping tablespoon Roasted Fresno Chiles (page 140)

1 teaspoon thinly sliced fresh Italian parsley leaves

Finishing-quality extra-virgin olive oil, about 1 tablespoon

roasted fresno chiles

*W*e use these fiery, sweet roasted chiles on the White Anchovy, Tomato, and Spicy Fresno Chiles pizza (page 139) and the Spicy Salami, Mozzarella, and Fresno Chiles pizza (below). If you are making a variety of pizzas, it might be convenient to include these two to use up all the peppers.

MAKES 2 HEAPING TABLESPOONS, OR ENOUGH FOR 2 PIZZAS

*A*djust the oven rack to the middle position and preheat the oven to 400°F.

Spread the chiles on a baking sheet, drizzle with the olive oil, season with salt, and toss to coat the chiles with the seasonings. Roast the chiles in the oven for 4 to 6 minutes, to wilt them slightly. Use the chiles or set aside to cool to room temperature, transfer to an airtight container, and refrigerate for up to three days.

¼ pound Fresno chiles (red jalapeño peppers; about 4), halved, stems and seeds removed, and sliced lengthwise ⅛ inch thick
1 tablespoon extra-virgin olive oil
Kosher salt

spicy salami, mozzarella, and fresno chiles

*N*o matter how creative we like to be with our pizzas, we also have a big place in our hearts for the classics such as this—essentially a pepperoni pizza with roasted chiles added for extra kick.

MAKES 1 PIZZA (SERVES 1)

SUGGESTED WINE PAIRING: CIRO ROSSO CLASSICO (CALABRIA)

*P*repare and stretch the dough and preheat the oven according to the instructions given in "Nancy's Scuola di Pizza" (page 128).

Brush the rim of the dough with olive oil and season the entire surface with salt. Ladle or spoon the sauce onto the center of the dough and use the back of the ladle or spoon in a circular motion to spread the sauce over the surface of the dough, leaving a 1-inch rim without any sauce. Scatter the roasted chiles and mozzarella cubes over the pizza, and lay the salami slices on top. Slide the pizza into the oven and bake until the cheese is melted and the crust is golden brown and crispy, 8 to 12 minutes. Remove the pizza from the oven, cut it into quarters, and serve.

1 round of Nancy's Pizza Dough (page 126)
1 tablespoon extra-virgin olive oil
Kosher salt
¼ cup *Passata di Pomodoro* (page 25) or tomato sauce
1 heaping tablespoon Roasted Fresno Chiles (above)
3 ounces low-moisture mozzarella, cut into ½-inch cubes
¾ ounce thinly sliced spicy hard salami (10 to 12 slices)

gorgonzola dolce, fingerling potatoes, radicchio, and rosemary

*T*his was one of the original ten pizzas we served at the Pizzeria. I knew I wanted to offer a potato pizza, and I love the combination of potatoes and Gorgonzola.

MAKES 1 PIZZA (SERVES 1)

SUGGESTED WINE PAIRING: PETITE ARVINE (VALLE D'AOSTA)

*P*repare and stretch the dough and preheat the oven according to the instructions given in "Nancy's Scuola di Pizza" (page 128).

Brush the rim of the dough with the olive oil and season the entire surface with salt. Lay the radicchio over the surface of the pizza. Break the potatoes into 1-inch chunks and scatter them over the radicchio. Scatter the Gorgonzola and mozzarella around the potatoes and sprinkle the rosemary over the pizza. Slide the pizza into the oven and bake until the cheese is melted and the crust is golden brown, 8 to 12 minutes. Remove the pizza from the oven, cut it into quarters, and serve.

1 round of Nancy's Pizza Dough (page 126)

1 tablespoon extra-virgin olive oil

Kosher salt

2 cups thinly sliced radicchio

6 ounces roasted fingerling potatoes (about 4 potatoes; see Smashed Potatoes with Rosemary, page 255)

3 ounces Gorgonzola *dolce*, crumbled

2 ounces low-moisture mozzarella, cut into ½-inch cubes

1 teaspoon fresh rosemary tufts

littleneck clams, garlic, oregano, parmigiano-reggiano, and pecorino romano

*C**lam pizza, a Connecticut tradition, is one of the specialties at Lombardi's in New York City, and having my first clam pie there is one of my most memorable pizza-eating experiences. We use a combination of Parmigiano and pecorino to finish this pizza, but if you want to use only one, pick your favorite.*

MAKES 1 PIZZA (SERVES 1)

SUGGESTED WINE PAIRING: VERDICCHIO DEI CASTELLI DI JESI
(THE MARCHES)

*T*o prepare the clams, put them in a small sauté pan or saucepan with 1 cup of water over high heat. Cover the pan, reduce the heat to medium, and cook the clams until they steam open, 3 to 4 minutes. Turn off the heat and remove the clams from the juice, discarding any clams that didn't open. Discard the juice, shuck the clams, and discard the shells. Drain the clams in a colander and let them sit in the colander to release excess liquid for about 5 minutes. Transfer the clams to a small bowl. Stir together the garlic and the oil. Add half of the oil-garlic mixture to the clams, reserving the remaining mixture to dress the pizza, and stir to coat the clams with the seasonings. You can prepare the clams up to this point up to several hours in advance. Transfer the clams to an airtight container and refrigerate until you are ready to use them.

To make the pizza, prepare and stretch the dough and preheat the oven according to the instructions given in "Nancy's Scuola di Pizza" (page 128).

Brush the rim of the dough with the olive oil and season the entire surface with salt. Add a pinch of the sliced parsley or oregano leaves to the bowl with the clams and stir to combine. Spread the remaining tablespoon of the oil-garlic mixture over the pizza, leaving a 1-inch rim without any oil. Scatter the clams over the pizza, slide the pizza into the oven, and bake until the crust is golden brown, 8 to 12 minutes. Remove the pizza from the oven and cut it into quarters. Sprinkle the dried oregano over the pizza, and use a microplane or another fine grater to grate a light layer of Parmigiano-Reggiano and another of pecorino romano over the surface. Sprinkle the red pepper flakes and the remaining parsley or oregano leaves over the pizza, drizzle with the finishing-quality olive oil, and serve.

for the clams
20 littleneck clams (about 1 pound)
1 garlic clove, chopped
2 tablespoons extra-virgin olive oil

for the pizza
1 round of Nancy's Pizza Dough (page 126)
1 tablespoon extra-virgin olive oil
Kosher salt
1 heaping tablespoon thinly sliced fresh Italian parsley leaves or whole fresh oregano leaves
1 teaspoon dried oregano (preferably Sicilian on the branch)
Wedge of Parmigiano-Reggiano, for grating
Wedge of pecorino romano, for grating
1/4 teaspoon red pepper flakes
Finishing-quality extra-virgin olive oil, about 1 tablespoon

fennel sausage, panna, and scallions

his is my number-one favorite Pizzeria Mozza pizza, and it's a direct rip-off of the Norcia pizza they serve at Pellicano. Sausage and panna, or cream, is a classic combination in Umbria. The summer I discovered this pizza I ordered it every time I went to Pellicano, in an effort to figure out what was in the white sauce that was smeared on the crust. When I asked, they told me "panna." I knew panna was cream, but I couldn't understand how they could put cream on pizza. Finally, I went back to the kitchen to see for myself, and what I saw was that the cream had been whipped, making it spreadable. Whipping cream for a pizza was such a foreign idea to me that when I started playing with pizzas for the restaurant, I tried to avoid it. I made this pizza with crème fraîche and later with mascarpone—anything not to put whipped cream on a pizza—but the whipped cream was definitely the best.

MAKES 1 PIZZA (SERVES 1)

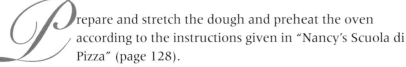

SUGGESTED WINE PAIRING: ROSSO CONERO (THE MARCHES)

repare and stretch the dough and preheat the oven according to the instructions given in "Nancy's Scuola di Pizza" (page 128).

Roll the fennel sausage meat into two 2-ounce balls and place them on a baking sheet. Place the baking sheet in an oven preheated to 500°F for 6 minutes, to partially cook the sausage and render the fat. Remove the sausage from the oven and set aside to cool slightly while you prepare the pizza.

Brush the rim of the dough with the olive oil and season the entire surface with salt. Spoon the cream into the center of the dough and use the back of the spoon in a circular motion to spread it over the surface of the dough, leaving a 1-inch rim without any cream. Break each ball of sausage into 4 pieces and scatter the pieces over the pizza. Scatter the cheese, then the scallions around the sausage. Slide the pizza into the oven and bake until the cheese is melted and the crust is golden brown and crispy, 8 to 12 minutes. Remove the pizza from the oven, sprinkle it with the fennel pollen, cut it into quarters, and serve.

1 round of Nancy's Pizza Dough (page 126)

4 ounces Fennel Sausage, uncooked (page 137)

1 tablespoon extra-virgin olive oil

Kosher salt

¼ cup heavy whipping cream, whipped to soft peaks (page 274)

1 ounce low-moisture mozzarella, cut or torn into ½-inch cubes

3 scallions, thinly sliced on an extreme bias starting at the green ends and moving toward the root ends (white and green parts) or ½ cup very thinly sliced red onion

1 tablespoon fennel pollen (see page 19)

long-cooked broccoli, caciocavallo, and peperoncino

*L*ong-cooked broccoli is one of my all-time favorite vegetable preparations, so I had to find a way to work it onto a pizza. Normally I don't like broccoli on pizza because whenever I've seen it, it's just been dropped onto the pizza raw, and often with a whole mix of other uncooked vegetables that don't go with each other or with pizza. Here, the broccoli is cooked until it has a buttery texture, so it works with the crust instead of just sitting on top of it. We use a mix of mozzarella and caciocavallo cheese, a Sicilian cheese similar to mozzarella that has been dried and aged for a few weeks, so it has a funky aged flavor that goes well with the broccoli. If you can't find caciocavallo cheese, look for scamorza, or use all mozzarella in its place.

MAKES 1 PIZZA (SERVES 1)

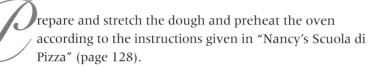

SUGGESTED WINE PAIRING: AGLIANICO DEL VULTURE (BASILICATA)

*P*repare and stretch the dough and preheat the oven according to the instructions given in "Nancy's Scuola di Pizza" (page 128).

Brush the rim of the dough with the olive oil and season the entire surface with salt. Scatter the caciocavallo and mozzarella over the pizza, leaving a 1-inch rim without any topping. Tear the broccoli into 2-inch pieces, keeping the florets intact as much as possible, and lay the pieces on the cheese. Slide the pizza into the oven and bake until the cheese is melted and the crust is golden brown and crispy, 8 to 12 minutes. Remove the pizza from the oven, sprinkle the red pepper flakes over the surface, cut it into quarters, and serve.

1 round of Nancy's Pizza Dough (page 126)

1 tablespoon extra-virgin olive oil

Kosher salt

3 ounces caciocavallo, grated

1 ounce low-moisture mozzarella, cut into 1/2-inch cubes

4 ounces Long-cooked Broccoli (page 259)

1/4 teaspoon red pepper flakes

funghi misti, fontina, taleggio, and thyme

If we were one of those pizzerias that give wacky names to each pie, this mixed mushroom pizza would be called "The Vegas Guys," or "Peter's Pizza." Our editor, Peter Gethers, has a group of guys he goes to Las Vegas with every year for some sort of guy reunion weekend. They meet in Los Angeles and the tradition is that they choose a different restaurant to eat dinner in the night before they leave for Vegas. I'm flattered that for the last few years, they've quit chowing around and held their dinner consistently in the private dining room in the Pizzeria, called the Jack Warner Room. They were particularly excited about this pizza. It's a pretty straightforward mushroom pie, but the fact that we roast the mushrooms before adding them to the pizza, and the combination of taleggio and fontina cheeses that top it, make it especially flavorful.

MAKES 1 PIZZA (SERVES 1)

SUGGESTED WINE PAIRING: FUMIN (VALLE D'AOSTA)

To prepare the mushrooms, adjust the oven rack to the middle position and preheat the oven to 400°F.

Combine the mushroom slices on a baking sheet, drizzle with the olive oil, season with salt and pepper, and toss to coat the mushrooms with the seasonings. Spread the mushrooms in a single layer on the baking sheet and roast them in the oven until they are golden brown and slightly wilted, 8 to 10 minutes. Use the mushrooms or set aside to cool to room temperature, transfer to an airtight container, and refrigerate for up to two days.

To make the pizza, prepare and stretch the dough and preheat the oven according to the instructions given in "Nancy's Scuola di Pizza" (page 128).

Brush the rim of the dough with the olive oil and season the entire surface with salt. Scatter the mushrooms over the pizza, leaving a 1-inch rim without any topping. Scatter the fontina, taleggio, and mozzarella cheeses over the mushrooms, and then sprinkle with the thyme leaves. Slide the pizza in the oven and bake until the cheese is melted and the crust is golden brown and crispy, 8 to 12 minutes. Remove the pizza from the oven and cut it into quarters. Use a microplane or another fine grater to grate a light layer of Parmigiano-Reggiano over the surface of the pizza, and serve.

for the mushrooms

¼ pound jumbo white mushrooms, cleaned, stems trimmed, and sliced ¼ inch thick

¼ pound shiitake mushrooms, cleaned, stems removed, and sliced ¼ inch thick

1 3- to 4-ounce portobello mushroom, cleaned, stem removed, black feathery gills scraped out with a spoon and discarded, and sliced ¼ inch thick

¼ cup plus 2 tablespoons extra-virgin olive oil

Kosher salt and freshly ground black pepper

for the pizza

1 round of Nancy's Pizza Dough (page 126)

1 tablespoon extra-virgin olive oil

Kosher salt

1 ounce fontina, cut into ½-inch cubes

1 ounce taleggio, cut or torn into ½-inch pieces

1 ounce low-moisture mozzarella, cut into ½-inch cubes

1 teaspoon fresh thyme leaves

Wedge of Parmigiano-Reggiano, for grating

fresh goat cheese, leek, scallions, garlic, and bacon

Years ago I discovered a little place in San Francisco that made the most delicious green onion focaccia that I loved and never forgot. When the Pizzeria was conceived, I knew I wanted to offer one with green onions in memory of that one. In trying to invent my green onion pizza, I remembered my days at Spago, where they made a goat cheese and red pepper pizza that was really popular. Goat cheese and bacon is a great combination, as is goat cheese and browned garlic. And then there were those green onions . . . That mishmash of inspirations is how this pizza came to be. The garlic is the same that we use in the Olives al Forno (page 37). While you're at it, you might want to make enough for both, since the olives would be a great accompaniment to a pizza party.

MAKES 1 PIZZA (SERVES 1)

SUGGESTED WINE PAIRING: SAUVIGNON (ALTO ADIGE)

To prepare the leek, remove the tough outer leaves and trim and discard the root end and the dark green leaves so you are left with only the white and pale green part of the leek. Cut the leek into 3-inch segments, cut the segments in half lengthwise, and cut each half into julienned strips. Melt the butter with the olive oil in a small sauté pan over medium-low heat. Add the leek, season with salt, and cook, stirring often to prevent it from browning, until it is wilted and translucent, 5 to 7 minutes.

To make the pizza, prepare and stretch the dough and preheat the oven according to the instructions given in "Nancy's Scuola di Pizza" (page 128).

Brush the rim of the dough with the olive oil and season the entire surface with salt. Scatter 6 tablespoons of the sautéed leek over the surface of the pizza, leaving a 1-inch rim without any topping, and scatter the scallions. Break the goat cheese into 1-inch chunks and scatter them over the leek and scallions. Scatter the garlic cloves over the leek. Cut the bacon slices in half crosswise and rumple two halves onto each quadrant of the pizza. Slide the pizza into the oven and bake until the cheese is melted and the crust is golden brown and crispy, 8 to 12 minutes. Remove the pizza from the oven, and sprinkle the chives over the pizza. Cut the pizza into quarters, taking care not to cut through the bacon, and serve.

for the leek

1 medium leek, rinsed thoroughly
2 tablespoons unsalted butter
1 tablespoon extra-virgin olive oil
Kosher salt

for the pizza

1 round of Nancy's Pizza Dough (page 126)
1 tablespoon extra-virgin olive oil
Kosher salt
4 scallions, thinly sliced on an extreme bias starting at the green ends and moving toward the root ends (white and green parts)
1½ ounces fresh goat cheese
10 cloves of Garlic Confit (page 38)
4 thick slices applewood-smoked bacon
1 teaspoon minced chives

bianca with fontina, mozzarella, sottocenere al tartufo, and sage

This is a basic three-cheese pizza, the only surprise being the truffle-infused sottocenere cheese. Friend-of-Mozza Michael Krikorian orders this pizza with Fennel Sausage (page 137) on top. His version has become so popular that regular customers now know they can order the same thing if they ask for the "Michael."

MAKES 1 PIZZA (SERVES 1)

SUGGESTED WINE PAIRING: VALPOLICELLA CLASSICO SUPERIORE (VENETO)

Pour enough olive oil into a small skillet or saucepan to 1 inch deep and line a small plate with paper towels. Heat the oil over medium-high heat until a pinch of salt sizzles when dropped into it. Add the whole sage leaves and fry for about 30 seconds, until crisp and bright green. (If you overcook them, they turn brown and ugly.) Use a slotted spoon to remove the sage from the oil, transfer to the paper towels to drain, and season with salt. Strain the sage-infused oil through a fine-mesh strainer and reserve it to fry sage another time or to drizzle over grilled meats or vegetables. The sage can be fried up to several hours in advance. Store it in an air-tight container at room temperature.

Prepare and stretch the dough and preheat the oven according to the instructions given in "Nancy's Scuola di Pizza" (page 128).

Brush the rim of the dough with the 1 tablespoon of olive oil and season the entire surface with salt. Spoon the cream onto the center of the dough and use the back of the spoon to spread it over the surface of the dough, leaving a 1-inch rim without any cream. Sprinkle the chopped sage over the cream, cover with the shredded sottocenere, and scatter the fontina and mozzarella cubes over the pizza. Slide the pizza into the oven and bake until the cheese is melted and the crust is golden brown and crispy, 8 to 12 minutes.

Remove the pizza from the oven and carefully tilt it over a plate to drain the excess oil. Discard the oil. Cut the pizza into quarters, scatter the fried sage leaves over the surface, and serve.

1 tablespoon extra-virgin olive oil, plus more for frying the sage leaves

Kosher salt

¼ cup whole fresh sage leaves, plus 1 teaspoon chopped fresh sage leaves

1 round of Nancy's Pizza Dough (page 126)

2 tablespoons heavy whipping cream, whipped to soft peaks (page 274)

3½ ounces sottocenere al tartufo, shredded

1 ounce fontina, cut into ½-inch cubes

1 ounce low-moisture mozzarella, cut into ½-inch cubes

stracchino with artichokes, lemon, and olives

This is a wonderful example of a vegetarian dish that isn't at all compromised by its lack of meat. We scatter artichoke leaves over the surface of the pizza so you get the flavor of artichoke in every bite. The mild flavor of the stracchino contrasts nicely with the bitterness of the artichokes.

MAKES 1 PIZZA (SERVES 1)

SUGGESTED WINE PAIRING: GRILLO (SICILY)

To prepare the artichokes, fill a large bowl with water. Cut the lemon in half, squeeze the juice into the water, and drop the lemon halves into the water.

Remove the outer leaves from the artichokes until you are left with only the light green centers. Cut off the tough stem ends, leaving as much as 1 or 2 inches attached. Using a vegetable peeler or a small sharp knife, shave the artichoke stems, revealing the light green inner stems. Cut ½ inch to ¾ inch off of the tip ends of the leaves so they have flat tops, and discard all of the trimmed leaves and bits. Cut above the bottom to release all the leaves, unravel the leaves and place them in the acidulated water to prevent them from turning brown. Thinly slice the stems and add them to the acidulated water. To prepare the artichokes in advance, transfer them, along with the acidulated water, to an airtight container and refrigerate until you're ready to use them or for up to two days. Drain the leaves and stems. Dry out the bowl and return the artichokes to the bowl. Add the olive oil, parsley, and garlic and toss to coat the artichokes with the seasonings.

To prepare the pizza, prepare and stretch the dough and preheat the oven according to the instructions given in "Nancy's Scuola di Pizza" (page 128).

Brush the rim of the dough with the olive oil and season the entire surface with salt. Scatter the artichoke leaves over the surface of the pizza to cover, leaving a 1-inch border of the pizza with no topping. Scatter the stracchino, mozzarella, and olives over the artichoke leaves. Slide the pizza into the oven and bake until the cheese is melted and the crust is golden brown and crispy, 8 to 12 minutes. Remove the pizza from the oven and cut it into quarters. Sprinkle the parsley over the pizza and use a microplane or another fine grater to grate lemon zest over the surface. Grate a light layer of Parmigiano-Reggiano over the pizza, scatter the arugula over the top, and serve.

for the artichokes
1 lemon

4 ounces baby artichokes (2 to 3 artichokes)

1 tablespoon extra-virgin olive oil

1 tablespoon thinly sliced fresh Italian parsley leaves

1 large garlic clove, finely chopped

for the pizza
1 round of Nancy's Pizza Dough (page 126)

1 tablespoon extra-virgin olive oil

Kosher salt

2 ounces stracchino, torn into small chunks

½ ounce low-moisture mozzarella, cut into ½-inch cubes

1 ounce pitted Taggiasche or Niçoise olives

1 teaspoon thinly sliced fresh Italian parsley leaves

1 lemon

Wedge of Parmigiano-Reggiano, for grating

½ cup loosely packed arugula (preferably wild arugula)

buricotta with peperonata and oregano

The richness of peperonata contrasted with the mild flavor of ricotta is so perfect we found a way to offer it in both the Pizzeria and the Osteria (see Peperonata with Ricotta Crostini, page 87). We use buricotta, which looks pretty because the cheese holds its shape when it's baked, but if you can't get buricotta, the pizza will be equally good made with quality fresh ricotta. In a perfect world your ricotta will get blackened in places like a perfectly roasted marshmallow.

MAKES 1 PIZZA (SERVES 1)

SUGGESTED WINE PAIRING: AGLIANICO DEL TABURNO ROSATO (CAMPANIA)

Prepare and stretch the dough and preheat the oven according to the instructions given in "Nancy's Scuola di Pizza" (page 128).

Brush the rim of the dough with the olive oil and season the entire surface with salt. Spread the peperonata over the pizza, leaving a 1-inch rim without any topping. If you are using ricotta, put it in a bowl and stir it vigorously to fluff it up. Place one segment of the buricotta or spoon the ricotta into each quadrant of the pizza. Slide the pizza into the oven and bake until the crust is golden brown and crispy, 8 to 12 minutes. Remove the pizza from the oven and cut it into quarters, taking care not to cut through the cheese. Scatter the oregano leaves over the pizza, drizzle the finishing-quality olive oil over the cheese, sprinkle with sea salt, and serve.

1 round of Nancy's Pizza
  Dough (page 126)
1 tablespoon extra-virgin
  olive oil
Kosher salt
1 cup peperonata (see
  page 87)
4 ounces buricotta, cut into
  4 equal segments,
  or fresh ricotta
1 teaspoon fresh oregano
  leaves
Finishing-quality extra-
  virgin olive oil, about
  1 tablespoon
Maldon sea salt or another
  flaky sea salt, such as
  fleur de sel

potato, egg, and bacon

In the Pizzeria kitchen we refer to this as the "breakfast pizza" because of the traditional combination. We don't cut through the egg because the whole egg looks pretty in the center of the pizza when we bring it to the table. And that way our customers can have the thrill of breaking the yolk themselves.

MAKES 1 PIZZA (SERVES 1)

SUGGESTED WINE PAIRING: CARSO VITOVSKA (FRIULI)

Steam the potatoes until they are easily pierced with a fork, about 20 minutes. Remove the potatoes and set them aside until they are cool enough to touch. Use a small, sharp knife to remove the peel from the potatoes and discard the peels. Slice the potatoes into ¼-inch-thick rounds and place them in a small bowl. Use the potatoes or set them aside to cool to room temperature, transfer them to an airtight container, and refrigerate for up to two days.

Prepare and stretch the dough and preheat the oven according to the instructions given in "Nancy's Scuola di Pizza" (page 128).

Brush the rim of the dough with the olive oil and season the entire surface with salt. Scatter the mozzarella, the sottocenere, and fontina cubes over the surface of the pizza. Scatter the scallion slices over the cheeses, lay the potato slices on top of the scallions, and sprinkle the potato slices with salt. Cut the bacon slices in half crosswise and lay one half onto each quandrant of the pizza. Sprinkle 1 teaspoon of the thyme leaves over the pizza and place the pizza in the oven for 5 minutes, or until the pizza is halfway cooked. Crack the egg into a small bowl, remove the pizza from the oven and slide the egg onto the center of the pizza. Return the pizza to the oven until the crust is golden brown, 5 to 7 minutes. Remove the pizza from the oven and cut it into quarters, stopping at the edge of the egg so it stays intact, and making sure that each slice of pizza gets a piece of bacon. Sprinkle the egg with the sea salt, sprinkle the remaining thyme leaves over the pizza, and serve.

3 ounces small Yukon Gold potatoes (about 1½ potatoes)

1 round of Nancy's Pizza Dough (page 126)

1 tablespoon extra-virgin olive oil

Kosher salt

2 ounces low-moisture mozzarella, cut into ½-inch cubes

3 ounces shredded sottocenere al tartufo

1 ounce fontina, cut into ½-inch cubes

4 scallions, thinly sliced on an extreme bias starting at the green ends and moving toward the root ends (white and green parts)

2 thick slices applewood-smoked bacon

1½ teaspoons fresh thyme leaves

1 extra-large farm-fresh egg

Maldon sea salt or another flaky sea salt, such as fleur de sel

primi

clockwise from top left: pici, squid ink *chitarra, chitarra,* spaghetti, green dough tagliatelle, *raviolo,* orecchiette, gnocchi, gnudi, *fiorentini,* linguini, *francobolli, fregola sarda, corzetti stampati, maltagliati,* green dough garganelli, garganelli

I believe that pasta is one of the most misunderstood foods in this country, and cooking pasta correctly is a gospel that needs to be spread. Before Matt went to New York to work for Mario at Del Posto, we both thought about pasta the way most Americans do. We thought of the noodle as secondary, a vehicle for the sauce. But what Matt, and subsequently I, learned from Mario and the chefs who work for him was that in any pasta dish, the noodle is the star. Pasta that has been made, cooked, and dressed correctly can be so good, and yet so few places get it right. At Mozza, I think we get it right.

There are many intricacies and subtleties to making pasta correctly. The toothsomeness of the noodle, the choice of the shape and texture of the noodle for a particular sauce, the amount of sauce, and the way it dresses the noodle all affect the outcome. (More on this throughout this chapter.) After six months in New York, Matt came home with more than just good recipes or tips on how to make pasta. He had learned an entire approach to pasta that I had not known existed. I was so completely won over by Matt's enthusiasm—not to mention the dishes themselves—that we decided to make pasta the core of the Osteria menu. We have about twenty pasta dishes on the menu at any time, and we offer a pasta tasting menu daily. Almost every table orders pasta, and often they get several to share.

So often, when it comes to dressing pasta, it seems like anything goes. Many home cooks and restaurants alike use pasta as a chance to clean out the refrigerator. Not so with our pasta dishes, each of which, like the pizzas, were put together with great deliberation and attention paid to the combination of flavors, textures, and colors.

The recipes in this chapter include: filled pasta shapes, fresh pasta dishes, and those that use dried pasta. Many of those that use dried pasta, such as *Bavette Cacio e Pepe* (page 201) and Spaghetti *alla Gricia* (page 198), call for a short list of ingredients, many of which you could easily keep on hand, so they make convenient, delicious last-minute meals. Fresh pasta dishes are a different story. Not only does it take time and effort to make the pasta itself, but in most instances where fresh pasta is used, such as ragùs and filled pasta shapes, the sauces or fillings are also time-consuming. This isn't meant to discourage you, because I think each and every one of these dishes is worth the time it takes to make it. I just want to encourage you to do as an Italian would: choose the right pasta dish for the right occasion.

In the traditional Italian style, our pasta portions are based on first-course servings, with the idea that you will be following with a main course.

Everything I know about pasta I learned from working with Mario and his team of chefs at Del Posto, Babbo, and Lupa. Through them, my eyes were opened to the beauty and complexity of pasta. At the Pizzeria, Nancy had already elevated pizza to exactly where she wanted it to be, and after my Del Posto experience, I knew I wanted to do the same thing at the Osteria with pasta. I can only hope that I have done "the family" justice, both in our pasta program at Mozza and with my attempts to pass that along to you.

- We like our fresh pasta to have a springy, toothsome quality to it that you don't get from most fresh pasta. The way we achieve that is to knead the dough. At the restaurant, we mix the dough for 45 minutes to 1 hour in a standing mixer, but for the home cook, we recommend kneading by hand for 20 to 25 minutes. This saves not just time but also the motor in your mixer.
- To roll the pasta dough, adjust a pasta sheeter gauge to the thickest setting.
- Dust a baking sheet with semolina.
- Remove the pasta dough from the refrigerator and cut it into quarters.
- Dust one segment of the dough lightly with flour and pass it through the pasta sheeter, dusting the dough with flour again as it passes through the sheeter, to create long sheets. Adjust the sheeter to the next thinnest setting and pass the dough through again. Continue to pass the dough through the sheeter in this way until you have passed it through the gauge specified in the recipe.
- Place the sheeted dough on the prepared baking sheet and repeat, sheeting the remaining segments in the same way and dusting the sheeted pasta with semolina to prevent the sheets from sticking together.
- Use the shapes or place the baking sheet in the freezer for several hours until the pasta is frozen. Try to resist the temptation to freeze them for any longer than 2 weeks. The freezer will dehydrate the pasta, causing it to crack and break and lose its toothsome texture.
- We find that freezing the pasta helps it keep its shape when cooked. (No need to thaw it before adding it to the boiling water.)

- Make sure to boil enough water so you don't crowd the pasta in the pot. It's ideal to use a 6-quart pasta pot with a strainer insert.
- Salt the water. As Italians say, "Salt the water to taste like the ocean." To achieve the saltiness of the water that we use in the kitchen at Mozza, you can rely on a formula of 1 tablespoon per quart of water. It may seem like a lot of salt, but you want it to permeate the noodle. Besides, salt is cheap, and most of it goes down the drain.
- Likewise, wait to put the pasta in the water until all your guests are ready to eat. That means seated, with wine. Once the pasta is out of the water, everything goes really fast. And the last thing you want is for your pasta to get cold while the table is still being set.
- Stir the pasta when you add it to the water so it doesn't stick together. Then leave it alone while it cooks to prevent it from falling apart. This is especially important with fresh pasta.
- Cook pasta al dente. *Al dente* literally translates "to the tooth." In reference to pasta, it refers to pasta that you can feel under your teeth when you bite into it, as opposed to pasta that is so mushy that to eat it you don't need teeth at all.
- Drain the pasta quickly, leaving a little water still dripping from the pasta, then quickly add it to the pan with the sauce. You don't want to let pasta sit in a colander in the sink, and never rinse it.
- When you're cooking the pasta with the sauce as we call for you to do in all of these recipes, the goal is to stain the pasta with the sauce. This step, called *macchiare,* "to stain," allows the flavors of the sauce to permeate the pasta rather than to simply dress it.
- Be organized. Before you drop in the pasta, make sure you have the tools you will need handy—a colander, a strainer, or tongs for draining the pasta (if you are not using a pasta pot; directions are given for this in the recipes), a rubber spatula for stirring the pasta with the sauce, and a grater if the recipe calls for cheese.
- When we cook the pasta with the sauce, we often add water—a simple step that can make the difference between an unappealing, sticky sauce and one that looks glistening and delicious. We use the water the pasta was cooked in, which has the added benefit of having the flavor of the noodles and salt. We use plain water for the orecchiette and gnudi dishes, because the pasta water would make them too salty.
- We give you exact amounts of sauce to dress each pasta dish. The idea is to have just enough sauce to coat the pasta nicely and not be dry, but not so much that the sauce leaks out onto the plate.

- All of our ragùs make enough for approximately sixteen first-course servings. They freeze well, and since ragù takes several hours to cook, it seems silly to make less.

- If you want to make any of the pasta dishes in quantities larger than those we give you, toss the pasta with the sauce in batches no larger than those we give you. (This means you will use two sauté pans if you want to make eight servings.) Otherwise, you will crowd the pan and end up with gluey pasta, broken shapes, and a big mess.

- Eat, slurp, enjoy, but whatever you do, please don't cut the noodles. When I was in Bologna with Mario, I ordered tagliatelle bolognese, and I heard Mario saying, "Don't cut the noodle, dude." I didn't know he was talking to me. He'd never spoken to me directly like that. He kept repeating himself and finally I looked up and I said, "What? Me?" He goes, "Yeah. Don't ever cut the noodle." Then he explained. "Think about it. Somebody's grandmother is back in the kitchen making that thing by hand. You don't want to show her disrespect."

basic pasta dough

We use this dough to make all of our filled pasta shapes such as Fresh Ricotta and Egg Ravioli with Brown Butter (page 175) and Francobolli di Brasato al Pomodoro *with Basil and Ricotta Salata* al Forno *(page 177).*

MAKES 1 1/4 POUNDS

Put the flour, eggs, and egg yolks in the bowl of a standing mixer fitted with the paddle attachment and mix on low speed until the dough comes together. Turn off the mixer, remove the paddle attachment, and replace it with the dough hook. Scrape down the sides of the bowl and beat the dough with the dough hook on medium speed until it forms a ball, about 5 minutes. Dust a flat work surface with flour. Turn the dough out onto the dusted surface and gently knead it for 20 to 25 minutes, until the ball begins to feel elastic and the surface of the dough feels smooth and silky. Wrap the dough in plastic wrap and refrigerate to rest for at least 45 minutes and up to overnight before sheeting it (any longer and the dough will discolor).

2 1/4 cups all-purpose flour, plus more for dusting

3 extra-large eggs

6 extra-large egg yolks

semolina dough

This dough is more toothsome than any of our other pasta dough because it is fortified with semolina, a by-product of milling durum wheat flour, which is what the majority of dried pasta is made of. We use it to make orecchiette and pici, both of which need a strong dough to hold their shape.

MAKES A SCANT 2 POUNDS

Combine the flour, semolina, and water in the bowl of a standing mixer fitted with the paddle attachment and mix on low speed until the dough comes together. Turn off the mixer, remove the paddle attachment, and replace it with the dough hook. Scrape down the sides of the bowl and beat the dough with the dough

2 1/2 cups all-purpose flour, plus more for dusting

1 3/4 cups semolina

1 1/4 cups water

hook on medium speed until it forms a ball, about 5 minutes. Dust a flat work surface with flour. Turn the dough out onto the dusted surface and gently knead it for 20 to 25 minutes, until the ball begins to feel elastic and the surface of the dough feels smooth and silky. Wrap the dough in plastic wrap and refrigerate to rest for at least 45 minutes and up to overnight before sheeting it (any longer and the dough will discolor).

dry dough

We use dry dough to make the pastas that we serve with our ragùs. *It gets shaped into* maltagliati, *garganelli,* corzetti stampati, *and tagliatelle (all described later), as well as other short shapes. We call it dry dough because it feels dryer than our basic pasta dough since it is made with only egg yolks and no whites.*

MAKES 14 OUNCES

*P*ut the flour in the bowl of a standing mixer fitted with the paddle attachment and begin to run the machine at low speed. With the mixer running, add the egg yolks gradually, mixing until the dough comes together. Turn off the mixer and dust a flat work surface with flour. Turn the dough out onto the dusted surface, form it into a ball, and gently knead it for 20 to 25 minutes, until the ball begins to feel elastic and the surface of the dough feels smooth and silky. Wrap the dough in plastic wrap and refrigerate to rest for at least 45 minutes and up to overnight before sheeting it (any longer and the dough will discolor).

1½ cups all-purpose flour, plus more for dusting
12 extra-large egg yolks (16 ounces of yolks), whisked together in a medium bowl

green dough

It's very traditional to use ortiche, or "nettles," to make green pasta such as this one. Despite the fact that they are often called "stinging nettles," they don't really sting, but they do have a bristly texture that can irritate your skin. If you wash them first, they won't bother you as you pick the leaves off the stems. Another solution is to wear thin rubber gloves. If you can't find nettles, spinach is an acceptable substitute. In either case, the greens have so much water in them (no matter how much you try to squeeze it all out) that we use very few eggs in this dough.

MAKES 1 1/2 POUNDS

Kosher salt
2 pounds fresh nettles picked from the stems, or spinach leaves
2 extra-large eggs
3 1/2 cups all-purpose flour, plus more for dusting

Fill a large saucepan with water, bring it to a boil over high heat, and add enough salt so it tastes like the ocean. Fill a large bowl with ice water and place a fine-mesh strainer in the sink.

Plunge the nettles or spinach leaves into the boiling water and cook them for 1 minute, until they turn bright green and tender. Drain the leaves in the strainer and immediately plunge them in the strainer into the ice water to cool. Lift the greens out of the water and place them in the center of a clean dishtowel. Close the dishtowel to form a bundle with the greens inside and, holding the bundle over the sink, twist the towel as tightly as you can to wring out the excess water.

Put the eggs in the jar of a blender or the bowl of a food processor fitted with a metal blade. Pull the nettle or spinach leaves apart slightly (they will be in a tight ball after having been wrung out) and add them to the blender. Blend the eggs and greens on low speed to begin to combine them. Gradually increase the speed, pulsing if necessary to loosen the mixture, until it is a very fine, homogenous purée.

Put the flour in the bowl of a standing mixer fitted with the paddle attachment. Add the purée and mix on low speed until the dough comes together. Turn off the mixer, remove the paddle attachment, and replace it with the dough hook. Scrape down the sides of the bowl and beat the dough with the dough hook on medium speed until it forms a ball, about 5 minutes. Dust a flat work surface with flour. Turn the dough out onto the dusted surface, form it into a ball, and gently knead it for 20 to 25 minutes, until the ball begins to feel elastic and the surface of the dough feels smooth and silky. Wrap the dough in plastic wrap and refrigerate to rest for at least 45 minutes and up to overnight before sheeting it (any longer and the dough will discolor).

black dough

This is the Basic Pasta Dough with the addition of squid ink. The ink makes the pasta black and also infuses it with a subtle seafood flavor. You may want to wear plastic gloves while making this pasta; otherwise, the black ink will stain your hands for days.

You can buy squid ink or cuttlefish ink at Italian and specialty food stores; if you can't find it, you can't make this dough. Use a quality store-bought squid ink pasta, preferably fresh, instead.

MAKES 11 OUNCES

Put the flour in the bowl of a standing mixer fitted with the paddle attachment and begin to run the machine at low speed. With the motor running, gradually add the egg yolks and the squid ink, mixing until the dough comes together. Turn off the mixer, remove the paddle attachment, and replace it with the dough hook. Scrape down the sides of the bowl and beat the dough with the dough hook on medium speed until it forms a ball, about 5 minutes. Dust a flat work surface with flour. Turn the dough out onto the dusted surface and gently knead it for 20 to 25 minutes, until the ball begins to feel elastic and the surface of the dough feels smooth and silky. Wrap the dough in plastic wrap and refrigerate to rest for at least 45 minutes and up to overnight before sheeting it (any longer and the dough will discolor).

1½ cups plus 2 tablespoons all-purpose flour, plus more for dusting
10 extra-large egg yolks
1 teaspoon squid ink or cuttlefish ink

In Italy, which pasta is served with which sauce is governed by strict rules and age-old traditions. Ragùs are traditionally served with fresh egg pasta because the richness of the ragù stands up to the richer, heavier noodle. Long strands of dry pasta, such as linguine and spaghetti, are used for simple, slippery sauces that will coat the noodle. Short shapes are paired with sauces that contain ingredients that require you stab into them with a fork; pasta with holes, such as rigatoni, penne, and garganelli, are used when you want to trap little bits of a sauce, such as the minced meat in bolognese, inside the tubes, and the *rigate*, or ridges, on the outsides of pasta such as penne are not for decoration but to help the sauce cling to the noodle. While we do not always adhere to tradition when choosing which shape of pasta to serve with a particular sauce, we do pay close attention to the way the noodle and the sauce interact.

In the very back of the Osteria kitchen where we store all our dry goods, we have a small room that we call the pasta room. There, two or three employees are busy all day long sheeting pasta and turning it into the fresh pasta shapes described below. I love watching them, and the way their hands work so quickly and methodically to make these intricate shapes so beautifully and consistently.

orecchiette

Orecchiette, meaning "little ears," are small dome-shaped disks. They are the most common shape in Puglia. They're used in many regional dishes there, including the one that inspired our Orecchiette with Fennel Sausage and Swiss Chard (page 180). Although this shape doesn't look as intricate as some of the others, it is one of the most difficult to shape, which is probably why so few restaurants make their own. Following our instructions, you can't fail. To get the desired texture on the surface of the pasta, we suggest you use a plastic cutting board. At the Osteria, we use a wooden cutting board that has been deliberately scored with a knife, which gives the orecchiette the texture we want.

MAKES 8 SERVINGS

$\mathcal{S}$lice the round of dough into 1-inch-thick slabs and cut each slab into 1-inch-wide slabs. Roll each section on a clean, dry work surface into a tube ¼ inch thick, and set aside. Dust the work surface with flour, and return the tubes to the dusted surface. Use a long knife or a straight-edged rolling pastry cutter to cut the dough into 1-inch-long pieces, discarding the misshapen ends.

Dust a baking sheet lightly with semolina. Dust a plastic cutting board or other slightly textured surface very lightly with flour. Place one pasta segment on the cutting board with the cut end facing you. With the flat side of the tip of a table knife, gently press on the end of the segment closest to you and continue pressing away from you toward the other end of the segment, flattening the dough into a small disk about ¼ inch thick in the process. Pick up the disk and invert it onto your index finger so that the side of the dough you pressed on is facing down. Use the fingers of your other hand to pull the edges of the dough around the index finger, forming a caplike-shaped ear. Place the pasta shape on the prepared baking sheet and repeat, shaping the remaining dough segments in the same way. Use the orecchiette or cover the baking sheet with plastic wrap and refrigerate the pasta for up to one day. To freeze, place the baking sheet in the freezer until the pasta is firm to the touch. Transfer the pasta to sealable plastic bags, or an airtight container, dusting off the excess semolina, and freeze for up to two weeks (any longer and the pasta will dry out and crack).

Semolina Dough (page 162)
All-purpose flour, for dusting
Semolina, for dusting

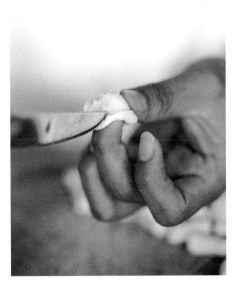

pici

Pici are long, hand-rolled strands from the Montalcino area of Tuscany, not far from my house. Also called umbrichella, *this pasta is the most typical shape in my region, so naturally I wanted to serve it at Mozza. Although it is not a regular item on the menu, we often use pici in place of the gnocchi in the Gnocchi with Duck Ragù (page 187).*

MAKES 8 SERVINGS

Roll the dough out to the third thickest setting on the pasta sheeter (number 3 using a KitchenAid attachment) according to the directions given in "Matt's Scuola di Pasta" (page 158). Dust a baking sheet lightly with semolina and dust a work surface with flour. Lay one pasta sheet on the flour-dusted surface and cut it into 5-inch squares. Stack the squares of dough and use a long knife to cut the dough into ⅛-inch-thick strips. Roll one strip on the countertop with your fingertips to create a strand about 10 inches long. Lay the strand on the semolina-dusted baking sheet and repeat, rolling the remaining strips in the same way and dusting the strands with semolina to prevent them from sticking together. Use the pici or cover the baking sheet with plastic wrap and refrigerate the pasta up to one day. To freeze, place the baking sheet in the freezer until the pasta is firm to the touch. Transfer the pasta to sealable plastic bags, or an airtight container, dusting off the excess semolina, and freeze for up to two weeks (any longer and the pasta will dry out and crack).

Semolina Dough (page 162)
Semolina, for dusting
All-purpose flour, for dusting

tagliatelle

Tagliatelle comes from the word tagliare, *which means "to cut," because the sheets of pasta are cut into long, flat strands similar to fettuccine but wider. Tagliatelle is a traditional shape in the Emilia-Romagna region, and traditionalists believe tagliatelle verde (made with green dough) is the only pasta to toss with ragù bolognese, the official ragù of the region. We make tagliatelle with Green Dough to serve with Stinging Nettle Tagliatelle with Lamb Ragù, Taggiasche Olives, and Mint (page 192).*

MAKES 6 SERVINGS TAGLIATELLE, OR 8 SERVINGS GREEN TAGLIATELLE

Roll the dough out to the thinnest setting on the pasta sheeter (number 8 using a KitchenAid attachment) according to the directions given in "Matt's Scuola di Pasta" (page

Dry Dough (page 163) or
Green Dough (page 164)
Semolina, for dusting
All-purpose flour, for dusting

158). Dust a baking sheet with semolina and dust a flat work surface with flour. Lay one sheet of dough on the flour-dusted surface and use a long knife or straight-edged rolling pastry cutter to trim the edges of the sheet to make a rectangle with straight edges. Stack the remaining sheets on top of one another, dusting each layer. Using the first sheet as a template, cut the remaining sheets so you have a stack of rectangular pasta sheets. Discard the irregular ends. Cut the rectangles crosswise into ¼-inch-wide strips that are as long as the sheet is wide. Place the strips on the prepared baking sheet, dusting them with semolina between layers to prevent sticking. Use the tagliatelle or cover the baking sheet with plastic wrap and refrigerate the pasta up to one day. To freeze, place the baking sheet in the freezer until the pasta is firm to the touch. Transfer the pasta to sealable plastic bags, or an airtight container, dusting off the excess semolina, and freeze for up to two weeks (any longer and the pasta will dry out and crack).

maltagliati

*M*altagliati *means "badly cut," and is so named because the pieces are cut from the sheet of dough in random shapes. In order for us to ensure that the pasta cooks evenly, however, ours only look randomly cut but are actually all cut to the exact same shape and size.*

MAKES 6 SERVINGS

*R*oll the dough out to the second thinnest setting on the pasta sheeter (number 7 using a KitchenAid attachment) according to the directions given in "Matt's Scuola di Pasta" (page 158). Dust a baking sheet with semolina and dust a flat work surface with flour. Place one sheet on the flour-dusted work surface and use a hard-edged ruler as a guide to trim and discard the edges of the pasta sheets so you're left with perfect rectangles. Starting from one corner and moving to the opposite corner, use a straight-edged rolling pastry cutter to make a cut across the pasta. Using the ruler as a guide, make similar parallel cuts 1 inch apart from the original cut. Do the same in the opposite direction to form diamond-shaped pasta. Place the cut pasta on the semolina-dusted baking sheet and continue cutting the remaining sheets in the same way. Use the *maltagliati* or cover the baking sheet with plastic wrap and refrigerate the pasta up to one day. To freeze, place the baking sheet in the freezer until the pasta is firm to the touch. Transfer the pasta to sealable plastic bags, or an airtight container, dusting off the excess semolina, and freeze for up to two weeks (any longer and the pasta will dry out and crack).

Dry Dough (page 163)
Semolina, for dusting
All-purpose flour, for dusting

garganelli

Garganelli, which comes from the word **gargala,** *meaning "trachea," are hollow ridged tubes, similar to penne. We prefer garganelli for our ragù bolognese (see page 189) over the more traditional tagliatelle because we like the way the small bits of sauce stick to the ridges on the outside and get tucked inside the tubes. Since garganelli are also a specialty of Bologna, we think that we haven't done too much injustice to tradition. To make this shape you'll want to have a thin plastic pen on hand. We remove the ink cartridge just to be safe, and you might want to do the same.*

MAKES 6 SERVINGS

Roll the dough out to the third thinnest setting on the pasta sheeter (number 6 using a KitchenAid attachment) according to the directions given in "Matt's Scuola di Pasta" (page 158). Dust a baking sheet lightly with semolina and dust a work surface with flour. Lay one sheet of pasta on your work surface and use a long knife or straight-edged rolling pastry cutter to cut the edges straight. Use the knife or rolling cutter to cut each sheet into 1½-inch-wide strips and then into 1½-inch squares. Place the squares on the

Dry Dough (page 163)
Semolina, for dusting
All-purpose flour,
for dusting

prepared baking sheet, dusting them with semolina to prevent them from sticking together.

Fold a clean, dry kitchen towel a few times to form a bed and place a ridged gnocchi or pasta board on the towel. Place one square on the board with the point facing the edge of the board. Pick up the pen and place it on the pasta at the point closest to you. Push down on the pen gently and roll it away from your body so the pasta wraps around the pen to form a tube with a ridged exterior. Slide the tube off the pen onto the prepared baking sheet and repeat, rolling the remaining pasta squares in the same way. Use the garganelli or cover the baking sheet with plastic wrap and refrigerate the pasta up to one day. To freeze, place the baking sheet in the freezer until the pasta is firm to the touch. Transfer the pasta to sealable plastic bags, or an airtight container, dusting off the excess semolina, and freeze for up to two weeks (any longer and the pasta will dry out and crack).

corzetti stampati

Corzetti stampati, or "stamped coins," are a traditional pasta shape of Genoa, made using a wooden stamp to imprint a design onto the "coins." Corzetti are usually served with the most famous Genoese pasta dish: basil pesto with green beans and potatoes. Matt and I shirked that tradition and serve ours with a Sicilian dish, pasta with eggplant and tomato sauce, instead. If you can't find a stamp, you could get away with making unstamped coins using a 2- to 2½-inch cookie cutter.

MAKES 6 SERVINGS

Roll the dough out to the third thinnest setting on the pasta sheeter (number 6 using a KitchenAid attachment) according to the directions given in "Matt's Scuola di Pasta" (page 158). Dust a baking sheet lightly with semolina and dust a work surface with flour. Use a cookie cutter the same size as your stamp to cut the dough into rounds, and then use the stamp to imprint the pasta coins. Carefully lift the coins and place them on the prepared baking sheet, dusting with semolina to prevent them from sticking together. Repeat, stamping as many *corzetti* as the dough allows. Use the *corzetti* or cover the baking sheet with plastic wrap and refrigerate the pasta up to one day. To freeze, place the baking sheet in the freezer until the pasta is firm to the touch. Transfer the pasta to sealable plastic bags, or an airtight container, dusting off the excess semolina, and freeze for up to two weeks (any longer and the pasta will dry out and crack).

Dry Dough (page 163)
Semolina, for dusting
All-purpose flour,
for dusting

spaghetti alla chitarra

*C*hitarra *means "guitar" in Italian, and the shape, a specialty of Abruzzo, gets its name from the device with which it's made—a wooden frame strung with metal wire like a guitar. The way it works is that a sheet of pasta dough is pressed down onto the strings, which cut the sheet into long, square spaghetti-like strands. We make* chitarra *alternately this way and by cutting the sheets with a long knife.*

MAKES 6 SERVINGS OF REGULAR SPAGHETTI
OR 4 SERVINGS BLACK SPAGHETTI

*R*oll the dough out to the third thickest setting on the pasta sheeter (number 5 using a KitchenAid attachment) according to the directions given in "Matt's Scuola di Pasta" (page 158). Dust a baking sheet lightly with semolina and dust a work surface with flour. Lay one sheet of the dough on top of a *chitarra* and use a rolling pin to roll the length of the pasta, pressing it into the strings to form thin strips. (Alternatively, to cut the strands by hand, roll the dough out to the thinnest setting on a pasta machine—8 on a KitchenAid mixer—and place the sheets on the baking sheet, dusting lightly with semolina between each sheet. When you've rolled all of the pasta dough, trim the edges of one sheet to make a rectangle with straight edges. Using the first sheet as a template, cut the remaining sheets so you have a stack of rectangular pasta sheets. Cut the rectangles crosswise into 1/16-inch-wide strips that are as long as the sheet is wide.) Use the spaghetti or cover the baking sheet with plastic wrap and refrigerate the pasta up to one day. To freeze, place the baking sheet in the freezer until the pasta is firm to the touch. Transfer the pasta to sealable plastic bags, or an airtight container, dusting off the excess semolina, and freeze for up to two weeks (any longer and the pasta will dry out and crack).

Dry Dough (page 163) or Black
Dough (page 165)
Semolina, for dusting
All-purpose flour, for dusting

gnocchi

*W*hen people talk about good gnocchi, you always hear about how "light" they are, but I find that just because gnocchi are light doesn't mean they're good. More often than not, gnocchi taste and feel to me like boiled mashed potatoes or mushy dumplings. It wasn't until

I had good gnocchi, which, in addition to being light, had some texture and springiness to them, that I realized how good they could be. Matt worked really hard to ensure that our gnocchi had those qualities. This dough is very starchy and sensitive, so the gnocchi must be formed and served the same day the dough is made. You must use russet potatoes.

MAKES 8 SERVINGS

*A*djust the oven rack to the middle position and preheat the oven to 350°F.

Spread a ¼-inch layer of salt on a baking sheet. Rinse the potatoes, roll them in the salt, and place them, on the salt-covered baking sheet, in the oven to bake until they're very soft, about 1½ hours. Remove the potatoes from the oven and use a small knife to remove half of the peel, discarding the peel. Squeeze the potatoes out of the peel into a food mill or potato ricer and discard the remaining peel. Pass the potatoes through the food mill or potato ricer into a large bowl. Sprinkle the 2 teaspoons of salt over the potatoes and cut the salt in with the tines of a fork, sweeping through the potatoes from side to side with the tips of the tines to avoid compressing the potato.

Drizzle the egg over the potatoes and cut it into the potatoes in the same way. Pass the potato and egg mixture through the food mill again into a large bowl. Sprinkle the potatoes with some of the flour, adding the flour gradually and cutting it in with the fork in the same manner, adding more flour as soon as the flour you have added is integrated and the dough begins to look wet again. Form the dough into a brick about 1 inch thick, patting down on the top of the dough to make it square. Turn the brick out onto a baking sheet, cover it with plastic wrap, and refrigerate for 30 minutes.

Remove the dough from the refrigerator, and cut the dough brick into 1-inch-long segments. Lightly flour a flat work surface and roll the segments into ½-inch-thick tubes. Dust the tubes generously with flour and line them up side by side. Cut the tubes into 1-inch segments. Dust the work surface again with flour. One at a time, pick up one of the cut segments with one hand and a large dinner fork with the other. Holding the fork so that the tines are resting on the work surface and the convex (arched) side is facing out, and using your thumb, roll the gnocchi down the length of the fork to create ridges. Place the ridged gnocchi on the prepared baking sheet and repeat, forming the remaining segments in the same way. Use the gnocchi or cover the baking sheet with plastic wrap and refrigerate for up to 8 hours.

2 teaspoons kosher salt, plus about 1½ cups salt for baking sheet and for boiling gnocchi

3½ pounds russet potatoes

1 extra-large egg, lightly beaten

2 cups all-purpose flour, plus more for dusting

fresh ricotta and egg ravioli with brown butter

I'm generally turned off when people describe food as being "sexy," but sexy is the best description I have for this warm, luscious, pillowy raviolo. *The word* raviolo *is the singular for* ravioli, *and this is one big, square* raviolo *filled with ricotta and a raw egg yolk. We are not at all ashamed to tell you that this is a direct rip-off from Michael Tusk, the chef and owner of Quince restaurant in San Francisco. The first time I had it, I thought it was one of the best things I had ever eaten, and for sure the single best pasta dish I'd ever put in my mouth. When our servers bring this to the table, they suggest to the guests that they cut into the* raviolo *starting from the center so the egg pours out onto the plate into the pool of browned butter that the* raviolo *sits in. It's sexy. What else can I say? We recommend you use farm-fresh eggs with bright orange yolks. You will need a 3 × 3-inch fluted cookie cutter or a fluted pastry cutter to make these.*

SERVES 8

SUGGESTED WINE PAIRING: TREBBIANO D'ABRUZZO (ABRUZZI)

To make the ravioli, combine the ricotta and Parmigiano-Reggiano in a medium bowl, and sprinkle with the salt, sugar, and nutmeg. Stir to combine the seasonings with the cheese. Stir in the cream, adding more if necessary to obtain the consistency of soft-serve ice cream. (You can make the filling up to two days in advance. Transfer it to an airtight container and refrigerate until you are ready to assemble the ravioli.) Scoop up ⅓ cup of the ricotta filling and form it into a disk about ½ inch high and 2¼ inches in diameter. Set the disk on a plate and repeat, forming the remaining ricotta into a total of 8 disks. Set them aside while you prepare the dough for the ravioli.

To make the ravioli, cut eight 4-inch-square pieces of parchment and dust two baking sheets with semolina. Roll the dough out to the third thinnest setting on a pasta sheeter (number 6 using a KitchenAid attachment) according to the directions given in "Matt's Scuola di Pasta" (page 158), stacking the sheets of dough on one of the parchment-lined baking sheets. When you have rolled out all of the dough, dust a flat work surface with flour and lay one sheet of the dough on the floured surface. Place three or four ricotta disks on the dough, leaving 4 inches between each disk and 1½ to 2 inches of dough on all the sides of the outer disks. Use the back of a spoon or your fingers to make a crater deep enough to hold an egg yolk in the

for the ravioli

1 pound fresh ricotta (about 2 cups)

¾ cup freshly grated Parmigiano-Reggiano

1 teaspoon kosher salt

1 teaspoon sugar

1 teaspoon freshly grated nutmeg

3 tablespoons heavy whipping cream, plus more as needed

Semolina for dusting

Basic Pasta Dough (page 162)

All-purpose flour for dusting

8 extra-large farm-fresh eggs

for finishing and serving the pasta

Kosher salt

1½ cups (3 sticks) unsalted butter

18 fresh sage leaves

Wedge of Parmigiano-Reggiano, for grating

center of each disk. Separate one egg, reserving the white and carefully sliding the yolk into one crater. Repeat, filling the remaining 2 or 3 disks in the same way (you don't need to reserve any more whites). Lay a second sheet of dough directly behind the first and use a rolling pastry cutter, starting at the edge of the dough nearest your body and moving in a straight line directly away from you, making one long cut through both sheets of dough between two disks of ricotta. Continue making cuts down the sheet of dough between the disks. Using a pastry brush, brush egg white around each cheese disk. Lift one segment of dough from the back sheet and lay it on top of the corresponding front segment of dough. Without lifting the *raviolo,* cup both hands around the cheese so that the edges of your pinky fingers press down around the cheese, sealing the *raviolo* closed. Repeat, covering and sealing the remaining ravioli. Use a 3 × 3-inch fluted cookie cutter or fluted pastry wheel to cut each *raviolo,* discarding the scraps of dough around it. Place the ravioli on the prepared baking sheet and repeat, assembling the remaining ravioli in the same way. Cover the baking sheet with plastic wrap and refrigerate until you are ready to boil them, or for up to 8 hours.

Fill two wide pots with 6 quarts of water each. Add 6 tablespoons of salt to each pot and bring to a boil over high heat. Have a slotted spat-

ula or slotted spoon and a clean dishtowel handy for lifting the ravioli out of the water.

While the water is coming to a boil, make the brown butter sauce. Place the butter and sage leaves in a medium saucepan and cook over medium-high heat for 3 to 5 minutes without stirring, swirling the pan occasionally to brown the butter evenly and prevent it from burning, until the bubbles subside and the butter is dark brown with a nutty, toasty smell. Reduce the heat to low to keep the butter warm while you cook the pasta.

Remove the ravioli from the refrigerator and, one at a time, lift the parchment holding each *raviolo* off the baking sheet and gently drop the *raviolo* with the paper into the water, adding 4 ravioli to each pot. (The parchment will quickly separate and will be easy to remove from the water.) When you have dropped all the ravioli, remove and discard the parchment paper, partially cover the pots to return the water to a boil quickly, and keep it boiling. Cook the ravioli for 4 minutes.

With a clean dishtowel in one hand and a slotted spoon or spatula in the other, lift one *raviolo* out of the water and onto the dishtowel to blot it dry, and then carefully place it in the center of a dinner plate. Repeat with the remaining ravioli. Pour the brown butter over the ravioli, dividing it evenly. Place one of the sage leaves on top of each *raviolo,* discarding the remaining leaves. Use a microplane or another fine grater to grate a light dusting of Parmigiano-Reggiano over each *raviolo,* and serve.

francobolli di brasato al pomodoro with basil and ricotta salata al forno

*F*rancobolli *is Italian for "postage stamps," and that's what these small, filled pasta shapes look like. They are filled with braised short ribs that we whip with Parmigiano and then top with a simple tomato sauce. The reason for you to make this is the same reason we make it: to use leftover* Brasato. *This recipe makes more ravioli than you will need for four servings. You can either freeze the remaining ravioli or double the sauce recipe. If you double the sauce recipe, toss the sauce with the ravioli four servings at a time.*

Ricotta salata is ricotta cheese that has been pressed and salted. The result is a hard, bright white grating cheese with a much stronger flavor than fresh ricotta. Matt got the idea to bake the cheese in a very hot oven, which gives it a smoky flavor.

*P*reheat the oven to 500°F. Place the hunk of cheese you are working with (I recommend using a piece about the size of a slice of cheesecake) on a baking sheet and bake until the underside is almost black, about 20 minutes. Turn the cheese over and bake it for another 10 to 15 minutes to brown the other side. Remove the cheese from the oven and set it aside to cool to room temperature. It will keep, refrigerated, for at least a week.

To make the filling, shred the short rib meat, discarding the sinew and bones. Place the meat and the braising liquid or water in a skillet over medium-high heat and cook, stirring occasionally to keep the sauce from sticking and breaking the meat apart as it cooks, until it is warmed through. Transfer the contents of the pan to the bowl of a food processor fitted with a metal blade or the jar of a blender and purée. Turn the purée out into a medium bowl and stir in the Parmigiano-Reggiano. Transfer the filling to an airtight container and refrigerate for at least 1 hour to chill, or for up to three days. When you are ready to make the *francobolli,* transfer the filling to a pastry bag or a sealable plastic bag with a ½-inch hole cut out of the corner.

Dust two baking sheets with semolina. Roll out the dough to the third thinnest setting on a pasta sheeter (number 6 using a KitchenAid attachment) according to the directions given in "Matt's Scuola di Pasta" (page 158), stacking the sheets on one of the semolina-dusted pans and dusting with additional semolina between each sheet. When you have sheeted all of the dough, dust a flat work surface with flour. Using a 1¾-inch square cookie cutter, press down lightly on the dough to score it into as many squares as you can fit, making sure not to actually cut into the dough. Squeeze 1 teaspoon of the filling in the center of each square. When you have finished piping the filling onto one sheet of dough, use a pastry brush to paint a circle of egg white around each dollop of filling. Lay a second sheet of dough on top of the first, stretching it slightly to cover the filling and lining up the edges of the two sheets as much as possible. Use the same cookie cutter to cut a square around each of the mounds, with the filling directly in the center. One by one, pick up a *francobollo* and gently squeeze out the air pockets before pressing it closed. If you are a stickler for uniformity,

for the ricotta salata al forno
Wedge of ricotta salata

for the *francobolli*
8 ounces braised short ribs (1 rib, weighed without the bone) (*Brasato al Barolo with Polenta and Horseradish Gremolata,* page 230), plus 1 cup reserved braising liquid or water
¼ cup plus 2 tablespoons freshly grated Parmigiano-Reggiano
Semolina, for dusting
Basic Pasta Dough (page 162)
All-purpose flour, for dusting
1 extra-large egg white

for finishing and serving the pasta
Kosher salt
2 tablespoons extra-virgin olive oil
4 garlic cloves, crushed
1 cup *Passata di Pomodoro* (page 25)
4 whole large fresh basil leaves, plus several fresh micro or miniature basil leaves (if unavailable, use additional large leaves)
2 tablespoons finishing-quality extra-virgin olive oil

use the cutter to recut the squares. Place the finished *francobolli* in a single layer on the second prepared baking sheet and repeat with the remaining dough and filling. If you are not cooking the *francobolli* immediately, cover the baking sheet with plastic wrap and refrigerate until you are ready to boil them or for up to one day. (To freeze the *francobolli*, place the baking sheet in the freezer until the *francobolli* are firm to the touch, then transfer them to sealable plastic bags or an air-tight container, dusting off the excess semolina in the process, and place them in the freezer for up to two weeks.)

To prepare the pasta, fill a pasta pot or large stockpot with 6 quarts of water, add 6 tablespoons of salt, and bring the water to a boil over high heat. If you are not using a pasta pot, place a colander in the sink or have a large wire strainer handy.

While the water is coming to a boil, make the sauce. Combine the olive oil and garlic in a large sauté pan over medium-high heat. Season the garlic with salt and cook, stirring until it is golden brown, about 1½ minutes. Turn off the heat and add the *passata*, the four large basil leaves, and a pinch of salt. Return the heat to medium and cook for 1 minute, stirring to incorporate the ingredients and emulsify the sauce. Turn off the heat while you cook the pasta.

Remove the *francobolli* from the refrigerator or freezer and drop them into the boiling water. Stir to prevent the pasta from sticking together, partially cover the pot to return the water to a boil quickly and keep it boiling, and cook the pasta until it's al dente, about 2 minutes. About 30 seconds before the pasta is done, place the sauce over high heat. Lift the pasta out of the cooking water, or reserve 1 cup of the water and drain the pasta, and immediately add it to the pan with the sauce. Add 2 tablespoons of the reserved water and cook the pasta with the sauce for 2 minutes, stirring gently, staining the noodle with the sauce, and adding more of the reserved pasta water if necessary. Turn off the heat and add the finishing-quality olive oil, stirring vigorously and shaking the pan to emulsify the sauce. Remove and discard the basil leaves and garlic cloves.

Pile the *francobolli* in the center of each of four plates, dividing them evenly, and spoon any remaining sauce over the pasta. Use a microplane or another fine grater to grate a light layer of the ricotta salata over each serving. Scatter tiny basil leaves or snip larger leaves over the *francobolli*, and serve.

orecchiette with fennel sausage and swiss chard

Before we opened the Osteria, Matt made all of the dishes he wanted to put on the pasta menu for us to taste together. When he made this dish—his version of a classic from Puglia—I was absolutely convinced that the pasta program we were committing to was a good idea, and that Matt was absolutely the one to execute it. Evidently I'm not alone because this has been our most popular pasta since the day we opened. The chard you will prepare for this dish makes more than you will need for four servings, as does the Fennel Sausage recipe. It would be a good recipe to double and serve to a crowd—just remember to prepare the sauce and toss it with the pasta in two separate sauté pans.

SERVES 4

SUGGESTED WINE PAIRING: ROSSO CONERO (THE MARCHES)

To prepare the chard, pull the leaves from the ribs. Roughly chop the leaves and set aside. Cut off and discard the very ends of the ribs and slice the ribs ¼ inch thick.

Heat the olive oil in a large sauté pan over medium-high heat until it is almost smoking and slides easily in the pan, 2 to 3 minutes. Add the chard ribs, season with salt, and sauté for 2 to 3 minutes, until barely translucent. Add the onion, garlic, and chiles, and season with salt. Sauté the vegetables for about 10 minutes, adding water to the pan (as much as 1 cup total), stirring often to prevent the vegetables browning. (You add water to the pan so you can sauté and sweat the onion without browning it, but you never want the onion swimming in water—just enough so the pan isn't dry.) Add the chard leaves, season with salt, and fold the leaves in with the onion for 1 or 2 minutes to wilt them slightly. Reduce the heat to low, cover, and cook for 15 to 20 minutes, stirring from time to time, until the chard leaves are very dark green and the onion, leaves, and stems are one soft, homogenous mixture. Turn the vegetables out onto a cutting board and chop, cutting first in one direction and then perpendicular to the first direction, until the vegetables are finely chopped to the point of being almost puréed. Measure out a heaping ¼ cup of the vegetables for the pasta dish. Use the rest as an excuse to prepare this dish again in the very near future, or spoon a heaping spoonful under a piece of grilled fish, topped with a spoonful of Salsa Verde (page 261).

for the chard

1 bunch Swiss chard
¼ cup extra-virgin olive oil
Kosher salt
½ large yellow Spanish onion, thinly sliced
12 garlic cloves, thinly sliced lengthwise
2 dried arbol chiles

for finishing and serving the pasta

¾ pound Fennel Sausage (page 137)
½ teaspoon Aleppo pepper
1 cup Basic Chicken Stock (page 27), or ¼ cup salted pasta water mixed with ¼ cup plain water
3 tablespoons unsalted butter
Kosher salt
12 ounces Orecchiette (page 166)
3 tablespoons finishing-quality extra-virgin olive oil
¼ cup plus 2 tablespoons freshly grated Parmigiano-Reggiano
2 teaspoons fennel pollen (see page 19)
2 tablespoons Toasted Bread Crumbs (page 74)

To make the sauce, heat a sauté pan over high heat for about 2 minutes until it's very hot. Add the sausage to the pan and cook it undisturbed for about 2 minutes, until the meat is seared. Stir the meat and cook for another 4 minutes, breaking it into pea-size pieces, until it is cooked through. Add the chopped chard and cook for 2 to 3 minutes to warm it through, stirring the chard into the sausage as it cooks. Sprinkle the pepper over the chard and sausage, add the chicken stock, and cook the sauce for 2 minutes, stirring constantly, to bring the ingredients together. Add the butter, stir until it melts, and turn off the heat while you cook the pasta.

Fill a pasta pot or large stockpot with 6 quarts of water, add 6 tablespoons of salt, and bring the water to a boil over high heat. If you are not using a pasta pot, place a colander in the sink or have a large wire strainer handy to lift the pasta out of the pot.

Remove the orecchiette from the refrigerator or the freezer and drop them into the boiling water. Stir to prevent the pasta from sticking together, partially cover the pot so the water returns to a boil quickly and continues boiling, and cook the pasta until it's al dente, about 2 minutes. About 1 minute before the pasta is done, place the sauce over high heat. Lift the pasta out of the cooking water or drain it and immediately add it to the pan with the sauce. Cook the pasta with the sauce together for 1 to 2 minutes, stirring with a rubber spatula, until the sauce is thick, adding fresh water to the pan if the pasta looks dry or sticky instead of slippery and glistening. Turn off the heat and add the finishing-quality olive oil, Parmigiano-Reggiano, and fennel pollen, stirring vigorously and shaking the pan to emulsify the sauce.

Pile the orecchiette in the center of each of eight plates, dividing it evenly, and spoon any sauce left in the pan over the pasta. Sprinkle a generous tablespoon of bread crumbs over each serving, and serve with the remaining bread crumbs on the side.

corzetti stampati with eggplant, olives, and fresh ricotta

*Y*ears ago my friend Paul Schrade gave me a wooden pasta stamp, which I never used. Since I'm a baker, I occasionally thought about using it to make a pretty cookie, but I never thought to use it for its intended use: to imprint corzetti stampati, or "stamped coins." Then about a year after Mozza opened, when I'd run out of projects to nudge Matt about, I broke out the stamp and told Matt to get to work. Rather than follow the traditional Genoese route of serving corzetti with green beans, potatoes, and pesto, Matt came up with a version of Pasta alla Norma—Sicily's most famous pasta dish that combines tomato sauce, eggplant, and sheep's milk ricotta—using the corzetti in place of the spaghetti or penne traditionally used. We use Japanese eggplant and slice it into medallions, which work really nicely with the flat "coins." No Italian in his right mind would ever take a shape from Genoa and toss it with a sauce from Sicily, but that's one of the advantages of being American. Though we try to be respectful of tradition, we are not bound by it. Think of it as Italian fusion—and enjoy.

SERVES 6

SUGGESTED WINE PAIRING: CARIGNANO DEL SULCIS (SARDINIA)

*P*lace the eggplant slices in a bowl and season them with salt and pepper. Heat ¼ cup of the oil in a large sauté pan over medium-high heat until the oil is almost smoking and slides easily in the pan, 2 to 3 minutes. Place half of the eggplant in the pan, increase the heat to high, and cook for about 1½ minutes, until the eggplant is deep brown and slightly crisp on one side. Turn the eggplant slices with tongs and add the garlic, making sure it touches the pan and not the eggplant. Season the garlic with salt, add 2 tablespoons of the remaining olive oil, and sauté the garlic and eggplant together, stirring constantly so the garlic doesn't burn, until the garlic is light golden, 1 to 2 minutes. Remove the eggplant slices and garlic to a plate. Add the remaining 2 tablespoons of olive oil to the pan and cook the second batch of eggplant in the same way as the first, leaving it in the pan. (You will not add garlic to the second batch.) Turn off the heat and return the first batch of eggplant and the garlic to the pan. Add the *passata,* red pepper flakes, and about 1 cup of water, or enough water that the sauce is loose enough to easily coat the pasta. Turn off the heat while you cook the pasta.

¾ pound Japanese eggplant, sliced ¼ inch thin
Kosher salt and freshly ground black pepper
½ cup extra-virgin olive oil
10 garlic cloves, thinly sliced
1 cup *Passata di Pomodoro* (page 25) or tomato sauce
¾ teaspoon red pepper flakes
1 cup fresh sheep's milk ricotta (preferably)
9 ounces *Corzetti Stampati* (page 171)
½ cup Arbequina or Ligurian olives
⅓ cup thinly sliced fresh Italian parsley leaves
2 tablespoons finishing-quality extra-virgin olive oil

Fill a pasta pot or large stockpot with 6 quarts of water, add 6 table-spoons of salt, and bring the water to a boil over high heat. If you are not using a pasta pot, place a colander in the sink or have a large wire strainer handy to lift the pasta out of the pot.

Put the ricotta in a small bowl and stir it vigorously with a spoon to fluff it up. Set it aside at room temperature while you cook the pasta.

Remove the *corzetti* from the refrigerator or freezer and drop them into the boiling water. Stir to prevent the pasta from sticking together, partially cover the pot so the water returns to a boil quickly and con-tinues boiling, and cook the pasta until it's al dente, about 2 minutes. About 1 minute before the pasta is done, place the sauce over high heat. Lift the pasta out of the cooking water, or reserve 1 cup of the water and drain the pasta, and immediately add it to the pan with the sauce. Add 2 tablespoons of the reserved water and cook the pasta with the sauce for 2 minutes, stirring gently with a rubber spatula so you don't tear the pasta, to stain the pasta with the sauce and thicken the sauce slightly, adding more of the reserved pasta water if necessary for the sauce to be glistening and easily coat the pasta. Turn off the heat and stir in the olives and parsley. Add the finishing-quality olive oil, stirring vigorously and shaking the pan to emulsify the sauce, tak-ing care not to tear the pasta in the process.

Spoon the *corzetti* and eggplant in the center of each of six plates, dividing them evenly, and spoon any sauce remaining in the pan over the pasta. Spoon 3 tablespoons of ricotta in one mound in the center of each serving of *corzetti,* and serve.

maltagliati with wild boar ragù

ild boar, called cinghiale, *is hunted and sold all over Umbria, so as a born-again Umbrian I would feel as if I were betraying my experience of Italy if I didn't include this ragù at my restaurant. Cutting the boar is the hardest part of this recipe, and it isn't hard at all. The ideal is to buy frozen wild boar and cut it while it's only partially defrosted, when it's easier to cut.*

MAKES 1 QUART OF RAGÙ, OR ENOUGH FOR 16 SERVINGS;
PASTA WITH SAUCE SERVES 6

SUGGESTED WINE PAIRING: MONTEFALCO ROSSO (UMBRIA)

To make the ragù, cut the meat into ½-inch cubes. Place the meat in a nonreactive baking dish, season it with the salt and pepper, and toss to coat the meat all over with the seasonings. Cover the dish with plastic wrap and refrigerate for at least 1 hour and up to overnight.

Combine the Soffritto, olive oil, anchovies, and rosemary in a large saucepan over low heat and cook for 2 to 3 minutes to soften the rosemary and meld the flavors. Increase the heat to medium high. Move the vegetables to create a bare spot in the pan, add the tomato paste to that spot, and cook for 1 minute, stirring, to caramelize the tomato paste slightly. Add the wine, increase the heat to high, and boil the wine until the pan is almost dry, about 15 minutes. Add the tomato sauce, 2 cups of the chicken stock, and the red pepper flakes, and bring the sauce to a simmer. Add the meat, return the sauce to a simmer, reduce the heat to low and simmer the ragù, adding more chicken stock from time to time to keep the ragù from getting too thick or sticking to the bottom of the pan, until the meat is tender, about 4 hours. To test for doneness, put a cube of meat on a plate. If you can smash it easily with the back of the spoon, it's done; otherwise, continue cooking. When the ragù is done, turn off the heat and let it rest for about 10 minutes.

Ladle 1 cup of the ragù into the bowl of a food processor fitted with a metal blade or the jar of a blender. Pulse several times to chop the meat but not quite purée it. Return the chopped meat to the pan and stir to combine. If necessary, return the pot to medium heat and cook the ragù until the sauce is thick. Use ragù or allow it to cool to room temperature, transfer it to an airtight container, and refrigerate for up

for the wild boar ragù

- 2 pounds boneless boar shoulder or lamb or venison shoulder
- 2 teaspoons kosher salt, plus more to taste
- ½ teaspoon freshly ground black pepper
- 1 cup Soffritto (page 28)
- 2 tablespoons extra-virgin olive oil
- 4 anchovy fillets (preferably salt-packed), rinsed, backbones removed if salt-packed, and finely chopped
- 1 tablespoon finely chopped fresh rosemary needles
- 1 tablespoon double-concentrated tomato paste
- 2 cups dry red wine
- 1½ cups Basic Tomato Sauce (page 24)
- 3 cups Basic Chicken Stock (page 27), plus more as needed
- 1 teaspoon red pepper flakes

(continued)

maltagliati with wild boar ragù *(continued)*

to three days; freeze it for as long as three months. Warm the ragù over medium heat before serving, adding enough water to loosen it to a saucelike consistency.

To finish and serve the pasta, fill a pasta pot or large stockpot with 6 quarts of water, add 6 tablespoons of salt, and bring the water to a boil over high heat. If you are not using a pasta pot, place a colander in the sink or have a wire strainer handy.

While the water is coming to a boil, combine 1½ cups of the ragù with the tomato sauce, butter, and ½ cup of the salted pasta water in a large sauté pan over medium heat. Cook the sauce, stirring occasionally, until the butter is melted and the sauce is warmed through, adding more pasta water if necessary to obtain a loose, saucelike consistency. Reduce the heat to low while you cook the *maltagliati*.

Remove the *maltagliati* from the refrigerator or freezer and drop them into the boiling water. Stir to prevent them from sticking together, partially cover the pot so the water returns to a boil quickly and continues boiling, and cook the pasta until it's al dente, about 2 minutes. About 1 minute before the pasta is done, place the sauce over high heat. Lift the pasta out of the cooking water, or reserve 1 cup of the water and drain the pasta, and immediately add it to the pan with the sauce. Cook the pasta with the sauce for 2 minutes, stirring gently with a rubber spatula so you don't tear the pasta, to stain the pasta with the sauce, adding some of the reserved pasta water if the pasta is dry and sticky instead of slippery and glistening. Turn off the heat and gently stir in the parsley. Add the finishing-quality olive oil, stirring vigorously and shaking the pan to emulsify the sauce, taking care not to tear the pasta in the process. Add the grated Parmigiano-Reggiano and pecorino romano and stir to combine.

Spoon the *maltagliati* in the center of each of six plates, dividing them evenly, and spoon any sauce remaining in the pan over the pasta. Use a microplane or another fine grater to grate a light layer of Parmigiano-Reggiano over each plate, and serve.

for finishing and serving the pasta

Kosher salt

¾ cup Basic Tomato Sauce (page 24)

3 teaspoons unsalted butter

12 ounces *Maltagliati* (page 169)

⅓ cup thinly sliced fresh Italian parsley leaves

¼ cup plus 2 tablespoons finishing-quality extra-virgin olive oil

3 tablespoons freshly grated Parmigiano-Reggiano, plus a wedge for grating

3 tablespoons freshly grated pecorino romano

gnocchi with duck ragù

*W*e serve this rich, meaty ragù alternately with gnocchi (page 172) and pici (page 168). When the ragù is tossed with gnocchi, the flavor becomes like a rich and delicious meat-and-potatoes dish. It manages to be exotic and familiar at the same time. We use only duck legs and not the whole duck because the meat from the legs is more moist and lends itself better to long cooking. You will probably have to special-order the legs from your poultry purveyor, so when you do, make sure to ask for the livers, too. Alternatively, you can make this ragù with one whole duck, cut into pieces. Not only will this be easier to find but also you're guaranteed to get the liver with it.

MAKES 1 QUART OF RAGÙ, OR ENOUGH FOR 16 SERVINGS;
GNOCCHI WITH SAUCE SERVES 8

SUGGESTED WINE PAIRING: BARBERA D'ASTI (PIEDMONT)

*P*lace the duck legs in a nonreactive baking dish and season them with the salt and pepper on all sides. Cover the dish with plastic wrap and refrigerate for at least an hour and up to overnight.

Heat the oil and garlic together over medium-high heat in a large Dutch oven or large sauté pan and cook the garlic, stirring constantly to prevent it from browning, until it's softened, 2 to 3 minutes. Stir in the Soffritto and cook it for 1 minute. Move the vegetables to create a bare spot in the pan, add the tomato paste to that spot, and cook for 1 minute, stirring, to caramelize the tomato paste slightly. Add the wine, chicken stock, livers, sage, and duck legs and bring the liquid to a boil. Reduce the heat and simmer the duck legs for about 1½ hours, until the duck is tender and falling off the bones. Turn off the heat and let the duck cool to room temperature in the braising liquid.

Transfer the duck and the braising liquid to an airtight container, or cover the pot, and refrigerate until you are ready to make the ragù. You can make the duck to this point up to a day in advance.

Remove the legs from the braising liquid, and pour the liquid into a medium saucepan. Pull the meat off the bones, discarding the bones, and shred the meat, picking out and discarding any tendons or other unsavory bits as you work the meat through your fingers. Add the meat to the pan with the braising liquid and bring the liquid to a boil over high heat. Reduce the heat and simmer the meat in the liquid, breaking it up as it cooks, until the liquid is reduced and the sauce has

for the duck ragù

4 duck legs (or one whole duck, cut up), skinned, cut apart at the joint, visible fat removed, rinsed and patted dry (about 1¾ pounds)

1½ teaspoons kosher salt, plus more to taste

½ teaspoon freshly ground black pepper, plus more to taste

2 tablespoons extra-virgin olive oil

2 garlic cloves, thinly sliced

½ cup Soffritto (page 28)

5 tablespoons double-concentrated tomato paste

2 cups dry red wine

3 cups Basic Chicken Stock (page 27), enough to cover the duck legs by ½ inch

3½ ounces duck livers, finely chopped (about 2 livers), or chicken livers

4 fresh sage leaves

(continued)

a thick, ragù-like consistency. Taste for seasoning and add salt and pepper, if desired. Use the ragù or allow it to cool to room temperature, transfer it to an airtight container, and refrigerate it for up to three days; freeze it for as long as three months. Warm the ragù over medium heat before serving, adding enough water to loosen it to a saucelike consistency.

To finish the gnocchi, fill a pasta pot or large saucepan with 6 quarts of water, add 6 tablespoons salt, and bring it to a boil over high heat. If you are not using a pasta pot, place a colander in the sink or have a wire strainer handy for lifting the pasta out of the water.

While the water is coming to a boil, combine 2 cups of ragù with the tomato sauce, butter, and ½ cup of the salted pasta water in a large sauté pan over medium heat and cook, stirring occasionally, until the butter is melted and the sauce is warmed through, adding more of the pasta water, if necessary, to obtain a loose, saucelike consistency. Turn the heat off while you cook the gnocchi.

Remove the gnocchi from the refrigerator and drop them into the boiling water. Stir to prevent the gnocchi from sticking together, partially cover the pot so the water returns to a boil quickly and continues boiling, and cook the gnocchi for 2 to 3 minutes, until they float to the top. About 1 minute before the gnocchi is done, place the sauce over high heat. Lift the gnocchi out of the cooking water, or reserve 1 cup of the water and drain the gnocchi, and immediately add them to the pan with the sauce. Cook the gnocchi with the sauce for 2 minutes, stirring gently with a rubber spatula so you don't smash the gnocchi, adding some of the reserved water if necessary for the sauce to be glistening and to easily coat the gnocchi. Turn off the heat and gently stir in the parsley. Add the finishing-quality olive oil, stirring vigorously and shaking the pan to emulsify the sauce. Add the grated Parmigiano-Reggiano and pecorino romano and stir to combine.

Spoon the gnocchi onto each of eight plates, dividing them evenly, and spoon any sauce remaining in the pan over the gnocchi. Use a microplane or another fine grater to grate a light layer of Parmigiano-Reggiano over each plate, and serve.

**for finishing and
  serving the gnocchi**

Kosher salt

1 cup Basic Tomato Sauce
  (page 24)

1 tablespoon plus 1 teaspoon
  unsalted butter

28 ounces Gnocchi
  (page 172; about
  96 gnocchi) or 24 ounces
  Pici (page 168)

½ cup thinly sliced fresh
  Italian parsley leaves

½ cup finishing-quality
  extra-virgin olive oil

¼ cup freshly grated
  Parmigiano-Reggiano,
  plus a wedge for grating

¼ cup freshly grated pecorino
  romano

garganelli with ragù bolognese

*P*rior to his working at Del Posto, Matt went to Italy with Mario for a story for Gourmet. *The premise of the story was that Mario was taking his chefs and the general manager from Del Posto to Italy, specifically to the center of Emilia-Romagna, to show them what it was like to eat there. They ate sixty-two courses in five days and Matt had a lot of dishes to talk about, but the one he was most excited about was the ragù bolognese he had at Diana, a restaurant just outside the main* piazza *in Bologna. It was as if his eyes had just been opened. He called me right after that meal: "It was rich but delicate and with a touch of sweetness," he told me. When they got back to New York, while Matt was relegated to the soup station of the kitchen, Mark Ladner and Mark's team at Del Posto attempted to create a bolognese that captured the spirit of the one at Diana. When Matt tasted Mark's version, he called me again, excited: "They did it!" he said. "They nailed it." And that—the Del Posto version of the Diana bolognese—was what Matt was going for when we opened Mozza. Having eaten at Diana myself, I can also tell you that Matt nailed it. When making bolognese, the most important thing is to go slow. You never want the meat to cook directly against the pan, because you want to braise the meat, not brown it. The "secret" to it is the Soffritto, which takes several hours to make—so give yourself time.* This *is slow food!*

MAKES OVER 1 QUART OF RAGÙ OR ENOUGH FOR MORE THAN 16 SERVINGS; PASTA WITH SAUCE SERVES 6

SUGGESTED WINE PAIRING: SANGIOVESE DI ROMAGNA (EMILIA-ROMAGNA)

*T*o make the ragù, combine the oil and garlic in the bowl of a miniature food processor fitted with a metal blade or the jar of a blender and purée. Add the pancetta and purée, stopping to scrape down the sides of the bowl or jar occasionally, until the ingredients form a homogenous paste. Transfer the pancetta-garlic paste to a large sauté pan and cook over medium heat until the fat from the pancetta is rendered, about 5 minutes, stirring constantly to prevent the garlic from browning. Stir in the Soffritto and cook for about 1 minute. Move the vegetables to create a bare spot in the pan, add the tomato paste to that spot, and cook for 1 minute, stirring, to caramelize the tomato paste slightly. Add the veal and pork; season with the salt, pepper, and nutmeg; and cook, stirring occasionally, until all the juices released from the meat have cooked off and the pan is almost dry, about 10 minutes. Add the wine, increase the heat to

for the ragù bolognese

2 tablespoons extra-virgin olive oil

8 garlic cloves

2½ ounces pancetta, roughly chopped or ground

1 cup Soffritto (page 28)

½ of a 4.5-ounce tube (¼ cup plus 1 tablespoon) double-concentrated tomato paste

1 pound ground veal

1 pound ground pork

2 teaspoons kosher salt, plus more to taste

(continued)

medium high, and cook until the wine has evaporated and the pan is almost dry, about 10 minutes. Add the chicken stock, bring it to a simmer, reduce the heat, and simmer the meat with the stock for about 2 hours, stirring occasionally to prevent the meat from sticking to the bottom of the pan, until the stock has almost all cooked off but the pan is not completely dry. Add the milk and simmer until the ragù returns to a thick, saucy consistency, 30 to 40 minutes. Use the ragù, or allow it to cool to room temperature, transfer it to an airtight container, and refrigerate it for up to three days; freeze it for as long as three months. Warm the ragù over medium heat before serving, adding enough water to loosen it to a saucelike consistency.

To finish and serve the pasta, fill a pasta pot or large stockpot with 6 quarts of water, add 6 tablespoons of salt, and bring the water to a boil over high heat. If you are not using a pasta pot, place a colander in the sink or have a wire strainer handy for lifting the pasta out of the water.

While the water is coming to a boil, combine 1½ cups of the ragù, the chicken stock, and butter in a large sauté pan over medium heat. Stir the ingredients to combine and heat, stirring occasionally, until the butter is melted and the sauce is warmed through, adding more chicken stock, if necessary, to obtain a loose, sauce consistency. Turn off the heat while you cook the garganelli.

Remove the garganelli from the refrigerator or freezer and drop them into the boiling water. Stir to prevent the pasta from sticking together, partially cover the pot so the water returns to a boil quickly and continues boiling, and cook the pasta until it's al dente, about 2 minutes. About 1 minute before the pasta is done, place the sauce over high heat. Lift the pasta out of the cooking water, or reserve 1 cup of the water and drain the pasta, and immediately add it to the pan with the sauce. Cook the pasta with the sauce for 2 minutes, stirring gently with a rubber spatula so you don't tear the pasta, to stain the pasta with the sauce, adding some of the reserved pasta water if the pasta is dry and sticky instead of slippery and glistening. Turn off the heat and add the finishing-quality olive oil, stirring vigorously and shaking the pan to emulsify the sauce. Add the grated Parmigiano-Reggiano and pecorino romano and stir to combine.

Pile the garganelli in the center of each of six plates, dividing them evenly, and spoon any sauce remaining in the pan over the pasta. Use a microplane or another fine grater to grate a light layer of Parmigiano-Reggiano over each plate, and serve.

½ teaspoon freshly ground black pepper
¼ teaspoon freshly grated nutmeg
1 cup dry white wine
3 cups Basic Chicken Stock (page 27)
¾ cup whole milk

for finishing and serving the pasta
Kosher salt
¾ cup Basic Chicken Stock (page 27), plus more as needed or pasta-cooking water
3 teaspoons unsalted butter
12 ounces Garganelli (page 170)
6 tablespoons finishing-quality extra-virgin olive oil
3 tablespoons freshly grated Parmigiano-Reggiano, plus a wedge for grating
3 tablespoons freshly grated pecorino romano

stinging nettle tagliatelle with lamb ragù, taggiasche olives, and mint

*T*raditionally, lamb shanks such as those in this recipe would be braised and served in all their glory, and subsequently, making lamb ragù would be a way to turn a relatively small amount of left-over meat into tomorrow night's pasta dinner. We braise the lamb just so that we can pull it apart and turn it into ragù. It's a decadent thing to do, and results in a luxurious and delicious pasta. Enjoy.

MAKES 1 QUART OF RAGÙ OR ENOUGH FOR 16 SERVINGS;
PASTA WITH SAUCE SERVES 6

SUGGESTED WINE PAIRING: LACRIMA DI MORRO D'ALBA (THE MARCHES)

*T*o marinate the lamb, combine the olive oil, rosemary, garlic, salt, and pepper in a small bowl. Place the lamb shanks in a nonreactive baking dish or a large bowl and rub the marinade into all sides of the lamb. Cover the dish or bowl with plastic wrap and place it in the refrigerator to marinate the lamb for at least several hours and up to overnight.

To make the ragù adjust the oven rack to the middle position and preheat the oven to 350°F.

Heat 2 tablespoons of the olive oil in a large Dutch oven or large, ovenproof sauté pan over medium-high heat until the oil is almost smoking and slides easily in the pan, 2 to 3 minutes. Remove the lamb from the marinade and wipe off the marinade. Sear the lamb shanks, turning the shanks so they brown evenly, about 15 minutes total. Remove the lamb shanks to a plate. Add the remaining ¼ cup of olive oil to the pan you cooked the lamb in and heat until it's almost smoking. Add the onion, carrot, and celery, and sauté, stirring often, until the vegetables are soft and the onion is tender and translucent, 8 to 10 minutes. Add the garlic and cook for about 1 minute, stirring constantly to prevent it from browning. Add the anchovies and bay leaf. Move the vegetables to create a bare spot in the pan, add the tomato paste to that spot, and cook for 1 minute, stirring, to caramelize the tomato paste slightly. Add the wine, increase the heat to high, and boil the wine for about 2 minutes, until it has reduced by half. Add the tomatoes and their juice and cook for about 2 minutes to meld the flavors. Return the lamb shanks to the pan as well as any juices that have released onto the plate they were resting on. Add enough stock so that only 1 inch of the lamb is visible. Nestle the rosemary sprig between the shanks. If you have commercial-grade plastic wrap, which won't

for marinating the lamb
½ cup extra-virgin olive oil
¼ cup chopped fresh rosemary needles
¼ cup chopped fresh garlic
1 heaping tablespoon of kosher salt
1 teaspoon freshly ground black pepper
2 lamb hind shanks (about 1½ pounds each)

for the ragù
¼ cup plus 2 tablespoons extra-virgin olive oil
1 yellow Spanish onion, roughly chopped (about 1-inch pieces)
1 large carrot, peeled and roughly chopped (about 1-inch pieces)
1 celery rib, roughly chopped (about 1-inch pieces)
3 garlic cloves, smashed and roughly chopped
3 to 4 anchovy fillets (preferably salt-packed), rinsed and backbones removed if salt-packed

melt in the oven, cover the pan with plastic wrap. In either case, cover the pan tightly with aluminum foil and place the lid on the pot if it has one. Place the pan in the oven and cook the lamb until it is tender and falling off the bones, about 3½ hours. Remove the pan from the oven and remove the foil and plastic if you are using it, being careful not to burn yourself from the steam that will arise from the pan. Set aside to allow the lamb shanks to cool to room temperature in the braising liquid; transfer to an airtight container and refrigerate until you are ready to make the ragù.

Lift the lamb shanks from the braising liquid to a plate. Pour the liquid through a fine-mesh strainer into a medium saucepan, pressing down on the vegetables in the strainer to extract as much liquid as you can from them, and discard the contents of the strainer. Skim the fat from the braising liquid. Remove and discard the fat cap before proceeding.

Pull the meat off the lamb shanks and carefully pick through the meat to remove any sinew and bones. Put the pulled meat in the saucepan with the braising liquid and bring to a boil over high heat. Reduce the heat to medium and cook the lamb with the braising liquid, stirring to prevent the sauce from sticking to the bottom of the pan, and breaking up the meat as it cooks, until the meat and sauce have combined into a thick, saucelike consistency. The time will vary from 10 to 20 minutes depending on how much braising liquid you started with. Use the ragù or allow it to cool to room temperature, transfer to an airtight container, and refrigerate for up to three days; freeze it for as long as three months. Warm the ragù over medium heat before serving, adding enough water to loosen it to a saucelike consistency.

If you are not using a pasta pot, place a colander in the sink or have tongs handy for lifting the pasta out of the water.

While the water is coming to a boil, combine 1½ cups of the ragù, the tomato sauce, butter, and chicken stock in a large sauté pan over medium heat. Stir the ingredients to combine and heat, stirring occasionally, until the butter is melted and the sauce is warmed through. Reduce the heat while you are cooking the tagliatelle.

Remove the tagliatelle from the refrigerator or freezer and drop it into the boiling water. Stir to prevent the strands from sticking together, partially cover the pot so the water returns to a boil quickly and continues boiling, and cook the pasta until it's al dente, about 2 minutes. About 1 minute before the pasta is done, place the sauce over high heat. Lift the pasta out of the cooking water, or reserve 1 cup of the water and drain the pasta, and immediately add it to the pan with the sauce. Cook the pasta with the sauce for 2 minutes, stirring

1 dried bay leaf

1 tablespoon double-concentrated tomato paste

1 cup dry white wine

1 14 ounce-can whole peeled tomatoes (preferably San Marzano), crushed (including juice)

4 cups Basic Chicken Stock (page 27), or as needed

1 long fresh rosemary sprig

for finishing and serving the pasta

1½ cups Basic Tomato Sauce (page 24)

2 tablespoons unsalted butter

¾ cup Basic Chicken Stock (page 27)

12 ounces Tagliatelle (page 168)

½ cup pitted Taggiasche or Niçoise olives (about 40 olives)

⅓ cup thinly sliced fresh Italian parsley leaves

⅓ cup thinly sliced fresh mint leaves

¼ cup plus 2 tablespoons finishing-quality extra-virgin olive oil

3 tablespoons freshly grated Parmigiano-Reggiano, plus a wedge for grating

3 tablespoons freshly grated pecorino romano

gently so you don't tear the pasta, to stain the pasta with the sauce, adding some of the reserved pasta water if the pasta is dry and sticky instead of slippery and glistening. Turn off the heat and gently stir in the olives, parsley, and mint. Add the finishing-quality olive oil, stirring vigorously and shaking the pan to emulsify the sauce. Add the grated Parmigiano-Reggiano and pecorino romano and stir to combine.

Use tongs to lift the tagliatelle out of the pan and onto the center of each of six plates, dividing the pasta evenly, and twirling it as it falls onto the plate to form a tight mound. Spoon any sauce left in the pan over the pasta and use a microplane or another fine grater to grate a light layer of Parmigiano-Reggiano over each plate, and serve.

ricotta gnudi with chanterelles

*G*nudi *are little dumplings, like gnocchi, but made with ricotta instead of potatoes. Most places don't do gnudi justice. They are often mushy and heavy, instead of light and fluffy, like these. This recipe makes 36 to 40 gnudi, or enough for 6 to 8 people as a first course. The dough does not keep well, so you need to plan on serving a crowd, or serve hearty, main-dish-size portions.*

SERVES 6 TO 8

SUGGESTED WINE PAIRING: ALBANA DI ROMAGNA SECCO (EMILIA-ROMAGNA)

*T*o make the gnudi, combine the ricotta, Parmigiano-Reggiano, egg, butter, and nutmeg in a large mixing bowl and use a rubber spatula to gently fold the ingredients together. Sprinkle the flour over the ricotta mixture and gently fold in the flour from the edges inward, scraping down the sides of the bowl as you work; you are not really working the dough as much as you are simply allowing the ricotta mixture to absorb the flour. When all the flour has been absorbed and it is no longer visible, use one hand to gently bring the dough together into a ball, dusting the sides of the bowl and the dough lightly with flour as you work. Roll the dough around in the floured bowl so the outside isn't sticky.

Dust a baking sheet with flour. Gently tear off a ½-ounce piece of dough, dust your hands lightly with flour, and roll the dough gently into a ball slightly smaller than a Ping-Pong ball and place it on the baking sheet. Repeat until you have rolled all of the dough. Cover the baking sheet with plastic wrap and refrigerate for up to 8 hours.

for the gnudi

1 pound fresh ricotta cheese

¼ cup freshly grated
   Parmigiano-Reggiano

1 extra-large egg,
   lightly beaten

2 teaspoons unsalted butter,
   melted and cooled slightly

¼ teaspoon freshly
   ground nutmeg

1 cup all-purpose flour,
   plus more for dusting

(continued)

To finish and serve the gnudi, fill a large stockpot with 6 quarts of water, add 6 tablespoons of salt, and bring the water to a boil over high heat. If you are not using a pasta pot, place a colander in the sink or have a wire strainer handy for lifting the gnudi out of the water.

While the water is coming to a boil, make the sauce. Heat the olive oil in 2 large sauté pans over medium-high heat until the oil is almost smoking and slides easily in the pans, 2 to 3 minutes. Add the mushrooms, cut side down, dividing them evenly between the two pans. Season the mushrooms with salt and sauté without turning them and stirring them as little as possible without burning them, until they are golden brown. Turn the mushrooms and cook them for about 1 minute on the other side to brown them slightly. Reduce the heat to low, add the garlic and thyme, season the garlic with salt, and cook for 30 seconds to 1 minute, stirring constantly so the garlic doesn't brown. Add the butter, dividing it evenly between the pans, and add ½ cup of fresh water to each pan. Increase the heat to medium to melt the butter and bring the liquid to a simmer, stirring constantly with a rubber spatula to emulsify the sauce. Add the spinach in handfuls, dividing it evenly and gently folding it in with the mushrooms until it barely wilts. Turn off the heat while you cook the gnudi.

Remove the gnudi from the refrigerator and drop them into the boiling water. Stir to prevent the gnudi from sticking together, partially cover the pot so the water returns to a boil quickly and continues boiling, and cook until they float to the top, about 4 minutes. About 1 minute before the gnudi are done, place the sauce over high heat. Lift the gnudi out of the cooking water or drain them and immediately add them to the pans with the sauce, dividing them evenly. Cook the pasta with the sauce for 2 minutes, stirring gently with a rubber spatula so you don't smash the gnudi, to coat them with the sauce, adding some fresh water if necessary for the sauce to be glistening and easily coat the gnudi. (Adding the water you cooked the gnudi in will make the dish too salty.) Add the finishing-quality olive oil evenly to the two pans and simmer for another minute, stirring vigorously, until the sauce is emulsified and creamy looking.

Pushing the gnudi to the side, spoon some of the mushrooms and spinach from the pans into the center of each plate to create a bed for the gnudi. Divide the gnudi among the plates, and spoon any vegetables or sauce left in the pan over the gnudi. Use a microplane or another fine grater to grate a light layer of Parmigiano-Reggiano over each plate, and serve.

**for the sauce and
for serving the gnudi**
Kosher salt
½ cup extra-virgin olive oil
1 pound chanterelles, cleaned and cut into rough 2-inch segments (if the mushrooms are less than 2 inches across, leave them whole)
8 large garlic cloves, thinly sliced lengthwise
2 teaspoons fresh thyme leaves
½ cup (1 stick) unsalted butter, cut into pieces
10 cups baby spinach (about 2 pounds)
8 teaspoons (2 tablespoons plus 2 teaspoons) finishing-quality extra-virgin olive oil
Wedge of Parmigiano-Reggiano, for grating

squid ink chitarra with sea urchin, dungeness crab, and jalapeño

att makes a point to return to Italy every year for inspiration. On a recent trip, he happily returned with the idea for this sea urchin pasta dish, the only cold pasta we serve. I love sea urchins, or ricci. They are a delicacy of many seaside regions in Italy, such as Puglia and Sicily, but many aficionados say that the best sea urchins come from the waters off Southern California. Cooked lump crab meat is readily available at seafood stores and in the seafood sections of high-end grocery stores.

SERVES 4

SUGGESTED WINE PAIRING: VERMENTINO DEI COLLI DI LUNI (LIGURIA)

ombine the pine nuts, jalapeño peppers, onion, and olive oil in the bowl of a food processor or the jar of a blender and purée to form a paste. Scrape the paste into a bowl.

Fill a large saucepan or pasta pot with 6 quarts of water, add 6 table-spoons salt, and bring it to a boil over high heat. If you are not using a pasta pot, place a colander in the sink or have a pair of tongs handy to lift the pasta out of the water. Fill a medium bowl with ice water.

Reserve 4 of the best-looking sea urchin tongues for garnish and put the remaining 12 tongues, the crab meat, and ¼ cup of the jalapeño pesto in separate piles in a medium bowl, discarding the remaining pesto or reserving it for another use. Drizzle the pesto with ½ cup of the finishing-quality olive oil and set aside at room temperature while you cook the pasta.

Remove the *chitarra* from the refrigerator or freezer and drop it into the boiling water. Stir to prevent the strands from sticking together, partially cover the pot so the water returns to a boil quickly and con-tinues boiling, and cook the pasta until it's al dente, about 2 minutes. Lift the pasta out of the water or drain it and plunge it in the ice water, leaving it there for 5 or 10 seconds to stop it from cooking. Use tongs to lift the pasta out of the ice water, and transfer it to the bowl with the sea urchin and crab meat. Using a rubber spatula, gently fold the pasta to coat it with the sauce. Drizzle the lemon juice and sprinkle the sea salt over the pasta and gently fold the pasta to distribute the seasonings evenly.

Use tongs to lift the *chitarra* out of the bowl and onto the center of each of four plates, dividing the pasta evenly, and twirling it as it falls

¼ cup Toasted Pine Nuts (see page 63)

6 jalapeño peppers, stems removed

½ cup diced onion (about ½ a small onion)

¼ cup extra-virgin olive oil

Kosher salt

16 whole sea urchin tongues

8 ounces lump crab meat

½ cup finishing-quality extra-virgin olive oil, plus more for drizzling

½ pound black Spaghetti *alla Chitarra* (page 172), or quality store-bought squid ink pasta

2 teaspoons fresh lemon juice

1 teaspoon Maldon sea salt or another flaky sea salt, such as fleur de sel, plus more for topping the pasta

onto the plate to form a tight mound. Spoon the sea urchin and crab meat remaining in the bowl over the pasta. Place one of the reserved sea urchin tongues on top of each serving of pasta, drizzle ½ teaspoon of finishing-quality olive oil over and around each plate, top with a pinch of sea salt, and serve.

spaghetti alla gricia

I get really excited to be able to offer something that other restaurants are not offering, and that our clientele is not familiar with. So I was really excited when I was introduced to Spaghetti alla Gricia, spaghetti with guanciale and—depending on who you ask—maybe onion on a recent trip to Rome, at a trattoria known for traditional renditions of classic dishes, Al Moro. Alla Gricia is also known as "Amatriciana in bianco" because it is a "white," tomatoless version of that classic pasta dish. This is one case where I feel that substituting pancetta for guanciale just won't do. If you can't get guanciale where you live, find a mail-order source for it. It's worth it. And until the guanciale is delivered, make something else.

SERVES 4

SUGGESTED WINE PAIRING: CIRCEO ROSSO (LAZIO)

*F*ill a pasta pot or a large stockpot with 6 quarts of water, add 6 tablespoons of salt, and bring the water to a boil over high heat. If you are not using a pasta pot, put a colander in the sink or have a pair of tongs handy for lifting the pasta out of the water.

Cut the onion in half, separate the layers, and cut each layer into petals that are 1 inch wide across the middle. Put the onion petals in a large sauté pan with 1 cup of water and a big pinch of salt and cook the onion over high heat until the water evaporates, about 5 minutes. Add the *guanciale* and olive oil and cook over medium-high heat until the *guanciale* is crisp, about 3 minutes. Remove the pan from heat and add another cup of water, the red pepper flakes, and black pepper. Turn off the heat while you cook the spaghetti.

Drop the spaghetti into the boiling water, stir to prevent the strands from sticking together, partially cover the pot so the water returns to a

Kosher salt

1 large red onion

6 ounces *guanciale,* cut into ¼-inch-thick, 2-inch-long batons

¼ cup extra-virgin olive oil

1 teaspoon red pepper flakes

1 teaspoon fresh coarsely ground black pepper

12 ounces spaghetti

1 cup whole fresh Italian parsley leaves

2 tablespoons freshly grated Parmigiano-Reggiano

2 tablespoons freshly grated pecorino romano, plus a wedge for grating

boil quickly and continues boiling, and cook the pasta, using the time indicated on the package as a guide, until it's al dente. About 1 minute before the pasta is done, place the sauce over high heat. Lift the pasta out of the cooking water, or reserve 1 cup of the water and drain the pasta, and immediately add it to the pan with the sauce. Cook the pasta with the sauce for 2 minutes, stirring with a rubber spatula or tongs, to coat the pasta with the sauce, adding some of the reserved pasta water if the pasta is dry and sticky instead of slippery and glistening. Turn off the heat and stir in the parsley. Add the grated Parmigiano-Reggiano and pecorino romano and stir to combine.

Use tongs to lift the spaghetti out of the pan and onto the center of each of four plates, dividing the pasta evenly, and twirling it as it falls onto the plate to form a tight mound. Spoon any sauce left in the pan over the pasta and use a microplane or another fine grater to grate a light layer of pecorino romano over each plate, and serve.

linguine with clams, pancetta, and spicy fresno chiles

 att added pancetta to this classic dish. It's such a perfect addition that it feels as if it's always been there.

SERVES 4

SUGGESTED WINE PAIRING: VERMENTINO RIVIERA LIGURE DI PONENTE (LIGURIA)

Cut off and discard the stems from the chiles, cut in half, and place them in the bowl of a food processor fitted with a metal blade. Add the red onion, garlic cloves, and 2 tablespoons of the olive oil and purée, wiping down the sides of the bowl with a rubber spatula, if necessary. Use, or transfer to an airtight container for up to several days.

Place the yellow onion in a small saucepan with enough water to cover by 1 inch. Bring the water to a boil, reduce the heat, and simmer for about 1 hour or until the onion is mushy. Drain the onion, reserving the water, and transfer the onion to the bowl of a food processor fitted with a metal blade or the jar of a blender. Purée the onion, adding the reserved cooking water as needed to make a smooth purée.

4 Fresno chiles (red jalapeño peppers)
1/2 cup roughly chopped red onion (about 1/2 small onion)
4 garlic cloves, plus 1/4 cup thinly sliced garlic (about 8 large cloves)
1/4 cup extra-virgin olive oil
1/2 large yellow Spanish onion, diced (about 1 cup)

(continued)

Fill a pasta pot or a large stockpot with 6 quarts of water, add 6 tablespoons of salt, and bring the water to a boil over high heat. If you are not using a pasta pot, put a colander in the sink or have a pair of tongs handy for lifting the pasta out of the water.

While the water is coming to a boil, combine 2 cups of the wine and the clams in a large sauté pan over high heat. Cover the pan and cook the clams until they steam open, 3 to 4 minutes. Remove the clams from the liquid, discarding any that haven't opened. Strain the liquid through a fine-mesh strainer and reserve the liquid. Shuck half of the clams and leave the other half in their shells.

Combine the pancetta and 2 tablespoons of the olive oil in a large sauté pan over medium-high heat and cook, stirring the pancetta to brown it evenly, until the fat is rendered, about 5 minutes. Push the pancetta to one side and add the sliced garlic to the bare side of the pan. Season the garlic with salt, add ½ cup of the puréed onion (discarding or reserving the rest for another use), and cook the garlic and onion purée for about 1 minute, until the garlic is fragrant and the water has cooked out of the purée. Stir in 3 tablespoons of the chile paste and cook for 30 seconds. Add the remaining ½ cup of wine, ½ cup of the reserved liquid you cooked the clams in, and ½ cup of fresh water. Turn off the heat and add the scallions but don't stir them in. Turn off the heat while you cook the pasta.

Drop the linguine into the boiling water, stir to prevent the strands from sticking together, partially cover the pot so the water returns to a boil quickly and continues boiling, and cook the pasta, using the time indicated on the package as a guide, until it's al dente. About 1 minute before the pasta is done, place the sauce over high heat. Lift the pasta out of the cooking water, or reserve 1 cup of the water and drain the pasta, and immediately add it to the pan with the sauce. Cook the pasta with the sauce for 2 minutes, stirring with a rubber spatula or tongs, to coat the pasta with the sauce, adding some of the reserved pasta water if the pasta is dry and sticky instead of slippery and glistening. Turn off the heat and stir in the parsley. Drizzle in the finishing-quality olive oil.

Divide the clams that are still in their shells among four large soup plates or pasta plates. Use tongs to lift the linguine out of the pan and on top of the clams, dividing the pasta evenly, and twirling it as it falls onto the plate to form a tight mound. Spoon any sauce or clams left in the pan over the pasta, and serve.

Kosher salt

2½ cups dry white wine

48 littleneck clams (about 4½ pounds)

½ pound pancetta, cut into batons ¼ inch thick and 2 inches long

8 scallions, thinly sliced on an extreme bias starting at the green ends and moving toward the root ends (white and green parts)

12 ounces dry linguine

½ cup thinly sliced fresh Italian parsley leaves

4 teaspoons (1 tablespoon plus 1 teaspoon) finishing-quality extra-virgin olive oil

bavette cacio e pepe

This is a very simple Roman pasta dish made with nothing but black pepper and pecorino romano cheese. We believe in leaving traditional dishes alone, but we did make a couple of changes to this dish. We use bavette, *in place of spaghetti, which is the shape traditionally used. And we cut the pecorino with Parmigiano because pecorino is so pungent that it can be overwhelming on its own. The pepper for this dish must be coarsely ground. I recommend you use Tellicherry peppercorns, a fragrant, flavorful variety from India. Coarsely grinding or cracking the pepper for this dish is the perfect excuse for breaking out the mortar and pestle.*

SERVES 4

 SUGGESTED WINE PAIRING: CESANESE DI OLEVANO ROMANO (LAZIO)

Fill a pasta pot or a large stockpot with 6 quarts of water, add 6 tablespoons of salt, and bring the water to a boil over high heat. If you are not using a pasta pot, put a colander in the sink or have a wire strainer handy to lift the pasta out of the pot. Drop the *bavette* into the boiling water, stir to prevent the strands from sticking together, partially cover the pot so the water returns to a boil quickly and continues boiling, and cook the pasta, using the time indicated on the package as a guide, until it's al dente.

While the pasta is cooking, combine the olive oil, pepper, and ½ cup of the pasta cooking water in a large sauté pan. About 1 minute before the pasta is done, place the sauce over high heat. Lift the pasta out of the cooking water, or reserve 1 cup of the water and drain the pasta, and immediately add the pasta to the pan with the sauce. Cook the pasta with the sauce for 2 minutes, stirring with a rubber spatula or tongs, to stain the pasta with the sauce, adding some of the reserved pasta water if the pasta is dry and sticky instead of slippery and glistening. Turn off the heat and let the pasta rest in the pan for 1 minute. (Letting the pasta rest before you add the cheese prevents it from melting and becoming stringy.) Add the grated Parmigiano-Reggiano and pecorino romano, stirring vigorously and shaking the pan until the oil and cheese form a homogenous, emulsified sauce. Drizzle the finishing-quality olive oil over the pasta and stir quickly to combine.

Use tongs to lift the *bavette* out of the pan and onto the center of each of four plates, dividing the pasta evenly, and twirling it as it falls onto the plate to form a tight mound. Spoon any sauce left in the pan over the pasta. Coarsely grind black pepper over the pasta, if desired, and serve.

Kosher salt

12 ounces *bavette* or linguine *fine*

½ cup extra-virgin olive oil

1 tablespoon plus 1 teaspoon fresh coarsley ground black pepper, plus more to taste

¼ cup freshly grated Parmigiano-Reggiano

¼ cup freshly grated pecorino romano

4 teaspoons finishing-quality extra-virgin olive oil

fiorentini with guanciale, tomato, and spicy pickled peppers

*M*att got the inspiration for this dish from the Whole Hog Dinner that the restaurant Oliveto, in Oakland, hosts every year for chefs, food professionals, and friends from all over the world. One year they served pasta with cured pork, pickled peppers, and tomato sauce, which was so good that when we got back to Los Angeles, Matt decided to make his own version.

Fiorentini *means "Florentine," but here refers to a twisted short pasta shape made by Setar, an artisanal pasta producer in Napoli. If you can't find it, use another dried, artisanally produced pasta in its place, such as* maccheroni alla chitarra, *a big tube-shaped pasta from Napoli. The tubes collapse when they cook so they're like empty ravioli.*

SERVES 4

SUGGESTED WINE PAIRING: LAMEZIA ROSSO (CALABRIA)

*F*ill a pasta pot or a large stockpot with 6 quarts of water, add 6 tablespoons of kosher salt, and bring the water to a boil over high heat. If you are not using a pasta pot, place a colander in the sink or have a wire strainer handy to lift the pasta out of the water.

Combine the olive oil and *guanciale* in a large sauté pan over medium-high heat and cook until the *guanciale* is golden brown and crisp, about 3 minutes. Add the garlic, reduce the heat to medium, and cook for about 1 minute, until the garlic is light golden and fragrant, stirring constantly to prevent it from burning. Add the *passata*, sugar, and 1 teaspoon kosher salt and cook for about 1 minute, to dissolve the sugar and warm the sauce. Turn off the heat and add the basil while you cook the pasta.

Drop the pasta into the boiling water, stir to prevent it from sticking together, partially cover the pot so the water returns to a boil quickly and continues boiling, and cook the pasta, using the time indicated on the package as a guide, until it's al dente. About 1 minute before the pasta is done, place the sauce over high heat. Lift the pasta out of the cooking water, or reserve 1 cup of the water and drain the pasta, and immediately add it to the pan with the sauce. Cook the pasta with the sauce for 2 minutes, stirring with a rubber spatula to stain the pasta with the sauce, adding some of the reserved pasta water if the pasta is dry and sticky instead of slippery and glistening. Turn off the heat and

Kosher salt

1/4 cup extra-virgin olive oil

5 ounces *guanciale* or pancetta, cut into small dice

8 garlic cloves

2 cups *Passata di Pomodoro* (page 25) or tomato sauce

1 teaspoon sugar

12 large fresh basil leaves

12 ounces *fiorentini* or another artisanal pasta shape, such as *maccheroni alla chitarra*

1/2 cup thinly sliced fresh Italian parsley leaves

1/2 cup Spicy Pickled Peppers (page 204, or jarred), seeded and thinly sliced

1/4 cup finishing-quality extra-virgin olive oil

Wedge of Parmigiano-Reggiano, for grating

stir in the parsley and peppers. Add the finishing-quality olive oil, stirring vigorously and shaking the pan to emulsify the sauce.

Pile the pasta in the center of each of four plates, dividing it evenly, and spoon any sauce remaining in the pan over the pasta. Use a microplane or another fine grater to grate a light layer of Parmigiano-Reggiano over each plate, and serve.

spicy pickled peppers

*W*e pickle Fresno chiles (also called red jalapeño peppers) for the pasta dish Fiorentini *with* Guanciale, *Tomato, and Spicy Pickled Peppers (page 203). It seemed silly to have you pickle just enough peppers for one dish, since they will keep, refrigerated, for at least several weeks and probably much longer. Slice the peppers and add them to grilled cheese or sliced meat sandwiches, or use them in place of the roasted peppers on the pizza with White Anchovy, Tomato, and Spicy Fresno Chiles (page 139) or the Spicy Salami, Mozzarella, and Fresno Chiles pizza (page 140). If you can wait, the peppers are even better a few days after you make them.*

MAKES 1 QUART

*C*ombine the vinegar, honey, juniper berries, cloves, peppercorns, and bay leaves in a medium saucepan and bring the liquid to a simmer over high heat. Reduce the heat and simmer the brine for 10 minutes to meld the flavors. Add the chiles and increase the heat to high to return the brine to a boil. Reduce the heat and simmer the chiles until they soften slightly but still hold their shape, 4 to 6 minutes. Turn off the heat and set the chiles aside to cool in the brine. Use the chiles, or transfer them, along with the brining liquid, to an airtight container and refrigerate for up to several weeks.

4 cups white wine vinegar

2 tablespoons honey

1 teaspoon juniper berries

1 teaspoon whole cloves

2 teaspoons black peppercorns

2 dried bay leaves

¾ pound Fresno chiles (red jalapeño peppers), rinsed, stems left on

secondi

*S*econdo means "second" in Italian, and in this case *secondi* (plural for *secondo*) refers to main dishes. In Italy, *secondi* are very simple. Except at fancy restaurants, a typical *secondo* consists of grilled or roasted meat or fish, or a very simple braise. More often than not, *secondi* are served unadorned. You may get a slice of lemon or a few lettuce leaves on your plate, but none of the accompanying sides or sauces like those typically served in American restaurants. While our *secondi* are Italian in spirit, the way we present them, with a vegetable to enhance both the visual presentation of the dish and the diner's experience of eating it, and some kind of condiment, is more American.

   With the exception of a few items that are served as daily specials in the Pizzeria, the recipes in this chapter are for dishes served in the Osteria, which tend to be layered in terms of their flavor, and more refined in their presentations. This means that the majority of these recipes require several steps, often done over the course of two days. This is what makes the food at Mozza special, but it also requires organization and patience. My hope is that you look at the steps not as obstacles but as ways to spread the cooking out over time. If you do, I can assure you it will be a pleasure to put these dishes together for your family and friends.

grilled whole orata with fresh herbs and extra-virgin olive oil

The first time I ate at the Atelier of Joël Robuchon in Paris, I saw a whole fish delivered to another customer that I could tell had been boned and deep-fried. The skeleton had been removed but the head and tail, which flipped up so nicely on the plate, had been left intact. I watched in awe as the diner carved into the fish and ate it head to tail, without any of the usual fuss required to eat around the bones of a whole fish. I was so impressed that I told Matt I wanted to put something like that on the Osteria menu. He chose to grill the fish rather than fry it, but it's the same idea. We chose to use orata, *also called dorade or sea bream, a classic Mediterranean variety, because you see whole branzino on every Italian menu from California to Campagna, and we wanted to introduce our customers to something different. We wrap the fish in a fig leaf in the fall and a radicchio leaf the rest of the year before grilling it in order to contain the herbs stuffed inside the fish. Boning the fish is the most difficult part of making this dish—and I won't lie to you: it is tricky. I promise that with patience, a good sharp knife (preferably a fish knife or a 6-inch boning knife) and fish tweezers, you will be able to do it.*

SERVES 4

SUGGESTED WINE PAIRING: FIANO DI AVELLINO (CAMPANIA)

Fill a medium saucepan with water, bring it to a boil over high heat, and salt it to taste like the ocean, adding about 1 tablespoon of salt for each quart of water. Place a colander in the sink or have a wire strainer handy and fill a large bowl with ice water. If you are using fig leaves, make a triangular cut at the stem end to remove the tough portion of the stem, where it meets the leaf. Add the fig or radicchio leaves to the boiling water and cook for 1 minute, until they are slightly wilted and pliable. Drain the leaves in the colander or remove them with the strainer and plunge them into the ice water for about 1 minute, until they've cooled, to stop them from cooking. Remove the leaves from the water and place them on paper towels to drain. Pat the leaves with paper towels to dry completely.

Combine the chives, basil, parsley, and mint in a medium bowl. Drizzle with the ¼ cup olive oil, season with salt and pepper, and toss to combine the herbs and coat them with the seasonings.

Fill a large wide bowl with ice and place the fish on the ice.

Place one fish at a time on the cutting board, and if the fish still has

Kosher salt and freshly ground
  black pepper
8 large fig leaves or 12 large
  radicchio leaves
40 chives, trimmed and cut
  into 1-inch pieces
1¼ cups whole fresh basil
  leaves
1¼ cups whole fresh Italian
  parsley leaves
1¼ cups whole fresh mint
  leaves
¼ cup extra-virgin olive oil,
  plus more for the fish,
  leaves, and lemons
4 whole *orata* (dorade or
  sea bream), scaled and
  fins removed
2 lemons

Olio nuovo or finishing-quality
extra-virgin olive oil
Maldon sea salt or another
flaky sea salt, such as
fleur de sel

fins, use kitchen shears to cut them off; discard the fins. Place the fish so the belly is facing you and the head is facing left (if you are right-handed; left-handers put the fish in the opposite direction). With your knife parallel to the edge of the fish, the blade facing the belly, and the palm of your free hand resting on top of the fish to hold it in place, enter the fish under the tail, and make a decisive cut from the tail to the head along the top edge of the vertebrae, cutting deep enough to expose the spine. (You want to make that cut in one fluid motion; using a 6-inch knife, the cut will utilize the length of the knife.) Turn the fish so the belly is away from you. Again, with your free hand resting on the fish to hold it in place and the knife parallel to the fish, make an incision from the head to the tail in the same fashion as the cut you made on the belly side, again making sure the incision is on the top edge of the vertebrae, deep enough to expose the spine. Using kitchen shears parallel to the counter, enter the fish through the incision and, with small cuts perpendicular to the edge of the spine, snip the bones that are connected to the fillet to detach it from the spine. Return the fish to the original position with the belly closest to you and make the same snips with the scissors to the other side of the spine. Wipe down your cutting board with a wet towel and flip the fish, so the belly is still facing you but the bottom side is now facing up, and make the same incision to the belly that you did the first time, now working from the head to the tail, but still cutting on the top edge of the vertebrae, again cutting in one decisive motion, deep enough to expose the spine. (With the first set of incisions, you were releasing one fillet of the fish from the spine, and you are now releasing the other fillet.) Wipe down the cutting board again as needed, turn the fish so the spine is facing you, and make one last cut, from the head to the tail, as you did the other three cuts. Use the kitchen shears to make the same small cuts perpendicular to the edge of the spine to snip the bones that are connected to the second fillet to detach it from the spine. You have now detached both the top and bottom fillets from the spine. Turn the fish to its original position with the head facing left (for right-handers). With your knife perpendicular to the fish and the blade facing the tail, enter the fish through the incision that you made to cut through the skin of the top fillet so your knife ends up over the tail, releasing the top fillet at the tail so that the fish can be opened up. Flip the top fillet over the head of the fish to open the fish. Use the shears to snip through the spine at the head and tail ends of the fish and lift and discard the spine; the spine will come out in one full piece; if not, look for any bones that may still be attached to the fillets and snip them with your scissors. Run the knife underneath the rib cage, nes-

tled in the belly of the fish, to release the rib cage from the flesh and discard the rib cage. Using fish tweezers, remove and discard any visible bones from both fillets of fish. Place the fish on the ice and repeat, boning the remaining fish in the same way.

When you have boned all the fish, wipe down and dry the cutting board, and place one fish on the board, belly closest to you. Lift the top fillet of the *orata* to open it and expose the cavity, and stuff one quarter of the herb mixture (about 2 cups, loosely packed) inside. Close the fish over the herbs, place it back on the ice, and repeat with the remaining fish.

Lay two of the fig leaves or three of the radicchio leaves on a clean, dry cutting board. Lay one of the stuffed *orata* next to the leaves. Drizzle the fish with olive oil and drizzle the oil onto the leaf, making sure to get oil on the edges of the leaves, as it acts like glue, holding the leaves in place when you wrap them around the fish. Place the *orata* on the leaf at the edge closest to you and roll it away from you to wrap it with the leaves. Pat the leaves down to adhere and place the fish, sealed side down, in a nonreactive baking dish or on a large platter. Repeat with the remaining fish. When all the fish have been wrapped, place them, still on ice, in the refrigerator to chill for at least 10 minutes or up to several hours. You can prepare the fish up to this point up to two days in advance. Transfer them to a baking sheet or a plate, cover tightly with plastic wrap, and refrigerate until you are ready to use them.

Cut the lemons in half and cut ½ inch off the pointed ends so each lemon half has two flat surfaces. Brush both cut ends with olive oil.

Prepare a hot fire in a gas or charcoal grill or preheat a grill pan or heavy-bottomed skillet over high heat.

Remove the *orata* from the refrigerator and use a pastry brush to pat olive oil on both sides of each fish. (Don't brush the oil on or you might loosen the leaf.) Place the fish sealed side down on the grill or in the grill pan to cook for 7 to 8 minutes per side, turning carefully to keep the fish intact, until it is golden brown and the leaves are crisp.

While the fish are grilling, place the lemon halves with the larger, center side of the lemons facing down, on the grill or in the grill pan with the fish, for about 2 minutes, until golden brown. Turn and cook the smaller sides of the lemon for about 30 seconds just to warm them. Remove the *orata* to each of four plates and let them rest for 2 to 3 minutes before serving. Place one lemon half on each plate with the wider side facing up. Put bowls of *olio nuevo* or finishing-quality olive oil and sea salt on the side of each plate for people to personalize their fish, and serve.

pan-roasted sea trout with umbrian lentils and red cabbage sottaceto

I am a red wine drinker, so any fish preparation that can be enjoyed with red wine, such as this one, which is served with a rich lentil stew and pickled red cabbage, is a winner for me. Sea trout is a freshwater fish that drifted into the sea, so although it is trout, it looks and tastes like it wants to be salmon with pink flesh and the same moist, oily quality that you get from really good salmon. Sea trout is much more consistent in quality than salmon and also less expensive, so I hope you will enjoy this salmon alternative. Sottaceto means "pickled" in Italian. The cabbage here is slow-cooked in balsamic vinegar, so it's like a pickle, which cuts through the richness of the lentils and the fattiness of the fish. The recipes for the cabbage and lentils both make more than you will need for four servings of fish. You can double the number of fish fillets you prepare, or serve the remaining cabbage and lentils on the side. Since the cabbage is pickled, it will keep, refrigerated, for at least a week.

SERVES 4

SUGGESTED WINE PAIRING: ORVIETO SUPERIORE (UMBRIA)

To make the cabbage, warm the oil and garlic together in a large nonstick sauté pan over medium heat. Season with salt and sauté the garlic, stirring constantly to prevent it from browning, for about 2 minutes, until it begins to soften. Add the cabbage, season with salt and pepper, and cook, stirring frequently, for about 2 minutes, to wilt it slightly. Reduce the heat to low, add the vinegar, and simmer the cabbage 35 to 45 minutes, until the vinegar is reduced by about two-thirds and is thick and jammy. You don't need to stir the cabbage while it cooks, just let it slowly simmer and it will melt down into the vinegar. You can prepare the cabbage to this point up to three days in advance. Transfer it to an airtight container and refrigerate; bring to room temperature before serving.

Adjust the oven rack to the middle position and preheat the oven to 350°F. Season both sides of the trout with salt and pepper. Heat the olive oil in a large nonstick sauté pan over medium-high heat until the oil is almost smoking and slides easily in the pan, 2 to 3 minutes. Place the fish fillets in the pan skin side down and cook for 1 to 2 minutes, so the skin begins to brown and crisp. Place the pan in the oven and cook for about 4 minutes, until the skin is golden brown. (To check for doneness, look at the skin around the outer edges of the fish; you want it to be a rich, crunchy, french-fry brown around the sides.) Remove

for the cabbage
¼ cup extra-virgin olive oil
8 garlic cloves, thinly sliced
Kosher salt and freshly ground black pepper
¼ head of red cabbage, cored and thinly sliced (about 4 cups)
1 cup balsamic vinegar

for the fish
4 6-ounce fillets sea trout, skin on
Kosher salt and freshly ground black pepper
¼ cup extra-virgin olive oil
30 whole fresh Italian parsley leaves
Lentils Castelluciano (page 264)
2 tablespoons finishing-quality extra-virgin olive oil, plus more for drizzling
1 lemon

the pan from the oven and slide a spatula under each fillet to turn it, taking care not to tear the skin or burn yourself, as the pan will be searing hot. Return the pan to the oven and cook the fish for another minute. Remove the pan from the oven and let the fish rest in the pan for 2 minutes.

While the fish is cooking, combine ½ cup of the cabbage with the parsley in a small bowl and toss gently. Warm the lentils in a small saucepan over medium heat. Add enough water so they are the consistency of a thick porridge but not so thin that they will spread over the surface of the plate. Remove the lentils from the heat and drizzle in 2 tablespoons of the finishing-quality olive oil, stirring constantly for about a minute, until the lentils are creamy and emulsified.

Ladle ¼ cup of the lentils into the center of each of four plates. Lay the trout on top of the lentils, squeeze a few drops of lemon juice over each fish fillet and top with the cabbage and parsley, dividing it evenly. Drizzle each serving of fish with the finishing olive oil, and serve with the remaining cabbage on the side.

bacalà al forno with tomato, ceci, and rosemary

One of the things I like about Italian food in general is that it is not a wimpy cuisine; the flavors are bold and decisive, as you will see in this preparation of bacalà, *or salt cod. I first tried this classic preparation at Ristorante Da Delfina, at the same lunch where I also discovered Ribollita "Da Delfina" (page 115). I loved how hearty the dish was and how pronounced the flavors were. In keeping with the Florentine tradition of eating* bacalà *on Fridays, we serve this as the Friday* piatto *special in the Pizzeria, and in keeping with our tradition of cooking Pizzeria dishes in the pizza oven, this, too, is cooked in that oven. We start with fresh cod and salt-cure it in the style of old days, where the fish was cured as a way of preserving it. Ideally you will start with a center cut of cod, which will yield more even-size pieces, which will salinate evenly. The cod takes three days to cure, so plan accordingly.*

SERVES 4

 SUGGESTED WINE PAIRING: VERMENTINO DI GALLURA (SARDINIA)

To prepare the cod, place it on your work surface, pour 2 tablespoons of salt into your hand, and with your hand close to the fish, sprinkle the salt in an even layer over one side of the fillet. Turn the fish and repeat, sprinkling the other side with the remaining 2 tablespoons of salt. Place a rack on a baking sheet or roasting pan and place the cod on the rack. Wrap the baking sheet in plastic and place the cod in the refrigerator for three days to cure.

Fill a large bowl or nonreactive baking dish with water and place the cod in the water to soak for 1 hour, changing the water two or three times during that time. Remove the cod and pat it dry with paper towels. Place the cod on a cutting board and cut it down the center lengthwise. Cut each length into six equal pieces so you have 12 pieces total.

Adjust the oven rack to the middle position and preheat the oven to 350°F.

Heat ¼ cup of the olive oil in a large ovenproof sauté pan over medium heat. Add the garlic and sauté for 1 minute, stirring constantly to prevent it from browning. Add the *passata* and chopped rosemary and cook for about 5 minutes to heat through. Cut each roasted tomato half in half again and place them in the saucepan without stirring. (If you are using canned tomatoes, cut them into quarters.) Add the ceci, again without stirring, and place the fish on top of the ceci and sauce. Drizzle the fish with the 2 tablespoons of olive oil and bake until the fish is opaque and cooked through, about 15 minutes.

Pour enough olive oil into a small skillet or saucepan to fill it 1 inch deep and line a small plate with paper towels. Heat the oil over medium-high heat until a pinch of salt sizzles when dropped into it. Add the rosemary tufts and fry for about 30 seconds until they are crisp but not brown. Use a slotted spoon or strainer to remove the rosemary from the oil, transfer to the paper towels to drain, and season with salt. Strain the rosemary-infused oil through a fine-mesh strainer and reserve it to fry rosemary another time, to make a vinaigrette, or to drizzle over grilled meats or vegetables. The herbs can be fried up to several hours in advance. Store them in an airtight container at room temperature.

Remove the cod from the oven and place the sauté pan on the stovetop over medium-high heat. Add 1 cup of water and cook the sauce for 2 to 3 minutes, stirring gently without breaking up the fish.

Spoon the sauce onto the center of four plates, dividing it evenly. Place three pieces of fish on top of each serving of sauce, stacking them on top of one another in different directions. Scatter the fried rosemary

for the cod
1½ pounds cod fillet (preferably center cut)
¼ cup kosher salt
¼ cup extra-virgin olive oil, plus 2 tablespoons for drizzling
12 garlic cloves, thinly sliced
1 cup *Passata di Pomodoro* (page 25) or tomato sauce
1 heaping tablespoon chopped fresh rosemary needles
8 halves of Roasted Roma Tomatoes (page 26) or 4 canned whole peeled plum tomatoes (preferably San Marzano)
1 cup Ceci (page 96)

for the fried rosemary
Extra-virgin olive oil
1 cup fresh rosemary tufts
Kosher salt

for finishing and serving
1 lemon, halved
Garlic Mayonniase (optional; page 51)

over the fish, dividing it evenly, squeeze a few drops of lemon juice over each serving, and serve a ramekin of Garlic Mayonnaise on the side of each plate, if you are using it.

pan-roasted halibut pepe verde

I love a fish in meat's clothing, and that's what this is: a mild-flavored fish cooked in a rich veal jus. I got the idea for it at a restaurant called Ribollita, in Chiusi, the nearest large town to my house in Italy. There, they wrap a pork filet in lardo and then smother it with green peppercorn sauce. Eventually the lardo found its way onto fish instead of pork. We use veal stock that we have left over from making the Veal Breast Stracotto (page 235), but if you haven't made that dish recently, you can substitute any quality veal or beef stock.

SERVES 4

SUGGESTED WINE PAIRING: VERDICCHIO DI MATELICA (THE MARCHES)

*A*djust the oven rack to the middle position and preheat the oven to 350°F.

Combine the rosemary, garlic, and ¼ cup of the olive oil in the bowl of a miniature food processor or the jar of a blender and purée. Rinse the fish fillets, pat them dry with paper towels, and lay them in a single layer in a nonreactive baking dish. Pour the marinade over the fish and turn to coat with the marinade on all sides.

Combine the veal stock and peppercorns in a medium sauté pan over high heat. Bring the stock to a boil and continue to boil until it is glossy and has reduced by two-thirds, about 10 minutes. You want the liquid to be shiny and translucent with the consistency of a thick glaze or thin gravy. If you cook it for so long that it becomes dull and gravy-like, stir in enough water to obtain the desired consistency. Turn off the heat while you cook the fish. Just before serving, if the sauce has cooled, warm it over medium heat. Stir in the lemon juice just before serving.

Remove the fish fillets from the marinade and season on both sides with salt. Heat the remaining ¼ cup of olive oil in a large nonstick sauté pan over medium-high heat until the oil is almost smoking and

Heaping ¼ cup fresh rosemary needles

2 large garlic cloves

½ cup extra-virgin olive oil

4 6-ounce skinless halibut fillets (about 1½ inches thick) or any other mild white fish, such as branzino or striped bass

1½ cups veal stock (see Veal Breast *Stracotto*, page 235) or any quality veal or beef stock

¼ cup green peppercorns, soaked in water for 1 hour

1¼ teaspoons fresh lemon juice

Kosher salt

8 large outer leaves of butter lettuce or Boston lettuce

slides easily in the pan, 2 to 3 minutes. Place the fillets skin side down in the pan and cook for 1 to 2 minutes so the skin begins to brown and crisp. Place the pan in the oven and cook the fish for about 4 minutes, until the skin is golden brown. To check for doneness, look at the skin around the outer edges of the fish; you want it to be a rich, crunchy, french-fry brown around the sides. Remove the pan from the oven and slide a spatula under each fillet to turn it, taking care not to tear the skin or to burn yourself, as the pan will be searing hot. Return the pan to the oven and cook the fish for another minute. Remove the pan from the oven and remove the fish to a plate or cutting board.

Line a plate with paper towels. Without wiping out the pan, place it over high heat and, working in batches, place the lettuce leaves in the pan for 30 seconds to 1 minute to wilt them slightly. Remove the leaves to a paper towel and use another paper towel to gently pat them dry. Drape two lettuce leaves in the center of each of four large plates, overlapping them slightly. Lay the fish on the lettuce and spoon the sauce, including the peppercorns, over the fish, dividing it evenly.

guinea hen crostone with liver and pancetta sauce

Braised guinea hen served on a big piece of toasted bread and smothered in a rich, gravy-like sauce made of the hens' livers and pancetta is the house specialty of Ristorante Masolino, my favorite restaurant in Panicale. I felt I would be remiss in not including it on the menu at Mozza, and since we all know how generous and open the Italian people are, I was more than a little surprised when I asked Masolino's owner, Andrea, for the recipe for this dish, and he refused. Evidently he was not interested in sharing the secrets of his specialty with the world. So I did the only thing I could do. The summer before we opened Mozza I went to the restaurant countless times and each time forced someone in my party to order the guinea hen so I could have a bite and try to figure out how to make it—or how to tell Matt to make it.

This recipe requires a lot of preparation, so it's important to have all of your slicing and dicing done before you start cooking. You can get guinea hen thighs at poultry shops, or order it online from specialty sources such as D'Artagnan. If all you can get are thighs connected to the legs, use the legs to fortify your chicken stock. (Put the chicken stock and guinea legs in a stockpot, bring the stock to a boil over high heat, reduce the heat, and simmer for up to 2 hours, skimming off the foam that rises to the top.) As important as I believe it is for food to look as good as it tastes, I do not delude myself. I know that this dish is not going to win any beauty contests. Rest assured that what it lacks in beauty it makes up for in flavor. I think even Andrea would approve.

SERVES 4

SUGGESTED WINE PAIRING: SAGRANTINO DI MONTEFALCO (UMBRIA)

To prepare the hens, rinse them and pat dry with paper towels. Cut the legs from the thighs at the joint. Place the thighs in a nonreactive baking dish. Season the thighs with the salt and pepper, cover the dish with plastic wrap, and refrigerate overnight to cure, or for at least several hours.

To braise the guinea thighs, pour the flour on a plate or into a pie pan. Dredge the guinea hen thighs in the flour, patting off the excess flour. Heat ¼ cup of the olive oil in a Dutch oven or high-sided sauté pan large enough to hold the thighs in a single layer over medium-high heat until the oil is almost smoking and slides easily in the pan, 2 to 3 minutes. Place the guinea thighs skin side down in the pan and cook until golden brown, about 5 minutes per side, taking care not to rip the skin when you turn them. Remove the thighs to a plate and wipe out the pan.

Add the remaining ¼ cup of oil and heat it for about 1 minute, until the oil is almost smoking. Add the pancetta and cook to render the fat but not brown, 2 to 3 minutes. Add the onions and garlic, and cook until the onions are tender and translucent, about 10 minutes, stirring occasionally to prevent the onions and garlic from browning. Add the sage and rosemary, and season with freshly ground black pepper. (We don't add salt to this sauce because the salt on the thighs and in the pancetta is sufficient.) Cook the herbs with the onions and garlic for about 1 minute, stirring often, to soften the herbs. Add the livers, wine, lemon juice, capers, vinegar, and 4 cups of the stock to the pan. Return the guinea thighs to the pan skin side up, and add any juices that have collected on the plate on which they were resting. If there is not enough liquid to liberally cover the guinea thighs, add more stock as needed. Bring the liquid to a simmer over high heat. Reduce the heat and simmer the guinea thighs, uncovered, until they are fork-tender and the meat pulls away from the bone easily, 1 to 1½ hours. Remove the pan from the heat and carefully remove the thighs to a plate. When the thighs are cool enough to handle, remove the bone

for curing the hens

4 whole guinea hens (about 3½ pounds each)

4 teaspoons kosher salt, or 1 teaspoon for each pound of guinea thighs

1 teaspoon freshly ground black pepper

for braising the thighs

All-purpose flour, for dredging

½ cup extra-virgin olive oil, plus more for oiling the pan

¾ pound pancetta, diced

2 large yellow Spanish onions, diced (3 to 4 cups)

12 large garlic cloves, thinly sliced

3 tablespoons chopped fresh sage leaves

2 tablespoons chopped fresh rosemary needles

Freshly ground black pepper

1 pound guinea hen livers or chicken livers, veins removed and livers roughly chopped (approximately 2½ cups)

1 750-ml. bottle dry white wine

½ cup fresh lemon juice (from about 2 lemons), plus more as needed

(continued)

from each thigh, taking care to keep the thighs intact. Discard the bones. You can braise the guinea hen to this point up to five days in advance of serving it. Transfer the thighs and liquid to separate airtight containers and refrigerate until you are ready to serve them. Remove and discard the fat from the top of the braising liquid. Transfer it to a medium saucepan and proceed with the recipe.

Return the pan to high heat and bring the liquid to a boil. Boil the sauce, stirring occasionally to prevent it from sticking to the bottom of the pan, until it has reduced by half and is the consistency of thin gravy, 10 to 20 minutes. Pour 2 cups of the sauce into the bowl of a food processor fitted with a metal blade or the jar of a blender, taking care not to fill the bowl or jar more than halfway, as the hot liquid will expand. Holding a kitchen towel, keep the lid tight, if you are using a blender, and begin blending at low speed, increasing slowly to prevent an explosion. Purée until the sauce is smooth. Return the puréed sauce to the pan and stir to incorporate. Turn off the heat, taste for seasoning, and add salt or lemon juice, if desired.

Adjust the oven rack to the middle position and preheat the oven to 350°F.

Use olive oil to grease a baking dish just large enough to hold the bread slices in a single layer. Lay the bread in the baking dish and ladle the remaining 1 cup stock evenly over the bread. Place the baking dish in the oven and bake the bread until the bottom is golden brown and crisp, about 15 minutes. To check for doneness, lift a corner of the bread with a spatula, taking care as it tends to stick to the pan and you don't want to leave the crunchy bits in the pan.

Make the garnish while the bread is toasting. Combine the parsley, celery leaves, and lemon zest in a medium bowl. Drizzle the leaves with the finishing-quality olive oil, sprinkle with sea salt, and toss gently to coat with the seasonings.

Remove the toasts from the oven and carefully remove them from the baking dish, making sure not to leave the crispy part in the dish. Place each piece of toast bottom side up on a dinner plate and rest two guinea thighs on each piece of toast. Ladle a generous ½ cup of the sauce over each thigh so it runs off onto the *crostone*. Pile the garnish on each thigh, dividing it evenly, and serve the *crostone* with the remaining sauce on the side.

1 tablespoon capers (preferably salt-packed), soaked for 15 minutes if salt-packed, rinsed, and drained

1 tablespoon white wine vinegar

5 cups Basic Chicken Stock (page 27), plus more as needed

4 long ½-inch-thick slices from a loaf of *pane rustica* or another large, flat loaf of rustic white bread, such as ciabatta; or 8 slices from a *bâtard* or fat baguette, cut on an extreme bias to yield very long slices

for the garnish

¾ cup whole fresh Italian parsley leaves

¾ cup celery leaves (only the pale green leaves from the heart)

Zested strips of 3 lemons

1 tablespoon finishing-quality extra-virgin olive oil

Maldon sea salt or another flaky sea salt, such as fleur de sel

grilled quail wrapped in pancetta with sage and honey

If I had to name a signature secondo *at the Osteria, this* agrodolce *preparation of quail would be it. The quail are stuffed with a savory mixture of pancetta and herbs, and then drizzled with honey and aged* balsamico condimento. *When Matt and I travel to fund-raising and other food events around the country, this is the meat dish we most often choose to serve because it can be prepared ahead of time, and I've never met anyone—not even quail skeptics—who wasn't completely enamored of it. It's also easy to pair with wine. The gamey flavor of the bird and the pork can handle a big, fruity wine, and it doesn't overpower even the finest wines.*

SERVES 4

SUGGESTED WINE PAIRING: AMARONE DELLA VALPOLICELLA (VENETO)

To make the stuffing, warm the olive oil in a sauté pan over medium-high heat until the oil is almost smoking and slides easily in the pan, 2 to 3 minutes. Add the pancetta and cook to render the fat but not brown, 2 to 3 minutes. Add the onion, garlic, sage, rosemary, and thyme; season with the salt and pepper, and cook until the onion is tender and translucent, about 10 minutes, stirring occasionally to prevent the onion and garlic from browning. Remove the pan from the heat and set aside to cool to room temperature. Transfer the stuffing to an airtight container and refrigerate overnight or for at least 2 hours to chill.

To prepare the quail, rinse and pat dry with paper towels, checking for any remaining bones or feathers. Combine the onion, thyme, vinegar, honey, and pepper in a bowl or nonreactive baking dish large enough to hold all the quail. Place the quail in the marinade and turn to coat them on all sides. Cover with plastic wrap and place the quail in the refrigerator to marinate for at least 2 hours or up to overnight.

Remove the quail from the marinade, pat dry with paper towels, and lay them on a baking sheet. One at a time, lay a quail on your work surface, open up the legs, and spoon 2 tablespoons of stuffing inside the cavity. Cross the legs to close in the stuffing. Slide the skewer through the bottom leg and then through the top leg and rotate the skewer so it's perpendicular to the legs. Return the quail to the baking sheet and repeat, stuffing the remaining birds in the same way. Unravel the pancetta if it's from a round slice and stack two slices of pancetta on your work surface. Lay the quail on top of the pancetta

for the stuffing

2 tablespoons extra-virgin olive oil

3 ounces thick-sliced pancetta, diced

1 cup chopped Spanish onion (about ½ onion)

2 large garlic cloves, finely chopped

1 teaspoon chopped fresh sage leaves

1 teaspoon chopped fresh rosemary needles

1 teaspoon chopped fresh thyme leaves

¼ teaspoon kosher salt

¼ teaspoon freshly ground black pepper

for marinating and grilling the quail

8 semi-boneless quail

1 medium red onion, halved and thinly sliced

A small handful of fresh thyme sprigs (about 10 sprigs)

¼ cup balsamic vinegar

(continued)

and wrap it around the quail, moving along the body of the quail to cover as much as possible. Return the quail to the baking sheet and repeat, wrapping the remaining quail in the remaining pancetta. (You can prepare the dish to this point up to a day in advance. Wrap the baking sheet tightly in plastic wrap and refrigerate until you are ready to grill. Season with salt and pepper on both sides before grilling.)

To fry the sage leaves, pour enough olive oil into a small skillet or saucepan to fill it 1 inch deep and line a small plate with paper towels. Heat the oil over medium-high heat until a pinch of salt sizzles when dropped into it. Add the sage leaves and fry for about 30 seconds, until crisp but not browned. Use a slotted spoon to remove the sage from the oil, transfer to the paper towels to drain, and season with salt. Strain the sage-infused oil through a fine-mesh strainer and reserve it to fry sage another time or to drizzle over grilled meats or vegetables. (The sage can be fried up to several hours in advance. Store it in an air-tight container at room temperature.)

To prepare the radicchio, combine the vinegar, olive oil, salt, and pepper in a large bowl. Add the radicchio leaves and soak in the marinade while you grill the quail or for up to 24 hours.

Prepare a hot fire in a gas or charcoal grill or preheat a grill pan or heavy-bottomed skillet over high heat. Brush the grill grates or grill pan with olive oil.

Place the quail breast side down on the grill and cook for 4 to 5 minutes, until it is browned and the pancetta is crisp. Turn the quail, taking care to keep the pancetta intact, and cook for 4 to 5 minutes on the other side. Cook for another 3 to 5 minutes, turning them often to prevent the outsides from burning, until they are cooked to medium. To check for doneness, squeeze the quail at the thickest point; if the flesh feels firm, it is done. If the quail appear to be searing too quickly, move them to a cooler part of the grill or lower the heat on the grill pan so they can cook through before the outsides burn. Remove the quail to a plate to rest for about 5 minutes before serving. While the quail are resting, grill the radicchio for 1½ to 2 minutes, turning occasionally, until it is browned in places but not crisp.

To serve, remove the skewers and discard. Drape two radicchio leaves in the center of each plate, overlapping them. Lay one quail on each serving of radicchio and rest the other in another direction on top of the first. Drizzle 1 teaspoon of honey over and around each serving. Drizzle 1 teaspoon of the *balsamico* and 1 teaspoon of the finishing-quality olive oil, and scatter the fried sage leaves over each plate.

2 tablespoons mild-flavored honey, such as clover or wildflower

1 tablespoon freshly ground black pepper

8 bamboo skewers, soaked overnight or for at least 30 minutes

16 thin slices pancetta (about 1 pound)

Extra-virgin olive oil

for frying the sage
Extra-virgin olive oil
20 fresh sage leaves
Kosher salt

for the radicchio
2 tablespoons balsamic vinegar
2 tablespoons extra-virgin olive oil
½ teaspoon kosher salt
½ teaspoon freshly ground black pepper
16 radicchio leaves

for serving the dish
4 teaspoons honey, plus more to taste
4 teaspoons aged *balsamico condimento*, plus more to taste
Finishing-quality extra-virgin olive oil (about 4 teaspoons)

duck al mattone with pear mostarda

*O*ne of the unique and really great things about duck is that if you do everything right, you are able to get the skin deliciously crisp, as it is here. We borrowed the idea for cooking the duck from a similar dish that is served at Mario and Joe's Lupa Osteria Romana, in New York. We call it "al mattone," a term that refers to something (generally chicken) cooked under a brick, because it has the same crisp skin as if you had put pressure on the bird when you cooked it. We serve the duck with either a side of sautéed corn or Brussels sprout leaves. Even though we gave you recipes for both, the idea is that you make only the one that is in season. The duck also comes with a ramekin of pear mostarda, *a spicy Italian condiment whose sharp spiciness cuts through the richness of the duck and really makes the dish. To confit the ducks, buy rendered duck fat from the same source as you buy your ducks. We serve half a duck to each guest, but it's a dish that people often order, along with two or three* contorni, *to share. Served family style with the corn or Brussels sprouts, and two or three additional* contorni, *four duck halves could feed six or eight people. After cooking the ducks we like to rest them in the fat they were cooked in for at least 24 hours. Plan accordingly.*

SERVES 4 TO 8

SUGGESTED WINE PAIRING: BARBARESCO (PIEDMONT)

*T*o cure the duck, put the salt, brown sugar, red pepper flakes, and peppercorns in a large bowl and stir to combine. Place the ducks in a large nonreactive baking dish. Pack the cure on the ducks and use your hands to rub it all over. Cover the dish with plastic wrap and place the ducks in the refrigerator to cure overnight.

To confit the duck, adjust the oven rack to the middle position and preheat the oven to 300°F.

Remove the ducks from the refrigerator, rinse off the salt, and pat dry with paper towels. Place them in a medium Dutch oven or another pot large enough to hold them (it's okay if the ducks are stacked and not in a single layer). Add enough duck fat to cover the ducks by 1 inch and bring the fat to a gentle boil, uncovered, over medium heat. Turn off the heat and place an ovenproof baking dish or ovenproof plates on top of the ducks to keep them submerged. Place the lid on the pot or cover tightly with aluminum foil and put the ducks in the oven. About 30 minutes after you put them in the oven, uncover the pot to check to be sure the fat is not boiling. If it is, lower the oven

to cure and confit the duck
¾ cup kosher salt
½ cup brown sugar
2 tablespoons red pepper flakes
½ cup whole black peppercorns
4 duck halves
Rendered duck fat (8 to 10 cups, or enough to cover), liquefied at room temperature

(continued)

temperature to 250°F and check the fat again in another 15 minutes, lowering the heat again, if necessary, to prevent the fat from boiling. Cook for a total of 3½ to 4 hours, until the ducks are fork-tender. To check for doneness, insert a fork into the thigh of one duck half and wiggle the thigh. If it gives easily, it is done; if not, cover the pot and return the ducks to the oven for 30 minutes more before checking them again. Remove the pot from the oven, remove the lid, and let the ducks cool to room temperature in the fat. When they have cooled, cover the pot or transfer the ducks and fat to another container, making sure the ducks are submerged in the fat, and refrigerate overnight or for up to one week.

When you are ready to serve the ducks, remove them from the refrigerator and set aside at room temperature to allow the fat to liquefy. Alternatively, if they are in a pot that can go on the stove, melt the fat over low heat. Gently remove the ducks from the fat, taking care not to tear the skin or detach it from the meat, and pat them dry with paper towels. You do not want to pull the ducks out of solid fat, as you might separate the meat from the bones and the skin from the meat in the process.

Adjust the oven rack to the middle position and preheat the oven to 350°F. Place a baking sheet near the stove.

Heat the olive oil in a large nonstick sauté pan over medium-high heat until the oil is almost smoking and slides easily in the pan, 2 to 3 minutes. Turn the heat off and carefully slide two of the duck halves, skin side down, into the pan. You must turn off the heat before adding the ducks to the pan, as any moisture that drips off them into the oil will flare up and put your duck—and possibly you—in jeopardy. Increase the heat to medium high and press the breasts into the oil so the maximum surface area is in the oil. Cook the ducks undisturbed until the skin is crisp, 5 to 6 minutes. You may want to step away while they are frying, as the oil in the pan will splatter and pop while the ducks cook. When the skin sides of the duck are crisp, turn off the heat and drain the fat from the pan into a bowl, reserving it. Starting at the leg and moving toward the breast, carefully slide a spatula under one of the duck halves to lift it out of the oil and place it cooked side up on the baking sheet. Repeat, lifting the second duck half out of the pan and onto the baking sheet. Pour a splash of water on the baking sheet (not on the duck) and put the baking sheet in the oven while you cook the remaining duck halves.

Return the reserved fat to the pan and heat it over medium-high heat until the oil is almost smoking and slides easily in the pan. Cook

for finishing and serving the duck

¼ cup extra-virgin olive oil

4 or more lemon wedges, seeds removed

Pear *mostarda* (preferably Mostarda Mantovana by Casa Forcello)

for the corn

¼ cup rendered duck fat (clean fat, not that used to cook the ducks)

8 large garlic cloves, thinly sliced

Kosher salt

2 cups fresh-cut corn kernels (from 2 ears of corn)

¼ teaspoon red pepper flakes

3 scallions, thinly sliced on an extreme bias starting at the green ends and moving toward the root ends (white and green parts)

for the brussels sprouts

1 pound Brussels sprouts

¼ cup rendered duck fat (clean fat, not that used to cook the ducks)

Kosher salt

8 large garlic cloves, thinly sliced

1 cup Spanish sherry vinegar

the remaining two duck halves as you did the first two. When they are done, drain the fat from the pan and discard. Place the duck halves cooked side up on the baking sheet with the first two duck halves and return the baking sheet to the oven while you cook the vegetables.

To prepare the corn, heat the duck fat in a large sauté pan over medium-high heat until the fat is almost smoking and slides easily in the pan, 2 to 3 minutes. Add the garlic, season with salt, and sauté for about 30 seconds, stirring constantly so it doesn't brown. Add the corn kernels and the red pepper flakes, season the kernels with salt, and cook, stirring only as much as necessary to prevent the kernels from burning, until they are golden brown, slightly crisp, and popping in the pan, 4 to 5 minutes. Turn off the heat, add the scallions, and stir them for about 1 minute, until they wilt slightly. Taste for seasoning and add more salt, if desired. Divide the corn among individual ramekins or serve family style.

Alternatively, to prepare the Brussels sprouts, trim and discard the stem ends and cut the sprouts in half through the core. Use a small knife to carve out the cores, discarding the cores, and use your fingers to break the Brussels sprouts into loose leaves into a bowl.

Heat the duck fat in a large sauté pan over medium-high heat until the oil is almost smoking and slides easily in the pan, 2 to 3 minutes. Add the Brussels sprout leaves, season with salt, and cook, stirring often, until they are browned in places, about 2 minutes. Add the garlic and vinegar, and cook for about 1 minute, until the pan is dry. Add ¾ cup of water and cook, shaking the pan or stirring the leaves occasionally, until the pan is dry and the leaves are wilted. Taste for seasoning and add more salt, if desired. Divide the Brussels sprouts among individual ramekins or serve family style.

Remove the ducks from the oven, drain the water off the baking sheet and place one duck half on each of four plates, or place the ducks on a large platter to serve them family style. Nestle one lemon wedge alongside each duck half. Spoon the *mostarda* into individual small bowls or ramekins and serve one to each person, whether you are serving the ducks family style or individually.

variation: crisp duck leg with lentils castellucciano

*W*e serve this as a daily piatto *special in the Pizzeria with Lentils Castellucciano and fried sage sprinkled all around. We included it as a variation to the Duck* al Mattone *because the preparations of the duck, with the exception of cooking times, are identical.*

SERVES 6 TO 8

 SUGGESTED WINE PAIRING: PINOT NERO (ALTO ADIGE)

*C*ure and confit six to eight duck legs in the same manner as for Duck *al Mattone*, reducing the cooking time in the oven to about 2½ hours, or until the skin splits away from the muscle at the anklebone. Fry the duck legs in the same manner, but change the stovetop cooking time to 5 minutes on the first (skin) side and 1 minute on the second side. Pour a splash of water on the baking sheet around the legs and place them in the oven for 5 to 7 minutes, to heat them through. Fry 1 cup of sage leaves and 1 cup of rosemary tufts in the oil reserved from frying the ducks. Serve the duck legs on a bed of warm Lentils Castellucciano (page 264), drizzle finishing-quality olive oil around the lentils and scatter the fried herbs over the top. Serve with a lemon wedge on each plate.

grilled beef tagliata, rucola, and parmigiano-reggiano with aged balsamico condimento

*T*agliata, *which means "cut" and refers to a dish of sliced meat, is probably the most popular* secondo *at the Osteria. The* tagliata *I've been served in Italy has been dressed in different ways, ranging from chopped arugula to sautéed fresh porcini, to black pepper and Parmigiano, or just a drizzle of aged* balsamico condimento. *I am a salad nut, so the version we serve at the Osteria consists of thinly sliced steak and a pile of dressed arugula layered with thin slices of Parmigiano. When I make it for a crowd at home, I serve the meat on the cutting board and offer the arugula and Parmigiano in a big, wide salad bowl. This recipe calls for two types of balsamic vinegar: an inexpensive cooking-quality balsamic to marinate the steaks, and an aged* condimento-*grade* balsamico, *to drizzle on the steak. If you don't have an aged* balsamico *the other is no substitute.*

SERVES 4

SUGGESTED WINE PAIRING: MORELLINO DI SCANSANO (TUSCANY)

*C*ombine the balsamic vinegar, rosemary, and garlic in the bowl of a food processor fitted with a metal blade or the jar of a blender and pulse until the rosemary is finely chopped. Add the olive oil and pulse until all the ingredients are combined.

If you are using hanger steaks, lay one on a cutting board and use a large sharp knife to cut out the silver skin running down the center of each steak; in the process you will cut each hanger steak into two long, narrow pieces, each similar in shape to a tenderloin. Place the steaks in a large bowl or nonreactive baking dish. Pour the marinade over and turn to coat them on all sides. Cover tightly with plastic wrap and refrigerate for at least 1 hour and up to overnight. Remove the steaks from the refrigerator and bring to room temperature before grilling.

Prepare a hot fire in a gas or charcoal grill or preheat a grill pan or heavy-bottomed skillet over high heat.

Remove the steaks from the marinade, discard the marinade, and generously season the steaks with salt and pepper on both sides, using about 1 teaspoon of salt per pound of meat. Put the steaks on the grill or in the grill pan and cook until the meat is seared and deep brown on all sides, 5 to 6 minutes per side for medium rare. Remove the steaks to a platter or cutting board and let them rest for about 5 minutes before slicing. Use a sharp knife to carve the steaks diagonally against the grain into ½-inch-thick slices.

While the steaks are resting, use a large knife or a mandoline to cut the wedge of Parmigiano-Reggiano into very thin slices. Put the arugula in a large, wide bowl, sprinkle with salt and toss gently to distribute evenly. Drizzle the vinaigrette and toss gently to coat the leaves. Taste for seasoning and add more salt or vinaigrette, if desired.

Slide a long knife under one quarter of the steak slices and transfer them onto one of four dinner plates, gently fanning the slices out in a slightly curved line. Repeat, fanning the remaining steak slices on the other plates in the same way and drizzle the steaks with any juices that have collected on the cutting board. Lay a few slices of Parmigiano-Reggiano next to each serving of steak, in the space left by the curved line of the meat. Building the salad in two layers from here and, saving the largest slices for the top, pile a handful of arugula on each bed of cheese. Place another layer of Parmigiano-Reggiano slices on the arugula and top it with another handful of arugula. Lay the largest slices of Parmigiano-Reggiano on the finished salads. Sprinkle each serving of steak with a pinch of sea salt, drizzle each with 1 teaspoon of the *balsamico condimento* and the finishing-quality olive oil, and serve.

1 cup balsamic vinegar

½ cup whole fresh rosemary needles

8 whole garlic cloves

½ cup extra-virgin olive oil

4 hanger steaks (7 to 8 ounces each), or 2 to 2½ pounds flank steak

Kosher salt and freshly ground black pepper

Wedge of Parmigiano-Reggiano (about 4 ounces)

8 cups loosely packed arugula (preferably wild arugula; about ½ pound)

Lemon Vinaigrette (page 29), plus more to taste

Maldon sea salt or another flaky salt, such as fleur de sel

Aged *balsamico condimento*

Finishing-quality extra-virgin olive oil

brasato al barolo with polenta and horseradish gremolata

*I*n the last few years, it seems like there have been two requirements to opening a successful restaurant in Los Angeles. You have to offer a selection of decent wines by the glass, and you have to offer braised short ribs. You see short ribs served on the bone and off the bone; cooked with Indian spices, Asian spices, and Latin American spices; and served over mashed potatoes, polenta, and who knows what else. I don't roll my eyes when I see them on a menu because I know how good they can be. Once they're cooked, they're good for a few days, so they're convenient for the home cook. Braise them today; reheat them tomorrow. In the Italian spirit of not wasting any bit of food, shred the leftover meat to make Francobolli di Brasato al Pomodoro *(page 177).*

SERVES 6

SUGGESTED WINE PAIRING: BAROLO (PIEDMONT)

*P*lace the short ribs in a nonreactive baking dish or a large bowl and season them with salt and pepper on all sides, using approximately 1 teaspoon of salt per pound of meat. Cover the dish or bowl with plastic wrap and refrigerate for at least 1 hour and up to overnight.

Heat 2 tablespoons of the olive oil in a Dutch oven or large high-sided sauté pan over medium-high heat until the oil is smoking and slides easily in the pan, 2 to 3 minutes. Place the short ribs in the pan to sear on all three sides (it's not necessary to sear the bone side), until the meat is deep brown, about 5 minutes per side. If you can't squeeze all of the short ribs in the skillet at one time, sear them in two batches, adding more oil to the pan to sear the second batch if it's dry. Remove the short ribs to a plate.

Adjust the oven rack to the middle position and preheat the oven to 350°F.

Reduce the heat to medium, add the remaining 2 tablespoons of olive oil, and heat it until almost smoking. Add the onion, carrot, and celery and sauté, stirring often, until the vegetables are soft and the onion is tender and translucent, about 10 minutes. Add the garlic and cook for about 1 minute, stirring constantly to prevent it from brown-ing. Move the vegetables to create a bare spot in the pan, add the tomato paste to that spot, and cook for 1 minute, stirring, to caramelize the tomato paste slightly. Add the wine, increase the heat to high, and

6 beef short ribs
(about 1 pound each)

2 tablespoons kosher salt

2 teaspoons freshly ground
black pepper

¼ cup (4 tablespoons)
extra-virgin olive oil,
plus more as needed

1 medium onion, cut up
into large pieces

1 carrot, peeled and cut into
large pieces (about 2 inches)

1 celery rib, cut into roughly
2-inch pieces

3 garlic cloves, thinly sliced

1 tablespoon double-
concentrated tomato paste

1 750-ml. bottle dry red wine
(preferably Barolo)

1 14-ounce can peeled plum
tomatoes (preferably
San Marzano), including
their juice

4 cups Basic Chicken Stock
(page 27), plus more
as needed

boil the wine for about 20 minutes, until it is thick and jammy. Add the tomatoes and their juice and sauté for about 2 minutes to meld the flavors.

Return the short ribs bone side down to the pan. Add any juices that may have collected on the plate they were resting on and enough stock to come just to the top edge of the short ribs. Nestle the thyme, oregano, and rosemary sprigs in the liquid around the meat. Wrap the porcini in a doubled piece of cheesecloth, pull the corners toward the center, and tie it into a bouquet with a piece of cooking twine. Tuck the bouquet between the ribs, making sure the mushrooms are submerged in the liquid. If you have commercial-grade plastic wrap, which won't melt in the oven, cover the pan with plastic wrap. In either case, cover the pan tightly with aluminum foil and place the lid on it if it has one. Place the short ribs in the oven and cook until the meat is fork-tender and falling off the bones, about 3 hours. Remove the short ribs from the oven and remove the foil and plastic from the pan if you used it, being careful not to burn yourself with the steam that will rise from the pan. Set aside to allow the short ribs to cool in the braising liquid for at least 30 minutes.

Remove the short ribs from the braising liquid to a plate. Pour the contents of the pan, including the vegetables and the bouquet, through a fine-mesh strainer into a medium saucepan (or bowl if you are not serving the short ribs now). Press down on the vegetables and the bouquet to extract as much juice as you can from them. Discard the contents of the strainer. Remove the porcini from the cheesecloth, discard the cheesecloth, and add the mushrooms to the braising liquid. Gently pull each short rib off the bone and remove the sinewy tissue that connects the meat to the bone. Pick any meat left on the bone or from the connective tissue and reserve to make the *Francobolli di Brasato* al Barolo (page 177). You can prepare the short ribs to this point up to five days in advance. Cover the pot with plastic wrap or transfer the meat with the braising liquid to an airtight container and refrigerate until you are ready to serve it. (You will proceed slightly differently.)

If the short ribs are still warm from the braising liquid, bring the liquid to a boil over high heat, reduce the heat, and simmer until the liquid is the consistency of a thick glaze or thin gravy, stirring occasionally to prevent it from sticking to the pan; it will be thick enough to coat the back of a spoon.

If you have prepared the short ribs in advance and are rewarming them, preheat the oven to 350°F. If the short ribs have been in the refrigerator, remove and discard the fat from the liquid. Pour the liquid into a Dutch oven or stovetop-safe baking dish and warm it over

10 fresh thyme sprigs
10 fresh oregano sprigs
1 long rosemary sprig
½ ounce dried porcini
  mushrooms

for the garnish
¾ cup whole fresh Italian
  parsley leaves
¾ cup whole fresh celery
  leaves (only pale green
  leaves from the hearts)
Zested strips of 3 lemons
1 tablespoon finishing-quality
  extra-virgin olive oil
Maldon sea salt or another
  flaky sea salt, such as
  fleur de sel
Fresh peeled horseradish

Polenta (page 265)

medium heat, then place the short ribs bone side down in the dish. Place the dish in the oven for about 30 minutes, basting the meat with the sauce occasionally, until the meat is warmed through. Put the dish on the stovetop, and cook as directed above to thicken.

To make the garnish, combine the parsley leaves, celery leaves, and lemon zest in a medium bowl. Drizzle the leaves with the finishing-quality olive oil, sprinkle with sea salt, and toss gently to coat the leaves with the seasonings. Use a microplane or another fine grater to grate about 60 strokes of horseradish over the salad and toss gently.

Spoon ½ cup of the polenta in the center of each of six plates. Place one short rib on top of the polenta and ladle a generous ½ cup of the sauce over each short rib. Divide the porcini evenly among the servings and serve any remaining sauce on the side. Pile the garnish on top of the short ribs, dividing it evenly, and grate a few additional strokes of horseradish over each serving, and serve.

porcini-rubbed rib-eye bistecca

*W*e are not a steakhouse, so I'm always pleasantly surprised when our customers tell us that our rib-eye is their favorite steak in Los Angeles. We start with quality, conventionally raised meat, just like what you will be able to get at a good butcher. The reason our steak is so good is the rub we coat the meat with before grilling it. The rub contains dried porcini, which have a delicious, earthy flavor, and a tiny bit of sugar, which caramelizes on the grill and gives the steak a beautiful crust. More often than not our customers share it among two or three people along with two or three contorni, such as Smashed Potatoes with Rosemary (page 255), Cipolline with Thyme and Sherry Vinegar (page 254), and Sautéed Broccolini with Chiles and Vinegar (page 262) to eat along with it. We order our rib-eyes "frenched," which means that the meat is cut off the bone so the bone looks almost like a handle, which makes for a more unusual, elegant presentation. If you have a butcher who will do that for you, great. If not, it won't make a bit of difference in the flavor. Unlike a French preparation, served with a heavy Béarnaise sauce, ours is served with Italy's two best condiments: quality extra-virgin olive oil and aged balsamico condimento.

SERVES 4 TO 6

SUGGESTED WINE PAIRING: BRUNELLO DI MONTALCINO (TUSCANY)

*G*rind the porcini to a powder in several batches in a spice grinder. Turn the ground porcini out into a large mixing bowl. Put the red pepper flakes in the spice grinder, grind them until finely chopped, and add to the bowl with the porcini. Add the sugar, salt, and pepper, and stir to combine the ingredients. The rub will keep indefinitely, stored in an airtight container at room temperature, but it will lose its luster after about 30 days.

Wrap kitchen twine around the perimeter of each steak, and tie the ends closed in a bow. (This helps maintain the shape of the steak so it cooks more evenly.) Cut off and discard the excess twine and lay the steaks on a clean cutting board. Pour the rub onto a plate or pie pan. Place one steak in the rub and turn it to coat both sides and the edges in a generous, even layer with the rub. Place the prepared steak on a platter or baking sheet and repeat with the remaining steaks. Grill the steaks or cover tightly with plastic wrap and refrigerate for up to 4 hours. Remove the steaks from the refrigerator and bring them to room temperature before grilling.

Prepare a hot fire in a gas or charcoal grill or preheat a grill pan or heavy-bottomed skillet over high heat. Season both sides of the steaks liberally with salt and pepper, and sprinkle additional rub on any bare spots.

Place the steaks on the hottest part of the grill or in the grill pan to cook, turning every 6 to 8 minutes, for about 25 minutes for medium rare, or until they reach an internal temperature of 125°F. Remove the steaks to a cutting board or platter and let them rest for 10 to 15 minutes before serving. Remove and discard the twine. Serve the steaks whole or sliced against the grain. If you are moving the steaks from a cutting board to plates, drizzle them with the juices that have collected on the surface they were resting on. Serve with finishing-quality olive oil and *balsamico* on the side.

2 ounces dried porcini

1 tablespoon red pepper flakes

¼ cup sugar

2 tablespoons kosher salt, plus more for seasoning

2 tablespoons freshly ground black pepper, plus more for seasoning

4 rib-eye steaks (preferably frenched)

Finishing-quality olive oil

Aged *balsamico condimento*

lamb chops scottadito with insalata di fregola sarda, mint, and yogurt

his is an Italian interpretation of a grilled lamb entrée you might see at a Lebanese restaurant. Scottadito *means "burnt fingers" in Italian, and it refers to the fact that the lamb bones are meant to be picked up with your fingers while they're searingly hot. We serve the lamb with a tabbouleh-like salad made of* fregola sarda, *a bread crumb–size pasta shape from Sardinia so small it acts like a grain in the kitchen, and Greek yogurt.*

SERVES 4

SUGGESTED WINE PAIRING: CERASUOLO DI VITTORIA (SICILY)

o prepare the lamb, chop two-thirds of the lemon zest strips, reserving the remaining third for garnish, and place them in a bowl large enough to hold the lamb or in a nonreactive baking dish. Stir in the mint, sugar, salt, and pepper to combine. Add the lamb chops and turn to coat the meat on all sides with the seasonings. (You can prepare the chops to this point up to several hours in advance. Cover the bowl or dish tightly with plastic wrap and refrigerate until you're ready to grill them. Remove the lamb from the refrigerator and bring to room temperature before grilling.)

To prepare the *fregola*, fill a medium saucepan with water, bring it to a boil over high heat, and salt it to taste like the ocean, adding approximately 1 tablespoon of salt to each quart of water. Place a colander in the sink or have a wire strainer handy to lift the pasta out of the water. Add the *fregola*, stir to prevent it from sticking together, and cook, using the time indicated on the package as a guide, until al dente. Drain the *fregola*, and transfer it to a large bowl. Drizzle with a small amount of olive oil, toss to coat it with the oil, and set it aside to cool to room temperature.

Put the tomatoes in a small bowl and season them with salt. Add the onion, cucumber, mint, parsley, garlic, and the seasoned tomatoes to the bowl with the *fregola*. Squeeze the lemon and drizzle the vinaigrette over the salad. Toss to thoroughly combine the ingredients and coat them with the vinaigrette. Taste for seasoning and add more salt, if desired.

To prepare the yogurt sauce, stir the yogurt and olive oil together until combined.

for the lamb
Zested strips of 3 lemons
¼ cup thinly sliced fresh
    mint leaves
1 tablespoon sugar
1 teaspoon kosher salt
1 teaspoon freshly ground
    black pepper
12 lamb rib chops
    (about 2 pounds)

for the *fregola sarda* salad
Kosher salt
¼ cup *fregola sarda*
Extra-virgin olive oil
½ cup halved Sweet 100
    tomatoes, cut through
    the stem ends, or cherry
    tomatoes, quartered
½ cup finely diced red onion
¼ cup finely diced peeled
    cucumber
2 tablespoons thinly sliced
    fresh mint leaves
2 tablespoons thinly sliced
    fresh Italian parsley leaves
1 teaspoon grated garlic
1 lemon, halved
½ cup Lemon Vinaigrette
    (page 29), plus more
    to taste

To grill the lamb chops, prepare a hot fire in a gas or charcoal grill or preheat a grill pan or heavy-bottomed skillet over high heat.

Remove the lamb chops from the rub and season them with salt and pepper on both sides. Grill the lamb chops for about 2 minutes per side for medium rare, turning them only once. Remove the lamb chops to a plate.

Spoon 1 tablespoon of the yogurt sauce on each of four plates and spread it out to form a pool about 3 inches in diameter. Spoon the *fregola* on top of the yogurt, leaving a rim of the yogurt visible. Place three lamb chops on each plate, leaning one against the other like a fallen teepee. Top each serving with a tangle of reserved lemon zest and 3 of the mint leaves. Drizzle 1 teaspoon of the finishing-quality olive oil over and around each serving of lamb, sprinkle a pinch of paprika on each plate around the lamb, and serve.

for the yogurt sauce
¼ cup plus 2 tablespoons strained whole-milk Greek yogurt
1 tablespoon plus 1 teaspoon extra-virgin olive oil

for serving the lamb
Kosher salt and freshly ground black pepper
12 whole tiny fresh mint leaves
Finishing-quality extra-virgin olive oil
Smoked paprika

veal breast stracotto

*O*ne of my favorite daytrips from my house in Italy is to the town of Panzano in Chianti, to visit the world-famous butcher Dario Cecchini. Dario has been covered by every food publication imaginable, and since Bill Buford wrote about him in his memoir, Heat, Dario's shop has become a mecca for foodies traveling in Italy. To meet the demand of his fans, Dario now has three restaurants that people can visit while they're there: a steakhouse serving prime cuts, such as bistecca fiorentina, a classic preparation of a T-bone or porterhouse grilled over a wood fire; a hamburger restaurant, Dario Plus; and my favorite of the three, Solo Ciccia. This restaurant, whose name means "only meat," offers lesser cuts of meats prepared in a variety of ways, many of them cooked long and slow, or stracotto, like this dish. Veal breast isn't something you'll find at your average grocery store, so you'll have to get it from a butcher, and you will probably have to special-order it. Ask the butcher to save the bones he carved the breast from, as you'll use those to make the stock in which the meat is braised. While you're at it, have him roll and tie the breast for you, too. Even though this might be out of your ordinary shopping routine, the good news is that you'll end up with a rich, luxurious veal dish for not a lot of money.

SERVES 4

 SUGGESTED WINE PAIRING: BARBERA D'ALBA (PIEDMONT)

To season the veal, place the breast in a nonreactive baking dish and season it all over with the salt and pepper, using approximately 1 teaspoon of salt per pound of meat. If your butcher did not roll and tie the veal breast, roll it tightly lengthwise into a long log shape and tie it with kitchen twine in five or six places along the roll. Cover the dish tightly with plastic wrap and refrigerate for at least 1 hour and up to overnight.

Meanwhile, if you are making the stock, adjust the oven rack to the middle position and preheat the oven to 325°F.

Place the veal bones on a baking sheet and roast them, shaking the pan occasionally for even cooking, until they're evenly browned, about 1½ hours. Remove the baking sheet from the oven and transfer the bones to a large stockpot. Add the chicken stock and bring it to a boil over high heat, skimming off the foam that rises to the top. Add the leek, onion, and carrot, reduce the heat, and simmer the stock for 1 hour, skimming as needed. Remove the stock from the heat, pour it through a fine-mesh strainer, and discard the contents of the strainer. Use the stock, or set aside to cool to room temperature, transfer it to an airtight container and refrigerate for up to three days.

To braise the veal, adjust the oven rack to the middle position and preheat the oven to 350°F.

Cut the veal in half, if necessary, for it to fit in the pan. Heat ¼ cup of the oil over medium-high heat in a large Dutch oven or large, high-sided sauté pan until the oil is almost smoking and slides easily in the pan, 2 to 3 minutes. Place the veal in the pan to sear to deep brown on all sides, 10 to 15 minutes. Remove the veal to a plate.

Add 2 tablespoons of the remaining olive oil to the pan. Reduce the heat to medium low, add the prosciutto, and cook, stirring constantly, to render the fat but not to brown the prosciutto, 2 to 3 minutes. Increase the heat to medium, add the remaining ¼ cup of olive oil, and warm the oil for a minute or two before adding the celery, carrot, and onion. Season the vegetables with the pepper, and sauté until the vegetables are softened and slightly caramelized, 10 to 15 minutes. Add the garlic and sauté for 1 minute, stirring constantly to prevent it from browning. Move the vegetables to create a bare spot in the pan, add the tomato paste to that spot, and cook for 1 minute more, stirring, to caramelize the tomato paste slightly. Add the wine, increase the heat to high, and boil until it reduces by about half, about 5 minutes. Return the veal and any juices that have collected on the plate it was resting on to the pan. Pour in enough stock to come half to three-fourths of

for seasoning the veal
1 4-pound boneless veal breast, bones reserved
1 tablespoon plus 1 teaspoon kosher salt
1 teaspoon freshly ground black pepper

for the veal stock (optional)
8 cups Basic Chicken Stock (page 27)
1 leek, cleaned thoroughly and roughly chopped into 1-inch pieces
1 large Spanish onion, roughly chopped into 1-inch pieces
1 carrot, peeled and roughly chopped into 1-inch pieces

for braising the veal
½ cup plus 2 tablespoons extra-virgin olive oil
¼ pound prosciutto, ground or finely chopped
2 celery ribs, finely diced (about 1 cup)
1 large carrot, peeled and finely diced
Half of a large Spanish onion, finely diced
½ teaspoon freshly ground black pepper
3 garlic cloves, thinly sliced
2 tablespoons double-concentrated tomato paste
1 750-ml. bottle dry white wine
1 quart veal stock or Basic Chicken Stock (page 27), warmed if gelatinous

the way up the veal breast, about 4 cups. Increase the heat to medium high and bring the stock to a simmer. Turn off the heat. If you have industrial-strength plastic wrap, which won't melt in the oven, cover the Dutch oven or pan tightly with plastic wrap. In either case, cover tightly with aluminum foil and place the lid on if it has one. Place the veal in the oven for 2 hours. Remove the pot from the oven and uncover it. Add the turnips, nestling them in the sauce, return the lid to the pot, and place it back in the oven for about 1 hour, until the meat is fork tender and the vegetables are tender. Remove the veal from the oven and remove and discard the foil and plastic wrap (if you used it) from the pan, being careful not to burn yourself with the steam that will rise from the pan. Allow the meat to cool in the braising liquid for at least 30 minutes. You can prepare the veal to this point up to five days in advance. Cool the meat and turnips to room temperature in the braising liquid. Remove the vegetables and transfer them to an airtight container. Cover the pot with plastic or transfer the veal with the liquid to an airtight container and refrigerate until you are ready to serve it. (You will proceed slightly differently.)

If you have prepared the veal in advance and are rewarming it, pre-heat the oven to 350°F. Remove the veal and turnips from the refriger-ator. Remove and discard the fat from the liquid and pour it into a large Dutch oven or stovetop-safe baking dish and cook as directed below to thicken. Remove the string and slice the veal as directed below and lay the slices in the sauce, resting them on top of one another, domino fashion. Nestle the turnips around the veal and place the dish in the oven for about 30 minutes, basting the vegetables and the veal with the sauce occasionally, until the meat is warmed through.

If you are serving the dish the same day, remove the veal and turnips to a plate, skim the fat from the braising liquid, and bring the liquid to a boil over high heat. Reduce the heat and simmer the liquid until it is the consistency of a thick glaze or thin gravy, stirring occa-sionally to prevent it from sticking to the pan; it will be thick enough to coat the back of a spoon.

To make the garnish, combine the parsley leaves, celery leaves, and lemon zest in a medium bowl. Drizzle the leaves with the finishing-quality olive oil, sprinkle with sea salt, and toss gently to combine.

To serve, cut off and discard the string from the veal and cut it into eight slices of even thickness. Lay two slices of veal on each of four plates, resting one at an angle on top of the other. Nestle the turnips around the veal, dividing them evenly, and ladle the sauce over the meat. Pile the garnish on each serving, dividing it evenly, and serve.

4 turnips, halved or quartered depending on their size, or 8 baby turnips (about 2 pounds), or whole unpeeled baby carrots with 1-inch greens attached

for the garnish
3/4 cup whole fresh Italian parsley leaves
3/4 cup whole fresh celery leaves (only pale green leaves from the hearts)
Zested strips of 3 lemons
1 tablespoon finishing-quality extra-virgin olive oil
Maldon sea salt or another flaky sea salt, such as fleur de sel

veal sweetbreads piccata with artichokes

*W*hoever named sweetbreads had an ingenious idea—to give such a nice-sounding name to a part of the animal, the thymus gland, that doesn't sound all that appetizing. I've found that despite the clever name, otherwise open-minded eaters are often squeamish when it comes to eating sweetbreads—a shame, since they can be out of this world. These are seared so they have a crisp exterior and creamy interior. Sweetbreads and artichokes are a pretty typical Italian pairing, and one that I love. While this isn't a difficult dish to make, it does require several steps, so plan ahead.

SERVES 4

SUGGESTED WINE PAIRING: GRECO DI TUFO (CAMPANIA)

*T*o prepare the sweetbreads, place them in a nonreactive baking dish or large bowl and pour the milk over them, adding more if necessary to cover. Cover the dish with plastic wrap and place the sweetbreads in the refrigerator to soak overnight. Drain the sweetbreads and discard the milk. Rinse the sweetbreads under cool water and pat them dry with paper towels.

Heat the olive oil in a large saucepan over medium-high heat until it is almost smoking and slides easily in the pan, 2 to 3 minutes. Add the onion, fennel, and celery, and season with salt and sauté, stirring often, until the vegetables begin to soften, 3 to 5 minutes. Increase the heat to high, add the wine, vinegar, and peppercorns, and bring the liquid to a boil and boil until it reduces by half, about 15 minutes. Add the sweetbreads and add enough water to just cover. Place a large paper coffee filter or a piece of cheesecloth on the surface to keep the sweetbreads submerged and heat until you see the first few bubbles start to rise up from the surface. Reduce the heat to medium and simmer until an instant-read thermometer inserted into one of the sweetbreads registers 120°F to 125°F, removing the smaller sweetbreads from the liquid to the colander as they become done, 5 to 10 minutes.

Meanwhile, fill a large bowl with ice water and place a colander in the sink. Place a wire cooling rack inside a baking sheet. Plunge the sweetbreads in the ice water for 1 minute to cool completely. Lift the sweetbreads out of the ice water, pat dry with paper towels, and place them on the wire rack. Cover the baking sheet with plastic wrap and place a heavy baking dish on top of the sweetbreads and a bag of beans or a can of tomatoes on the dish to weigh it down. Place the weighted sweetbreads in the refrigerator for 1 to 2 hours.

for preparing the sweetbreads

2 pounds veal sweetbreads

2½ cups whole milk, plus more as needed

¼ cup extra-virgin olive oil

½ large or 1 small yellow onion, cut into 1-inch pieces

1 fennel bulb, cut into 1-inch pieces

1 celery rib, cut into 1-inch pieces

Kosher salt

2 cups dry white wine

¼ cup champagne vinegar

1 tablespoon whole black peppercorns

(continued)

To finish and serve the sweetbreads, adjust the oven rack to the middle position and preheat the oven to 350ºF.

Cut the artichokes in half crosswise at the stem. Thinly slice the stems lengthwise and place them in a bowl. Break apart the artichoke leaves to separate them and drop them into the bowl.

Remove the weights and the plastic wrap from the sweetbreads and discard the plastic. Use a small, sharp knife to cut away and discard any knotty pieces or silver skin from the sweetbreads. Cut the sweetbreads into 2- to 3-inch segments. Pat the sweetbreads dry with paper towels and season all over with salt and pepper.

Heat the grapeseed oil in a large sauté pan over medium-high heat until the oil is almost smoking and slides easily in the pan, 2 to 3 minutes. Sear the sweetbreads in the oil until they are deep brown and crisp all over, about 4 minutes, turning them to cook all sides. Remove the sweetbreads to a baking sheet or a large plate and place them in the oven to heat through, about 3 minutes, while you make the sauce. Wipe the pan out with paper towels and add the olive oil and garlic. Season the garlic with salt and sauté over medium-high heat for 2 to 3 minutes, stirring constantly to prevent it from browning, until it softens slightly and becomes fragrant. Add the wine, caperberries, red pepper flakes, sugar, and 1 teaspoon of salt, and cook, stirring often, until the liquid has burned off, the garlic is golden brown, and the sugar left in the pan begins to caramelize around the sides, about 8 minutes. Add the chicken stock, increase the heat to high, and bring it to a boil. Stir in the artichokes and butter, and cook, stirring occasionally, until the liquid reduces by half and the sauce thickens slightly, about 12 minutes. Turn off the heat. Drizzle the lemon juice into the pan, add the parsley, and stir to incorporate into the sauce.

Remove the sweetbreads from the oven. Use a slotted spoon to strain the artichoke leaves out of the liquid and spread them out in a circle about 6 inches diameter in the center of four plates, dividing them evenly. From here, building each serving in two layers, place a few leaves of *cavolo nero* on top of each serving of artichoke leaves. Nestle half of the sweetbreads on top of the *cavolo,* dividing them evenly, drizzle with half of the sauce, dividing the sauce evenly and leaving the caperberries in the pan. Build the second layer, starting with a few of the *cavolo* leaves, the remaining sweetbreads, and topped with a drizzle of the sauce, using all of the ingredients in the second layer. Nestle the caperberries and zested strips of lemon around and on top of the sweetbreads, and serve.

for finishing and serving the sweetbreads
12 Braised Artichokes
    (page 70)
Kosher salt
Freshly ground black pepper
½ cup grapeseed oil or
    another neutral-flavored oil,
    such as canola
¼ cup extra-virgin olive oil
8 large garlic cloves,
    thinly sliced
1 cup dry white wine
20 whole caperberries
2 teaspoons red pepper flakes
2 teaspoons sugar
1 cup Basic Chicken Stock
    (page 27)
¼ cup (½ stick) unsalted
    butter
Juice of 2 lemons
¼ cup thinly sliced fresh
    Italian parsley leaves
Sautéed *Cavolo Nero*
    (page 260)
Zested strips of 1 lemon

pan-roasted pork chops with olives and sambuca-braised fennel

This is a simple, straightforward secondo *whose flavor is 100 percent dependent on the quality of the pork you use. We use pork from heritage pigs, such as Berkshire and Red Wattle, which are the most moist and more flavorful than the pork you find at a conventional grocery store. Berkshire, also known as Kurobuta pork, is the variety most available to the consumer. You can get such pork at some butchers, at high-end grocery stores, and also by mail order from online sources. I guarantee you will find the difference in flavor worth the effort it takes to get it.*

SERVES 4

SUGGESTED WINE PAIRING: ETNA ROSSO (SICILY)

To prepare the fennel, adjust the oven rack to the middle position and preheat the oven to 400°F.

Cut the fennel fronds off the bulbs and reserve them to garnish the pork. Trim and discard the ends from the fennel and, with the bulb standing on the flat, root end, slice the bulbs lengthwise into ½-inch-thick slices. Combine the fennel, onions, garlic, and olives in a baking dish large enough to hold the fennel slices snugly. Drizzle with ¼ cup of the olive oil, sprinkle with the salt and pepper, and toss to combine the ingredients. Remove the fennel slices and create a bed of the onions, olives, and garlic. Lay the fennel slices on top of the onions, slightly overlapping the slices. Pour the Sambuca and chicken stock around the fennel and drizzle the remaining ¾ cup olive oil over the fennel. If you have industrial-strength plastic wrap, which won't melt in the oven, cover the dish tightly with plastic wrap. In either case cover the dish tightly with aluminum foil and place it in the oven to cook for 1 hour. Remove the dish from the oven and remove and discard the foil and plastic, if you used it, taking care not to burn yourself with the steam that will rise. Return the pan to the oven and cook until the fennel is browned and glazed looking, 1 hour to 1 hour 15 minutes. Remove the pan from the oven, leaving the oven on to cook the pork.

To prepare the pork, combine the salt, sugar, and 1 cup of water in a large nonreactive baking dish or large sealable plastic bag to make a brine. Add the pork chops and turn to coat them on all sides. Cover the dish with plastic or seal the bag and set aside for 1 hour. Remove the chops from the brine, discarding the brine. Pat the pork chops dry with

for the fennel

3 medium fennel bulbs (about 1 pound), with fronds

2 large yellow Spanish onions, thinly sliced (about 2 cups)

20 cloves thinly sliced garlic, about ½ cup

½ cup Arbequina, Ligurian, Taggiasche, or Niçoise olives

1 cup extra-virgin olive oil

1 tablespoon kosher salt

½ teaspoon freshly ground black pepper

2 cups Sambuca

1 cup Basic Chicken Stock (page 27)

for the pork

½ cup kosher salt

⅓ cup sugar

4 9- to 10-ounce boneless pork chops (about 1 inch thick)

4 teaspoons Fennel Rub (page 242)

¼ cup extra-virgin olive oil

¼ cup (4 tablespoons) finishing-quality extra-virgin olive oil

½ teaspoon fennel pollen

paper towels, and place them on a cutting board. Sprinkle each chop generously with 1 teaspoon of the fennel rub and use the sides of the chops to mop up the rub that falls onto your cutting board.

Heat the olive oil in a large ovenproof sauté pan over medium-high heat until it is almost smoking and slides easily in the pan, 2 to 3 minutes. Add the chops and cook until deep brown and caramelized on one side, 2 to 3 minutes. Turn the pork chops and place the pan in the oven for 5 minutes, to cook the pork through. Remove from the oven and let the chops rest in the pan for 2 minutes before serving.

Lay the braised fennel mixture in the center of each of four plates, dividing it evenly. Drizzle a spoonful of the braising liquid over each serving and lay a pork chop on top. Drizzle 1 tablespoon of the finishing-quality olive oil over and around each chop, sprinkle with a pinch of fennel pollen, lay several of the fennel fronds on top, and serve.

fennel rub

*W*e use this seasoning mix for the Pan-roasted Pork Chops with Olives and Sambuca-braised Fennel (page 241) and the Pork Ribs with Fennel and Apple Cider Vinegar (facing page). It will keep for months, so if you like pork with fennel, make double (or more) of this recipe.

MAKES ABOUT 1/3 CUP

*C*ombine the salt, pepper, and fennel seeds in a spice grinder and grind them into a powder. Use the rub or transfer to an airtight container and store at room temperature.

2 tablespoons kosher salt
2 tablespoons freshly ground black pepper
2 tablespoons fennel seeds

pork ribs with fennel and apple cider vinegar

ven though eating a slab of baby back ribs isn't an Italian tradition, I felt that, Italians being the pork lovers they are, we could justify serving ribs as long as they had an Italian sensibility. After much prodding by me and experimenting by him, Matt came up with these tender, juicy, peppery, fennely, vinegary, Italianish baby back ribs. It was his brilliant idea to saw the racks of ribs in half down the middle—something you'll have to ask a butcher to do for you. The riblets feel a bit closer to the single rib you might be served among the unusual cuts on a mixed grill plate in Umbria or Tuscany instead of something you'd get in a roadside barbecue joint. Italian? Not exactly. Delicious? Very. The coleslaw recipe makes twice as much dressing as you'll need to dress the slaw for four servings, but because it is an emulsified dressing made with one egg yolk, you can't make less.

SERVES 4

SUGGESTED WINE PAIRING: ETNA ROSSO (SICILY)

o prepare the ribs, remove and discard the silver skin from the bone side of each rack of ribs. Combine the salt, sugar, and 1 quart of water together in a baking dish large enough to hold the ribs in a single layer to make a brine. Submerge the ribs in the brine, cover tightly with plastic wrap, and refrigerate for 1 hour.

Adjust the oven rack to the middle position and preheat the oven to 350°F.

Remove the ribs from the brine, wipe the baking dish dry, and pat the ribs dry with paper towels. Place the ribs bone side up in a single layer in the baking dish, dust the bone side of the ribs with half of the fennel rub, and pat so the rub adheres to the meat. Turn the ribs and repeat on the other side, leaving the ribs bone side up in the dish. Combine the vinegar and honey in a medium bowl and pour it over the ribs. If you have industrial-strength plastic wrap, which won't melt in the oven, cover the dish tightly with plastic wrap. In either case cover tightly with aluminum foil and place the ribs in the oven to cook for 1½ hours. Remove the ribs from the oven and remove and discard the foil and plastic, if you used it, being careful not to burn yourself with the steam that will rise from the pan. Baste the ribs with the juices in the dish and return them to the oven, uncovered, for another 20 to 30 minutes, until they are deep brown and glazed looking.

for the ribs

2 racks of pork baby back ribs
    (2 to 2½ pounds), sawed
    in half lengthwise
½ cup kosher salt,
    plus more for seasoning
½ cup sugar
Fennel Rub (facing page)
1 cup apple cider vinegar
¼ cup honey

(continued)

To prepare the coleslaw, toast the celery seeds in a small sauté pan over medium-high heat, shaking the pan or stirring the seeds constantly, until they are golden and fragrant, about 1 minute. Transfer the seeds to a small bowl and set aside to cool to room temperature.

Combine the egg yolk, vinegar, lemon juice, whole-grain mustard, Dijon mustard, sugar, garlic, and ½ teaspoon salt in a medium bowl and whisk to combine the ingredients. Place a wet kitchen towel around the bottom rim of the bowl to hold it in place. Combine the grapeseed oil and olive oil and drizzle the oils a few drops at a time, whisking constantly to form an emulsion. When you have added half of the oil, begin to drizzle the oil in a slow, steady stream, continuing to whisk constantly, until all of the oil has been added. Taste for seasoning and add more salt, if desired. The dressing can be made up to three days in advance. Transfer to an airtight container and refrigerate until you are ready to serve the coleslaw.

Remove and discard the outer leaves from both cabbage halves and remove and discard the cores. Separate the leaves, stack two or three leaves on top of one another, and slice them lengthwise ¼ inch thick. Put the leaves into a large bowl and repeat with the remaining leaves.

Trim and discard the ends of the carrot and cut the carrot into 2-inch-long segments. Cut the carrot on a mandoline to create ⅛ inch slabs, discarding the rounded slabs (the first and last slices). Stacking the slabs two at a time, cut them into ⅛-inch-wide matchsticks, and add them to the bowl with the cabbage. Cut the parsnip in the same way as the carrot and add it to the same bowl. Holding the apple upright on your cutting board, cut it into four slabs around the core so you are left holding the core in the center. Discard the core. Cut the apple segments on the mandoline into ⅛-inch-wide slabs, discarding the rounded slices. Stack the slabs two at a time, cut them into ⅛-inch-wide matchsticks, and add them to the bowl with the vegetables. If you are not ready to serve the coleslaw, cover it with a damp paper towel and refrigerate until you are ready to serve it, or for up to several hours. Just before serving, season the coleslaw with salt and toss to distribute the salt. Drizzle ½ cup of the dressing over the coleslaw and toss to coat the slaw with the dressing. Taste for seasoning and add more dressing or salt, if desired.

To serve, lay two of the rib halves on each of four plates, crossing one over the other. Spoon or brush any glaze remaining in the pan over the ribs and sprinkle them with fennel pollen. Pile a heaping ½ cup of the coleslaw next to the ribs and serve the remaining coleslaw on the side.

for the coleslaw

1 heaping teaspoon celery seeds

1 extra-large egg yolk

1½ tablespoons red wine vinegar

1½ tablespoons (1 tablespoon plus 1½ teaspoons) fresh lemon juice

1 tablespoon whole-grain mustard

1 tablespoon Dijon mustard

1 heaping teaspoon sugar

1 garlic clove, grated or minced

½ teaspoon kosher salt, plus more for seasoning

¾ cup grapeseed oil or another neutral-flavored oil, such as canola

¼ cup extra-virgin olive oil

½ a small head of red cabbage (halved through the core)

½ a small head of green cabbage (halved through the core)

1 large carrot, peeled

1 large parsnip, peeled

1 Granny Smith apple

Fennel pollen, for serving

rabbit con salsiccia, roasted garlic, lemon, and rosemary

In Italy you see "coniglio," or rabbit, offered in even the humblest trattoria or osteria, and I can almost never resist ordering it. The flavor of rabbit meat is so subtle that my favorite preparations are those that really coax the flavor out, such as this one. We braise the legs in white wine and serve them with a rabbit and pancetta sausage. When you buy rabbit, ask your butcher to separate the legs from the body of the animal, to fillet the saddles, and to reserve the carcass. And if you don't have a meat grinder, ask your butcher to grind the loin and belly meat for the sausage as well. We got the method for curing the rabbits from the Zuni Café Cookbook, *a constant, inspiring resource for us. While nothing in this recipe is difficult, I won't lie to you: it is time consuming. But when it's all done and you serve and bite into the finished dish, I think you'll find it was worth it. If you want to spare yourself a little effort, skip the step of making the rabbit stock and use chicken stock in its place.*

SERVES 4

SUGGESTED WINE PAIRING: CHIANTI CLASSICO (TUSCANY)

If you are making the stock, adjust the oven rack to the middle position and preheat the oven to 325°F.

Place the rabbit bones and the leek, onion, and carrot on a baking sheet and roast, shaking the pan occasionally for even cooking, until they're evenly browned, about 1½ hours. Remove the baking sheet from the oven and transfer the bones and vegetables to a large stockpot. Add the chicken stock to the pot and bring to a boil over high heat, skimming off the foam that rises to the top. Reduce the heat and simmer for 1 hour, skimming as needed. Remove the stock from the heat, pour it through a fine-mesh strainer, and discard the contents of the strainer. Use the stock, or set it aside to cool to room temperature, transfer it to an airtight container, and refrigerate for up to three days.

To prepare the rabbit legs, place the legs in a nonreactive baking dish large enough to fit them in a single layer and season them all over with the salt. Set the legs aside at room temperature to cure for 1½ hours. Rinse the rabbit legs and the baking dish, wipe the legs and the dish dry, and return the legs to the dish. Pour the milk in the dish, adding more if necessary to cover the rabbit legs. Cover the dish with plastic wrap and place the legs in the refrigerator for 1 hour. (Soaking the rabbits in milk desalinates them.) Remove the legs from the refrigerator,

for the stock (optional)
Bones of 2 whole rabbits, quartered
1 leek, roughly chopped (about 1-inch pieces)
1 large Spanish onion, roughly chopped (about 1-inch pieces)
1 carrot, peeled and roughly chopped (about 1-inch pieces)
2 quarts Basic Chicken Stock (page 27)

for cooking the rabbit legs
2 whole rabbits, legs separated from the carcass (you will have 4 rabbit hind legs and 4 rabbit front legs; loins and bellies reserved for making the sausage)

(continued)

and remove them from the milk. Discard the milk, rinse the rabbit legs under water, and pat them dry with paper towels.

To make the sausage, place the rabbit loins and bellies in a nonreactive baking dish or a sealable plastic bag and season with the pepper, sugar, and 1 teaspoon of the salt. Cover the dish with plastic wrap or seal the plastic bag and place the rabbit in the refrigerator to cure, at least 3 hours or overnight.

One hour before you are ready to complete the sausage, place the rabbit loins and bellies and the pancetta in the freezer to chill. (This makes the meats easier to pass through the meat grinder.) Fill a large bowl with ice water and have a small bowl ready to set inside. Fit a meat grinder with a small die. Remove the rabbit and pancetta from the freezer and pass them together through the grinder into the smaller bowl. Place the bowl with the meat inside the bowl of ice and set aside to chill while you prepare the rest of the ingredients for the sausage.

Combine the oil, minced onion, garlic, and rosemary needles in a medium sauté pan over medium-high heat and sauté until the onion and garlic are soft and translucent but not browned, about 5 minutes, stirring constantly and adding a splash of water to the pan from time to time to prevent the onion and garlic from browning. Remove the bowl with the rabbit and pancetta from the ice water, reserving the ice water for dipping your hands into, and add the contents of the sauté pan to the smaller bowl. Season with the remaining 1 teaspoon of salt, pepper, and nutmeg and stir gently until the ingredients are combined. Add 2 tablespoons of the ice water and mix the meats and vegetables with your hands, adding more ice water, if necessary, to make the mixture sticky and tacky. Dip your hands in the bowl of ice water to prevent the meat from sticking to your fingers. Pick up a 1½-ounce portion and mold it into a 1-inch-thick patty. Place the patty on a baking sheet or plate and repeat with the remaining meat. (The sausages can be prepared to this point up to five days in advance. Cover tightly with plastic wrap and refrigerate the sausages until you are ready to braise them, or freeze for up to several months.)

To cook the rabbit legs, adjust the oven rack to the middle position and preheat the oven to 350ºF.

Heat 2 tablespoons of the olive oil in a large Dutch oven or high-sided, ovenproof sauté pan over medium-high heat until the oil is almost smoking and slides easily in the pan, 2 to 3 minutes. Add the rabbit legs to the pan in a single layer, reduce the heat to medium, and

3 tablespoons plus 1 teaspoon kosher salt

3 cups whole milk, plus more as needed

for preparing the sausage
Loins and bellies from 2 rabbits (about ¾ pound)

¼ teaspoon freshly ground black pepper, plus more for seasoning

¼ teaspoon sugar

2 teaspoons kosher salt

6 ounces pancetta

1 tablespoon extra-virgin olive oil

½ cup minced Spanish onion (about ¼ large onion)

½ teaspoon chopped garlic

½ teaspoon minced fresh rosemary needles

⅛ teaspoon freshly grated nutmeg

¼ cup ice water

for cooking the rabbit
3 tablespoons extra-virgin olive oil, plus more as needed

1 celery rib, roughly chopped (about 1-inch pieces)

1 large carrot, peeled and roughly chopped (about 1-inch pieces)

1 leek, rinsed and roughly chopped (about 1-inch pieces)

1 large Spanish onion, halved and thinly sliced

2 large garlic cloves

1 quart white wine

1 long, fresh rosemary sprig (about 6 inches)

(*continued*)

rabbit con salsiccia, roasted garlic, lemon, and rosemary *(continued)*

cook for 3 to 5 minutes on the first side, until they are golden brown.
(If you do not have a pan large enough to fit all of the legs, cook them
in two batches, cooking all of the hind legs in one batch and the
forelegs in another batch and adding more olive oil to the pan in
between batches, if necessary.) Turn the rabbit legs and cook them for
2 minutes on the other side. Remove the legs to a plate and add the
remaining 1 tablespoon of olive oil. Add the celery, carrot, leek, and
sliced onion and sauté for about 2 minutes, stirring often, until the
vegetables begin to soften. Add the garlic cloves and sauté for about
5 minutes, stirring occasionally, until golden brown and softened.
Add the wine, increase the heat to high, and cook until it reduces
by half, about 10 minutes. Return the rabbit legs, nestling them in
a single layer in the pan and place the rosemary and chile on top.
Alternatively, if your pan is not large enough to hold all of the legs,
pour the contents of the pan into a baking dish large enough to hold
them in a single layer. Gradually add the stock to just cover the rabbit.
If you have industrial-strength plastic wrap, which won't melt in the

1 dried arbol chile
3 cups reserved rabbit stock or
    Basic Chicken Stock
    (page 27), or as needed

**for finishing and serving
the rabbit**

2 tablespoons extra-virgin
    olive oil
20 garlic cloves
$1/2$ teaspoon red pepper flakes
$2 1/2$ cups reserved rabbit stock
    or Basic Chicken Stock
    (page 27)
Zested strips of 1 lemon
Sautéed *Cavolo Nero*
    (page 260)

oven, cover the pan or baking dish tightly with plastic wrap. In either case cover the dish tightly with aluminum foil and put the lid on the pot if it has one. Place the rabbit in the oven to braise for 1 hour to 1½ hours, until the meat is fork-tender and the joints move easily, checking for doneness after 1 hour. Remove the rabbit legs from the oven, remove the lid, and remove and discard the foil and plastic, if you used it, being careful not to burn yourself with the steam that will rise from the pan. Set the rabbit aside to cool in the braising liquid for at least 30 minutes. You can prepare the rabbit to this point up to five days in advance. Cool the rabbit in the braising liquid to room temperature. Cover the pot with plastic wrap or transfer the rabbit with the liquid to an airtight container and refrigerate until you are ready to serve it.

To finish the rabbit, if it is still warm from the braising liquid, heat the oil in a large sauté pan over medium-high until the oil is almost smoking and slides easily in the pan, 2 to 3 minutes. Add the sausages and cook them about 1 minute on each side, until they are golden brown. Remove the sausage to a plate lined with paper towels and drain the oil from the pan, leaving just enough to cover the bottom of the pan. Add the garlic, rosemary sprig, and red pepper flakes, and sauté for about 2 minutes, until the garlic is golden brown and slightly caramelized. Add the rabbit legs and 1 cup of the reserved rabbit stock or chicken stock. Increase the heat to high and bring the liquid to a boil. Turn off the heat, stir in the lemon zest strips, and place the pan in the oven, uncovered, until the meat is heated through, about 12 minutes. Remove the pan from the oven and remove the sausage from the pan. Place the pan over high heat, spooning the sauce over the rabbit as it cooks, until the sauce is thick and gravy-like and has reduced by about half, 7 to 9 minutes. Add the sausage back to the sauce to warm it from the residual heat in the pan.

If you have prepared the rabbit in advance and are rewarming it, preheat the oven to 350°F. Place the rabbit in the braising liquid in the oven about for 20 minutes, basting it with the sauce occasionally, until it is warmed through. Cook the sausage and sauce as directed above.

To serve, pile the *cavolo nero* in the center of each plate, dividing it evenly. Nestle one rabbit leg on each mound of the *cavolo* and rest the other leg against the first at a perpendicular angle. Place one sausage patty on either side of each serving of rabbit and lay the garlic cloves and rosemary sprig on top. Spoon the sauce over the rabbit, dividing it evenly.

contorni

Contorni are side dishes that are meant to be ordered alongside se-condi, or main dishes. In Italy, at least in the countryside where I spend my time, the list of contorni *is usually limited to a few simple seasonal basics, such as roasted potatoes and sautéed spinach, or bitter greens, such as rapini. We took liberties with our* contorni, *offering what we imagined our American audience would want to order with their main dishes. Some of these, such as the Roasted Beets with Horseradish Vinaigrette and Mâche (page 266) and Brussels Sprouts with Sherry Vinaigrette and Prosciutto Bread Crumbs (page 256), come from the antipasti section of the Pizzeria menu. Others, such as Polenta (page 265) and Lentils Castellucciano (page 264), are served as components to specific* secondi. *Any one of them would be delicious served at room temperature as part of a* tavola fredda, *or "cold table" of appetizers, which is closer to how they might be enjoyed in Italy.*

marinated shell beans with cherry tomatoes and oregano

Italians famously eat a lot of beans, so including shell beans on our menu was an obvious choice. Shell beans are so delicious and can be prepared in such a variety of ways, and yet you don't normally see them at conventional grocery stores. Looking for shell beans is a good excuse to visit your local farmers' market, which is where we find them in Los Angeles in the late summer and early fall. We use a mix of four types of shell beans—borlotti beans, cannellini beans, lima beans, and flageolet—because we like the range of sizes, colors, and flavors of the various beans. Properly cooking beans is about 90 percent of the battle, which is why we cook each type of bean sepa-rately; to spare yourself the effort, use fewer varieties of beans. If you don't have access to shell beans, or when shell beans are not in season, you could make this using dried beans. Refer to Ceci (page 96) for instructions. The recipe for the bouquet is for each pot of beans. You will need to make the same number as types of beans you are making.

SERVES 4 TO 6

Wrap the onion, garlic, and sage in a doubled piece of cheesecloth and tie it into a closed bundle with kitchen twine. Put each type of bean in a separate small or medium saucepan and add enough water to each pan to cover the

1 cup minced Spanish
yellow onion
(about ½ onion),
per bouquet

(continued)

beans by 1½ inches. Place one bouquet in each pan, stir in the olive oil, bring the water to a boil over high heat, and salt the water to taste like the ocean. Add approximately 1 tablespoon of salt for each quart of water. Reduce the heat and simmer the beans until they are tender and creamy, but not mushy, adding more water as needed, but never covering them by more than an inch and a half, 25 to 35 minutes. (Cooking them in this way yields richer tasting, creamier beans than if you were to just boil them in tons of water.) Turn off the heat and allow the beans to cool in the cooking liquid. Remove and discard the cheesecloth bundles. The beans can be prepared to this point up to one week in advance. If you are using the beans now, drain them, reserving the cooking liquid to use as a hearty, bean-flavored base for vegetable soup. To use them later, transfer the beans and the cooking liquid to an airtight container and refrigerate until you are ready to use them or up to 24 hours. Drain and bring the beans to room temperature before dressing them.

Combine the various beans in a large mixing bowl. Add the tomatoes, parsley, and oregano. Drizzle with the vinaigrette, season with salt and pepper, and stir gently to combine the ingredients, taking care not to crush the beans. Taste for seasoning and add more salt, pepper, or vinaigrette, if desired. Serve at room temperature.

6 large garlic cloves,
  thinly sliced, per bouquet
4 fresh sage leaves,
  per bouquet
1 pound fresh shell beans,
  such as borlotti, cannellini,
  lima, or flageolet (about
  3 cups shelled beans)
2 tablespoons extra-virgin
  olive oil
Kosher salt
Slow-roasted Cherry Tomatoes
  (page 67)
½ cup thinly sliced fresh
  Italian parsley leaves
¼ cup fresh oregano leaves
½ cup Lemon Vinaigrette
  (page 29), plus more
  to taste
Freshly ground black pepper

cipolline with thyme and sherry vinegar

ipolline are small, flat, sweet Italian onions. This agrodolce *preparation of cipolline is one of the staples of my Umbrian* tavola, *and
the most popular* contorno *at the Osteria, I think in part because
onions go with so many main dishes, and they are also easy to share. My dad
orders them every time he comes to the restaurant. I think he could make a meal
of nothing but these onions followed by a perfectly pulled espresso. In the summer when I can find them, I use long, red torpedo onions in place of cipolline.*

SERVES 4 TO 6

djust the oven rack to a position in the upper third of the
oven and preheat the oven to 425°F.

Fill a large saucepan with water, bring the water to a
boil over high heat, and salt it to taste like the ocean. Add approximately 1 tablespoon of salt for each quart of water. While the water is
coming to a boil, place a colander in the sink or have a wire strainer
handy for lifting the onions out of the water. Add the cipolline to the
boiling water and cook until they are just tender, about 3 minutes.
Drain the onions, or lift them out of the water, and run cold water over
them to cool, and drain again. Use a small knife to trim the ends off
and rub the cipolline with a dry dishtowel to remove the skins.

Stir the olive oil, sugar, and ¼ cup of the vinegar together in a large
sauté pan over medium heat. Add the cipolline and season them with
kosher salt and pepper. Toss to coat the onions with the seasonings,
and bring the liquid to a simmer. Turn off the heat, put the lid on the
pan, and place it in the oven to roast the cipolline for about 20 minutes, until soft. Remove the pan from the oven, uncover, and return
the cipolline to the oven to roast for another 10 minutes, uncovered,
basting a few times with the juices until they're lightly glazed.

Remove the pan from the oven and place it on the stove. Turn the
heat to medium high, season the cipolline with kosher salt and pepper,
and cook, shaking the pan to make sure they don't stick, and turning
them carefully with tongs, until they are lightly caramelized on both
sides, 4 to 5 minutes. Turn off the heat and add the remaining 2 tablespoons of vinegar and 2 tablespoons of water. Place the pan over
medium heat and cook the cipolline for 2 to 3 minutes, shaking the
pan frequently, until they are glazed and sticky. Turn off the heat,
sprinkle the thyme leaves over the cipolline, and toss or stir gently to
distribute the thyme. Transfer the onions to a serving dish and sprinkle
with sea salt. Serve warm or at room temperature.

Kosher salt and freshly ground
    black pepper
1 ½ pounds cipolline or
    red torpedo onions
¼ cup extra-virgin olive oil
1 teaspoon sugar
¼ cup plus 2 tablespoons
    Spanish sherry vinegar
2 tablespoons fresh thyme
    leaves
Maldon sea salt or another
    flaky sea salt, such as
    fleur de sel

smashed potatoes with rosemary

*T*he summer before we opened Mozza, Matt came to stay with me at my house in Italy. We went to a luncheon at the Tuscan winery Arnaldo Caprai, where we were served rosemary-scented potatoes that inspired these. Smashing the potatoes gives them more surface area, which means more crispy bits—my favorite part.

SERVES 4 TO 6

*C*ombine the potatoes, chopped rosemary, butter, garlic, salt, and ¼ cup of the olive oil in a large sauté pan over medium heat. When the butter melts, stir to combine, then cover the pan with a lid and cook the potatoes until they are tender when pierced with a fork, about 30 minutes. Uncover the pan, remove the potatoes from the pan, and set them aside to cool slightly. Remove the garlic with a slotted spoon and discard, reserving the oil and butter in the pan. When the potatoes are cool enough to touch, one at a time, place the potatoes on a flat surface and use the heel of your hand to smash them ½ inch thick, pressing evenly to prevent the potatoes from breaking apart. Slide the potatoes off the surface rather than lifting them, to help keep them intact. You can prepare the potatoes to this point up to several hours in advance. Proceed just before you are ready to serve them.

Add 2 tablespoons of the remaining olive oil to the oil-butter mixture, or enough so the fat in the pan is ½ inch deep, and heat over medium-high heat until the oil is almost smoking and slides easily in the pan, 2 to 3 minutes. If the oil begins to bubble, reduce the heat slightly. Working in two or more batches, add the smashed potatoes in a single layer to the pan, season with salt, and cook until they are deep brown and crisp, about 3 minutes per side. Remove the potatoes to paper towels to drain and season them with sea salt. Add the remaining 2 tablespoons of oil to the pan, or more as needed, and heat before adding the second batch. Cook the remaining potatoes in the same way.

To fry the rosemary, pour enough olive oil into a small skillet or saucepan to fill it 1 inch deep and line a small plate with paper towels. Heat the oil over medium-high heat until a pinch of salt sizzles when dropped into it. Add the rosemary and fry for about 30 seconds until crisp but not brown. Use a slotted spoon to remove the rosemary from the oil, transfer to the paper towels to drain, and season with salt. Strain the rosemary-infused oil through a fine-mesh strainer and reserve it to fry rosemary another time, to make vinaigrettes, or to driz-

2 pounds fingerling potatoes (about 20 small potatoes; or substitute small Yukon Gold potatoes)

¼ cup roughly chopped fresh rosemary needles

¼ cup (½ stick) unsalted butter

8 large garlic cloves, smashed with the flat side of a knife

2 teaspoons kosher salt, plus more as needed

½ cup extra-virgin olive oil, plus more as needed

Maldon sea salt or another flaky sea salt, such as fleur de sel

5 to 7 rosemary branches

zle over grilled meats or vegetables. (The rosemary can be fried up to several hours in advance. Store it in an airtight container at room temperature.) Serve warm, with the fried rosemary branches scattered on top.

brussels sprouts with sherry vinaigrette and prosciutto bread crumbs

russels sprouts get a bad rap. People say they hate Brussels sprouts more than any other food, other than lima beans; in both cases, I believe the reason is that the vegetables are so rarely prepared well. We sear our Brussels sprouts so they get nicely browned while maintaining their unique texture and vibrant green color, then we toss them in sherry vinaigrette and top them with bread crumbs laced with prosciutto and herbs. Judging by the number of people who absolutely love these, I would say we have converted many a Brussels sprout hater with this preparation. The recipe for the prosciutto bread crumbs makes about 1 cup, which is more than you will need for this dish, but since it calls for such a variety of herbs, it seems silly to make a smaller portion and have so many herbs left over—better to have the bread crumbs left over. They are delicious sprinkled on any roasted vegetables. If you don't have time to prepare the bread crumbs, the Brussels sprouts are still delicious without them.

SERVES 4 TO 6

o make the bread crumbs, adjust the oven rack to the middle position and preheat the oven to 350°F. Line a plate with paper towels.

Combine the prosciutto and olive oil in a large sauté pan over medium-high heat and cook, stirring frequently, until the prosciutto is brown and crisp, about 5 minutes. Turn off the heat and transfer the prosciutto to the paper towels to drain. Add the bread crumbs to the pan you cooked the prosciutto in and toss to coat the bread crumbs with the oil in the pan. Scatter the bread crumbs on a baking sheet and place them in the oven to toast for 12 to 15 minutes, until they are light golden brown, stirring them once or twice during cooking time so they brown evenly. Remove the bread crumbs from the oven but leave the oven on. Add the prosciutto, chervil, chives, and tarragon to the baking sheet with the bread crumbs and stir to combine. Return the

for the prosciutto bread crumbs

¼ pound prosciutto, ground or finely chopped

2 tablespoons extra-virgin olive oil

1 cup finely ground bread crumbs (from about 5 ounces of crustless bread)

½ cup finely chopped fresh chervil leaves

½ cup finely minced fresh chives

⅓ cup finely chopped fresh tarragon leaves

bread crumbs to the oven for 10 minutes, stirring them once or twice during that time so they cook evenly, until they are golden brown and crisp. Set them aside to cool to room temperature. Use the bread crumbs, or transfer them to an airtight container, and store them at room temperature for up to two days. Bring the bread crumbs to room temperature before using them.

To make the vinaigrette, combine the vinegar, shallots, salt, and pepper in a small bowl, and set aside for about 5 minutes to allow the shallots to marinate in the vinegar. Add the oil in a slow, steady stream, whisking constantly to combine. Taste for seasoning and add more salt or vinegar, if desired. Use the vinaigrette or transfer it to an airtight container and refrigerate it for up to three days. Bring the vinaigrette to room temperature, whisk to recombine the ingredients, and taste again for seasoning before using.

To cook the Brussels sprouts, put them in a large bowl, drizzle them with ½ cup of the olive oil, season with the salt and pepper, and toss to coat with the seasonings.

Heat ½ cup of the remaining olive oil in a large sauté pan over medium heat until the oil is almost smoking and slides easily in the pan, 3 to 4 minutes. Working in two or more batches, place the Brussels sprouts cut side down in a single layer in the oil and sauté them for 2 to 3 minutes on each side, until they are golden brown on both sides and tender but not mushy, using tongs to turn the sprouts as they brown. Remove the sprouts to a plate or baking sheet as they are done. When you've removed the first batch of sprouts, add the remaining 2 tablespoons of oil to the pan and cook another batch. Repeat until all of the Brussels sprouts are cooked, adding more oil as necessary. You can prepare the Brussels sprouts to this point up to several hours in advance. Transfer them to an airtight container and keep them at room temperature until you are ready to serve them.

When you are ready to serve the Brussels sprouts, drizzle them with the vinaigrette, squeeze a few drops of lemon juice over them, and toss to coat the sprouts with the seasonings. Taste for seasoning and add more salt, if desired. Transfer the Brussels sprouts to a serving platter or dish, sprinkling each layer of sprouts lightly with the bread crumbs. Sprinkle ¼ cup of bread crumbs over the top and serve, serving the remaining bread crumbs on the side or reserving them for another use. Serve warm or at room temperature.

for the sherry vinaigrette
½ cup Spanish sherry vinegar
¼ cup finely chopped shallots
2 teaspoons kosher salt
1 teaspoon freshly ground
    black pepper
¼ cup extra-virgin olive oil

for the brussels sprouts
2 pounds Brussels sprouts,
    stem ends trimmed, outer
    leaves removed, and
    sprouts halved
1 cup plus 2 tablespoons
    extra-virgin olive oil,
    plus more as needed
1 tablespoon kosher salt
½ teaspoon freshly ground
    black pepper
Half of a lemon

cauliflower gratinate

For this rich side dish, one of the originals from the Pizzeria, we simmer the cauliflower in cream and then put it in the pizza oven to brown the top. I've never met anyone who didn't like it. Butter, cream, garlic, cauliflower . . . what's not to like?

SERVES 4 TO 6

Adjust the oven rack to the middle position and preheat the oven to 450°F. Lightly butter a large baking dish, preferably one nice enough to present at the table.

Trim and discard the cauliflower leaves, cut the florets off the core, discard the core, and cut the florets into 1½-inch pieces.

Warm the butter, olive oil, onion, garlic, and 1 teaspoon of the salt in a heavy-bottomed saucepan over medium heat and cook until the onion begins to soften, 3 to 4 minutes, stirring often to prevent the garlic from browning. Add the cauliflower, cream, and the remaining teaspoon of salt, increase the heat to high, and bring the cream to a boil. Reduce the heat to low and simmer the cauliflower until it is tender, 10 to 12 minutes. Pour the cauliflower through a fine-mesh strainer, reserving the cream. Return the cream to the saucepan and simmer it over medium heat until it reduces by one-third and becomes the consistency of thin gravy, taking care that the cream doesn't brown. Return the cauliflower to the saucepan and stir gently to combine with the cream. Transfer the cauliflower and cream to the prepared baking dish and bake for 30 minutes, or until the top is golden brown. Remove the cauliflower from the oven and set aside for a few minutes to cool slightly before serving. Serve warm.

2 tablespoons unsalted butter, plus more for buttering the baking dish

1 large head of cauliflower (about 1½ pounds)

2 tablespoons extra-virgin olive oil

1 Spanish onion, halved through the core and sliced ¼ inch thick

10 garlic cloves, thinly sliced

2 teaspoons kosher salt

2 cups heavy whipping cream

long-cooked broccoli

*W*hen you read "Long-cooked Broccoli," note that this is distinctly different from the soggy, overcooked broccoli that you might remember from the school cafeteria. Here, the broccoli is cooked deliberately long and slow—almost poached—in olive oil with a lot of onion and garlic. Cooking it this way makes the broccoli tender, buttery, and flavorful. It's one of my all-time favorite vegetable preparations. We use it to top the Long-cooked Broccoli, Caciocavallo, and Peperoncino pizza (page 146), and we also offer it as an antipasto at the Pizzeria.

SERVES 4 TO 6

*T*rim off and discard the tough ends of the broccoli. Cut off the heads and separate the heads into roughly 2-inch pieces. Peel the broccoli stems with a vegetable peeler or a sharp knife, discard the peelings, and slice the stems lengthwise into ½-inch-thick slabs. Slice each slab lengthwise into ½-inch-wide batonettes.

Combine the onion, garlic, chile, and ¼ cup of the olive oil in a large sauté pan over medium heat; season with the salt and pepper and sauté until the onion begins to soften, 4 to 5 minutes. Add the broccoli stems and sauté for 2 to 3 minutes to soften them slightly. Add the broccoli heads and ¾ cup of the remaining olive oil and cook for 2 to 3 minutes, stirring to prevent the vegetables from browning and so they wilt evenly. Reduce the heat to low, and add the remaining ½ cup of olive oil. Cook, gently stirring only as necessary to prevent the broccoli from sticking to the pan but not so much or so vigorously that the broccoli heads fall apart, until the broccoli is very tender but still holding its shape, 45 minutes to 1 hour. Taste for seasoning and add more salt, if desired. Carefully lift the broccoli out of the oil and transfer it to a platter to serve. Reserve the oil to make the dish a second time or use it to sauté or drizzle over vegetables. Serve warm or at room temperature.

2½ pounds broccoli
1 large Spanish onion, halved through the core and sliced ¼ inch thin
½ cup thinly sliced garlic cloves
1 dried arbol chile
1½ cups extra-virgin olive oil
1 tablespoon kosher salt
½ teaspoon freshly ground black pepper

sautéed cavolo nero

Cavolo nero, a variety of kale, means "black cabbage" in Italian and is a staple of Tuscan cooking. It has a distinct, earthy flavor that I love and that complements many of our heartier preparations.

SERVES 4 TO 6

Fill a large pot with water, bring it to a boil over high heat, and salt it to taste like the ocean, adding about 1 tablespoon of salt for each quart of water. Place a colander in the sink or have a strainer handy to lift the *cavolo* out of the water. Fill a large bowl with ice water. Add the *cavolo nero* to the boiling water and cook until it is bright green and tender, about 2 minutes. Drain the *cavolo* or lift it out of the water and quickly plunge it in the ice water for about 1 minute, to cool completely. Lift the *cavolo* out of the ice water and gently wring it in your hands to squeeze out all the excess water. (You can prepare the *cavolo* to this point up to two days in advance. Transfer to an airtight container and refrigerate until you are ready to finish it.)

Heat the olive oil in a large sauté pan over medium-high heat until the oil is almost smoking and slides easily in the pan, 2 to 3 minutes. Add the shallots, season with salt, and sauté for about 30 seconds to soften, stirring constantly to prevent them from browning. Add the *cavolo nero*, separating the leaves as you add them to the pan if they have compressed from squeezing them. Season the *cavolo* with salt and sauté for 2 to 3 minutes, stirring constantly to coat the greens with the seasonings. Serve warm.

Kosher salt
1 bunch *cavolo nero* (or another variety of kale), leaves pulled from the stems and stems discarded
¼ cup extra-virgin olive oil
¼ cup finely chopped shallots

yellow wax beans stracotto in soffritto with salsa verde

I think the heart and soul of Italian cooking is coaxing the true flavor out of raw ingredients, and that's what we do with these beans. Stracotto means "long cooked," and for this recipe, yellow wax beans, a summer vegetable usually prepared al dente, are simmered long and slow with our deeply caramelized soffritto. You'll want to make this dish only if you already have soffritto in your refrigerator and when yellow wax beans are in season. You could also use yellow Romano beans.

SERVES 4 TO 6

Heat the oil in a large sauté pan over medium-high heat until it is almost smoking and slides easily in the pan, 2 to 3 minutes. Add the beans, sprinkle with ¼ teaspoon of the salt, and cook for about 2 minutes, until they are slightly browned. Move the beans to create a bare spot in the pan, add the tomato paste to that spot, and cook for 1 minute, stirring, to caramelize. Add the Soffritto and anchovies, and stir to combine the ingredients and to coat the beans with the Soffritto. Reduce the heat to low, season the beans with the remaining ¼ teaspoon of salt, and cook for about 2 minutes. Add 1 cup of water to the pan, and simmer the beans until they are very tender, about 20 minutes for wax beans and 30 minutes for Romano beans. If there is still water in the pan, remove the lid, increase the heat to high, and cook until the water evaporates. Serve the beans warm or at room temperature. Transfer the beans to a serving dish, spoon ¼ cup of salsa verde over them, and serve with the remaining salsa verde on the side.

- 2 tablespoons extra-virgin olive oil
- 1 pound yellow wax beans or yellow Romano beans, ends trimmed
- ½ teaspoon kosher salt
- ½ teaspoon double-concentrated tomato paste
- ½ cup Soffritto (page 28)
- 2 anchovy fillets (preferably salt-packed), rinsed, backbones removed if salt-packed, and minced
- ½ cup Salsa Verde (recipe follows)

salsa verde

This recipe makes twice what you need for the Yellow Wax Beans Stracotto in Soffritto, but it is one of those things that is difficult to make in smaller quantity. Spoon what you have left over on grilled fish, vegetables, or chicken.

MAKES ABOUT 1 CUP SALSA

Combine the anchovies, capers, garlic, salt, and half of the olive oil in the bowl of a food processor fitted with a metal blade or the jar of a blender. Add half of the parsley, mint, and marjoram leaves and pulse until the herbs are finely chopped. Turn off the machine and scrape down the sides of the bowl with a rubber spatula. Add the remaining herbs and the remaining olive oil and purée, stopping as soon as the ingredients form a homogenous paste, and adding more olive oil, if necessary, to obtain a loose, spoonable salsa. (You want to stop the machine as soon as you achieve the desired consistency, as the blade will heat the garlic and give it a bitter flavor. Also, overprocessing the salsa verde will incorporate too much air, making it fluffy and also too smooth. I like to see some flecks of herbs in my salsa verde.) Turn the salsa verde out into a bowl and stir in the lemon juice. Taste for seasoning and add more salt or lemon juice if desired. Use the

- 6 anchovy fillets (preferably salt-packed), rinsed, backbones removed if salt-packed, and finely chopped
- 2 heaping tablespoons capers (preferably salt-packed), soaked for 15 minutes if salt-packed, rinsed and drained
- 3 garlic cloves
- ½ teaspoon kosher salt, plus more to taste
- ⅔ cup extra-virgin olive oil
- ¾ cup packed fresh Italian parsley leaves
- ⅓ cup packed fresh mint leaves
- ¼ cup packed fresh marjoram leaves
- 1½ teaspoons fresh lemon juice, plus more to taste

salsa or transfer it to an airtight container and refrigerate for up to two days—any longer and it will lose its pretty green color and vibrant flavor. Bring the salsa to room temperature, stir to recombine the ingredients, and taste again for seasoning before serving.

sautéed broccolini with chiles and vinegar

Using vinegar and chiles in an aggressive way is something Matt picked up from Mario, and I love it. I have a thing for acidic food in general—vinegar in particular. If you were to follow me around the kitchen at Mozza as I tasted various sauces and condiments, what you would hear most often is, "It needs salt" or "It needs acid." This needs neither. Broccolini, also called baby broccoli, looks similar to broccoli but with longer, thinner stalks and smaller florets. It's a hybrid between conventional broccoli and Chinese broccoli and is slightly sweeter than broccoli. We also make this dish with Romanesco, an Italian heirloom variety of cauliflower.

SERVES 4 TO 6

Cut off and discard the dry ends of the broccolini. Cut off about 2 inches from the stems; reserve the stems but keep the stems and heads separate.

Heat 2 tablespoons of the olive oil in a large sauté pan over medium-high heat until the oil is almost smoking and slides easily in the pan, 2 to 3 minutes. Add the broccolini stems, season with salt, and cook them for 1 to 2 minutes until they begin to brown. Add the remaining 2 tablespoons of olive oil and the florets, season them with salt, and cook, stirring the broccolini or shaking the pan occasionally, for about 2 minutes, until the florets begin to brown and soften. Remove the pan from the heat, add ½ cup of water, cover, reduce the heat to medium low, and steam the broccolini until the water is evaporated and the broccolini is tender, about 2 minutes. Add the garlic and cook for 1 to 2 minutes until it is golden brown, stirring frequently to prevent the garlic from burning. Turn off the heat, add the vinegar and red pepper flakes, stir to combine them with the broccolini, and let the broccolini cook with the vinegar for about 1 minute from the residual heat of the pan. Taste for seasoning and add more salt, if desired. Serve warm.

1 pound broccolini
(about 2 bunches)
¼ cup extra-virgin olive oil
Kosher salt
6 garlic cloves, thinly sliced
lengthwise
⅓ cup red wine vinegar
½ teaspoon red pepper flakes

roasted carrots siciliana

Currants and pine nuts are a classic combination in Sicilian cuisine, so even though I may never see carrots such as these on a restaurant menu in Sicily, the combination feels Sicilian to me. You could make many different vegetables, such as broccoli or cauliflower, using this recipe. It is an ideal vegetable preparation to serve at parties because it can be made ahead of time, and everyone loves it. This dish looks especially pretty made with a mix of carrots in different shapes and colors—such as white, yellow, red, or purple—and carrots that are round, like a golf ball.

SERVES 4 TO 6

Adjust the oven rack to the middle position and preheat the oven to 450°F.

Scrub the carrots and trim and discard the stems, leaving the last ¾ inch of the stems attached. Place the carrots in a large bowl, drizzle with the olive oil, sprinkle with the salt and pepper, and toss to coat the carrots with the seasonings. Spread the carrots in a single layer on a baking sheet and place them in the oven to roast until they are golden in spots and tender but not mushy, shaking the pan occasionally during cooking time so they cook evenly, 10 to 15 minutes.

To fry the rosemary, pour enough olive oil into a small skillet or saucepan to fill it 1 inch deep and line a small plate with paper towels. Heat the oil over medium-high heat until a pinch of salt sizzles when dropped into it. Add the rosemary and fry for about 30 seconds, until it's crisp but not brown. Use a slotted spoon to remove the rosemary from the oil, transfer to the paper towels to drain, and season with sea salt. Strain the rosemary-infused oil through a fine-mesh strainer and reserve it to fry rosemary another time, to make vinaigrettes, or to drizzle over grilled meats or vegetables. (The rosemary can be fried up to several hours in advance. Store it in an airtight container at room temperature.)

Remove the carrots from the oven. Spoon ¼ cup of the relish over them and toss gently to distribute the relish. To serve, place a layer of carrots on a platter and spoon some of the relish remaining on the baking sheet over the carrots. Build another layer with the carrots perpendicular to the first layer. Add more of the relish and build a third layer. Spoon the remaining tablespoon of relish over the carrots and scatter the fried rosemary over and around them. Serve warm or at room temperature.

1 pound small to medium carrots (with the tops on, not whittled carrots)

2 tablespoons extra-virgin olive oil, plus more for frying

1 teaspoon kosher salt

¼ teaspoon freshly ground black pepper

¼ cup fresh rosemary tufts

Maldon sea salt or another flaky sea salt, such as fleur de sel

¼ cup plus 1 tablespoon Currant and Pine Nut Relish (page 71)

lentils castellucciano

We exclusively use Umbrian lentils in our restaurants, which are smaller than common brown lentils and are various shades of brown to green. Castelluccio, the town where the lentils come from, is a two-and-a-half-hour, winding, hilly drive over the Apennine Mountains from my house. Once you get there, you don't feel like you're in Umbria—or Italy—at all. There are no sunflowers. No rolling green hills. The landscape is crater-like, with fields and fields of flowering lentils. It feels more like you're on the moon, or in Oz. When I visited with a group of friends, we ate lunch at the one trattoria in town. Of course they offered lentils, and I was surprised to find them cooked in a much heartier way than I had ever seen lentils prepared before, almost like a stew or a ragù, with pork sausage, another delicacy of that region. This is Matt's rendition of the lentils we had that day.

SERVES 6 TO 8

Heat the olive oil in a large sauté pan or a stockpot over medium-high heat until the oil is almost smoking and slides easily in the pan, 2 to 3 minutes. Add the prosciutto and cook to render the fat but not brown, 2 to 3 minutes. Add the onion, carrot, and celery, season with salt and pepper, and sauté for about 10 minutes, until the vegetables have softened and the onion is translucent. Add the garlic and cook for 1 to 2 minutes, until it is fragrant, stirring constantly to prevent it from browning. Move the vegetables to create a bare spot in the pan, add the tomato paste to that spot, and cook for 1 minute, stirring, to caramelize the tomato paste slightly. Add the lentils and 3 cups of the stock; increase the heat to high and bring the stock to a boil. Reduce the heat and simmer the lentils, stirring occasionally, until most of the stock is absorbed, about 30 minutes. Add 2 more cups of the stock and simmer, stirring occasionally, until it is absorbed, about 30 minutes. Continue to cook the lentils in this way, adding 1 or 2 cups of stock as necessary so the lentils are covered and soupy but not drowning, until they are tender and creamy, 1 hour 15 minutes to 1 hour 45 minutes. If you have used all the liquid and the lentils are not done, continue cooking, using water in place of stock. When the lentils are done, if there is too much liquid in the pan, increase the heat to medium to cook it off until the lentils are creamy but not soupy. Taste for seasoning and add salt and pepper, if desired. (You can prepare the lentils to this point up to three days in advance. Set the lentils aside to cool to room temperature, transfer to an airtight container and refrigerate the lentils until you are ready to

¼ cup extra-virgin olive oil

¼ pound prosciutto, finely chopped

1 large Spanish onion, finely chopped

1 large carrot, peeled and finely chopped

1 celery rib, finely chopped

1½ teaspoons kosher salt, plus more to taste

½ teaspoon freshly ground black pepper, plus more to taste

2 large garlic cloves, minced

1 tablespoon double-concentrated tomato paste

1 pound Umbrian lentils (about 2½ cups) or lentilles du Puy or beluga lentils

2 quarts Basic Chicken Stock (page 27)

¼ cup finishing-quality extra-virgin olive oil

serve them. Just before serving, warm the lentils over medium heat, stirring often and adding enough water to loosen the lentils to a creamy consistency.) Drizzle the finishing-quality olive oil into the lentils, stirring vigorously, until the lentils are creamy and emulsified, about 1 minute. Serve warm or at room temperature.

polenta

*P*olenta, which is cooked cornmeal, takes the place of mashed potatoes at the Italian table as a comforting, starchy side dish. To cook polenta correctly, you have to go by the texture, not the time, as the cooking times will vary depending on how the corn was milled and how fresh it is. We start with a whole-grain polenta, Anson Mills Rustic Polenta Integrale. Like any whole grain, it still has the germ and the bran, which gives it a more earthy flavor. It takes about three hours to cook so it's definitely something to save for when you're in the mood for slow cooking. We cook the polenta—with all that stirring that polenta is so known for—until you can't feel the grain under your teeth. The texture of the finished polenta is almost custardy. Matt uses Italian sparkling mineral water to make polenta because he thinks the minerals in the water add to the flavor of the polenta. When making the polenta to serve Brasato *al Barolo with Polenta and Horseradish Gremolata (page 230), omit the Parmigiano-Reggiano in this recipe.*

SERVES 4

*C*ombine the water and salt in a large saucepan and bring to a boil over high heat. Gradually add the polenta, whisking constantly. Stir in the olive oil and bring the water back to a boil. Reduce the heat and cook the polenta at a very low simmer until it's creamy, for 40 minutes to 3 hours, adding more water to the pot as needed. You can prepare the polenta to this point up to three days in advance. Set the polenta aside to cool to room temperature, transfer to an airtight container, and refrigerate until you are ready to serve it. Just before serving, warm the polenta over medium heat, stirring often and adding enough water to loosen the polenta to a creamy consistency. Drizzle the ¼ cup finishing-quality olive oil into the polenta, stirring vigorously to emulsify. Transfer the polenta to a serving dish or individual dishes. Drizzle a thin layer of additional finishing-quality olive oil and coarsely grind fresh pepper over the top. Use a microplane or another fine grater to grate a thin layer of Parmigiano-Reggiano over the polenta, and serve warm.

3½ cups Italian sparkling mineral water (or tap water), plus more as needed

1 tablespoon kosher salt

½ cup polenta (preferably whole grain or from an artisan mill)

2 tablespoons extra-virgin olive oil

¼ cup finishing-quality extra-virgin olive oil

Fresh coarsely ground black pepper

Wedge of Parmigiano-Reggiano, for grating

roasted beets with horseradish vinaigrette and mâche

I don't like many beet preparations because they tend to be too sweet for me, but the horseradish that these are tossed with fixes that. In the Pizzeria, we present these beets as an antipasto, which is how we give them to you here. In the Osteria, we serve the same beets as part of a composed plate, spooned over burrata, topped with toasted walnuts that have been tossed in walnut oil, fried paper-thin sliced beets, and mâche. We used to dress the beets with freshly grated horseradish, but I found the spiciness to be really inconsistent. Then I was introduced to a jarred, prepared horseradish, Atomic—it really has that horseradish burn. I love it. It's one of the rare instances where fresh isn't best.

SERVES 4

To cook the beets, adjust the oven rack to the middle position and preheat the oven to 400°F.

Place the beets in a baking dish large enough to fit them in a single layer. Drizzle the beets with the olive oil, season them with the salt and pepper, and toss to coat the beets with the seasonings. Cover the dish with foil and place it in the oven to cook the beets for about 1 hour (for medium-size beets), until they are easily pierced with a knife. Remove the beets from the oven, and remove the foil, being careful not to burn yourself from the steam that will rise. Set the beets aside until they are cool enough to touch. Rub the beets with a clean dishtowel to remove their skins and cut the beets into ½-inch-thick slices. Stack a few slices on top of each other and cut the slices into ½-inch batonettes, and then into ½-inch cubes. Transfer the cubed beets to a medium mixing bowl. (The beets can be prepared to this point up to one day in advance. Transfer to an airtight container and refrigerate until you're ready to serve them. Bring the beets to room temperature before serving.)

To make the dressing, combine the vinegar, mustard, salt, and pepper, and whisk. Add the oil in a slow steady stream, whisking constantly to form an emulsion. Pour the dressing over the beets, and toss to coat them with the dressing. Add 2 tablespoons of the horseradish and toss again to distribute the horseradish. Taste for seasoning and add more salt, pepper, or horseradish, if desired. Transfer the beets to a serving platter and scatter the mâche leaves over the top, or use scissors to snip the chive in 1-inch pieces over the beets. Serve at room temperature.

for cooking the beets

1 pound red beets, stems removed and discarded, scrubbed, and patted dry
2 tablespoons extra-virgin olive oil
1 teaspoon kosher salt
¼ teaspoon freshly ground black pepper

for dressing and serving the beets

1½ tablespoons apple cider vinegar
1½ tablespoons Dijon mustard
¾ teaspoon kosher salt, plus more to taste
½ teaspoon freshly ground black pepper, plus more to taste
3 tablespoons extra-virgin olive oil
2 tablespoons to ¼ cup prepared horseradish (preferably Atomic)
Mâche or 12 fresh chives for garnish

pancetta-wrapped radicchio al forno with aged balsamico condimento

*T*he perfect example of how good a few simple ingredients, combined and prepared correctly, can be. When we can get it, our preferred variety for this is radicchio di Treviso, which has an oblong head. The roasted heads look so pretty lined up on a platter that they make the perfect addition to an outdoor meal served family or buffet style. As always, the quality of the *balsamico* you use is essential to the quality of the finished dish.

SERVES 4 TO 8

*A*djust the oven rack to the middle position and preheat the oven to 500°F.

Remove and discard the outer leathery leaves from the radicchio. Cut the radicchio heads in half through the core, leaving the core intact, and cut each half through the core again into four wedges. Starting ½ inch below the tip of one radicchio wedge, wrap one piece of pancetta around it, leaving ½ inch at the core end of each wedge exposed. Lay the radicchio on a baking sheet and repeat with the remaining radicchio and pancetta, making sure the wedges are lined up in a single layer without touching each other.

Place the radicchio in the oven to bake for 14 minutes. Remove the baking sheet from the oven and turn the wedges over. Return the radicchio to the oven and bake until the pancetta is crisp and browned in places. Remove the baking sheet from the oven and transfer the radicchio to a serving platter, laying the wedges side by side facing alternate directions. Pour the fat rendered from the pancetta from the baking sheet into a small bowl. Add the *balsamico,* stir to combine with the fat, and drizzle over the radicchio. Use a microplane or another fine grater to grate a light dusting of Parmigiano-Reggiano over the radicchio, and serve warm.

2 large heads of radicchio
8 thin slices pancetta
    (about ½ pound)
1 tablespoon aged *balsamico condimento*
Wedge of Parmigiano-Reggiano, for grating

dolci

*B*ecause pastry is where my expertise lies and where I am the most confident, I knew exactly what I wanted when it came to developing the desserts for Mozza. First, because the restaurants were going to be side by side, I wanted the desserts in the Osteria and those in the Pizzeria to be easily distinguishable from each other. And second, I wanted the desserts to feel Italian, but not to be Italian. I hope I don't get banished from Italy for saying it, but my reasoning is simple: desserts tend to be my least favorite part of an authentic Italian meal.

I wanted the diner to feel, though he or she had never eaten such a thing in Italy, that maybe, were they to travel to the right region and eat in the right restaurant, they could find such a dessert, *someday.* Whereas the savory dishes in this book are Italian dishes with an American touch, the desserts are the reverse. They are essentially American with Italian touches—and Italian names. The Butterscotch *Budino* (page 272) is basically butterscotch pudding. *Torta Della Nonna* (page 276) is cheesecake. The *Bombolini* (page 293) are a dressed-up version of jelly doughnuts, and *Fritelle di Riso* (page 283) was Dahlia Narvaez's and my way of offering rice pudding in an Italian restaurant.

Because these are restaurant desserts, even the simpler Pizzeria creations are assembled of various components, which are made by a team of people, in stages. To make any one of these in its entirety will take some time and organization. This isn't meant to discourage you, but to encourage you to plan ahead. Dahlia, our head pastry chef at both restaurants, has broken each recipe into its individual components and told you which components can be made ahead of time. Very little has to be done at the last minute. That's how we are able to serve these desserts to our guests within a reasonable amount of time, and that is how you will be able to offer them to your guests at home.

At both restaurants, in addition to our composed desserts, we offer a plain serving of gelato or sorbetto, served with a *pizzelle*, or waffle cookie, as well as an assorted cookie plate. For that reason, even though many of the *gelati* and biscotti are elements of composed dishes, we separated them in this book to encourage you to make these when you aren't up for the task of the more complicated desserts. Cookies especially make a wonderful dessert for a large crowd or open-house type of gathering. The cookie doughs can be baked earlier in the week (or even earlier, if kept in the freezer), the cookies baked earlier in the day, and a selection of cookies, displayed at room temperature on platters and cake stands, look so pretty and inviting.

butterscotch budino with
caramel sauce and maldon sea salt

*B*efore we opened either restaurant, Dahlia and I scoured our *favorite Italian cookbooks to get ideas for desserts we might want to offer. The one that seemed to be in every book was* budino, *or pudding. We decided to serve butterscotch pudding because we both love American butterscotch pudding. It immediately became our signature dessert in the Pizzeria. And it still is the most talked about, written about, dreamed about, and ordered dessert we offer—at either restaurant.*

Two things to keep in mind for the success of the pudding are, first, that you heat the sugar in a heavy-bottomed saucepan so you can cook it sufficiently without it burning. But the real "secret," which our intrepid recipe tester Lyn Root taught us, is that if the smoke alarm in your house doesn't go off while you're cooking the sugar, chances are you haven't cooked the caramel long enough. We serve these in glasses, such as highball glasses, which look really pretty because you can see the different layers of ingredients. It's also convenient in that you probably have plenty of such glasses at home. You will need twelve heat-resistant 8-ounce glasses or 7-ounce ramekins to make this.

SERVES 12

SUGGESTED WINE PAIRING: RECIOTO DI SOAVE (VENETO)

*F*ill a large bowl with ice water and set a smaller bowl inside. Set a fine-mesh strainer in the smaller bowl.

To make the *budino,* stir the cream and milk together in a medium bowl. In another medium bowl, whisk the egg yolks, egg, and cornstarch together. Combine the brown sugar, salt, and ½ cup of water in a large, heavy-bottomed saucepan over high heat. Cook the sugar, without stirring, swirling the pan occasionally for even cooking, until the sugar is smoking, nutty smelling, and a very dark caramel color, 10 to 12 minutes. (Don't be alarmed: the sugar will become foamy and lava-like with slow-bursting bubbles.) Reduce the heat to low and immediately add the cream-milk mixture in a thin, steady stream, stirring with a whisk as you add it. This stops the cooking process and prevents the sugar from burning. This will cause the sugar to seize, or

for the *budino*

3 cups heavy whipping cream
1½ cups whole milk
3 extra-large egg yolks
1 extra-large egg
⅔ cup cornstarch
1 cup plus 2 tablespoons
    dark brown sugar
1½ teaspoons kosher salt
5 tablespoons unsalted butter
2 tablespoons Scotch whiskey

harden. Increase the heat to high and cook until the seized sugar has dissolved and the mixture is liquid again, 5 to 7 minutes. Turn off the heat. Ladle out 1 cup of the hot cream and sugar mixture and gradually add it to the bowl with the eggs, whisking constantly to prevent the cream mixture from cooking the eggs. Continue adding the cream to the eggs until you have added half of the cream. Gradually add the contents of the bowl to the saucepan with the remaining caramel, stirring constantly with a whisk, and cook the custard over medium heat until it is thick enough to coat the back of a spoon. Remove the custard from the heat and whisk in the butter and whiskey.

Pour the custard through the strainer into the bowl set in the ice, and ladle it into the glasses or ramekins, leaving at least 1 inch of space at the top of each *budino*. Place the *budini* on a baking sheet and refrigerate for several hours to chill. (The *budini* can be prepared to this point up to three days in advance.) Remove the baking sheet from the refrigerator, cover each *budino* with plastic wrap, and return the *budini* to the refrigerator until you are ready to serve them.

To serve, if the caramel sauce has cooled, warm it over medium heat until it returns to a loose saucelike consistency and is barely warm but not hot. Remove the *budini* from the refrigerator and spoon 1 tablespoon of the sauce on each *budino*. Sprinkle with a pinch of sea salt and top each with a big dollop (about 2 tablespoons) of the whipped cream. Place each *budino* on a small plate, ideally lined with a small napkin or doily, and place two Rosemary Pine Nut Cookies, if you are using them, alongside each glass on the plate.

for serving the budino

¾ cup Caramel Sauce (recipe follows)

Maldon sea salt or another flaky sea salt, such as fleur de sel

Whipped Cream (page 274)

24 1¼-inch Rosemary Pine Nut Cookies (optional; page 327)

caramel sauce

*T*his recipe makes far more than you will need for the Butterscotch Budino *with Caramel Sauce and Maldon Sea Salt (facing page) or the Caramel* Coppetta *with Marshmallow Sauce and Salted Spanish Peanuts (page 296), but caramel is something you can't make in small batches.*

MAKES ABOUT 2 CUPS

*P*our the cream into a medium saucepan. Using a small, sharp knife, split the vanilla bean lengthwise. Use the back of the knife to scrape out the pulp and seeds and add the scrapings and the bean to the saucepan with the cream. Heat the cream over high heat until it just begins to boil. Turn off the heat and add the butter, stirring until it melts.

Combine the sugar, corn syrup, and ¼ cup of water in a large, heavy-bottomed saucepan over medium-high heat, and cook without stirring, swirling the pan for even cooking and brushing down the sides of the pan with a pastry brush to remove the sugar crystals until the sugar becomes a medium amber color, about 10 minutes. Remove the caramel from the heat. Remove the vanilla bean from the cream mixture and discard the bean. Gradually add the cream mixture to the caramel, whisking constantly to thoroughly combine, taking care as the mixture will steam and bubble. Serve the caramel sauce, or set it aside to cool to room temperature. Transfer to an airtight container and refrigerate for up to one month. Before serving, warm the sauce in a small saucepan over medium-low heat, stirring constantly to melt it.

1 cup heavy whipping cream
1 whole vanilla bean
4 tablespoons (½ stick) unsalted butter
1 cup sugar
¼ cup light corn syrup

whipped cream

*W*hipping cream is all about the details. Perfectly whipped cream is cloudlike and light, but if you go just a little too far, it becomes too stiff—on its way to turning into butter. I fold in a bit of crème fraîche or sour cream when serving whipped cream on desserts because I love the tang that it adds, and it guarantees a smooth, dense, and shiny cream. If you are whipping cream to put on a pizza, do not add the crème fraîche; simply continue whipping the cream until it is thick and mousselike.

MAKES ABOUT 2 CUPS

*P*our the whipping cream into a chilled bowl and whip it with a chilled whisk until it thickens to soft peaks. Do not overwhip the cream, as it will become curdled. Add the crème fraîche and gently beat it until the whipped cream is thick and mousselike. (Use the cream or cover the bowl and refrigerate until you're ready to serve it or for up to several hours. Before serving, whip gently to stiffen if it separated.)

1 cup very cold heavy whipping cream
¼ cup plus 1 tablespoon crème fraîche or sour cream

torta della nonna

Torta della Nonna, or "grandmother's tart," is traditionally a two-crusted tart filled with pastry cream that is seen in almost every trattoria in Italy. Dahlia and I knew we wanted to include a version, but luckily, the name gave us a lot of room to be creative. As long as it was reminiscent of something a grandmother would make—meaning homey, simple, and comforting, like this cheesecake version that Dahlia created—I felt we could call it Torta della Nonna.

Honey is an obvious pairing with cheese in Italy, so we serve this dessert with three different types of honey on the side: a sweet, delicate, floral honey, such as wildflower honey; a bitter honey (also referred to as savory honey), such as buckwheat or chestnut honey; and honey in the comb. The crust that we use for this torta, Pasta Frolla, *is a typical Italian pastry dough used in many classic Italian desserts. In keeping with the Italian spirit, I make it with Italian leavening. You will need an 11-inch flan ring (a straight-sided, bottomless tart ring) for the tart and one that is slightly smaller (we use an 8-inch ring) to cut a circle for the top crust.*

SERVES 8 TO 10

 SUGGESTED WINE PAIRING: MARSALA VERGINE RISERVA (SICILY)

*T*o make the crust, combine the flour, confectioners' sugar, butter, leavening, and salt in the bowl of a standing mixer fitted with a paddle attachment, and mix on low speed until the butter and dry ingredients form a coarse cornmeal consistency, about 2 minutes. Add the egg yolks and vanilla, if you are using it, and mix on medium speed until the dough is smooth, 2 to 3 minutes. Dust a flat work surface with flour and turn the dough out onto it. Knead the dough for a few minutes until it comes together into a ball. Wrap the dough in plastic wrap and refrigerate it for at least 1 hour and up to three days; or freeze it for up to two months. (Defrost the dough overnight in the refrigerator.)

Remove the dough from the refrigerator. Dust a flat work surface with flour, cut the dough into chunks, and knead the dough on the countertop to soften it, until it is the texture of Play-Doh. Cut off a ⅓ cup portion (about 3.2 ounces) of dough, wrap it in plastic wrap and return it to the refrigerator.

Line a baking sheet with parchment paper, butter the inside of an 11-inch flan ring, and place the ring on the baking sheet. Remove the

for the crust

1½ cups unbleached pastry flour or unbleached all-purpose flour, plus more for dusting

¾ cup confectioners' sugar, plus more for dusting

½ cup (1 stick) cold, unsalted butter, cut into cubes

¼ teaspoon Italian leavening, such as Bench Mate, Pane Angel, or Rebecchi, or ⅛ teaspoon baking soda and ⅛ teaspoon baking powder

Pinch of kosher salt

4 extra-large egg yolks

¼ teaspoon vanilla extract (if not using Italian leavening)

(continued)

remaining dough from the refrigerator. Dust your work surface and rolling pin with flour and roll the dough out to 2 inches larger than the ring, and to a thickness of ⅛ to ¼ inch. Gently fold the dough in quarters and place it on top of the flan ring, placing the point in the center and gently unfolding the dough so the ends are flopped over the ring. Gently push the dough down to fit inside the ring, pressing into the crease around the inside circumference so the dough fits snugly against the corners and sides. (Don't stretch the dough to fit or it will shrink during baking.) Dip the knuckle of your index finger in flour and use it to press the dough into the crease to create a straight edge, not sloping sides. Roll the rolling pin over the top of the flan ring to cut the dough. Pull off the trimmed dough and discard. Place the tart shell in the refrigerator to chill for at least 30 minutes and up to one day.

Remove the ⅓ cup of dough from the refrigerator and place it between two sheets of parchment paper. Roll it into an 8-inch circle about ¹⁄₁₆ inch thick. Place the dough sandwiched between the parchment paper on a baking sheet and put it in the freezer to chill until it is firm but not frozen, about 30 minutes.

Adjust the oven rack so it is in the lowest position and preheat the oven to 350°F and line another separate baking sheet with parchment paper.

Remove the sheet of dough that you rolled very thinly from the freezer, lay it on a flat work surface, remove the top sheet of parchment paper, and use the 8-inch ring to cut a circle out of the dough, working quickly so that it stays cold. Pull away and discard the scraps of dough around the circle and cut the circle into eight or ten equal wedges as you would a pie—however many servings you want the tart to make. Still working quickly, use a metal spatula to carefully lift the wedges one at a time and place them on the prepared baking sheet, leaving about 2 inches between each. Brush the wedges with the egg white. Scatter 2 tablespoons of the pine nuts over the wedges, dividing them evenly, and gently press the nuts into the wedges to make sure they adhere; reserve the remaining pine nuts for serving with the tart.

Bake the wedges until they're golden brown, about 8 minutes, rotating the pan in the middle of the baking time so the cookies brown evenly. Remove the baking sheet from the oven and place it on a wire cooling rack until the wedges cool, and dust them lightly with powdered sugar.

To make the filling, combine the cream cheese, goat cheese, butter, and mascarpone in the bowl of a standing mixer fitted with a paddle

All-purpose flour, for dusting
Unsalted butter, for the pan
1 extra-large egg white
⅓ cup toasted pine nuts
    (page 63)

for the filling
10 ounces Philadelphia-
    style cream cheese
1 cup mild-flavored fresh
    goat cheese, such as
    Coach Farms goat cheese
5 tablespoons unsalted butter,
    at room temperature
¼ cup mascarpone cheese
¼ cup plus 1 tablespoon
    unbleached pastry flour
    or unbleached all-purpose
    flour
1 teaspoon kosher salt
3 extra-large eggs
1 cup granulated sugar
1¼ teaspoons pure vanilla
    extract

for serving the tart
Honeycomb
Two types of single-flower
    honeys, such as chestnut
    honey and wildflower honey

attachment and mix on low speed until the ingredients are combined and the mixture is smooth and creamy, scraping down the sides of the bowl with a rubber spatula occasionally, about 2 minutes. Add the flour and salt, mix on low speed to incorporate, and transfer to a large mixing bowl.

Combine the eggs and sugar in the bowl you mixed the cheeses in. (There's no need to wash the bowl.) Exchange the paddle attachment for the whisk attachment on your mixer and beat the eggs and sugar together until the eggs are thick and fluffy and the sugar is dissolved, about 5 minutes. Add the vanilla and beat just to incorporate. Gently fold one-third of the egg mixture into the cheese, using the flat side of a spatula to smash the cheese and break up the density of the cheese with the egg. Add another third of the egg mixture, folding it in with a light hand so the eggs stay light and fluffy. Fold in the remaining egg mixture, mixing until the ingredients are combined but there are still visible lumps of cheese in the mix. (The filling can be made up to four days in advance. Transfer it to an airtight container and refrigerate until you are ready to bake the tart.)

Remove the tart shell from the refrigerator and pour the filling into the shell to fill it ⅛ inch from the top. (You may not use all of it but you don't want to overfill the ring; discard the excess.) Place the baking sheet with the tart on it in the oven to bake for about 40 minutes, rotating the baking sheet halfway through the baking time for even browning, until the filling is set and the top is golden brown. Remove the baking sheet from the oven and set it aside to cool slightly. Cut the tart into the same number of wedges that you cut cookie wedges. You can serve the tart warm, or set it aside to cool to room temperature. (To rewarm the tart, place the whole tart or individual slices on a baking sheet and put it in a 350°F oven until it is warmed through; about 5 minutes for slices, about 15 minutes for a whole tart.)

Just before serving, place the cookie wedges on the tart with the outside edges of the cookies about 1 inch from the edge of the tart. Lift the flan ring off the tart. Use a large knife to cut between the cookies, creating even slices using the cookies as a guide. Use a metal spatula to carefully transfer each wedge to a dessert plate. Spoon 1 teaspoon of honeycomb on one side of each wedge. Spoon 1 teaspoon of each of the two honeys into circles about the size of silver dollars on either side of each wedge. Scatter a few of the reserved pine nuts in the center of each pool of honey, but not the honeycomb, and serve.

pumpkin and date tart
with bourbon gelato

*W*hen you've worked with food as long as I have, and have come up with as many desserts as I have, you get to a certain point where many of the dishes you construct are compilations of things you've done previously. When we opened Mozza, I had done a cream-filled date tart that I really loved, so I urged Dahlia to rearrange some of its components, and to her credit she came up with this sophisticated rendition of pumpkin pie. We serve it with walnut cookies that are a twist on a Greek walnut cookie that I included in a previous book.

Pumpkin purée is one of the few canned items that I endorse, the reason being that it is totally pure—there are no weird ingredients in it, just pumpkin. Also, from my experience, roasting a pumpkin and puréeing it myself doesn't yield more delicious results than canned. You will need an 11-inch flan ring (a straight-sided bottomless tart ring) to make this.

SERVES 8 TO 10

SUGGESTED WINE PAIRING: ALBANA DI ROMAGNA DOLCE (EMILIA-ROMAGNA)

*T*o make the crust, whisk the egg yolk and cream together in a small bowl. Combine the flour, sugar, and butter in the bowl of a standing mixer fitted with a paddle attachment, and mix on low speed until the butter and dry ingredients form a fine cornmeal consistency, about 2 minutes. Add the egg yolk and cream, and mix on medium speed until the dough is smooth, 2 to 3 minutes. Dust a flat work surface with flour and turn the dough out onto it. Knead the dough for a few minutes until it comes together into a ball. Wrap the dough in plastic wrap and refrigerate it for at least 1 hour and up to three days; or freeze it for up to two months. (Defrost the dough overnight in the refrigerator.)

Line a baking sheet with parchment paper, butter the inside of an 11-inch flan ring, and place the ring on the baking sheet. Remove the dough from the refrigerator. Dust a flat work surface with flour, cut the dough into chunks, and knead the dough on the countertop to soften it, until it is the texture of Play-Doh. Dust your work surface again with flour and dust a rolling pin with flour and roll the dough out to 2 inches larger than the ring and to a thickness of ⅛ to ¼ inch. Gently fold the dough in quarters and place it on top of the flan ring, placing the point in the center and gently unfolding the dough so the ends are

for the crust
1 extra-large egg yolk
2 tablespoons heavy whipping cream
1¼ cups plus 2 tablespoons unbleached pastry flour or unbleached all-purpose flour, plus more for dusting
¼ cup sugar
½ cup (1 stick) chilled unsalted butter, cut into small chunks, plus more for the pan and the parchment paper

flopped over the ring. Gently push the dough down to fit inside the ring, pressing into the crease around the inside circumference so the dough fits snugly against the corners and sides. (Don't stretch the dough to fit or it will shrink during baking.) Dip the knuckle of your index finger in flour and use it to further press the dough into the crease, creating a straight edge, not sloping sides. Roll the rolling pin over the top of the flan ring to cut the dough. Pull off the trimmed dough and reserve it to patch any cracks in the crust after it is baked. Place the tart shell in the refrigerator to chill for at least 30 minutes and up to one day.

To make the filling, fill a large bowl with ice water and set a smaller bowl inside. Set a fine-mesh strainer in the smaller bowl. Whisk the egg yolks and sugar together in a medium bowl until they're smooth. Combine the cream, cinnamon, and nutmeg in a medium saucepan over high heat. When the cream just begins to boil, turn off the heat. Ladle 1 cup of the cream out of the pot and gradually add it to the bowl with the eggs, whisking constantly to prevent the cream from cooking the eggs. Gradually add the contents of the bowl to the saucepan with the remaining cream, stirring with the whisk. Cook the filling over medium heat, stirring constantly with the whisk, until it is thick enough to coat the back of a spoon, making sure it doesn't boil, or the eggs will curdle. Pour the filling through the strainer into the bowl set in the ice. Stir in the pumpkin purée and set aside to cool to room temperature. If a layer of foam has formed on the top of the fill-ing, skim it off and discard. You can prepare the filling up to three days in advance. Transfer it to an airtight container and refrigerate until you are ready to bake the tart.

Adjust the oven rack to the middle position and preheat the oven to 300°F.

Remove the prepared tart shell from the refrigerator. Lightly grease one side of a sheet of parchment paper and place it buttered side down on the tart shell. Pour pie weights or uncooked rice or beans into the shell, pressing them into the corners of the shell to prevent the corners from rising when the shell is baked. Place the tart shell on a baking sheet and bake it until light golden, about 25 minutes, rotating the baking sheet halfway through the cooking time so the tart browns evenly. Remove it from the oven and use a large spoon to carefully remove the weights. Peel off and discard the parchment paper and return the tart shell to the oven to bake until it is a rich golden brown and uniform in color, 15 to 20 minutes. Remove the tart shell from the oven and set it aside to cool to room temperature. (Leave the oven on.)

for the filling
5 extra-large egg yolks
¼ cup plus 2 tablespoons sugar
1½ cups plus 1 tablespoon heavy whipping cream
¼ teaspoon ground cinnamon
¼ teaspoon freshly grated nutmeg
½ cup pumpkin purée
8 to 10 plump Medjool dates

for serving the tart
Bourbon Gelato (page 311)
Bourbon, for drizzling
Toasted Walnut Biscotti (optional; page 324)

Check for cracks in the shell where the filling could leak out and smear a small amount of raw dough into the cracks so the crust is sealed. Add the scraps to the remaining disk of dough.

Submerge the dates in a bowl of hot tap water to loosen the skins. Remove the dates from the water and peel off and discard the skins. Remove the pits, reshape the dates, and pat them dry with a paper towel. Lay the dates on the tart shell about 1 inch from the edge of the tart pan, spacing them evenly so each slice of the tart will contain a whole date. Pour the filling into the prepared shell to fill it flush to the top. (You may not use all of the filling.) Place the baking sheet in the oven, taking care not to let the filling spill over the sides, and bake the tart at 300°F for 25 to 30 minutes, rotating the baking sheet during baking time so the tart cooks evenly, until it is almost set. (The very center will jiggle a bit when you gently shake the tart.) Remove the tart from the oven and allow it to cool slightly. Serve the tart warm or set it aside to cool to room temperature. (I like it best warm.)

To serve, lift the flan ring off the tart and cut the tart into eight or ten wedges, as many as the number of dates you used. Use a spatula to carefully transfer each wedge to a dessert plate. Nestle a scoop of gelato next to the tart, drizzle the gelato with a few drops of bourbon, and place two walnut biscotti on the side, if you are serving them.

fritelle di riso with nocello-soaked raisins and banana gelato

*T*hink of this dessert as sweet, crunchy rice pudding–filled ravioli. It is composed of many elements, none of which are difficult to make and all of which, apart from the frying, can be prepared in advance. But you need to plan ahead and make the various elements in stages. To make the sauce, look for quality, plump raisins, such as flame raisins, a moist and flavorful variety that we find at our local farmers' markets. We use cannoli dough in this recipe, which gets really crisp and blistered after it's fried. We run the dough through a pasta sheeter, but if you don't have one, you can roll the dough thin using a rolling pin on a lightly dusted surface. You will need a 3-inch square cookie cutter (preferably fluted) to make these.

SERVES 8

SUGGESTED WINE PAIRING: RAMANDOLO (FRIULI)

*F*ill a large bowl with ice water, place a smaller bowl inside, and set a fine-mesh strainer in the smaller bowl. To make the pastry cream, beat the egg yolks and sugar together in the bowl of a standing mixer fitted with a whisk attachment, stopping to scrape down the sides of the bowl once or twice, until the mixture is very thick, pale yellow, and a ribbon forms when the beater is lifted from the bowl, about 2 minutes. Pour the flour and cornstarch into a sifter and sift them into the bowl with the eggs. Whisk on low speed just to combine.

Pour the milk into a large saucepan. Using a small sharp knife, split the vanilla bean lengthwise. Use the back of the knife to scrape out the pulp and seeds and add the scrapings and the bean to the saucepan with the milk. Heat the milk over high heat. When the milk just begins to boil, turn off the heat. Ladle 1 cup of the milk out of the pot and gradually add it to the bowl with the eggs, whisking constantly to prevent the milk from cooking the eggs. Remove the vanilla bean from the saucepan. Gradually pour the egg-milk mixture back into the saucepan with the remaining milk, stirring constantly with a whisk. Cook the pastry cream over medium heat, stirring constantly with the whisk, until it bubbles in the center and is the thickness of custard, about 3 minutes. Remove the pastry cream from the heat and pour it through the strainer into the bowl set in the ice. Place a sheet of plastic wrap directly on top of the pastry cream and press it down to prevent a

for the pastry cream
7 extra-large egg yolks
(2 whites reserved for
assembling the *fritelle*)
1/2 cup sugar
**2 tablespoons unbleached
all-purpose flour**
2 tablespoons cornstarch
2 cups whole milk
1 whole vanilla bean

for the rice
2 cups whole milk
1/2 cup arborio rice
1/4 cup granulated sugar
1/4 teaspoon kosher salt
1 cinnamon stick
**1/8 teaspoon freshly grated
nutmeg**
1 vanilla bean

(continued)

skin from forming. Let the pastry cream cool completely in the ice bath. You can prepare the pastry cream up to five days in advance. Transfer it to an airtight container and refrigerate until you are ready to use it.

To prepare the rice, combine the milk, rice, sugar, salt, cinnamon stick, and nutmeg in a medium saucepan. Use a paring knife to split the vanilla bean lengthwise. Use the back of the knife to scrape out the pulp and seeds, and add the scrapings and the pod to the saucepan with the milk. Stir to combine the ingredients and bring the milk to a boil over high heat. Reduce the heat to low, cover the pot with a tight-fitting lid or aluminum foil, and cook the rice at a low simmer, without stirring, until it is cooked through and what liquid remains is thick and creamy, about 40 minutes. Turn off the heat, uncover the rice, and let it cool to room temperature. Remove and discard the cinnamon stick and the vanilla bean. You can prepare the rice up to five days in advance. Transfer it to an airtight container and refrigerate until you are ready to use it.

To make the raisin sauce, whisk the cornstarch with ½ cup of water in a small bowl. Combine the raisins and Nocello in a small saucepan and bring the Nocello to a simmer over low heat. (Over higher heat, the alcohol could ignite.) Simmer the raisins for about 10 minutes, until they are plump. Turn off the heat and gradually add the cornstarch and water, whisking constantly. Increase the heat to medium and cook the sauce until it thickens, 2 to 3 minutes. Set aside to cool slightly before serving. Serve warm. You can prepare the sauce up to three days in advance. Set it aside to cool to room temperature, transfer to an airtight container, and refrigerate until you are ready to serve it. Before serving, warm the sauce in a small saucepan, stirring occasionally and adding a few tablespoons of Nocello or water, if necessary, to loosen the sauce.

When you are ready to assemble the *fritelle*, stir the sweet rice and the pastry cream together in a medium bowl. Cover and refrigerate while you sheet the dough.

Dust a clean, flat work surface with flour and line two baking sheets with parchment paper. Whisk the egg whites together in a small bowl and have a pastry brush handy.

Place one sheet of the prepared, sheeted cannoli dough on the floured work surface. Use a 3-inch square fluted cookie cutter to cut squares as close as you can to one another, and making sure to press down firmly to cut all the way through the dough. When you have cut

for the raisin sauce
2 teaspoons cornstarch
1 cup large raisins
   (preferably flame raisins)
1 cup Nocello liqueur or rum
   or brandy

for assembling and
   serving the *fritelle*
All-purpose flour, for dusting
2 extra-large egg whites
   (reserved from above)
2 recipes Cannoli Dough
   (page 286)
Grapeseed oil or other neutral-
   flavored oil, such as canola
   oil, for deep-frying
½ cup granulated sugar
1 teaspoon ground cinnamon
Banana Gelato (page 312)
Confectioners' sugar,
   for dusting

all the squares from one sheet of dough, carefully pull each square away, discarding the scraps, and place the squares in a single layer on one of the prepared baking sheets. Repeat, cutting the remaining dough in the same way; cut a total of 24 squares for 8 servings.

Dust the work surface again with flour and place two or three of the squares on the floured surface. (You need to assemble these a few at a time, not assembly-line fashion, otherwise your work area will get too messy.) Brush the edges of each square with the egg white. Neatly spoon 1 heaping tablespoon of the rice filling into the center of each square. When you have filled the squares in front of you, lightly flour your fingertips. Carefully lift one corner of one square and fold it in half diagonally. Use the corner of the cookie cutter to press on and seal the two cut sides of each triangle closed and taking care not to press so hard that you cut through the dough. (Alternatively, you can seal the *fritelle* using the tines of a fork.) Place the filled *fritelle* on the second prepared baking sheet and place them in the refrigerator as you prepare the remaining *fritelle*. You can prepare the *fritelle* to this point up to one day in advance. Cover the baking sheet with plastic wrap and refrigerate the *fritelle* until you are ready to fry them.

Fasten a deep-fry thermometer to the side of a medium saucepan and fill the saucepan 3 to 4 inches deep with oil. Heat the oil over medium-high heat until the thermometer registers 350°F. While the oil is heating, line a baking sheet with paper towels and have a clean plate handy. Stir the granulated sugar and cinnamon together in a small bowl. If the raisin sauce has cooled, warm it over medium heat, then turn the heat to low to keep the sauce warm while you fry the *fritelle*.

Working in batches and taking care not to overcrowd the pan, carefully drop the *fritelle* into the oil in a single layer and fry until they are golden brown and blistered, turning them so they brown evenly, 3 to 4 minutes. Use a slotted spoon or tongs to remove the *fritelle* from the oil and transfer them to the paper towels to drain. While they're still hot but have cooled enough to handle, toss the *fritelle* in the bowl with the cinnamon sugar and remove them to the plate. Add more oil to the pan if it has dropped below 3 inches and wait for the oil to heat to 350°F before frying the remaining *fritelle* in the same way.

To serve the *fritelle*, spoon a tablespoon of the raisin sauce in the center of each of eight or ten plates. Using a 2¾-inch oval ice cream scoop, nestle a scoop of gelato on top of each serving of sauce and spoon ½ tablespoon of raisin sauce on top of the gelato. Place two *fritelle* side by side next to each serving of gelato and place the third *fritella* in the opposite direction on top of the first two. Dust the *fritelle* lightly with confectioners' sugar, and serve.

cannoli dough

We "borrowed" this recipe from our friend and Italian culinary mentor, Lidia Bastianich. Since it is an Italian tradition to pass recipes down through the generations of a family, and since Lidia's son, Joe, is one of the three partners who own Mozza, we felt that this was not just okay but also the Italian thing to do. We hope Lidia feels the same way.

MAKES ENOUGH FOR 8 SERVINGS OF *FRITELLE DI RISO* OR
ABOUT 40 *CANNOLI DI GELATO*

Whisk the wine, olive oil, and vinegar in a medium bowl to combine. Put the flour, sugar, and salt in the bowl of a standing mixer and mix at low speed just to combine. With the mixer still running, add the wet ingredients, reserving 1 tablespoon, and continue to run the mixer on low speed until the dough comes together. Add the reserved liquid if the dough feels hard and dry, otherwise discard it. (Alternatively, to make the dough by hand, combine the dry ingredients in a large bowl, and combine the wet ingredients in a separate bowl. Turn the dry ingredients out onto your work surface and create a well in the center. Pour the wet ingredients into the well and mix with your hands, working from the outside in, to bring the dough together.) Turn the dough out onto a lightly floured work surface and knead it for a few minutes to bring it together. Form the dough into a ball, wrap it in plastic wrap, and place it in the refrigerator to chill for at least an hour and up to a week.

Adjust a pasta sheeter gauge to the thickest setting (number 8 using a KitchenAid attachment). Line a baking sheet with parchment paper and cut two or three more sheets of parchment paper roughly the same size.

Remove the dough from the refrigerator and cut it into quarters. Dust one segment of the dough lightly with flour and pass it through the pasta sheeter, dusting the dough with flour as it passes through, to create long sheets. Adjust the sheeter to the next thinnest setting and pass the dough through again. Continue to pass the dough through the sheeter in this way until you have passed it through the thinnest gauge. Place the sheeted dough on the prepared baking sheet, dust it with flour, and place another sheet of parchment on top. Pass the remaining sheets of dough through the sheeter in the same way, separating each sheet of dough by a sheet of parchment paper to prevent them from sticking together.

1/3 cup dry red wine

2 tablespoons extra-virgin olive oil

1 teaspoon white wine vinegar

1 1/2 cups unbleached pastry flour or unbleached all-purpose flour, plus more for dusting

2 tablespoons sugar

1/4 teaspoon kosher salt

cannoli di gelato

Cannoli are one of the most widely known Italian desserts in this country, so naturally I wanted to find a way to include them in our repertoire. Traditional cannoli are tubes of fried pastry filled with ricotta cheese, and, often, bits of chocolate or dried fruit. When made right and served when the shells are still crisp, cannoli can be delicious, and when Dahlia came up with the idea of stuffing the shells with gelato, I knew she'd hit on something even better. They're like little elegant ice cream cones where you get crunchy cone in every bite. We serve them three to a plate, each filled with a different gelato, with complementary dessert sauces and chopped nuts. Serving this kind of selection would be extremely challenging to do at home, but even one flavor of gelato and one type of dessert sauce will still make a really special presentation and a delicious dessert. The cannoli dough makes enough for four servings, but the dessert sauce our gelati and sorbetti recipes make are enough for exponentially more cannoli. So to serve a crowd, just double or quadruple the dough recipe. You will need a 3-inch square cookie cutter (preferably fluted) and small cannoli forms to make these. To get away with buying fewer forms, you can fry the cannoli shells in batches.

MAKES ABOUT 32 CANNOLI DI GELATO, OR ENOUGH FOR 10 3-PIECE SERVINGS

SUGGESTED WINE PAIRING: MOSCATO DI PANTELLERIA (SICILY)

Spray the cannoli forms one at a time thoroughly with cooking spray. Line a baking sheet with parchment paper. Whisk the egg whites together in a small bowl and have a pastry brush handy.

Place one sheet of the prepared, sheeted cannoli dough on a floured work surface. Use a 3-inch square fluted cookie cutter to cut squares as close as you can to one another, making sure to press firmly on the cutter to cut all the way through the dough. When you have cut all the squares from one sheet of dough, carefully pull each square away, discarding the scraps, and place the squares in a single layer on the prepared baking sheet. Repeat, cutting the remaining sheets of dough in the same way, cutting 3 squares for each serving.

Flour your work surface again and, working four at a time, lay the squares of dough on the floured surface with one edge of each square parallel to the edge of the work surface. Brush the top edge of each square with the egg white. Lay one cannoli form in the center of each square, parallel to the edge, and roll it away from you so the dough

for the cannoli

Unflavored nonstick cooking spray

2 egg whites

Cannoli Dough (facing page)

All-purpose flour, for dusting

Grapeseed oil or other neutral-flavored oil, such as canola oil, for deep-frying

Gelati, sorbetti, sauces, and nuts of your choice

(continued)

wraps around the form. Gently press the dough where you brushed egg white to seal the cannoli closed. Place the dough-wrapped form on the baking sheet with the dough squares and repeat, wrapping the remaining forms in the same way. If you have more squares of dough than forms, place the dough in the refrigerator until you've fried and removed the shells from the forms you already rolled.

Fasten a deep-fry thermometer to the side of a medium saucepan and fill the saucepan 3 to 4 inches deep with oil. Heat the oil over medium-high heat until the thermometer registers 350°F. While the oil is heating, line a baking sheet or a plate with paper towels.

Working in batches and taking care not to overcrowd the pan, carefully drop the dough-wrapped cannoli forms into the oil in a single layer and fry until the cannoli are golden brown and blistered, turning them so they brown evenly, 4 to 5 minutes. Use tongs to lift the cannoli from the oil and transfer them to the paper towels to drain. Add more oil to the pan if it has dropped below 3 inches deep and wait for the oil to heat to 350°F before frying the remaining cannoli. When the cannoli are cool enough to handle, hold on to the metal form with a dishtowel and gently put your other hand around the cannoli, gripping it gently as you pull it so that it doesn't break as you slide it off, and return it to the baking sheet. If you are reusing the forms, place them in a bowl of ice water to chill. Dry thoroughly and spray them with cooking spray before wrapping them with dough and frying them in the same way. When you have fried all the cannoli shells, set them aside to come to room temperature. (This would be the perfect time to spin the *gelati* or *sorbetti* if you haven't already.)

When you have fried all of the cannoli, line a baking sheet that will fit in your freezer with parchment paper. (If you have fried all the dough squares, turn the parchment from the baking sheet so the clean side is facing up and use it to line the baking sheet.)

While the gelato is still soft (within several hours of spinning it in an ice cream maker), spoon it into a large pastry bag or a large sealable plastic bag with a ½-inch opening. Holding a *cannolo* shell in one hand and the pastry bag in the other, pipe the gelato or sorbetto into one end of the *cannolo* to fill it halfway. Turn the *cannolo* and pipe the gelato or sorbetto into the other side to fill it. Each *cannolo* will take about 3 tablespoons of gelato or sorbetto. Place the filled *cannolo* on the prepared baking sheet and repeat, piping the remaining gelato into the remaining shells in the same way. Place the baking sheet in the freezer to freeze the cannoli for at least 1 hour until firm, or up to several

suggested combinations

Salty Caramel Gelato (page 306) with Caramel Sauce (page 273) and Salted Spanish Peanuts (see Caramel *Coppetta* with Marshmallow Sauce and Salted Spanish Peanuts, page 296)

Chocolate Sorbetto (page 314) with Hot Fudge Sauce (page 316) and cacao nibs (see page 314)

Greek Yogurt Gelato (page 313) with Maraschino cherries and chopped pistachios

hours. The cannoli can be prepared up to one day in advance, wrapped tightly in plastic.

Remove the cannoli from the freezer. One by one, place the cannoli on a cutting board and use a large sharp knife to trim off the edges of the gelato, making a clean, sharp edge. Discard (or eat!) the trimmed gelato. Dip the ends in nuts, cacao nibs, or coconut, if you are using them.

Serve the cannoli three to a plate, laying them side by side. Spoon a teaspoon of each desired dessert sauce on each plate and lay one *cannolo* on top or each pool of sauce. Spoon a little more sauce over the top of each. Sprinkle the corresponding nuts over the sauce on each *cannolo,* and serve.

rosemary olive oil cakes with olive oil gelato

The first time I encountered olive oil cake was at Capezzana, an olive oil– and wine-producing estate in Tuscany. Olive oil cake was the house cook's signature morning dessert. I had never heard of such a thing and it sounded strange to me, but when I took a bite, it made perfect sense. It was a very simple sponge-type cake in which the butter had been replaced by olive oil, and it was delicious. Since it's all about the olive oil, the better the quality, the better the cake. For drizzling over the gelato, this is the time to bring out the best olive oil you have—and use olio nuovo *when it's in season. We bake the batter in tiny teacake molds, which means more surface area—and the slightly crispy exterior is my favorite part. The teacake molds we use are sold in a pan, like a muffin tin, at cookware shops. Alternatively, you could use individual teacake molds. This batter keeps well, and you'll have plenty of olive oil ice cream, so double the recipe to feed a crowd or if you think you might want to bake more later in the week. We serve the cakes with Olive Oil Gelato, which is equally unusual and delicious.*

MAKES ABOUT 32 CAKES, OR ENOUGH TO SERVE 8 TO 10

SUGGESTED WINE PAIRING: MOSCATO DI TRANI (PUGLIA)

To make the olive oil cakes, sift the flour, sugar, baking soda, and baking powder together into a large mixing bowl. Combine the milk, olive oil, and eggs in a separate large bowl, whisking to break up the egg yolks.

Create a well in the center of the dry ingredients and gradually pour the wet ingredients into the well, using a whisk to draw the dry ingredients from the edges to the center. Continue adding the wet ingredients and whisking the batter until the wet and dry ingredients are incorporated and the batter is smooth. If the batter remains lumpy, pour it through a fine-mesh strainer to get rid of the lumps. Transfer it to an airtight container and refrigerate until you're ready to bake the cakes. Stir in the orange zest and rosemary just before baking.

Adjust the oven rack to the middle position. Generously grease a tray of teacake molds with cooking spray or with olive oil. Place the prepared molds in the oven and preheat the oven and the molds to 350°F.

Remove the molds from the oven and, taking care not to burn yourself, fill each mold with the cake batter flush with the rim. Place the molds on a baking sheet and bake the cakes until they are browned, firm to the touch, and a toothpick inserted into the center comes out clean, 25 to 30 minutes. Remove the cakes from the oven and set them aside until they are cool enough to handle, about 5 minutes. While the cakes are still warm, loosen them with a small, sharp knife and turn them out onto a clean surface. To bake another batch of cakes, you don't need to wash the pan. Spray it again generously with cooking spray, and preheat it before adding more batter. Serve warm. (You can bake the cakes up to several hours in advance of serving them. To rewarm the cakes, put them on a baking sheet and place them in a 350°F oven for about 5 minutes, until they are heated through.)

To serve, spoon 1 small scoop of gelato on each plate. Drizzle each serving of gelato with ½ teaspoon of finishing-quality olive oil and sprinkle with a pinch of sea salt. Arrange three cakes in a triangle formation on each plate, nestling them next to the gelato. Place the fourth cake on top to form a pyramid, and dust the cakes lightly with confectioners' sugar and serve.

for the olive oil cakes

2 cups plus 2 tablespoons unbleached pastry flour or unbleached all-purpose flour

1½ cups granulated sugar

½ teaspoon baking soda

½ teaspoon baking powder

1½ cups whole milk

1½ cups finishing-quality extra-virgin olive oil

3 extra-large eggs

Grated zest of 1 orange

2 tablespoons chopped fresh rosemary needles

Unflavored nonstick cooking spray or olive oil

for serving the cake

Olive Oil Gelato (page 307)

Olio nuovo or finishing-quality extra-virgin olive oil

Maldon sea salt or another flaky sea salt, such as fleur de sel

Confectioners' sugar, for dusting

bombolini with berry marmellata, lemon curd, and vanilla gelato

veryone loves doughnuts, so it didn't surprise me when these bombolini, Italian for "little doughnuts," turned out to be the most popular dessert at the Osteria. You're likely to find some version of sweet fried dough in every Italian region. That said, ours is made with a brioche-style dough that's fried to order and served with a berry marmellata, *or compote, and lemon curd—not at all Italian, but reminiscent of jelly doughnut combinations that Americans know and love. For the* marmellata, *we use mountain huckleberries from Oregon; you can use blueberries, blackberries, or boysenberries, or a combination—as you like.*

MAKES 36 *BOMBOLINI* OR ENOUGH FOR 8 SERVINGS

 SUGGESTED WINE PAIRING: MOSCATO ROSA (ALTO ADIGE)

*T*o make the dough, warm the buttermilk in a saucepan over low heat just enough to take the chill off.

Using a small, sharp knife, split the vanilla bean lengthwise. Use the back of the knife to scrape out the pulp and seeds and smear the scrapings on the butter. Discard the bean or use it to infuse a sauce, gelato, or sugar.

Put the yeast in the bowl of a standing mixer. Pour the buttermilk over the yeast and let it sit for 1 to 2 minutes to activate the yeast. Add one of the eggs and 1 cup of the flour, and use your hands to mix the ingredients into a paste. Sprinkle another 1 cup flour over the paste but don't stir it in. Cover the bowl tightly with plastic wrap and set the bowl aside in a warm place until the surface of the flour cracks, about 10 minutes. The time will vary greatly depending on the temperature and humidity.

When the dough is ready, add the granulated sugar, salt, 1½ cups of the remaining flour, the remaining 5 eggs, and the nutmeg to the bowl with the dough. Fit the mixer with the dough hook and mix the ingredients on low speed for 1 to 2 minutes to combine. Increase the mixer speed to medium high and continue to mix the dough for 5 minutes. Turn off the mixer, add the remaining ½ cup flour, and mix the dough on medium-high speed until it leaves the sides of the bowl and wraps itself around the hook; it will be smooth, shiny, and slightly sticky. Reduce the mixer speed to low and, a few tablespoons at a time, add the butter with the vanilla pulp and seeds, adding more butter only after what you have added has been incorporated. After all the

for the *bombolini* dough
⅓ cup buttermilk

1 vanilla bean

1 cup (2 sticks) unsalted butter, softened at room temperature, but not greasy

2½ teaspoons active dry yeast

6 extra-large eggs, at room temperature

4 cups all-purpose flour, plus more as needed

⅓ cup granulated sugar

1 teaspoon kosher salt

½ teaspoon freshly grated nutmeg

Unflavored nonstick cooking spray or neutral-flavored oil, such as grapeseed oil or canola oil

(continued)

butter has been added, increase the mixer speed to medium high and beat the dough for 2 to 3 more minutes, until it pulls away from the sides of the bowl and wraps itself around the dough hook again, sprinkling 3 to 4 tablespoons of flour into the bowl, if necessary, to encourage the dough away from the sides.

Spray a large mixing bowl with nonstick cooking spray or grease it lightly with oil and turn the dough out into the bowl. Cover the bowl tightly with plastic wrap and set the dough aside in a warm place until it doubles in size, 2 to 2½ hours.

Line a baking sheet with parchment paper and dust it with flour. Dust a flat work surface with flour and gently turn the dough out onto it. Pat the dough out to ¾ inch thick, transfer it to the prepared baking sheet, and refrigerate for 1 hour.

Remove the dough from the refrigerator and use a 2-inch round cookie cutter to cut the dough on the baking sheet, making the cuts as close as possible as you cannot reuse the scraps of dough. Pull away and discard the scraps of dough so just the rounds are left on the baking sheet. Dust the tops lightly with flour, wrap the baking sheet in plastic wrap, and refrigerate until 1½ hours before you are ready to fry the *bombolini,* or for at least 1 hour and no more than 4 hours.

To make the *marmellata,* place a fine-mesh strainer in a large bowl. Whisk the cornstarch with 1 cup of water in a small bowl. Combine the orange juice, berries, granulated sugar, cinnamon sticks, and nutmeg in a large, heavy-bottomed saucepan. Using a small, sharp knife, split the vanilla beans lengthwise. Use the back of the knife to scrape out the pulp and seeds and add the scrapings and the beans to the pan with the berries. Place the berries over high heat. When they just begin to boil, pour them through the strainer set in the bowl. Remove the cinnamon sticks and vanilla beans from the strainer and return them to the saucepan you cooked the berries in. Transfer the berries to a bowl and add the juice back to the saucepan. Return the saucepan to high heat and bring the juice back to a boil. Turn off the heat and gradually add the cornstarch and water, whisking constantly. Return the heat to high and bring the juice back to a boil, whisking constantly. Continue boiling the juice until it is thick enough to coat the back of a spoon. Return the berries to the pot and bring the juice back to a boil. Reduce the heat and simmer the berries in the juice, stirring occasionally, until the *marmellata* is thick and syrupy, about 10 minutes. Set aside to cool slightly before serving. Serve warm. You can prepare the *marmellata* up to three days in advance. Set it aside to cool to room

for the berry *marmellata*

¼ cup cornstarch

4 cups strained fresh orange juice

2 cups huckleberries, blueberries, blackberries, or boysenberries, fresh or defrosted frozen

½ cup granulated sugar

4 cinnamon sticks

⅛ teaspoon fresh nutmeg

2 whole vanilla beans

for frying and serving the *bombolini*

Grapeseed oil or another neutral-flavored oil, such as canola oil, for deep-frying

½ cup granulated sugar

1 teaspoon ground cinnamon

1 cup Lemon Curd (page 295)

1 cup Whipped Cream (page 274)

Vanilla Gelato (page 305)

Confectioners' sugar, for dusting

temperature, transfer to an airtight container, and refrigerate until you are ready to serve it. Before serving, warm the *marmellata* in a small saucepan, stirring occasionally and adding a few tablespoons of water if necessary to loosen it.

An hour and a half before you are ready to serve the *bombolini,* remove the dough from the refrigerator, unwrap the baking sheet, and set it aside at room temperature, until the dough rounds double in size.

To fry the *bombolini,* fasten a deep-fry thermometer to the side of a medium saucepan and fill the saucepan 3 to 4 inches deep with oil. Heat the oil over medium-high heat until the thermometer registers 350°F. While the oil is heating, line a baking sheet with paper towels and have a clean plate handy. Stir the granulated sugar and cinnamon together in a small bowl.

Working in batches and taking care not to overcrowd the pan, carefully drop the *bombolini* into the oil in a single layer and fry until they are golden brown, 2 to 3 minutes, turning them so they brown evenly. Use a slotted spoon to remove the *bombolini* from the oil and transfer them to the paper towels to drain. When the *bombolini* are just cool enough to handle, toss them in the bowl with the cinnamon-sugar and transfer them to the plate. Repeat with the remaining dough rounds, making sure the oil is at the proper temperature before adding them to the pot.

To serve, if the *marmellata* has cooled, warm it in a medium saucepan over medium heat, stirring often. Combine the lemon curd and whipped cream and stir gently so they're streaky but not combined. Drop a heaping ¼ cup of the lemon cream onto each plate. Use the back of a spoon to create a crater in the center of each and spoon 3 tablespoons of *marmellata* next to the lemon cream. Arrange three *bombolini* in a triangle formation on the *marmellata* and place the fourth *bombolini* on top to create a pyramid. Nestle a 1½-ounce scoop of gelato in the crater you created in the lemon cream and dust the *bombolini* lightly with confectioners' sugar.

lemon curd

*T*his is a simple and foolproof recipe for the creamiest, lemoniest curd *you'll ever taste. It makes more than you will need for the* Bombolini *with Berry* Marmellata, *Lemon Curd, and Vanilla Gelato (page 293), but you can use the leftovers in countless ways: serve it atop Greek Yogurt Gelato (page 313) or as a dessert sauce for Cannoli di Gelato (page 287), or do the English thing and spoon it onto warm scones.*

MAKES ABOUT 2 CUPS

lemon curd *(continued)*

*S*et a stainless steel bowl over a pot of water or fill the bottom of a double boiler with water, making sure the water doesn't touch the top vessel, and bring the water to a simmer over medium heat. Fill a large bowl with ice water and set a smaller bowl inside. Set a fine-mesh strainer into the smaller bowl.

Combine the lemon zest, lemon juice, sugar, eggs, and egg yolks in the stainless steel bowl or the top of the double boiler and whisk to combine the ingredients and break up the egg yolks. Place over the simmering water and cook, stirring occasionally with the whisk, until the lemon curd is thick and gelatinous, about 6 minutes, occasionally scraping down the sides of the bowl with a rubber spatula. Remove the lemon curd from the heat, and drop the butter in a few tablespoons at a time, stirring so it melts into the curd. Pour the curd through the strainer into the bowl set over the ice water. Cover the lemon curd with plastic wrap, pressing the plastic down onto the curd to prevent a skin from forming and cool to room temperature. Transfer the lemon curd to an airtight container and place it in the refrigerator to chill for at least 30 minutes and up to three days.

Grated zest of 4 lemons
1 cup strained fresh lemon
    juice (about 4 lemons)
¾ cup sugar
3 extra-large eggs
3 extra-large egg yolks
½ cup (1 stick) unsalted butter,
    at room temperature

caramel coppetta with marshmallow sauce and salted spanish peanuts

*E*very restaurant menu has at least one or two items that can't be taken off lest customers riot. This sundae and the Butterscotch Budino (page 272) are those items for us, which just goes to prove that caramel and salt are a winning combination. In Italy, coppetta refers to an unadorned dish of gelato, but we took liberties with the definition with this sundae. It's a good dessert to serve to a crowd, since the recipes for the caramel, marshmallow sauce, and gelato make enough for twelve or more. To increase the yield, just increase the amount of peanuts that you toast.

SERVES 6

SUGGESTED WINE PAIRING: LAMBRUSCO FRIZZANTE DOLCE (EMILIA-ROMAGNA)

Adjust the oven rack to the middle position and preheat the oven to 325°F.

Put the nuts on a baking sheet, drizzle them with the oil, sprinkle them with the salt, and toss to coat the nuts with the seasonings. Spread the nuts out into an even layer and toast them in the oven until they are dark mahogany in color, 35 to 40 minutes, shaking the pan occasionally so they brown evenly. Remove the nuts from the oven and set aside to cool to room temperature. Use the nuts or transfer them to an airtight container for up to two days.

Spoon ½ teaspoon of marshmallow sauce in the center of each dessert plate to keep the *pizzella* in place, and lay one *pizzella* on each plate. Scoop two small scoops of gelato on top of each *pizzella*. Spoon 1 tablespoon of marshmallow sauce on top of one of the scoops of gelato and spoon a tablespoon of caramel sauce on the other. Scatter ¼ cup of peanuts on top of each serving of marshmallow sauce, push them down slightly to adhere, and serve.

1½ cups Spanish peanuts, with their skins on
1 tablespoon plus 2 teaspoons grapeseed oil or peanut oil
1 tablespoon kosher salt
Marshmallow Sauce (recipe follows)
8 Pizzelle (page 320)
Salty Caramel Gelato (page 306)
Caramel Sauce (page 273), warmed

marshmallow sauce

Marshmallow sauce is one of those things that can't be made in a small batch. It must be served the day it is made, so making it is a great excuse to feed the Caramel Coppetta *with Marshmallow Sauce and Salted Spanish Peanuts (facing page) to a crowd.*

MAKES 2 CUPS

Place the egg whites in the bowl of a standing mixer fitted with a whisk attachment and mix them on low speed until they form soft peaks.

While the eggs are beating, fasten a candy thermometer to the side of a medium saucepan. Combine the sugar, corn syrup, and ½ cup of water in the saucepan and cook over high heat, brushing down the sides of the pot to remove the sugar crystals, for 5 to 8 minutes, until the temperature reads 231°F. Increase the mixer speed to high and continue to whip the whites until they form stiff peaks. Turn off the mixer until the sugar reaches 234°F. Return the mixer to high speed and pour the hot sugar syrup in a thin, steady stream along the sides of the bowl to combine it with the egg whites. When all of the syrup has been added, continue to beat until soft peaks form. Do not overwhip, or the marshmallow sauce will be too stiff. You want the sauce to be a spoonable consistency but not so loose that it is runny. Add the vanilla and beat to incorporate it. Transfer the marshmallow sauce to a medium bowl and set it aside to cool to room temperature before serving.

2 extra-large egg whites
1 cup sugar
1 cup light corn syrup
1 teaspoon pure vanilla extract

strawberry and fig jam crostate
with meyer lemon panna cotta and saba

*I*t's impossible to walk into any bakery in Italy without seeing a lattice-covered jam-filled tart called a crostata, so when I penciled out a short list of the desserts I would want to make at Mozza, it was only natural that crostata was on that list. For the longest time, I just couldn't decide how I wanted to serve it. An unadorned crostata seemed fine for a bakery, but it looked too naked on the plate to serve alone at the Pizzeria. At the same time, I was struggling with how to incorporate another Italian favorite, panna cotta, into our repertoire. Somehow, in the course of all of my experimenting, I got the idea to substitute the creaminess of gelato, the most obvious accompaniment to a fruit tart, with the creaminess of panna cotta, and I put the crostata and panna cotta together. It worked, solving both problems at the same time. We drizzle the panna cotta with saba, Sardinian grape must. What we created was a dessert built of all Italian elements that, though you would never see them together in Italy, somehow work. I'm proud of that.

The recipe makes twelve crostate, four more than you will serve with the panna cotta. I based the yield on the number of crostate the dough would make—and I figured you could find someone to eat the extras. You will need twelve ½-cup miniature brioche molds to make the panna cotta, though you could use 2-ounce ramekins—your panna cotta will taste just as good, it just won't look as pretty. The crostata dough is the same as the Pasta Frolla (page 276) with toasted sesame seeds added. Dahlia and I got the idea when she was working on a sesame-seed biscotti. We didn't like the biscotti enough to include them in our repertoire, but we really liked the subtle flavor and crunch that the seeds added to the dough.

SERVES 12

SUGGESTED WINE PAIRING: BRACHETTO D'ACQUI (PIEDMONT)

*T*o make the crust, toast the sesame seeds in a small skillet over medium-high heat for 1 to 2 minutes, until they are fragrant. Transfer them to a plate to cool to room temperature.

Combine the flour, confectioners' sugar, butter, leavening, and salt in the bowl of a standing mixer fitted with a paddle attachment and mix on low speed until the butter and dry ingredients form a coarse cornmeal consistency, about 2 minutes. Add the egg yolks and vanilla, if you are using it, and mix on medium speed until the dough is smooth,

for the crust

2 teaspoons white sesame seeds

1½ cups unbleached pastry flour or unbleached all-purpose flour, plus more for dusting

¾ cup confectioners' sugar

(continued)

2 to 3 minutes. Dust a flat work surface with flour and turn the dough out onto it. Knead the dough for a few minutes until it comes together into a ball. Wrap the dough in plastic wrap and refrigerate it for at least 1 hour, and up to three days; or freeze it for up to two months. (Defrost the dough overnight in the refrigerator.)

To make the filling, combine the figs, strawberries, sugar, and lemon zest strips in a small saucepan. Use a small, sharp knife to split the vanilla bean lengthwise. Scrape the pulp and seeds out with the back side of the knife and add the scrapings and the bean to the saucepan. Add enough water to cover the fruit and bring it to a boil over high heat. Reduce the heat and simmer the figs until they're tender and the liquid is syrupy and golden, about 30 minutes. Remove the pot from the heat, and set aside to cool to room temperature. Remove and discard the lemon zest strips and the vanilla bean. Transfer the figs and the liquid to the bowl of a food processor fitted with a metal blade and purée. (You can prepare the jam up to a week in advance. Transfer it to an airtight container and refrigerate until you are ready to make the *crostate.* Warm it over low heat to a spreadable consistency.)

Line two baking sheets with parchment paper. Remove the dough from the refrigerator, dust a flat work surface with flour, cut the dough into chunks, and knead the dough on the countertop to soften it, until it is the texture of Play-Doh. Dust your work surface again with flour and dust a rolling pin with flour and roll the dough out to ¼ inch thick. (Depending on the size of your countertop, you may have to roll the dough out in two batches. Cut the dough in half and refrigerate one half while you are rolling the other.) With a five-inch-diameter plate or can as a stencil, use a knife or bench scraper to cut around the stencil to create large circles of dough. You should be able to cut all 12 *crostate* from the first rolling of dough; if not, bring the scraps together into a ball and reroll the dough to cut what you need. Reserve the scraps of dough to decorate the *crostate.*

Roll the edges of each dough round toward the center to create a rim about ⅛ inch thick. (This is a single roll around; your fingers might feel too big to do this, but work slowly and with care and you get a nice rim.) If the jam has cooled to the point where it is too thick to spread, warm it over low heat just to loosen it. Spoon 1 heaping tablespoon of the jam onto each *crostata.* Dip a small offset spatula in hot water and use it to spread the jam out toward the rim of the *crostata.*

Dust your work surface again with flour. Break off a segment of dough about the size of a Ping-Pong ball and roll it on the floured sur-

½ cup (1 stick) cold, unsalted butter, cut into cubes
¼ teaspoon Italian leavening, such as Bench Mate, Pane Angel, or Rebecchi, or ⅛ teaspoon baking soda and ⅛ teaspoon baking powder
Pinch of kosher salt
4 extra-large egg yolks
¼ teaspoon vanilla extract (only if not using Italian leavening)

for the filling
1 cup halved dried figs, stems removed and discarded
1 cup dried strawberries
⅓ cup granulated sugar
Peeled zest strips of 1 lemon (peeled using a vegetable peeler)
1 whole vanilla bean

for the panna cotta
¾ cup strained fresh Meyer lemon juice or conventional lemon juice
1 tablespoon granulated unflavored gelatin
Unflavored nonstick cooking spray
1½ cups plus 1 tablespoon plus 1½ teaspoons heavy whipping cream
¼ cup plus 2 tablespoons granulated sugar
Pinch of kosher salt
1 cup plus 2 tablespoons buttermilk
Grated zest of 1 Meyer lemon

Saba or aged *balsamico condimento*, for drizzling

face with your fingertips to create a long, thin tube about ¼ inch thick, or twice as thick as spaghetti. Lay the strand of dough across the center of one of the tarts. Roll two more strands and lay them on either side of the first, evenly spaced to the edges of the *crostata*. Lay three strands in the other direction at an angle, creating a diamond design on top. Continue to roll the dough and place the strands on the *crostate* to finish decorating all eight *crostate,* discarding any excess dough when you have finished. Trim the dough at the edges of the *crostate* with your fingers and discard. Use a large spatula to carefully lift each circle of dough onto the prepared baking sheets, placing six on each sheet. Cover the baking sheets with plastic wrap and refrigerate the *crostate* for 30 minutes, until the dough is firm, or up to one day.

Adjust the two oven racks so that one is in the top third of the oven and the other is in the bottom third, and preheat the oven to 350°F.

Bake the *crostate* for 20 to 25 minutes, until the crusts are golden brown, rotating the baking sheets both from front to back and from the upper to lower racks halfway through baking time so the *crostate* brown evenly. Remove the baking sheets from the oven and set aside to cool to room temperature before removing from the baking sheets.

To make the panna cotta, stir the lemon juice and gelatin granules together in a small bowl until the gelatin dissolves. (If you are using gelatin sheets, place them in a bowl of ice water to soften.) Spray eight ½-cup miniature brioche molds (or 2-ounce ramekins) with nonstick cooking spray. Place the molds on a baking sheet and refrigerate to chill while you prepare the panna cotta. Fill a large bowl with ice water and set a smaller bowl inside. Set a fine-mesh strainer in the smaller bowl.

Combine the cream, sugar, and salt in a large saucepan. Stir to combine the ingredients and heat over medium-high heat until the cream just begins to bubble. Turn off the heat. Add the buttermilk, lemon zest, and the lemon juice–gelatin mixture and stir until all of the ingredients are incorporated. Pour the panna cotta through the strainer into the bowl set over ice and set aside to cool to room temperature.

Ladle the cream mixture into the molds, filling them 1-inch deep. You may not use all of the cream. Return the molds to the refrigerator to chill until the panna cotta is set, at least 2 hours and up to overnight.

To serve, place the *crostate* in the center of each of twelve large plates. Remove the panna cotta from the refrigerator and fill a bowl with hot water. Working one at a time, carefully dip the bottom of each mold into the hot tap water to loosen the panna cotta. Turn it out directly onto the *crostate* so the edges of the panna cotta are flush with the *crostate*. Drizzle 1 tablespoon of *saba* over each panna cotta so that it cascades down the sides.

If there is one thing I would like to make sure to get across with this book, it is to clear up the common misconception that gelato is the Italian word for "ice cream." Yes, like ice cream, gelato is a creamy dairy-based frozen confection. But gelato is its own thing, and it deserves that respect.

The difference between gelato and American ice cream is that first, gelato has much less butterfat (and also, incidentally, fewer calories) than ice cream. American ice cream, which is based on French *glace,* is typically made with equal parts cream and milk—and sometimes even more cream than milk—and often a high percentage of egg yolks. Gelato, on the other hand, is made mostly of milk, and fewer and often no egg yolks. Second, gelato has far less air incorporated into it. In cheap American ice cream, the percentage of air can be up to 95 percent whereas in gelato the range is 35 to 45 percent, making it denser than ice cream. Lastly, commercial gelato is kept at a warmer temperature than ice cream, resulting in a product with a brighter, more immediate flavor.

As much as I have become a convert to gelato, I debated whether or not to include gelato recipes in this book. I didn't want to add to the gelato myth and confusion by doing what so many cookbook authors do; give recipes for ice cream and call it gelato. In order to give gelato the creamy consistency that French-style ice cream gets from the addition of egg yolk and the use of so much cream, modern gelato contains stabilizers and emulsifiers. These products, while all natural (at least in a good *gelatera*), are not available to even the savviest Internet consumer. If I was going to include gelato recipes in this book, I was determined to figure out how to translate those qualities for the home cook.

Dahlia and I set about trying to re-create the density and smooth texture of gelato using everyday ingredients such as cornstarch, corn syrup, and dry milk powder. We set up two inexpensive home ice cream makers side by side in the pastry kitchen, and for months Dahlia used them to spin the bases that she created. When Dahlia thought she had figured out a gelato base for a particular flavor, she would make two bases that were similar with a slight variation, and she would spin them in these machines to see how they would turn out for the home cook. After months of experimenting, countless batches of trial and error, tinkering with a tablespoon more or less of this or that, Dahlia

succeeded in making a product that I was happy with and that we could proudly call gelato.

Fruit-based *sorbetti* are more complicated, as they rely on a specific ratio of water to sugar to hold together. We struggle from season to season, and even from batch to batch, as the water content in fruit varies, and we often have to throw out entire batches that don't set properly; for this reason, we decided to include those *sorbetti*— chocolate and coconut—that don't contain fresh fruit.

In all of these recipes, we recommend you serve the *gelati* within an hour or so of spinning them. Since the home ice cream maker doesn't incorporate as much air into the base as a commercial American ice cream maker does, the just-spun gelato is very similar in texture and temperature to gelato found in Italy, but after several hours in the freezer it becomes rock-hard and icy.

We serve our *gelati* and *sorbetti* in ice-cold silver-plated dessert cups. We use a paddle instead of an ice cream scoop to scrape the gelato into the cup and we serve up to three flavors in one bowl, separated by a *Pizzelle* (page 320) that is stuck in the center. It's a simple dessert, but so pretty and satisfying.

vanilla gelato

*A*mericans think of vanilla as "plain" ice cream, the connotation often being that it is boring. But vanilla, if it's done well, is neither plain nor boring. Although they are expensive, it's worth the extra money to buy large, plump vanilla beans, which will impart significantly more flavor than lesser-quality beans. My favorite are Tahitian.

MAKES 1 QUART

*F*ill a large bowl with ice water and set a smaller bowl inside. Set a fine-mesh strainer in the smaller bowl. Whisk the egg yolks and cornstarch together in a medium bowl. Combine the milk, sugar, milk powder, corn syrup, and salt in a medium (4-quart) saucepan and whisk to break up and dissolve the milk powder. Using a small, sharp knife, split the vanilla beans lengthwise. Use the back of the knife to scrape out the seeds and pulp and add the scrapings and the beans to the pan with the milk. Heat the milk mixture over high heat until it begins to bubble and immediately turn off the heat. Slowly add ½ cup of the hot milk mixture to the bowl with the eggs, whisking constantly. Continue to add the milk ½ cup at a time, whisking constantly, until you have added about half of the milk, or enough to warm the eggs slightly. Pour the egg and milk mixture into the pot with the milk, return the pot to medium-low heat, and cook, stirring constantly with the whisk or a wooden spoon, taking care not to let the custard boil or the eggs will curdle, until the gelato base thickens enough to coat the back of a spoon.

Pour the gelato base through the strainer into the bowl set over the ice water and discard the vanilla beans. Stir in the vanilla extract and set aside to cool to room temperature. Transfer the base to an airtight container and refrigerate for at least several hours and up to three days.

Remove the base from the refrigerator, pour it into a bowl, and stir in the cream. Pour the base into the bowl of an ice cream or gelato maker and spin it according to the machine instructions. Serve the gelato straight from the maker or transfer it to an airtight container and place in the freezer until you're ready to serve it. Serve the gelato within a few hours of spinning it, before it hardens.

6 extra-large egg yolks
¼ cup cornstarch
3 cups whole milk
¾ cup plus 2 tablespoons sugar
¼ cup nonfat dry milk powder
2 tablespoons light corn syrup
½ teaspoon kosher salt
2 whole vanilla beans
2 teaspoons pure vanilla extract
1 cup heavy whipping cream

salty caramel gelato

ike the Butterscotch Budino (page 272), this gelato marries the sweet flavor of caramel with a touch of salt, a combination I love. It is the base of the Caramel Coppetta, a sundae composed of Marshmallow Sauce and Salted Spanish Peanuts (page 296). Even made in a home ice cream maker, it comes out dense and creamy, and I would say one of the real successes of a long gelato-making project involving a team of gelato-obsessed taste testers.

MAKES 1 QUART

ill a large bowl with ice water and set a smaller bowl inside. Set a fine-mesh strainer in the smaller bowl. Whisk the egg yolks and cornstarch together in a medium bowl. Combine the milk, milk powder, corn syrup, salt, and ¾ cup plus 2 tablespoons of the sugar (reserving 1 cup of the sugar to make the caramel) in a medium (4-quart) saucepan and whisk to break up and dissolve the milk powder. Using a small, sharp knife, split the vanilla beans lengthwise. Use the back of the knife to scrape out the seeds and pulp and add the scrapings and the beans to the pan with the milk. Heat the milk mixture over high heat until it begins to bubble and then immediately turn off the heat. Slowly add ½ cup of the hot milk mixture to the bowl with the eggs, whisking constantly as you add it. Continue to add the milk ½ cup at a time, whisking constantly, until you have added about half of the milk, or enough to warm the eggs slightly. Pour the egg and milk mixture into the pot with the milk, return the pot to medium-low heat, and cook, stirring constantly with the whisk or a wooden spoon, taking care not to let the custard boil or the eggs will curdle, until the gelato base thickens enough to coat the back of a spoon.

Pour the gelato base through the strainer into the bowl set over the ice water and discard the vanilla beans. Stir in the vanilla extract and set aside to cool to room temperature.

Meanwhile, to make the caramel, combine the remaining 1 cup sugar with ½ cup of water in a small saucepan (preferably with a light-colored bottom) and cook the sugar over high heat without stirring, brushing down the sides of the pan with a wet pastry brush to remove the sugar crystals and tilting the pan so the sugar cooks evenly, until it is dark brown and smoking, 15 to 20 minutes. Gradually add the burnt sugar to the base, whisking constantly until the sugar is thoroughly

6 extra-large egg yolks

¼ cup cornstarch

3 cups whole milk

¼ cup nonfat dry milk powder

2 tablespoons light corn syrup

¾ teaspoon kosher salt

1¾ cups plus 2 tablespoons sugar

2 whole vanilla beans

1 teaspoon pure vanilla extract

1 cup heavy whipping cream

combined and the gelato base is a homogenous color. Transfer the base to an airtight container and refrigerate for at least several hours and up to three days.

Remove the base from the refrigerator, pour it into a bowl, and stir in the cream. Pour the base into the bowl of an ice cream or gelato maker and spin it according to the machine instructions. Serve the gelato straight from the maker or transfer it to an airtight container and place in the freezer until you're ready to serve it. Serve the gelato within a few hours of spinning it, before it hardens.

olive oil gelato

When we decided to take on the challenge of making real Italian gelato for the restaurants, olive oil was the first flavor I knew I wanted to make. It's one of the most talked-about and raved-about flavors at Mario and Joe's pizzeria, Otto, in New York. Plus, I love the flavor of olive oil so much that there was no way I would pass up an opportunity to use it in a dessert. The olive oil isn't even cooked here, so you'll really taste the flavor. Pull out all the stops when choosing the olive oil—and use olio nuovo *when it's available.*

MAKES 1 QUART

Fill a large bowl with ice water and set a smaller bowl inside. Set a fine-mesh strainer in the smaller bowl. Whisk the egg yolks and cornstarch together in a medium bowl. Combine the milk, sugar, milk powder, corn syrup, and salt in a medium (4-quart) saucepan and whisk to break up and dissolve the milk powder. Heat the milk mixture over high heat until it begins to bubble and immediately turn off the heat. Slowly add ½ cup of the hot milk mixture to the bowl with the eggs, whisking constantly as you add it. Continue to add the milk ½ cup at a time, whisking constantly, until you have added about half of the milk, or enough to warm the eggs slightly. Pour the egg and milk mixture into the pot with the milk, return the pot to medium-low heat, and cook, stirring constantly with the whisk or a wooden spoon, until the gelato base thickens enough to coat the back of a spoon.

Pour the gelato base through the strainer into the bowl set over the ice water and set aside to cool to room temperature. Transfer the base

6 extra-large egg yolks
¼ cup cornstarch
3 cups whole milk
¾ cup plus 2 tablespoons sugar
¼ cup nonfat dry milk powder
2 tablespoons light corn syrup
½ teaspoon kosher salt
1 cup heavy whipping cream
¾ cup finishing-quality extra-virgin olive oil

to an airtight container and refrigerate for at least several hours and up to three days.

Remove the base from the refrigerator, pour it into a bowl, and stir in the cream and olive oil. Pour the base into the bowl of an ice cream or gelato maker and spin it according to the machine instructions. Serve the gelato straight from the maker or transfer it to an airtight container and place it in the freezer until you're ready to serve it. Serve the gelato within a few hours of spinning it, before it hardens.

stracciatella gelato

*S*tracciatella *comes from the verb* stracciare, *which means "to tear apart." Italians use the word for several foods, including the inside of* burrata *cheese, a soup in which the egg is dropped into hot broth, and this gelato, which consists of plain gelato, known as* "fior di latte," *or "flower of milk," with dark chocolate "shreds" strewn throughout. Ariana Flores, the assistant pastry chef for both restaurants, is always happy when this flavor goes back into rotation. It's her favorite to eat, but I also think she likes the process of drizzling the chocolate over the ice cream to make the shreds. I love how plain* stracciatella *is—that it's basically just milk, without even egg yolks or vanilla, which American chocolate chip ice cream generally contains—and I like the bright white color of it. If you want to make* fior di latte, *an Italian classic, simply omit the chocolate portion of this recipe. I especially like it topped with toasted pine nuts (page 63).*

MAKES 1 QUART

*F*ill a large bowl with ice water and set a smaller bowl inside. Set a fine-mesh strainer in the smaller bowl. Whisk the cornstarch and 1 cup of the milk together in a medium bowl until the cornstarch dissolves. Combine the sugar, milk powder, corn syrup, salt, and the remaining 3 cups of milk in a medium (4-quart) saucepan over high heat. Whisk to break up and dissolve the milk powder and heat the milk until it just begins to bubble. Turn off the heat and gradually add the milk-cornstarch mixture, whisking constantly. Return the heat to high and bring the milk back to a boil. Reduce the heat to medium high and cook, stirring constantly with the

3 tablespoons cornstarch
4 cups whole milk
1/2 cup sugar
1/4 cup nonfat dry milk powder
1/4 cup light corn syrup
1/8 teaspoon kosher salt
1/2 cup heavy whipping cream
2 to 4 ounces dark chocolate, cut into pieces

whisk, until the gelato base thickens slightly, 4 to 5 minutes. It will get viscous but will not thicken enough to coat the back of a spoon.

Pour the gelato base through the strainer into the bowl set over the ice water and set aside to cool to room temperature. Transfer the base to an airtight container and refrigerate for at least several hours and up to three days.

Place a medium stainless steel bowl in the freezer. Remove the base from the refrigerator, pour it into a separate bowl, and stir in the cream. Pour the base into the bowl of an ice cream maker and spin it according to the machine instructions.

Set a stainless steel bowl over a pot of water or fill the bottom of a double boiler with water, making sure the water doesn't touch the top vessel, and bring the water to a simmer over medium heat. Add the chocolate to the bowl or double boiler and let it melt, without stirring. Turn off the heat.

Take the stainless steel bowl out of the refrigerator. Spoon the gelato out of the ice cream maker into the bowl. Use a spoon to drizzle one-quarter of the melted chocolate over the gelato in thin strands. Use a large metal spoon or metal spatula to break up the chocolate strands and fold them into the gelato. Drizzle another quarter of the chocolate over the gelato and cut it into the gelato in the same way. Continue until you've used all of the chocolate. Cover the bowl and return the gelato to the freezer to firm slightly before serving. Serve it within a few hours of spinning it, before it hardens.

meyer lemon gelato

Meyer lemons are thought to be a hybrid between lemons and Mandarin oranges. They have a sweet perfume and a sweeter flavor than regular lemons. They're originally from China, but those of us who live and cook in Southern California consider them our own. I get so excited every January when I spot these smooth-skinned citrus at the farmers' market.

MAKES 1 QUART

3 tablespoons cornstarch
4 cups whole milk
½ cup plus 2 tablespoons sugar
¼ cup nonfat dry milk powder
¼ cup light corn syrup
⅛ teaspoon kosher salt
Grated zest of 2 Meyer lemons
1¼ cups strained fresh Meyer lemon juice
½ cup heavy whipping cream

Fill a large bowl with ice water and set a smaller bowl inside. Set a fine-mesh strainer in the smaller bowl. Whisk the cornstarch and 1 cup of the milk together in a medium bowl until the cornstarch dissolves. Combine ½ cup of sugar, the milk powder, corn syrup, salt, and the remaining 3 cups of milk in a medium (4-quart) saucepan over high heat. Whisk to break up and dissolve the milk powder and heat the milk until it just begins to bubble. Turn off the heat and gradually add the milk-cornstarch mixture, whisking constantly. Return the heat to high and bring the milk back to a boil. Reduce the heat to medium high and cook, stirring constantly with the whisk, until the gelato base thickens slightly, 4 to 5 minutes. It will get viscous but will not thicken enough to coat the back of a spoon.

Pour the gelato base through the strainer into the bowl set over the ice water and set aside to cool to room temperature. Transfer the base to an airtight container and refrigerate for at least several hours and up to three days.

Remove the base from the refrigerator and pour it into a large bowl. Stir the lemon zest, the lemon juice, and remaining 2 tablespoons sugar together in a small bowl until the sugar dissolves. Add the lemon juice mixture and the cream to the bowl with the base and whisk to combine. Pour the base into the bowl of an ice cream or gelato maker and spin it according to the machine instructions. Serve the gelato straight from the maker or transfer it to an airtight container and place it in the freezer until you're ready to serve it. Serve the gelato within a few hours of spinning it, before it hardens.

bourbon gelato

I love alcohol-flavored gelato because the alcohol cuts the richness of the dairy and also allows the gelato to get super-cold. But because alcohol doesn't freeze, if you add too much to the gelato it won't freeze at all. After making many versions with varying amounts of booze, we determined that the recipe below contains the maximum amount of alcohol that will freeze in a home ice cream maker. If it's still not boozy enough for you, do as I do: drizzle a few drops of bourbon over the top.

MAKES 1 QUART

Fill a large bowl with ice water and set a smaller bowl inside. Set a fine-mesh strainer in the smaller bowl. Whisk the cornstarch and 1 cup of the milk together in a medium bowl until the cornstarch dissolves. Combine the sugar, milk powder, corn syrup, salt, and the remaining 3 cups of milk in a medium (4-quart) saucepan over high heat. Whisk to break up and dissolve the milk powder and heat the milk until it just begins to bubble. Turn off the heat and gradually add the milk and cornstarch mixture, whisking constantly. Return the heat to high and bring the milk back to a boil. Reduce the heat to medium high and cook, stirring constantly with the whisk, until the gelato base thickens slightly, 4 to 5 minutes. It will get viscous but will not thicken enough to coat the back of a spoon.

Pour the gelato base through the strainer into the bowl set over the ice water and set aside to cool to room temperature. Transfer the base to an airtight container and refrigerate for at least several hours and up to three days.

Remove the base from the refrigerator, pour it into a large bowl, and stir in the cream and bourbon. Pour the base into the bowl of an ice cream or gelato maker and spin it according to the machine instructions. Serve the gelato straight from the maker or transfer it to an airtight container and place it in the freezer until you're ready to serve it. Serve the gelato within a few hours of spinning it, before it hardens.

3 tablespoons cornstarch
4 cups whole milk
1/2 cup sugar
1/4 cup nonfat dry milk powder
3 tablespoons light corn syrup
1/8 teaspoon kosher salt
1/2 cup heavy whipping cream
1/4 cup plus 3 tablespoons bourbon, plus more for drizzling

banana gelato

*T*he key to this gelato is to use super-ripe bananas—the blacker the better. Liz Hong, one of our line cooks who tested this recipe, let the bananas ripen for over a week before they were as black as we wanted them. Roasting the bananas before puréeing them is a little trick I use to prevent the bananas from turning brown when they're added to the base.

MAKES 1 QUART

*A*djust the oven rack to the middle position and preheat the oven to 350°F.

Place the bananas, in their peels, on a baking sheet and roast them in the oven for 20 to 25 minutes, until the banana peels are black and split, the bananas are mushy, and their juices are running out onto the baking sheet. Remove the bananas from the oven and set them aside to cool to room temperature.

Remove the banana pulp from the peels to a bowl. Squeeze the peels over the bowl to release any residual juices. Weigh out 8 ounces of banana and discard the rest or reserve it for another use. (If desired, transfer the purée to an airtight container for up to three days.)

Fill a large bowl with ice water and set a smaller bowl inside. Set a fine-mesh strainer in the smaller bowl. Whisk the cornstarch and 1 cup of the milk together in a medium bowl until the cornstarch dissolves. Combine the sugar, milk powder, corn syrup, salt, and the remaining 3 cups of milk in a medium (4-quart) saucepan over high heat. Whisk to break up and dissolve the milk powder and heat the milk until it just begins to bubble. Turn off the heat and gradually add the milk-cornstarch mixture, whisking constantly. Return the heat to high and bring the milk back to a boil. Reduce the heat to medium high and cook, stirring constantly with the whisk, until the gelato base thickens slightly, 4 to 5 minutes. It will get viscous but will not thicken enough to coat the back of a spoon.

Pour the gelato base through the strainer into the bowl set over the ice water and set aside to cool slightly. Pour half of the base into the bowl of a food processor fitted with a metal blade or the jar of a blender, add the bananas, and purée until smooth. Pour the gelato-banana mixture into the bowl with the plain gelato base and stir to combine. Transfer the base to an airtight container, and refrigerate for at least several hours and up to three days.

3 overripe medium bananas
3 tablespoons cornstarch
4 cups whole milk
1/2 cup sugar
1/4 cup nonfat dry milk powder
1/4 cup plus 2 tablespoons light corn syrup
1/8 teaspoon kosher salt
1/2 cup heavy whipping cream

Remove the base from the refrigerator, pour it into a large bowl, and stir in the cream. Pour the base into the bowl of an ice cream or gelato maker and spin it according to the machine instructions. Serve the gelato straight from the maker or transfer it to an airtight container and place it in the freezer until you're ready to serve it. Serve the gelato within a few hours of spinning it, before it hardens.

greek yogurt gelato

*T*he difference between thick, creamy Greek yogurt and the yogurt you see most often in this country is that Greek yogurt has been strained, separating the yogurt from the whey, the liquid that often sits on top of conventional yogurt. It makes all the difference in the richness and flavor of this gelato. Fortunately you can find Greek yogurt today in most grocery stores. Unlike the commercial frozen yogurts that contain a long list of ingredients whose names you can't pronounce (none of which is yogurt), our frozen yogurt consists of nothing but yogurt and sweeteners (sugar and corn syrup) and a pinch of salt. Yogurt isn't a traditional Italian ingredient, but in the years that I've been going to Italy, yogurt gelato has begun appearing in gelato cases and is now almost as likely to be seen as pistachio or stracciatella.

MAKES 1 QUART

*C*ombine the yogurt, sugar, corn syrup, and salt in a large bowl and stir to combine. (The gelato base can be made up to this point up to three days in advance.) Pour the base into the bowl of an ice cream or gelato maker and spin it according to the machine instructions. Serve the gelato straight from the maker or transfer it to an airtight container and place it in the freezer until you're ready to serve it. Serve the gelato within a few hours of spinning it, before it hardens.

4 cups strained whole-milk Greek yogurt

¾ cup sugar

¼ cup plus 2 tablespoons light corn syrup

¼ teaspoon kosher salt

chocolate sorbetto

This deep, dark chocolate sorbetto is so rich and thick, it's hard to believe there is no dairy in it. There is so much chocolate in it that, while it's smooth and delicious straight out of the maker, if you let it sit in the freezer for more than an hour or so, it becomes so hard you'd have to use a chisel to get a bite. Cacao nibs are the dry, toasted pieces of cacao beans left after the husks have been removed. I like them for the crunch and the bitter cocoa flavor they add. Cacao nibs are available in the baking section of specialty markets and from online sources, but if you can't find them, your sorbetto will still be good plain and smooth.

MAKES 1 QUART

Fill a large bowl with ice water and set a smaller bowl inside. Set a fine-mesh strainer in the smaller bowl. Whisk the cornstarch with 1 cup of the water in a medium bowl until the cornstarch is dissolved. Combine the sugar, cocoa powder, corn syrup, salt, and the remaining 3 cups of water in a medium (4-quart) saucepan over high heat and bring to a boil, whisking constantly. Turn off the heat and add the cornstarch and water mixture in a steady stream, whisking constantly. Return the saucepan to high heat and cook the sorbetto base, stirring constantly with the whisk, until it thickens to the consistency of pudding, 3 to 5 minutes. Turn off the heat and stir in the chopped chocolate and the whiskey.

Pour the sorbetto base through the strainer into the bowl set over the ice water and set aside to cool to room temperature. Transfer the base to an airtight container and refrigerate for at least several hours and up to three days.

Remove the sorbetto base from the refrigerator and pour it into the bowl of an ice cream or gelato maker. Spin the base according to the machine instructions until it has thickened considerably and is nearly done. With the machine still running, add the cacao nibs, if you are using them, and spin the sorbetto for another minute or two to distribute them evenly. Serve the sorbetto straight from the maker or transfer it to an airtight container and place it in the freezer until you're ready to serve it. Serve the sorbetto within a few hours of spinning it, before it hardens.

¼ cup cornstarch

4 cups water

½ cup plus 2 tablespoons sugar

½ cup cocoa powder

¼ cup light corn syrup

¼ teaspoon kosher salt

4 ounces bittersweet chocolate (minimum 66% cacao), finely chopped

2 tablespoons whiskey or 1 teaspoon pure vanilla extract

½ cup cacao nibs (optional)

coconut sorbetto

Another pure product, this sorbetto consists of nothing but coconut milk and sweeteners. My favorite way to eat it is alongside Chocolate Sorbetto (facing page), or with Hot Fudge Sauce (page 316) and toasted almonds, so it's like the frozen dessert version of an Almond Joy candy bar.

MAKES 1 QUART

*F*ill a large bowl with ice water and set a smaller bowl inside. Set a fine-mesh strainer in the smaller bowl. Whisk the cornstarch and 1 cup of the coconut milk together in a medium bowl until the cornstarch dissolves. Combine the sugar, corn syrup, salt, and the remaining coconut milk in a medium (4-quart) saucepan over high heat and bring the coconut milk to a boil, whisking constantly. Turn off the heat and add the coconut milk–cornstarch mixture in a steady stream, whisking constantly. Return the saucepan to high heat and bring the milk back to a boil, stirring constantly with the whisk. Reduce the heat and simmer the coconut milk for 5 minutes, stirring constantly with the whisk. The coconut milk will thicken very slightly.

Pour the sorbetto base through the strainer into the bowl set over the ice water and set aside to cool to room temperature. Transfer the base to an airtight container and refrigerate for at least several hours and up to three days.

Remove the sorbetto base from the refrigerator and pour it into the bowl of an ice cream or gelato maker. Spin the sorbetto according to the machine instructions and serve straight from the maker or transfer it to an airtight container and place it in the freezer until you're ready to serve it. Serve the sorbetto within a few hours of spinning it, before it hardens.

1 tablespoon cornstarch

2 14-ounce cans unsweetened coconut milk (about 3 1/2 cups)

1/2 cup plus 2 tablespoons sugar

1/4 cup light corn syrup

1/4 teaspoon kosher salt

hot fudge sauce

Combine the cocoa powder, corn syrup, sugar, coffee extract, and 1 cup plus 2 tablespoons of water in a medium saucepan over medium-high heat and cook, stirring constantly with a whisk to prevent the cocoa from burning, until the fudge sauce bubbles and is thick enough to coat the back of a spoon, about 5 minutes. Turn off the heat, add the chocolate, and stir until the chocolate is melted, 1 to 2 minutes. Stir in the brandy and set the fudge in a warm place until you are ready to serve it. Alternatively, let the fudge sauce cool to room temperature and then transfer it to an airtight container and refrigerate it until you're ready to serve it, or for up to several weeks. Before serving, warm the fudge sauce over medium-low heat, stirring constantly to prevent it from scorching.

1½ cups cocoa powder
1 cup light corn syrup
¾ cup sugar
1½ tablespoons coffee extract
1 pound bittersweet chocolate (minimum 66% cacao), chopped
⅓ cup brandy or 2 tablespoons pure vanilla extract

meyer lemon gelato pie

We change our gelato pies throughout the seasons—we make strawberry in the summer, pumpkin in the fall. We've experimented with others, such as caramel, banana, and coconut. But as good as they all are, the Meyer Lemon is the standout. The graham cracker crust, candied citrus peel, and champagne vinegar sauce turn a simple, familiar dessert into one with many layers of flavor and texture. It's one of my favorite desserts. The recipe for the graham crackers makes double what you will need for one pie, and the vinegar sauce makes even more than double what you will need, so plan to make this recipe twice within a short period.

Making your own graham crackers is optional in this recipe. Use 1 cup of commercial graham cracker crumbs, if you prefer. If you are making the graham crackers, whisk the honey, milk, and vanilla together in a small bowl. Combine the flour, brown sugar, baking soda, and salt in the bowl of a standing mixer fitted with the paddle attachment and mix on low speed until the ingredients are incorporated. Add the frozen butter and mix until it is the texture of coarse wet meal. (You can also make this in the bowl of a food processor fitted with a metal blade.) Add the honey-milk mixture and mix until the dough comes together.

Lightly flour a flat work surface and turn the dough out onto it. Pat the dough into a rectangle 1 inch thick, wrap tightly in plastic wrap, and refrigerate for 2 hours or as long as three days or freeze for up to two months.

Have two baking sheets handy and cut four pieces of parchment paper to fit the baking sheets. Divide the dough in half; rewrap one half and return it to the refrigerator. Roll the remaining dough between two sheets of the parchment paper to ⅛ inch thick. Place the dough, including the parchment, on one of the baking sheets and place it in the refrigerator to chill until firm, about 2 hours. Repeat, rolling and chilling the second ball of dough.

Adjust the oven rack to the upper and lower positions and preheat the oven to 350°F.

Remove the dough sheets from the refrigerator and remove and discard the top layers of parchment paper. Bake until the dough is lightly browned and slightly firm to the touch, about 25 minutes, switching the baking sheets from the upper and lower racks and rotating them from front to back halfway through so the crackers brown evenly. Remove the baking sheets from the oven and set aside to cool to room temperature.

To make the crust, break up the graham crackers in the bowl of a food processor fitted with a metal blade. Process the crackers to fine crumbs and then turn them out into a large bowl. Measure 1 cup of the crumbs. (Transfer the remaining crumbs to an airtight container and store at room temperature for up to several days or in the freezer for up to several months.) Add the butter, sugar, and cinnamon, and stir to combine. Press the crumbs into the bottom and sides of a 9-inch glass or foil pie plate to form an even crust. Place the crust on a baking sheet and bake until it is firm, about 8 minutes. Remove from the oven and set it aside to cool to room temperature. Place the crust in the freezer until you are ready to fill it, or for up to a week.

Spoon the gelato into the prepared pie shell and use an offset spatula or rubber spatula to create a wavy surface. Place the pie in the freezer for several hours or overnight, to freeze completely.

To make the candied lemon zest, use a vegetable peeler to peel long, irregular strips from the lemons, reserving the lemons for another use. Put the strips in a small saucepan, cover with water, and bring to a boil over high heat. Drain the strips in a fine-mesh strainer. Return them

for the graham crackers

⅓ cup mild-flavored honey, such as clover or wildflower

5 tablespoons whole milk

2 tablespoons pure vanilla extract

2½ cups plus 2 tablespoons unbleached pastry flour or unbleached all-purpose flour, plus more for dusting

1 cup packed dark brown sugar

1 teaspoon baking soda

¾ teaspoon kosher salt

7 tablespoons (3½ ounces) cold unsalted butter, cut into 1-inch cubes and then frozen

for the crust and filling

1 cup (2 sticks) unsalted butter, melted

1 cup sugar

¼ teaspoon ground cinnamon

Meyer Lemon Gelato (page 310)

for the candied lemon zest

2 lemons

1¾ cups sugar

2 tablespoons light corn syrup

for the champagne vinegar sauce

2 cups sugar

1 whole vanilla bean

½ cup champagne vinegar

2 tablespoons unsalted butter, cut into cubes

Whipped Cream (page 274)

to the saucepan, cover again with water, and repeat, bringing to a boil and straining the strips twice more, for a total of three times.

Combine the sugar, corn syrup, and 2 cups water in a small, heavy-bottomed saucepan and bring to a boil over high heat. Dip a pastry brush in water and brush down the sides of the pot to remove the sugar crystals. Add the zest strips, reduce the heat, and simmer, brushing the sides occasionally, until the zest is tender, translucent and candied, about 20 minutes. Turn off the heat and set the saucepan aside to cool to room temperature. Transfer the strips to an airtight container and store them at room temperature for up to several weeks.

To make the champagne vinegar sauce, combine the sugar and ½ cup of water in a large, heavy-bottomed saucepan over high heat and bring to a boil without stirring. Dip a pastry brush in water and brush down the sides of the pan to remove the sugar crystals. Use a small, sharp knife to split the vanilla bean lengthwise. Use the back of the knife to scrape out the pulp and seeds and add the scrapings and the bean to the saucepan with the sugar. Continue to cook the sugar without stirring, brushing down the sides of the pan occasionally and swirling the pan so the sugar cooks evenly, until the sugar begins to brown, about 5 minutes. Gently stir the sugar and cook it, stirring, until the caramel is translucent and amber colored. Turn off the heat and stir in the vinegar. The mixture will spatter and it may seize and harden. Return the saucepan to medium-high heat and boil the sugar and vinegar until the sauce melts if it has seized, and then thickens slightly, about 5 minutes. Turn off heat and add the butter a few pieces at a time, whisking gently, until all of the butter is incorporated.

Fill a large bowl with ice water and set a smaller bowl inside. Set a fine-mesh strainer in the smaller bowl. Pour the sauce through the strainer into the bowl set in the ice. Remove and discard the vanilla bean and whisk the sauce occasionally to prevent the butter from separating, until the sauce cools and is syrupy. Use the sauce, or transfer it to an airtight container and refrigerate for up to several weeks. Reheat the sauce over low heat and cool it until it is syrupy before serving.

To serve the pie, use a large knife dipped in hot water to cut it into 6 or 8 equal wedges. Spoon 1 tablespoon of the champagne vinegar sauce on the bottom of each plate and use the back of the spoon to spread it into a circle about 5 inches diameter. Place a pie wedge in the center of each plate and spoon another tablespoon of the sauce on top of each slice. Spoon 2 heaping tablespoons of whipped cream on top of the sauce and top each slice with three pieces of candied lemon peel.

pizzelle

*P*izzelle, *which some say are the original cookie, are thin waffle cookies from the Abruzzo region of Italy. They're made of a simple batter of flour, eggs, sugar, and butter, and are cooked in a* pizzelle *iron (available at cooking supply stores and online sources) that is either electric, like a waffle iron, or handheld over the stove, which is what we use. Note that this recipe makes enough batter for 16* pizzelle. *They should be served the day they're made, but the batter lasts for a week in the refrigerator so you can reserve the extra batter to cook fresh* pizzelle *whenever you want them. We serve* pizzelle *with the Caramel* Coppetta *with Marshmallow Sauce and Salted Spanish Peanuts (page 296) and also sticking out of each serving of gelato or sorbetto. Thin wafer cookies are often served in a* coppetta *of gelato in Italy, and it just makes the presentation more festive.*

MAKES ABOUT 16 PIZZELLE

*T*oast the anise seeds in a small skillet over medium-high heat, shaking the pan constantly so they don't burn, for about 1 minute, until they are golden brown and fragrant. Pour the seeds onto a plate and set them aside to cool to room temperature.

Combine the sugar, egg whites, vanilla, and salt in a medium bowl and whisk until the ingredients are smooth. Add the butter and whisk to incorporate. Add the flour and anise seeds, and whisk until the flour is no longer visible. Transfer the batter to an airtight container and refrigerate to chill for at least 2 hours or as long as one week.

Spray the inside surfaces of an electric or handheld *pizzelle* iron with nonstick cooking spray. Preheat the *pizzelle* iron over medium-high heat. Spoon 1 tablespoon of batter in the center. Close the iron and cook until it is deep golden on each side, 2 to 3 minutes, turning often. Open the iron and, using a small spatula or knife, carefully remove the *pizzelle* to a flat surface to cool. Use the spatula or knife to scrape off any excess cooked batter along the edges of the iron and repeat, spraying the iron with nonstick spray and preheating it before adding more batter, using the remaining batter to cook as many *pizzelle* as you are serving. When the *pizzelle* have cooled completely, transfer them to an airtight container and store them at room temperature for up to one day.

1 tablespoon anise seeds
1/3 cup sugar
2 extra-large egg whites
1 1/2 teaspoons pure vanilla extract
1/4 teaspoon kosher salt
1/4 cup (1/2 stick) unsalted butter, melted, plus more for brushing the *pizzelle* iron
1/3 cup unbleached all-purpose flour
Unflavored nonstick cooking spray

orange marmalade and almond crostate

*T*his is a cross between a cookie and a crostata. *Orange marmalade is one of the only fruit tart fillings that we don't make from scratch because there are so many good versions of orange marmalade available in stores. Almond meal is available in the baking section of specialty food stores. If you can't find it, grind fresh almonds in a food processor with a small amount of confectioners' sugar until the almonds are the texture of fine meal. You will need a 3¼-inch round cookie cutter to make these.*

MAKES 16 CROSTATE

*T*o make the crust, combine the flour, confectioners' sugar, almond meal, baking powder, leavening, and salt in the bowl of a food processor fitted with a metal blade and pulse to combine the ingredients. Add the butter and pulse until the crumbs are the consistency of fine wet meal. Whisk the cream, orange flower water, and egg yolk (reserve white for brushing tart later) together in a small bowl and add it to the bowl of the food processor. Pulse until the dough barely comes together. Dust a flat work surface with flour, turn the dough out onto it, and knead the dough for a few minutes until it comes together in a ball. Wrap the dough tightly in plastic wrap and refrigerate for at least 2 hours and up to three days, or freeze it for up to two months. (Defrost the dough overnight in the refrigerator.)

Adjust two oven racks so that one rack is in the top third of the oven and one in the bottom third and preheat the oven to 350°F. Line two baking sheets with parchment paper.

Remove the dough from the refrigerator. Dust a flat work surface with flour, cut the dough into chunks, and knead the dough on the countertop to soften it, until it is the texture of Play-Doh. Cut one-third of the dough from the ball, wrap it in plastic wrap, and return it to the refrigerator. Dust the work surface again with flour and dust a rolling pin with flour. Roll the dough out to ¼ inch thick. (Depending on the size of your countertop, you may have to roll the dough out in two batches. Cut the dough in half and refrigerate one half while you are rolling the other.) Cut the dough with a 3¼-inch round cookie cutter, making the cuts as close together as possible. Pull away the dough scraps from around the circles, bring the scraps together to form a ball, and reroll the dough to cut more circles. Discard the scraps left after rerolling the dough once. Use your fingers to carefully roll the edges of each round of dough toward the center to create a rim about ¼ inch

for the crust

2 cups plus 2 tablespoons unbleached all-purpose flour, plus more for dusting

¾ cup confectioners' sugar

½ cup plus 2 tablespoons almond meal

1½ teaspoons baking powder

1¼ teaspoons Italian leavening, such as Bench Mate, Pane Angel, or Rebecchi, or ⅝ teaspoon baking soda and ⅝ teaspoon baking powder

½ teaspoon kosher salt

12 tablespoons (1½ sticks) cold unsalted butter, cut into 1-inch cubes

2 tablespoons heavy whipping cream

1 tablespoon orange flower water

1 extra-large egg, white and yolk separated

(continued)

thick on each tart. (This is a single roll around; your fingers might feel too big to do this, but work slowly and with care and you will get a nice rim.) Transfer the finished tart shell to one of the prepared baking sheets and repeat with the remaining rounds of dough. Place the tart shells in the refrigerator while you prepare the filling.

To prepare the filling, stir the almond meal, egg whites, confectioners' sugar, cardamom, cinnamon, and nutmeg together in a small bowl.

Spoon 1 scant tablespoon of marmalade in the center of each tart shell and use a small offset spatula or the back of the spoon to spread the marmalade to the rim. Spoon 1 teaspoon of the almond filling into the center of each tart and spread it out slightly, leaving the marmalade visible around the edges of the tarts. (You may not use all of the almond filling.)

Remove the dough you placed in the refrigerator and dust a flat work surface and rolling pin with flour, and roll the dough out until it is almost paper thin, about $\frac{1}{16}$ inch thick. Use a 2¼-inch cookie cutter to cut out as many circles as you have tarts. Place one circle on top of each of the tarts. Brush each top circle lightly with the egg whites and scatter the almonds over the egg wash, dividing them evenly and pressing them down gently to adhere them to the tarts.

Bake the *crostate* for 20 to 25 minutes, until they are golden brown, rotating the baking sheets both from front to back and from the upper to the lower racks halfway through baking time so the *crostate* brown evenly. Remove from the oven and set aside to cool before removing the *crostate* from the baking sheets. Resist the temptation to break off the pieces of jam that may have spilled out around the crust during baking. It is a pretty detail.

for the tart filling

¾ cup almond meal or almond flour

2 extra-large egg whites

½ cup confectioners' sugar

½ teaspoon ground cardamom

½ teaspoon ground cinnamon

½ teaspoon freshly grated nutmeg

1 cup orange marmalade

⅔ cup thinly sliced unbleached almonds

toasted coconut biscotti

*T*he recipe for this was a gift to me from Fred Chino, one of the members of the Chino Farm family. Fred loves to bake—and he's really good at it. The first time I tried his coconut cookies, they were so good I couldn't stop eating them. Now we make a slight variation at Mozza2Go to make them feel more Italian. Even though I see the cookies every day, I still have a hard time resisting them. You will need a 2-inch round cookie cutter to make these.

MAKES ABOUT 30 COOKIES

Adjust the oven rack to the middle position and preheat the oven to 325°F. Line a baking sheet with parchment and cut another sheet of parchment the same size.

Spread the almonds in a single layer on a baking sheet and toast them until they are light golden and fragrant, 7 to 8 minutes, shaking the pan occasionally so the nuts brown evenly. Remove the almonds from the oven and let them cool to room temperature.

Stir the flour and cornstarch together in a medium bowl.

Combine the butter and granulated sugar in the bowl of a standing mixer fitted with a paddle attachment or a large mixing bowl and cream them together with the mixer on high speed until they are light and fluffy, stopping occasionally to scrape down the sides of the bowl with a rubber spatula, about 5 minutes. Add the vanilla and mix thoroughly. Add one egg yolk at a time, beating one egg yolk in thoroughly before adding the other. Add the flour-cornstarch mixture and the shredded, sweetened coconut and beat to incorporate all of the ingredients. Turn off the mixer and use a rubber spatula to fold in the toasted almonds.

Turn the dough out onto the prepared baking sheet. Press on the dough to flatten it to a 2-inch-thick rectangle. Cover the dough with another sheet of parchment paper, place the parchment-sandwiched dough on a flat work surface, and roll the dough out to a ½-inch thickness. Without removing the parchment paper, return the dough to the baking sheet and place it in the refrigerator to chill for at least 1 hour and up to overnight.

Remove the dough from the refrigerator and flip it to turn it out onto a flat work surface. Peel off both sheets of parchment paper and use them to line two baking sheets, with the clean side facing up. Cut the dough with a 2-inch round cookie cutter, making the cuts as close together as possible. Carefully lift the rounds of dough onto the prepared baking sheets, leaving about 1 inch between each cookie. When you have cut all the dough, gather what is left and reroll it and cut it in the same way. (If the dough is too soft to reroll, gather it into a ball and refrigerate it to chill it slightly before rolling it again.) Discard the scraps left after rerolling the dough once. Cover the baking sheets with plastic wrap and place them in the refrigerator to chill the dough for at least 1 hour and up to overnight. If all the cookies don't fit on two sheets, put them on a third parchment-lined baking sheet, if you have one, or place them on a sheet of parchment paper and refrigerate the dough while you bake the first batch. If you are reusing the baking sheet, set the cookies aside to cool slightly before removing them from

1 cup slivered almonds
2⅓ cups unbleached all-purpose flour
½ cup cornstarch
10 ounces (2½ sticks) unsalted butter, chopped
⅔ cup granulated sugar
2 teaspoons pure vanilla extract
2 extra-large eggs, whites and yolks separated
1½ cups shredded, sweetened coconut
1½ cups unsweetened, shaved coconut
Confectioners' sugar, for dusting

the baking sheet, then bake the second batch in the same way as the first.

Adjust two oven racks so that one rack is in the top third of the oven and one in the bottom third and preheat the oven to 300°F.

Brush the dough rounds with the egg whites, making sure to get the egg white to the edges but not on the sides. Using your fingers, pile as much of the unsweetened, shaved coconut as you can onto each cookie, about 2 tablespoons per cookie.

Bake the cookies for 45 to 50 minutes, until they are golden brown, switching the baking sheets from front to back and from the upper to the lower racks halfway through so the cookies brown evenly. Remove the cookies from the oven and set aside to cool completely before dusting lightly with confectioners' sugar.

toasted walnut biscotti

It seems like just about every culture has a version of a crumbly, melt-in-your-mouth cookie made with ground nuts. In Mexico, they make Mexican wedding cookies. In the American South, they have pecan sandies. These cookies are based on a Greek version made with ground walnuts. We press a walnut half into each cookie, which looks very pretty. You will need a 1-inch round cookie cutter to make these.

MAKES ABOUT 3 DOZEN COOKIES

Adjust the oven rack to the middle position and preheat the oven to 350°F.

Reserve 40 of the nicest-looking nut halves for topping the cookies and set them aside. Scatter the remaining ¼ cup of walnuts on a baking sheet and toast them in the oven until they are lightly browned, shaking the pan occasionally for even browning, about 10 minutes. Remove the walnuts from the oven and set them aside to cool to room temperature.

Warm the butter in a small saucepan over medium-high heat until it boils with large, loud, rapidly bursting bubbles. Reduce the heat to

¼ cup shelled walnut halves, plus 40 shelled walnut halves, about 1½ cups total
10 tablespoons (1 stick plus 2 tablespoons) unsalted butter

(continued)

medium and continue cooking for another 5 to 7 minutes, without letting it brown, until the butter becomes foamy and the bubbles are fewer and quieter. Remove from the heat and transfer to a bowl to cool. Skim the foam off the top and pour or spoon out ½ cup of the clarified butter, leaving the milk solids at the bottom of the bowl; discard the solids. Pour the ½ cup of clarified butter into a medium bowl and refrigerate the leftover butter for another use.

Stir the flour, baking powder, and a pinch of salt in a large mixing bowl and combine thoroughly.

Combine the toasted walnuts and sugar in the bowl of a food processor fitted with a metal blade and grind to a fine meal. Turn the meal out into the bowl with the flour and stir to thoroughly combine. Make a well in the center of the dry ingredients. Stir the walnut oil and vanilla into the bowl with the clarified butter and pour into the well. Use a whisk to combine the wet and dry ingredients, drawing the dry ingredients from the outer edges inward until the wet and dry ingredients are fully integrated. Dust a flat work surface with flour and turn the dough out onto it. Knead the dough for a few minutes until it comes together into a ball. Wrap the dough in plastic wrap and refrigerate for at least 3 hours and up to three days, or freeze for up to two months. (Defrost the dough overnight in the refrigerator.)

Adjust two oven racks so that one rack is in the top third of the oven and one in the bottom third and preheat the oven to 325°F. Line two baking sheets with parchment paper.

Remove the dough from the refrigerator. Dust a flat work surface with flour, cut the dough into chunks, and knead the dough on the countertop to soften it, until it is the texture of Play-Doh. Dust the work surface again with flour and dust a rolling pin with flour. Roll the dough out to ⅛ inch thick, adding more flour to the surface or the rolling pin if the dough is sticking. (Depending on the size of your countertop, you may have to roll the dough out in two batches. Cut the dough in half and refrigerate one half while you are rolling the other.) Cut the dough with a 2¼-inch round cookie cutter, making the cuts as close together as possible. Carefully lift the rounds of dough onto the prepared baking sheets, leaving about 1 inch between each cookie. When you have cut all the dough, gather what is left and reroll it and cut it in the same way. (If the dough is too soft to reroll, gather it into a ball and refrigerate it to chill it slightly before rolling it again.) Discard the scraps after rerolling it once. Place one walnut half, arched side up, in the center of each cookie. If all of the cookies don't fit on

½ cup plus 2 tablespoons unbleached pastry flour or unbleached all-purpose flour, plus more as needed

¼ teaspoon baking powder

Kosher salt

¼ cup sugar

¼ cup walnut oil, or grapeseed oil or another neutral-flavored oil, such as canola oil

½ teaspoon pure vanilla extract

two sheets, put them on a third parchment-lined baking sheet, if you have one, or place them on a sheet of parchment paper and refrigerate the dough while the first batch is baking. If you are reusing the baking sheets, set the cookies aside to cool slightly before removing them from the baking sheet, then bake the second batch in the same way as the first.

Bake the cookies for 14 to 16 minutes, until they are golden brown, rotating the baking sheets both from front to back and from the upper to lower racks halfway through cooking time so the cookies brown evenly. Remove the cookies from the oven and set them aside to cool completely.

rosemary pine nut cookies

*D*ahlia developed these cookies—shortbread topped with rosemary, pine nuts, and nougatine—to serve alongside the Butterscotch Budino (page 272) at the Pizzeria, to contrast with the smooth texture of the pudding. We now make two versions: the small cookies to serve alongside the budino in the Pizzeria and a larger version to sell individually for Mozza2Go. You will need a 1¼-inch or a 2½-inch cookie cutter to make these.

MAKES ABOUT 2½ DOZEN 1¼-INCH COOKIES OR
1½ DOZEN 2½-INCH COOKIES

*T*o make the nougatine topping, combine the cream, honey, and sugar in a small heavy-bottomed saucepan. Use a small, sharp knife to split the vanilla bean lengthwise. Use the back of the knife to scrape out the pulp and seeds and smear the scrapings onto the butter. Discard the bean or save it for another use. Add the butter with the vanilla scrapings to the saucepan and cook over high heat, stirring once or twice to ensure even cooking, until the mixture comes to a boil. Take the saucepan off the heat and add the flour, whisking constantly until smooth. Turn the mixture out into a bowl and fold in the pine nuts and rosemary sprig. Set the nougatine aside to cool to room temperature and remove the rosemary. The nougatine can be made up to a week in advance. Transfer it to an airtight container and refrigerate until you are ready to bake the cookies or for up to a week. Bring it to room temperature before using it.

for the nougatine topping
⅓ cup heavy whipping cream
1½ tablespoons mild-flavored honey, such as clover or wildflower
1½ tablespoons granulated sugar
1 whole vanilla bean
1 tablespoon unsalted butter
1½ tablespoons unbleached all-purpose flour, sifted
½ cup Toasted Pine Nuts (page 63)
1 fresh rosemary sprig

(continued)

To make the cookie dough, combine the butter and confectioners' sugar in the bowl of a standing mixer fitted with the paddle attachment and mix them at high speed until the mixture is creamy and smooth, stopping occasionally to scrape down the sides of the bowl with a rubber spatula, about 5 minutes. Add the vanilla and salt, and mix to incorporate. Add the flour and the polenta, and mix until thoroughly combined. Dust a flat work surface with flour and turn the dough out onto it. Knead the dough for a few minutes until it comes together into a ball. Wrap the dough tightly in plastic wrap and refrigerate for at least 2 hours and up to three days, or freeze it for up to two months. (Defrost the dough overnight in the refrigerator.)

Adjust two oven racks so that one rack is in the top third of the oven and one is in the bottom third. Preheat the oven to 350°F and line two baking sheets with parchment paper.

Remove the dough from the refrigerator. Dust a flat work surface with flour, cut the dough into chunks, and knead the dough on the countertop to soften it, until it is the texture of Play-Doh. Dust your work surface again with flour and dust a rolling pin with flour and roll the dough out to ¼ inch thick, adding more flour to the surface or the rolling pin if the dough is sticking. (Depending on the size of your countertop, you may have to roll the dough out in two batches. Cut the dough in half and refrigerate one half while you roll the other.) Cut the dough with a 1¼- or 2½-inch round cookie cutter, making the cuts as close together as possible. Carefully lift the rounds of dough onto the prepared baking sheets, leaving about 1 inch between each. When you have cut all the dough, gather what is left and reroll it and cut it in the same way. (If the dough is too soft to reroll, gather it into a ball and refrigerate it to chill it slightly before rolling it again.) Discard the scraps left after rerolling the dough once. If all of the cookies don't fit on two sheets, put them on a third parchment-lined baking sheet, if you have one, or place them on a sheet of parchment paper and refrigerate the dough while the first batch is baking. If you are reusing the baking sheets, set the cookies aside to cool slightly before removing them from the baking sheet, then bake the second batch in the same way as the first.

With the nougatine at room temperature, work it between your fingers, creating a thin disk about the size of a dime for smaller cookies, a quarter for the larger cookies. Place a circle of nougatine in the center of each circle of dough. Stick a few rosemary tufts on top of each

for the cookie dough
½ cup (1 stick) unsalted butter, at room temperature
½ cup plus 2 tablespoons confectioners' sugar
½ teaspoon pure vanilla extract
⅛ teaspoon kosher salt
¾ cup plus 2 tablespoons unbleached pastry flour or unbleached all-purpose flour, plus more for dusting
¼ cup polenta

2 heaping tablespoons rosemary tufts

cookie, making sure to pierce the dough with the rosemary so it doesn't fall off in the oven.

Bake the cookies for 10 minutes, switching the baking sheets on the upper and lower racks and rotating them from front to back halfway through cooking time so the cookies brown evenly. Remove the baking sheets from the oven and set aside to cool to room temperature.

chocolate and hazelnut maltagliati

Since we offer only one chocolate cookie on our assorted cookie plate, we made sure that cookie is as chocolatey as possible. We call them maltagliati, *which means "badly cut." In truth, the dough is not cut at all; the pieces are torn from a slab of chilled dough. In any case, the cookies are sure to please any dark-chocolate lover.*

MAKES ABOUT 4 DOZEN COOKIES

Adjust the oven racks so one rack is in the middle and preheat the oven to 325°F. Line a baking sheet with parchment paper and cut another piece of parchment the same size.

Place the hazelnuts on a baking sheet and toast them in the oven for 10 to 15 minutes, until they are golden brown and fragrant, shaking the pan occasionally so the nuts brown evenly. Remove the hazelnuts from the oven and set them aside until the nuts are cool enough to touch. Gather the nuts into a clean dishtowel and rub them together inside the towel to remove the skins.

Coarsely chop 1 pound of the chocolate and set it aside. Set a stainless steel bowl over a pot of water or fill the bottom of the double boiler with water, making sure the water doesn't touch the top vessel, and bring the water to a simmer over medium heat. Place the remaining 1 pound plus 6 ounces of chocolate in the bowl or the top of the double boiler. Melt it without stirring. Remove the chocolate from the heat and set it aside to cool slightly.

Combine the flour, baking powder, and salt in a medium bowl.

Using a standing mixer fitted with a paddle attachment, cream the butter and sugar together on high speed until light and fluffy, stopping occasionally to scrape down the sides of the bowl with a rubber spat-

2 cups hazelnuts
2 pounds plus 6 ounces bittersweet chocolate (minimum 66% cacao)
3/4 cup unbleached all-purpose flour
1 tablespoon baking powder
Pinch of kosher salt
12 tablespoons (1 1/2 sticks) unsalted butter, cut into cubes
2 1/4 cups sugar
5 extra-large eggs
1 cup cacao nibs (optional)

ula, about 5 minutes. Reduce the mixer speed to low and add the eggs one at a time, beating until each egg is incorporated into the batter before adding the next egg. Turn the mixer off and add the dry ingredients. Return the mixer speed to medium and beat the batter just until the flour is incorporated. With the mixer still running, slowly add the melted chocolate and mix until the chocolate is incorporated into the batter. Turn the machine off and remove the bowl from the stand. Add the toasted hazelnuts, chopped chocolate, and cacao nibs, if using, and stir to distribute evenly.

Dust a flat work surface with flour. Turn the dough out onto the floured surface and bring it together into a ball. To prepare the dough in advance, wrap it in plastic wrap and refrigerate up to three days, or freeze it for up to two months. (Defrost the dough overnight in the refrigerator.) Line a baking sheet with parchment paper. Turn the dough out on the baking sheet and place the second sheet of parchment on top of the dough. Use your hands to pat the dough out to an even ½-inch thickness. Cover the baking sheet with plastic wrap and refrigerate for at least 2 hours and up to three days.

Adjust two oven racks so that one rack is in the top third of the oven and one is in the bottom third and preheat oven to 350°F.

Remove the dough from the refrigerator and flip it to turn the dough out onto a flat work surface. Peel off both sheets of the parchment paper, and use them to line two baking sheets, with the clean side facing up. Use your hands to tear the dough into roughly 1½-inch pieces, and place the pieces on the prepared baking sheets, leaving about 2 inches between each. If all the cookies don't fit on two sheets, put them on a third parchment-lined baking sheet, if you have one, or place them on a sheet of parchment paper and refrigerate the dough while the first batch is baking. If you are reusing the baking sheets, set the cookies aside to cool slightly before removing them from the baking sheet, then bake the second batch in the same way as the first.

Bake the cookies for 10 to 12 minutes, until they are cracked on top and soft but not liquidy to the touch, rotating the baking sheets both from front to back and from the upper to lower racks halfway through cooking time so the cookies brown evenly. Remove the baking sheets from the oven.

Coffee is so important to life in Italy that I would be remiss in closing a cookbook on Italian cuisine without addressing it. Going to the bar for a morning coffee is an experience that you share with your friends, neighbors, and fellow villagers, and this is an activity of a strict routine. If you get to the bar at eight o'clock in the morning, you know more or less who is going to be there: the same people who were there yesterday and who will be there tomorrow. You order the same thing every day and you either down it standing up at the bar, or you pay the extra few cents and sit at a table and have a conversation or read the paper. Whether I'm in Italy or here, I love my morning cappuccino, but my passion doesn't compare to my dad's.

My dad, it would not be an exaggeration to say, is a coffee fanatic and has been ever since I can remember. A long time ago, way before Starbucks became a part of our culture and lingo, I remember my dad telling me that he could conceivably go to a restaurant, order a cup of coffee, and if it was good, that to him was proof that he was in a good restaurant. If the coffee was bad, that would be enough to turn him away. As a restaurateur I can tell you that there is some truth in my dad's simple test. When I was the pastry chef at Spago, Wolfgang used to tell me that my desserts were very important to the experience of the restaurant because that was the last thing people would have before they left the restaurant. At Mozza, we feel that way about coffee.

We start with beans from Intelligentsia, an artisanal coffee roaster based in Chicago, and then we have a barista at the Osteria—someone who is trained, skilled, knowledgeable, and passionate about making coffee and whose sole job is to make the drip coffee and espresso drinks. Our head barista, Jeremy Spencer, is probably one of the best baristas in Los Angeles or that I've ever known. He or another of our baristas makes the drinks, brings them to the table, and offers refills to those who order drip coffee. Although no self-respecting Italian would dream of drinking cappuccino after 11:00 a.m., our customers do, and Jeremy indulges them—and even draws designs and messages in the foam—this is known as "latte art." In Italy, it's an unwritten rule that you don't drink cappuccino after 11:00 a.m. (Macciato, which is *caffè* with a spoonful of foam on top, is the acceptable alternative if you don't like black coffee.) It's a rule I break every day at the restaurant at 5:30 p.m., when I start my shift. Breaking the rules—or at least bending them—is an American tradition that I relish.

acknowledgments

I gather there are some people who can sit down and write a cookbook essentially by themselves, but for *The Mozza Cookbook* it just about took a small *villaggio*. There were so many people instrumental in getting this book published.

First of all, thank you to Michael Krikorian, for being my e-mail liaison through this process, and for his sense of humor, which always helps to keep things in perspective.

Thank you to my co-authors Matt Molina and Carolynn Carreño.

Carolynn has an extraordinary way of conveying my thoughts about food onto a page. I kept her up for countless hours with late-night phone calls while she was on vacation in Italy and only once did she scream at me.

Carolynn was constantly in the kitchen consulting with chefs Chris Feldmeier, Chad Colby, Erik Black, Joe Marcos, Karla Mendoza, and Dave Almany, who provided her with the often tiny details that are vital for a restaurant's recipes to garner raves in the home kitchen. To all of them, *grazie*.

I could go on and on about Matt, but you'll read about him in the introduction.

My heartfelt thanks go to a brigade of recipe tasters spearheaded by Osteria server Lyn Root, who did the bulk of the testing. Also adding their time and talents were Emily Corliss, Elizabeth Hong, Tracey Harada, and Grace Lee. Paulina Techachal Gomez was particularly helpful with the pastas. You'll notice her lovely fingers shaping the pasta in the photographs.

Thanks also to Eric Alperin (mixologist extraordinaire) for implementing our intial cocktail program.

General Manager David Rosoff once again proved his expertise, superbly matching the food with the right wine. The staff at Mozza and I spent many a late night after service enjoying those food and wine pairings. Okay, mainly the wine. *Cin cin*, David.

Pastry chef extraordinaire Dahlia Narvaez was tireless in her insight with the dessert section, and, as always, added just the right notes. Her sous chefs, Ariana Flores and Sarah Asch, were a big support as well.

Office manager Kate Green was key in coordinating the communication between those involved in the book. She worked energetically and with much joy, though she did, however, threaten to force me to learn how to use a computer.

Sara Parenti very efficiently helped organize all the recipe files, put them into notebooks, and organized the files on Carolynn's computer. She was a pleasure to work with.

Photographer Sara Remington did a wonderful job with her portraits that help capture the soul of Mozza. And thanks to Iris Weinstein, who designed the book with style and grace.

Special thanks to my agent, Janis Donnaud, and my editor, Peter Gethers, who were there at the beginning as friends and advisers. Associate editor Christina Malach went above and beyond with her tenacious and exacting work. Production editor Maria Massey also worked extremely hard.

And finally, to Joe and Mario, without whom there wouldn't be a Mozza to begin with.

Thank you all.

nancy silverton

index

Page references in *italics* refer to illustrations.

pizza (*cont.*)

Bianca with Fontina, Mozzarella, Sottocenere *al Tartufo*, and Sage, *120*, 150

Buricotta with Peperonata and Oregano, *120*, 152

Dough, Nancy's, 126–27

Fennel Sausage, *Panna*, and Scallions, 144, *145*

Fresh Goat Cheese, Leek, Scallions, Garlic, and Bacon, *148*, 149

Funghi Misti, Fontina, Taleggio, and Thyme, *120*, 147

Gorgonzola *Dolce*, Fingerling Potatoes, Radicchio, and Rosemary, *120*, 142

Littleneck Clams, Garlic, Oregano, Parmigiano-Reggiano, and Pecorino Romano, 143

Long-cooked Broccoli, Caciocavallo, and Peperoncino, 146

Margherita: Mozzarella, Tomato, and Basil, *132*, 133

Marinara: Tomato, Sicilian Oregano, and Extra-virgin Olive Oil, 133–34

Meat Lover's: Bacon, Salami, Fennel Sausage, *Guanciale*, Tomato, and Mozzarella, 136–38

Nancy's scuola di, 128–29

le pizze bianche, 142–53

le pizze rosse, 133–41

Potato, Egg, and Bacon, 153

Prosciutto di Parma, *Rucola*, Tomato, and Mozzarella, 136

Spicy Salami, Mozzarella, and Fresno Chiles, 140, *141*

Squash Blossoms, Tomato, and Burrata, 134, *135*

Stracchino with Artichokes, Lemon, and Olives, 151

White Anchovy, Tomato, and Spicy Fresno Chiles, 139–40

Pizza Party (menu), 16

pizza stones, 128

Pizzelle, 320

Pizzeria Bianco (Phoenix), 123–24

Pizzeria Mozza (Los Angeles), ix, x, 3, 6–15, 87

decision to share recipes from, 10–11

development of pizzas at, 123–25

idea for, 6

menu of, 10, 15, 125

Pizza Bar at, 6–8

pizza oven at, 109

style of cooking at, 8

Wine Bar at, 6–8

Polenta, 265

pomegranate, in Sugar Plum, 34

porcini, 22

-rubbed Rib-eye *Bistecca*, 232–33

pork:

Chops, Pan-roasted, with Olives and Sambuca-braised Fennel, 241–42

Fennel Sausage, 137–38

Meatballs *al Forno*, *106*, 107–8

Meat Lover's: Bacon, Salami, Fennel Sausage, *Guanciale*, Tomato, and Mozzarella (pizza), 136–38

Ragù Bolognese, Garganelli with, 189–90, *191*

Ribs with Fennel and Apple Cider Vinegar, 243–44

Postino, Il, 34

potato(es):

Bacalà Mantecato (crostini), *30*, *48*, 49

Egg, and Bacon (pizza), 153

Fingerling, Gorgonzola *Dolce*, Radicchio, and Rosemary (pizza), *120*, 142

Grilled Octopus with Celery, Lemon and, *110*, 111–13

Smashed, with Rosemary, *250*, 255–56

prep techniques, 23

presentation, 29

primi (first courses), 13–15, 155–205

Bavette Cacio e Pepe, 201

Corzetti Stampati with Eggplant, Olives, and Fresh Ricotta, 183–84

Fiorentini with *Guanciale*, Tomato, and Spicy Pickled Peppers, *202*, 203–4

Francobolli di Brasato al Pomodoro with Basil and Ricotta Salata *al Forno*, 177–79

Fresh Ricotta and Egg Ravioli with Brown Butter, *174*, 175–77, *176*

Garganelli with Ragù Bolognese, 189–90, *191*

Gnocchi with Duck Ragù, 187–88

Linguine with Clams, Pancetta, and Spicy Fresno Chiles, 199–200

Maltagliati with Wild Boar Ragù, 185–86

Orecchiette with Fennel Sausage and Swiss Chard, 180–82, *181*

Ricotta Gnudi with Chanterelles, 194–96, *195*

Spaghetti *alla Gricia*, 198–99

Squid Ink *Chitarra* with Sea Urchin, Dungeness Crab, and Jalapeño, 197–98

Stinging Nettle Tagliatelle with Lamb Ragù, Taggiasche Olives, and Mint, 192–93

see also pasta doughs; pasta shapes, fresh

prosciutto, 92–93

Bread Crumbs, 256

di Parma, *Rucola*, Tomato, and Mozzarella (pizza), 136

-wrapped Breadsticks, 39

Prosecco, 33

Il Postino, 34

provolone, in Nancy's Chopped Salad, 94–97, *95*

Pudding (*Budino*), Butterscotch, with Caramel Sauce and Maldon Sea Salt, *268*, 272–74

Pumpkin and Date Tart with Bourbon Gelato, 280–82

q

Quail Wrapped in Pancetta, Grilled, with Sage and Honey, 221–22

Quince (San Francisco), 175

r

rabbit:
    con Salsiccia, Roasted Garlic, Lemon, and Rosemary, 245–49, *246*, *248*
    Stock, 245

radicchio:
    Gorgonzola *Dolce*, Fingerling Potatoes, and Rosemary (pizza), *120*, 142
    Grilled, 222
    Pancetta-wrapped, *al Forno* with Aged *Balsamico Condimento*, *250*, 267
    Tricolore with Parmigiano-Reggiano and Anchovy Dressing, 98
    White Beans alla Toscana with Extra-virgin Olive Oil and *Saba* (crostini), *30*, 44–46, *48*

ragùs, 160
    Bolognese, Garganelli with, 189–90, *191*
    Bolognese, in *Arancine* alla Bolognese, 42–43
    Duck, Gnocchi with, 187–88
    Lamb, Stinging Nettle Tagliatelle with, Taggiasche Olives, and Mint, 192–93
    prep tips for, 23
    Wild Boar, *Maltagliati* with, 185–86

Raisins, Nocello-soaked, *Fritelle di Riso* with Banana Gelato and, 283–86

ravioli, *154*
    Fresh Ricotta and Egg, with Brown Butter, *174*, 175–77, *176*

red cabbage:
    Coleslaw, 243, 244
    Sottaceto, 214

Red Wine–braised Squid with Garlic Mayonnaise, 118

Relish, Currant and Pine Nut, 71
    Roasted Carrots Siciliana, 263

Rib-eye *Bistecca*, Porcini-rubbed, 232–33

Ribollita (restaurant in Chiusi, Italy), 217

Ribollita "Da Delfina" (antipasto), *114*, 115–16

rice:
    Arancine alla Bolognese, 42–43
    Fritelle di Riso with Nocello-soaked Raisins and Banana Gelato, 283–86

ricotta, 60–61
    cow's milk, *54*, 57, 60–61
    Crostoni, Peperonata with, 87–89, *88*
    Fresh, and Egg Ravioli with Brown Butter, *174*, 175–77, *176*
    Fresh, *Corzetti Stampati* with Eggplant, Olives and, 183–84
    Fried Squash Blossoms with, 40–41
    Gnudi with Chanterelles, 194–96, *195*
    Homemade, 41
    Salata al Forno, *Francobolli di Brasato al Pomodoro* with Basil and, 177–79
    sheep's milk, *54*, 61
    Sheep's Milk with Hazelnut *Aillade*, Lemon, and Roasted Garlic Vinaigrette, 80–81
    see also buricotta

Ristorante Da Delfina (near Florence), 115, 215

Ristorante Masolino (Panicale, Italy), 218

Robuchon, Joël, 101, 210

Roscioli Antico Forno (Rome), 124

rosemary:
    Fried, 216
    Gorgonzola *Dolce*, Fingerling Potatoes, Radicchio and (pizza), *120*, 142
    Olive Oil Cakes with Olive Oil Gelato, 290–91
    Pine Nut Cookies, *268*, 327–29
    Smashed Potatoes with, *250*, 255–56

Rosoff, David, 12, 13

Rub, Fennel, 242

rucola, *see* arugula

rum:
    Meletti Smash, 35
    Il Postino, 34

s

saba, 22
    Strawberry and Fig Jam *Crostate* with Meyer Lemon Panna Cotta and, 298–301, *299*

sage:
    Bianca with Fontina, Mozzarella, Sottocenere *al Tartufo* and (pizza), *120*, 150
    Fried, 222

salads, 92
    Caprese, Mozza, 66–67
    Celery and Herb, Stracciatella with Celery-leaf Pesto and, 75–76
    Chopped, Nancy's, 94–97, *95*
    Coleslaw, 243, 244
    Fregola Sarda, 234
    Little Gem Lettuce with Dates, Red Onion, and Gorgonzola *Dolce*, 102–3
    Little Gem Lettuce with Summer Squash, Walnuts, and Pecorino, *100*, 101–2

a note about the authors

nancy silverton is the co-owner of Osteria Mozza, Pizzeria Mozza, and Mozza2Go in Los Angeles, where she makes her home. She is the founder of the La Brea Bakery and formerly owned and operated Campanile restaurant (recipient of the 2001 James Beard Award for Best Restaurant). She is the author of *A Twist of the Wrist, Nancy Silverton's Sandwich Book, Nancy Silverton's Pastries from the La Brea Bakery* (recipient of a 2000 Food & Wine Best Cookbook Award), *Nancy Silverton's Breads from the La Brea Bakery,* and *Desserts.* She has three children.

matt molina, a graduate of the Los Angeles Culinary Institute, began his career with Nancy Silverton at Campanile in Los Angeles. After six years, he went on to train at Del Posto in New York City in preparation for his role as executive chef of Pizzeria Mozza and Osteria Mozza. At both restaurants, Matt has received three stars from the *Los Angeles Times* and in 2008 he garnered Osteria Mozza a Michelin star. Matt has been nominated for Rising Star Chef, Best Chef Pacific, and Best New Restaurant at Osteria Mozza by the James Beard Foundation.

carolynn carreño is a James Beard Award–winning journalist and the coauthor of several cookbooks, including *Eat Me* (with Kenny Shopsin), *A Twist of the Wrist* (with Nancy Silverton), *Fresh Every Day* and *Sara Foster's Casual Cooking* (with Sara Foster), *100 Ways to Be Pasta* (with Wanda and Giovanna Tornabene), and *Once Upon a Tart* (with Frank Mentesana and Jerome Audureau). She lives in Los Angeles and New York.

a note on the type

The text of this book was set in a typeface called Méridien, a classic roman designed by Adrian Frutiger for the French type foundry Deberny et Peignot in 1957. Adrian Frutiger was born in Interlaken, Switzerland, in 1928 and studied type design there and at the Kunstgewerbeschule in Zurich. In 1953 he moved to Paris, where he joined Deberny et Peignot as a member of the design staff. Méridien, as well as his other typeface of world renown, Univers, was created for the Lumitype photo-set machine.

composed by North Market Street Graphics, Lancaster, Pennsylvania

printed and bound by C & C Offset Printing, Shenzhen, China

designed by Iris Weinstein

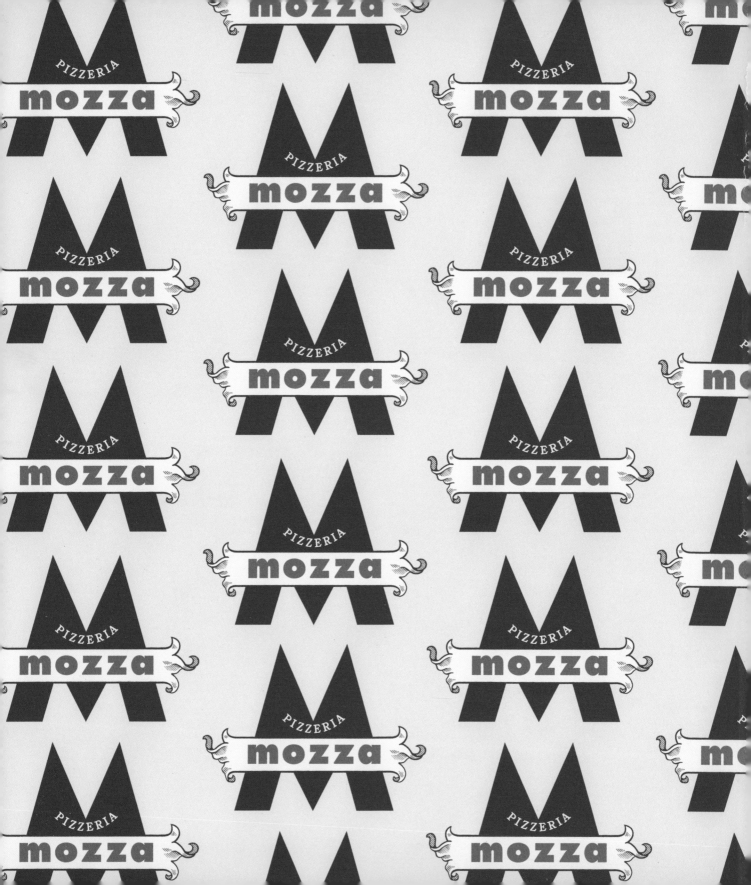